Legendary Watering Holes

NUMBER TEN:
CLAYTON WHEAT WILLIAMS
TEXAS LIFE SERIES

TEXAS A&M UNIVERSITY PRESS
COLLEGE STATION

RICHARD SELCER
DAVID BOWSER
NANCY HAMILTON
CHUCK PARSONS

Legendary Watering Holes
The Saloons That Made Texas Famous

COMPILED AND EDITED BY RICHARD SELCER

The paper used in this book meets the minimum requirements
of the American National Standard for Permanence of Paper for
Printed Library Materials, Z39.48-1984. Binding materials have
been chosen for durability.

∞

Library of Congress Cataloging-in-Publication Data

Legendary watering holes : the saloons that made Texas famous / Richard
Selcer . . . [et al.] ; compiled and edited by Richard Selcer.
    p. cm. — (Clayton Wheat Williams Texas life series ; no. 10)
  Includes index.
  ISBN 1-58544-336-0 (cloth : alk. paper)
  1. Bars (Drinking establishments) — Texas — History. I. Selcer,
Richard F. II. Series.
  TX950.57.T4L44 2004
  647.95764 — dc22
                             2004001180

Title page spread: Horseshoe Saloon, 1906. Courtesy Kansas Collection,
Kenneth Spencer Research Library, University of Kansas Libraries

Contents

	Acknowledgments	vii
INTRODUCTION	"Set 'Em Up!"	3
CHAPTER ONE	The Fine Art of Mixology BYRON JOHNSON AND SHARON PEREGRINE JOHNSON	43
CHAPTER TWO	Jack Harris's Vaudeville and San Antonio's "Fatal Corner" DAVID BOWSER	53
CHAPTER THREE	Ben Dowell's Saloon and the "Monte Carlo of the West" (El Paso) NANCY HAMILTON	123
CHAPTER FOUR	The "Free-Hearted Fellows" of the Iron Front (Austin) CHUCK PARSONS	169
CHAPTER FIVE	The White Elephant: Fort Worth's Saloon *par Excellence* RICHARD SELCER	227
EPILOGUE	"Last Call"	291
	Index	295

Acknowledgments

Every historical work is a collaborative effort no matter how many names appear on the front cover, and that truism applies especially to this book. I must start by acknowledging the contributions of my fellow authors: Chuck Parsons, David Bowser, and Nancy Hamilton. Without their expertise this book could never have been written. They know their saloons and their cities! I must also acknowledge their Job-like patience, as this project took at least three years longer than they ever imagined. Thanks to husband-wife team Byron and Sharon Peregrine Johnson who are probably the world's leading experts on western bartenders ("Mixologists"). I am eternally indebted to Bob Smith for his architectural and drawing talents. He brings a historian's mind and an architect's eye to his drawings. All the elevations, footprints, and street maps are Bob's work. Thanks to Clara Ruddell, Dalton Hoffman, Bob Smith, and James Kattner for providing pictures—Dalton, Bob, and Jim from their personal collections, and Clara from hours of diligent searching through local institutional collections for just the right pictures. Thanks to Bill Campbell for his unselfish "tech support" and unstinting encouragement. Thanks to Fort Worth Police Department historian Sgt. Kevin Foster for generously sharing the fruits of his own research in the form of stories and pictures. Thanks to western artist Jim Spurlock, a collaborator from my *Hell's Half Acre* period, for providing the beautiful artwork that illustrates the cover of this book. Thanks to the crack staff of the Fort Worth Public Library Local History and Genealogy Department for funneling information to me and looking up answers to obscure questions. A great big thanks to the editors and staff at Texas A&M University Press, for taking on this project in the first place and sticking with it through hot and cold. Finally, thanks to Mother Selcer and Lois Biege for being my biggest supporters during all the years it took to turn one of my whimsical ideas into a book.   —RICHARD SELCER

Many thanks to Jo Myler, Frank Faulkner, and the staff of the Texana Department of the San Antonio Public Library. Thanks to Martha Utterback, Elaine Davis, Cathy Herpich, and Dora Guerra of the Daughters of the Republic of Texas Library at the Alamo, and to Irene Andrade and the staff of the Bexar County Criminal Central Filing Office. Also, thanks to John Lovett, curator of the Rose Collection at the University of Oklahoma Library. Also, thanks of the most special and honorable note to Lupita Ramos, Frank Dickson, Ellen Maverick-Dickson, the late Maury Maverick, Jr., Rick Selcer, Chuck Parsons, John Ogden Leal, Bill Groneman, Chilton Maverick, Fred White, Sr., Docia Williams, Paula Allen, Larry and Yolanda Kirkpatrick, and Edward Coy Ybarra.   —DAVID BOWSER

Thanks to the staff of the Jane Burges Perrenot Research Center of the El Paso County Historical Society for assistance with photographs and especially to Richard Field of that group for his study of El Paso saloons.   —NANCY HAMILTON

I wish to acknowledge the contributions of the following people to the "Iron Front" chapter: Tom Bicknell of Crystal Lake, Illinois; Marley Brant of Marietta, Georgia; Craig Fouts of San Diego, California; Robert K. DeArment of Sylvania, Ohio; Gary Fitterer of Kirkland, Washington; Jens Kiecksee of Neuenkirchen, Germany; Robert G. McCubbin of Santa Fe, New Mexico; and Margaret Schlankey of the Austin History Center, Austin, Texas. The order of the listing is in no way indicative of the size of their contribution!   —CHUCK PARSONS

Legendary Watering Holes

Introduction
"Set 'Em Up!"

The English have always had their pubs, the Germans their beer halls, and the French their cabarets, but it took Americans to invent the "Wild West" saloon in the nineteenth century. The word itself was an import, but the concept was 100 percent American. "Saloon" came from the eighteenth-century French word *salon*, meaning a public meeting place; what Americans did was to take the basic concept and adapt it to our own unique frontier culture.[1] Though the saloon retained its basic function as a "public place," it became something more. In its New World incarnation it was a male bastion where men could escape the cares of the world to engage in the mindless pleasures of drinking, gambling, and, frequently, fighting.

The exact origins of the American saloon are impossible to determine. One historian says the saloon was "invented" in the tough Five Points neighborhood of New York City in the early nineteenth century.[2] If so, nobody ever claimed credit for it, but by 1848 the word "saloon" was part of the American vernacular—and by the end of the century it had become a synonym for drunkenness and violence.[3] Out West, the saloon was a place where the ordinary rules of polite society did not apply. In a typical frontier community, the first saloon went up before the first church, and invariably they outnumbered the churches as the town grew. They were more than just drinking establishments; they were community centers that doubled as polling places, courtrooms, and meeting halls. The opening of a new saloon in town was trumpeted with all the fanfare of a new theme park or mall in a later age. Today, the Western saloon is a cherished icon, celebrated in popular culture from Charles Russell paintings ("Painting the Town," 1898) to Hollywood movies (just name any "horse opera").

Before it was elevated to icon status, however, the Western saloon was an institution. Syndicated newspaper columnist Perry Stewart wrote a few years back, "Nothing says Old West like saloon," and while he based that statement more on casual observation than careful study, it still rings true.[4] It was in the West that the saloon evolved to its highest form. In its dual role as civic center and male retreat, the Western saloon was something more than its citified Eastern cousins. To begin with, it was identified with some of the more cultivated evils of the new industrial society, such as class conflict and socialist agitation.[5] Eastern, urban bars were hangouts for blue-collar workers, sailors, ward heelers, and radical agitators. The Western saloon, even at the end of the nineteenth century, still tended to be populated by romanticized types like the cowboy and the "sporting man." The latter was a popular name for the professional gambler, also sometimes referred to as "a knight of the green cloth."[6] Unlike the Eastern, urban tavern, the Western saloon was not a center of machine politics, labor activism, or organized prostitution either. Western saloons were still an affront to public decency, but their popular image was somehow less decadent on the other side of the Mississippi. By some twist of logic, a cowboy riding his horse right up to the bar or even "drilling" a double-dealing opponent sitting across the card table was more "civilized" than a gang of anarchist revolutionaries conspiring together or Irish labor organizers planning their next job action.

The reputation of a saloon was determined by its clientele more than anything else. The most famous watering hole in all of Western history was the Long Branch in Dodge City, Kansas, where such notables as Wyatt Earp, Bat Masterson, Chalk Beeson, William H. Harris, and Luke Short drank, played cards, and engaged in gunplay. Over a span of fourteen years starting in 1873, the Long Branch was at the heart of

Dodge City's wild 'n' woolly image. It was no coincidence that the most loyal customers of the Long Branch were Texas cowboys who drove longhorns up the Chisholm Trail and who knew a thing or two about saloons. In the Long Branch they found a home away from home. If Texans did not invent the Western saloon, they definitely perfected it in such towns as Dodge City, San Antonio, Austin, El Paso, and Fort Worth.

One myth that needs to be demolished is that Western saloons were populist establishments that welcomed any customer with money in his pocket. This is a romanticized fraud perpetrated at the time by Easterners in love with the myth of the "Old West" and treated as received wisdom today. Yet it was clearly never true across racial lines. No African American or Native American would have dared trespass in a white saloon without being invited, and the chances of that happening were nil. In towns with sizable Hispanic or Asian minorities, they also would have faced prejudice had they had the temerity to try to drink at the same bar as Anglo patrons.

It is only recently that historians and archaeologists seem amazed to discover that African Americans even had their own saloons! One such place was Brown's Saloon in Virginia City, Nevada, whose African American owner opened it in 1864 "near the town's red-light district." One archaeologist, after digging up and analyzing artifacts at the site, announced dramatically, "The mere existence of an African American saloon in a mining town of the Old West in northern Nevada alters our sense of the so-called Wild West."[7] On the contrary, it should come as no surprise that African Americans in Nevada and elsewhere across the West had their own saloons, for the simple reason that they were not allowed in white-owned establishments.

That same sort of bigotry applied not just across racial lines but also social lines, at least in towns with more than one saloon. It is only human nature to make class distinctions regardless of the organization or institution, and even the meanest classes of people can practice snobbishness. Saloons are no better and no worse than churches in this regard. Out west, the so-called "fancy saloons" that catered to gentlemen drew the line at buffalo hunters, cowboys, and any other workingman who changed clothes seasonally and bathed even less frequently. Brawling, loud-mouthed, malodorous types were met at the entrance by a

Not every "watering hole" was a fancy saloon. Some, like this little hole-in-the-wall place in Fort Worth's Hell's Half Acre, were simple working-man's bars. No casino games, clubrooms, or shoeshine boys here! From the author's collection

no-nonsense doorman and pointed toward the "tenderloin" section of town. That is why the fancy saloons had doormen and private "clubrooms" and why they were seldom if ever raided by the authorities. They policed themselves.[8]

The saloon business on the upper end of the scale included a number of familiar elements, some more essential to maintaining a profitable operation than others. Among the most essential elements were the "free" bar lunch, music, and bar tokens "good for one free drink."

The free bar lunch—forerunner of today's "happy hour" hors d'oeuvres spread—was a popular service that kept customers on the premises. Since the food was often heavily salted, the free lunch also tended to make customers drink more. In 1890 at a typical Fort Worth saloon, lunchtime customers could purchase a twelve-ounce glass of beer for a nickel and get a "nice bowl of soup" and a healthy serving of chili to go with it. If they followed the first beer up with another glass or three to help wash down the chili, so much the better.[9]

Any long bout of drinking always seemed to go better with musical accompaniment, a fact recognized by barkeeps across the West. Saloon music ranged from full-blown stage shows to an old, upright piano in the corner played indifferently by a no-talent "ivory thumper." Most places employed at least a piano man and a fiddle player, particularly if they had a dance floor. A full-scale band cost too much and took up too much room. Fort Worth's Waco Tap employed W. T. Andrews as its regular fiddle player and E. D. Winslow as its regular piano player. The piano player was normally accorded more respect as a musician if we are to judge by the fact that many of them adopted the title "Professor." At Fort Worth's Red Light Saloon in the late 1870s, Professor Marcross was the *maestro* of the ivories. Toward the end of the century, the most popular number in the barroom repertoire was the melancholy "After the Ball."

In the more upscale places like San Antonio's Vaudeville Saloon, where stage shows were a regular part of the program, the house band consisted of more than a fiddle player and a piano player. An expanded string section plus drums and even a brass section might be in the "pit." As for the quality of the stage shows, that varied widely, too, just like the quality of the musical accompaniment, from slew-footed chorus girls to polished vaudeville acts that traveled from town to town. Any place with a theater attached was considered a "fancy saloon," and such places were far outnumbered by joints that offered little more than a bar, a billiard table, and a few card tables.

Another essential element for any aspiring saloon was the bar token "good for one drink" more or less. It was a marketing device pure and simple, the nineteenth-century equivalent of today's newspaper discount coupon. Some were stamped "good for one free drink," while others had a fractional monetary value that was good toward the purchase of a drink. These little slugs had a long and honorable tradition in the saloon business, going back at least two hundred years to English pubs.[10] They were the cheapest and most effective form of advertising available in a pre-technological society, given out as change by bartenders. At some saloons late in the evening, the proprietor gave out tokens with a 12.5-cent face value which could be redeemed on the customer's next visit for a couple of drinks normally priced at 15 cents each.[11] Saloon tokens helped build a loyal clientele.

Other familiar elements of the Western saloon were popular with the boys but did not significantly affect the bottom line: "last call," interesting artwork on the wall, and brass spittoons.

Last call evolved when saloons began having to keep regular busi-

During their respective tenures running the Iron Front, Lon Martin and John B. Neff followed the usual practice of dispensing drink tokens liberally about town. The Martin token ("5 cents in trade") is a "German silver-round," while the Neff token ("Good for one drink") is a German silver octagon. In its day the Neff token would obviously have been more desirable, since it could be exchanged on a one-for-one basis. Courtesy *James Kattner, Texas Saloon Token Collection*

ness hours by city ordinance. Up until this turn-of-the-century crackdown, many saloons operated twenty-four hours a day, and seven-day weeks were not unknown. Where closing hours were in effect, 2:00 A.M. was customary. Shortly before 2:00 A.M., last call was loudly announced to all remaining customers still upright and with money in their pockets.

"Interesting" artwork for the majority of male customers meant pictures of scantily clad women, prize-fighters like James J. Corbett, and famous battles like "Custer's Last Stand". While the languid nudes painted by Adolphe William Bougereau (see especially *Nymphs and Satyr*) were considered no better than pornography by the art-collecting crowd, they were objects of romantic longing for lonely men gathered around the bar. Larger-than-life-size nudes displayed *en flagrante* were an affront to refined sensibilities the same way cigar smoking and swearing were. If anything, this made them more appealing. The only decision for proprietors of the better saloons was whether to invest in genuine paintings to hang on the walls; the more budget-conscious had to be satisfied with cheap lithographs, often furnished by the same brewers and distillers that stocked the bar. One barkeep who was a passable

York & Voltz's Senate Saloon in Junction City, Kansas, has all the elements of a first-class establishment: properly dressed bartender, electric lights, a cash register, and a brass rail along the bar. It loses points, however, by having simple buckets for spittoons. Courtesy *Pennell Collection of Kansas Collection, Kenneth Spencer Research Library, University of Kansas Libraries*

artist himself was Frenchman Adolphus Gouhenant. Gouhenant decorated the walls of his Dallas saloon with his own original works.[12]

A standard part of saloon furnishings were the brass spittoons strategically placed along the foot rail at the bar and elsewhere around the room. It took careful aim to put a stream of tobacco juice into one of these little pots even at normal "spitting distance." Signs on the wall advised patrons to "Use the spittoon," which the more refined users called "cuspidors."[13] Spittoons came in male and female versions, with the difference being the size of the opening—a piece of trivia known only to antique collectors today. The female spittoon had a wider opening, presumably because women were not so accurate in their aim! The presence of both male- and female-style spittoons in a place was not a sign of an open-door gender policy, just of whatever was most readily available when the place was furnished. Cleaning out spittoons regularly was one of the less-pleasant aspects of saloon housekeeping. The saloon was the last refuge of the functional spittoon in American society.

Some Western saloons solidified their image as a "male preserve" by keeping half-wild pets on the premises. The likelihood of finding such animals as panthers, wolves, and bears in residence at your favorite bar tended to be in direct proportion to the distance from the frontier. Thus, the practice is not recorded in "long-civilized" San Antonio but is recorded in Fort Worth, only a few years and not too many miles removed from the frontier. The Pacific Saloon in Fort Worth kept a pair of bear cubs on display in 1877 while another Fort Worth saloon kept a fully grown wolf in a cage. The Keg Saloon preferred a pet more appropriate to the town's early nickname ("Pantherville"), a panther. That animal, too, was confined in a cage, but on more than one occasion unwary customers got too close and were almost "scalped" for their carelessness. Such incidents did not seem to hurt business nor did they discourage the owner from keeping his pet.[14]

The heart of any saloon operation was what the bar served. Most Western saloons offered a limited assortment of liquid refreshment because their stock had to be hauled in by rail or freight wagon from one of the big eastern distillers. The typical frontier saloon of the mid-nineteenth century might stock whiskey, peach brandy, gin and bitters, in addition to some generic brand of beer. The "hard stuff" meant whiskey, and there was only one kind, the "house brand," which was delivered in barrels and then drawn off into bottles for display at the bar. Prebottled whiskey was too fragile and too expensive to have shipped in to frontier towns. A town like Dodge City, comparable in size to Fort Worth, Austin, or El Paso, could go through two to three hundred barrels of whiskey a year.[15] The stuff that came in barrels was vile enough to be rightly called "rotgut," "redeye," "cactus juice," "tangleleg," and "Kansas sheep dip" among other contemptuous names. The actual alcoholic content was often adulterated with molasses, tobacco juice, and even strychnine. Horace Greeley, after a tour of the West, called the stuff served in most saloons "dubious whiskey, colored and nicknamed to suit the taste of the customers."[16]

The better saloons in those towns with rail connections and regular deliveries were able to stock a wider assortment of liquid refreshment, catering to more refined tastes. Some customers preferred imported wines, cordials, or liqueurs, and a bar could charge premium prices for those. The standard retail price for a shot of whiskey served at the bar, not the fancy stuff, was twenty-five cents in the late nineteenth century.

This price did not change over many years except in some of the boom-towns and mining camps where the price of everything was inflated sky-high.

One of the more popular brands of whiskey in Texas was Monarch, which Chris Rintleman, owner of the Local Option Saloon in Fort Worth, bragged without a hint of irony had only "beneficial effects on its imbibers." In fact, said Rintleman, the second drink of Monarch "makes him an honest man!" [17]

Beer was still the most popular drink in Western saloons, and in the days before refrigeration came along, "fresh beer" was the highest recommendation a brew could have. "Fresh" did not mean "cold," however, because scarcely anybody's beer was truly cold by modern standards. When ice-making machinery finally arrived out west, it was brought in by the beer distributors. The same wagons that could be seen around town delivering beer also made ice deliveries to their customers. The connection between beer sales and ice was thus as solid as a block of frozen water.

Nonalcoholic beverages were quite limited, but so was the demand for them! Some saloons kept a jug of buttermilk on hand for the rare tee-totaler who wandered in. And by the 1880s, a few places, with a nod to the temperance reformers, were beginning to serve soda pop in bottles upon request. The product was provided by wholesale liquor dealers, such as Henry Strum of Dodge City, who saw a chance to expand their business without stirring up the temperance crusaders any more than they already were. Strum produced 14,400 bottles of soda pop per week, which he shipped all over Kansas and even into Texas. [18]

In the days before refrigeration, ice was a precious commodity in the saloon business, especially so in sultry Texas. It was expensive to import from northern climes and impractical to store.

Occasionally, a lucky weather break helped the cause, such as the freak hail storm that struck San Antonio on May 19, 1868. The next morning, the saloonkeepers were out gathering up all the hail stones they could find, which bounty kept them in ice-cold drinks for the next week or two. [19] Absent regular ice deliveries from heaven, saloons were dependent on a few commercial suppliers. Mechanical ice production did not have a significant impact on the saloon business until later in the

There was a remarkable symbiosis at work in the typical Western saloon, as can be seen in this Telluride, Colorado, establishment: the roulette wheel was run by a professional gambler; the shoeshine boy was an "independent contractor;" the bartender was a well-paid staff member; and the law officer probably took his cut of the proceeds off the top. Courtesy *Library of Congress*

century. Usually, saloons got their ice supplies from the same companies that supplied their beer, a practical arrangement that only strengthened the control the breweries had over the retail distributors.

In addition to the basics, first-class saloons offered a wide range of optional activities and services, most of them related to drinking or gambling. Tobacco in one form or another was an indispensable amenity. There was usually a box of cigars on the bar where the customer could help himself, paying the bartender. Some fancier establishments employed a "cigar girl" who circulated the room from table to table. In the larger saloons there was often a well-stocked tobacco stand or "apartment" on the premises. Beginning in the late 1870s, many saloons installed one of the new telephone machines at the bar for the use of customers. Shoe-shines and hair cuts were other popular services available in the better saloons.

In the cowtowns many places had a room in the back where cowboys (or anybody) who had imbibed too much could safely sleep off their binges. Larger places had one or more meeting rooms (called "clubrooms") for use by private parties and local fraternal organizations. All saloons had a billiard table or three, and some of them even had their own bowling alleys on the premises. Bowling took the form of either "nine-pins" or "ten-pins" and was considered as much a man's game as poker or billiards. Famed Western gunslinger John Wesley Hardin was a crackerjack bowler and even got into a shooting scrape in Trinity City, Texas, in 1872 over a game of ten pins.[20] Some places promoted themselves as "bowling saloons," and the alleys were not there for simple, wholesome recreation; they had the same purpose as roulette wheels— wagering.[21] Challengers in some parts of Texas were expected to put up five dollars to match skills with the reigning champ. In 1885 the state of Texas officially denoted nine- or ten-pins as a form of gambling, and prohibited the game. Weak enforcement, however, prevented the new law from having much effect on the popular saloon game but helped solidify its reputation as a low form of entertainment. In 1901 the legislature tried to tighten the law against "nine or ten pin alleys" in saloons but again with little effect.[22]

The same aroma of low morality that hung over bowling also applied to billiards, only more so because billiards was a much more popular saloon game. Virtually every Western saloon had a table or two in the back. Billiards (or pool) was nothing more than another game where men could test their skills and wager on the outcome. The same legislation that aimed to curb ten-pins also designated "pigeon hole tables" or "any gaming table" as illegal gambling facilities, but weak enforcement betrayed the good intentions of the legislators.[23] Every Texas town of any size had its "pool parlors" and "bowling alleys," which were nothing more than saloons with a twist.

Having the latest technology, such as refrigeration and telephone service, kept saloons up-to-date and gave those that could afford it an edge on the competition. The telephone proved only slightly less popular than a cold beer among the saloon crowd. Typically, saloons were the second town resident, after the doctor, to get a telephone as soon as that technology became available (after 1876). As service expanded and a central exchange was built, more saloons installed telephones. The rationale for such hook-ups, besides the novelty of the thing, was its practical usefulness. The bar-side telephone allowed Dad to check in at home and the "Missus" to call looking for Dad. On top of that, it was also a tool of the journalist trade because there was another telephone on the other end of that line at the city newspaper office.

Saloons were the best source for the latest news around town. The saloon was often the first place a newcomer stopped, and liquor is a notorious elixir for loosening tongues. The customers lined up along the bar could usually be depended upon to know the current hot tip or juicy rumor. Not only were saloons a place for hearing the latest news, they frequently *made* news of the violent or scandalous variety. Such an important source of news was not likely to be ignored by a shrewd newspaper editor. Some editors considered their local saloons a regular "beat" by assigning a "stringer" to make the rounds. One "round" tended to lead to another, and to help the reporter do his job, the editor supplemented his regular wages with "whiskey money." [24]

In a business based on customer satisfaction, the rule was, "give the customers what they want." This unwritten rule did not always extend to prostitutes, however, because they tended to bring more trouble than business into an otherwise semi-respectable place. Out of necessity, the prostitute herself was grudgingly tolerated by decent citizens as a member of the community, but disturbing the peace was not tolerated, and wherever men, women, and liquor got together, all hell tended to break loose. The sex-for-money trade, therefore, existed in the gray area of saloon culture; it was both there and not there.

In the public mind, the saloons and the prostitutes were always in cahoots, and some studies have shown that "the growth of prostitution in the United States [in the nineteenth century] paralleled the growth of the saloon." [25] But the reality is more complicated than that simple statement suggests. For one thing, the relevant studies have focused on urban America; a different set of rules existed out west. Secondly, most of the accusers were reformers with an axe to grind against both saloons and prostitutes.

Law and custom both kept women out of saloons. Most towns in Texas had ordinances on the books that made it "unlawful for any female or minor to enter a saloon" unless accompanied by a policeman or peace officer. Other ordinances emphasized that "lewd women" were not to be employed in saloons.[26] Local law was backed up by equally strong conventions against women in saloons. In Victorian America, women were usually regarded as an inhibition on male camaraderie, and "bad women" hanging around could cause a host of problems. Many barkeeps therefore barred all members of the gentler sex from the premises.[27] This practice was observed first-hand by Mrs. Fruzie Morton, a proper lady who grew up in Fort Worth before the turn of the century. Recalling the city of her childhood, Mrs. Morton said, "There were plenty of wide-open saloons and gambling houses, but women were not allowed in either . . . couldn't even look in the doors." Her recollections were supported by cowpuncher Tom Blevins, who recalled visiting a fancy Fort Worth saloon in 1874. In the main bar area downstairs, "There was no women . . . and never had been any." Furthermore, "no women from the outside was [*sic*] allowed to come in." However, the recollections of Fruzie Morton and Tom Blevins must be set against the testimony of saloon man Henry P. Shiel. The longtime Fort Worth law officer, who also happened to own a saloon in the city's Hell's Half Acre district from 1885 to 1891, testified in an 1894 court case that he rented some of the rooms in his saloon to prostitutes.[28]

The difference seems to be one of class. Shiel's place was a "joint" in the notorious tenderloin district. The self-styled "gentlemen's saloons" uptown drew the gender line at the door. This was not just true of Fort Worth but fancy saloons in towns all across the state.

The exceptions to this unwritten rule were the variety theaters (sometimes known as "concert saloons") with their stage shows and the "wine rooms" that were attached to many such places. The concert saloons, like Jack Harris's place in San Antonio and Joe Lowe's Centennial Theater in Fort Worth, were combination saloon–variety halls where burlesque-style shows were part of the regular fare.[29] Typically, they employed "actresses" who were expected to mix with customers when not on the stage. To enjoy a lady's company, the customer had to keep buying drinks for the two of them, which did wonders for bar receipts! It was common knowledge that many of the girls also entertained men after hours, so the line between saloons and prostitution was effectively blurred.

Since it was impossible to run a variety theater without female performers, the old-fashioned male "clubbiness" of the traditional saloon was hopelessly compromised. As late as 1910, municipal authorities in Texas were still wrestling with the problem of how to prevent the showgirls from mingling with the all-male audience and all that entailed. The solution at that point was to bar "theatrical performances" at any place that dispensed liquor or allowed women in the audience. This was the death knell of old-fashioned concert saloons in Texas.[30]

For saloons that wanted to maintain the males-only charade, the "wine room" was the cleverest dodge since the "gentlemen's club," not to mention a classic euphemism. In theory it was an apartment behind the main room reserved for "respectable female customers," which may also have been a classic oxymoron. The wine room usually had its own entrance so that no lady had to run the gauntlet of leering males in the front room. Wine rooms were probably introduced as an honest attempt to keep male and female drinkers separate without discriminating against either, but the original intention was soon forgotten. There were not enough "respectable" women drinkers to make separate facilities viable, and as a result wine rooms were soon taken over by the "other kind" of women.

The wine rooms and the concert saloons were just the most notable examples of how saloons tried to finesse the women-on-the-premises issue. It was more than a moral or ethical issue; it was also, in most towns, a legal issue as well. The mutual attraction between saloons and prostitution was simply too strong to keep them apart entirely. Men came to saloons, stated temperance reformer Frances Willard in delicate terms, to seek "fleshly indulgence."[31] And during one of the many local option elections in Texas, the Reverend J. T. Upchurch of Arlington railed that "The man who votes for the saloon votes to perpetuate [prostitution]." He went on to explain that "all the segregated vice districts in all the cities are either owned or controlled by the Licenced Liquor Traffic."[32]

It was a damning indictment of saloonkeepers, but not without some justification. Liquor-fueled activities such as gambling and drinking just segued naturally into illicit sex. When respectable women were shooed away from gentlemen's clubs, restaurants, and similar male resorts, the field was left wide-open to the "other" kind of women. That kind could always be found lurking in the wine rooms or hanging around just outside the back door. On a typical night, the girls did not have to wait long for business to find them. The deal between a saloon customer and a girl might be closed on the spot before being consummated somewhere else. By keeping the bawds at arm's length, this back-alley arrangement afforded a cover for all involved. The popular image of a saucy saloon girl sitting alongside a "swell" at the gaming table in the front room is largely a Hollywood creation.

Still, the natural alliance between management and working girls was no myth. Sometimes the alliance blossomed into love and marriage, as in the case of "Mollie," who was working as a "soiled dove" in Ellsworth, Kansas, in 1872 when she married saloonkeeper Joe Brennan. Joe gave Mollie a last name, but this did not prevent her from continuing in her profession.[33]

Saloonkeepers were businessmen, and any smart businessman knows his customers. In railroad towns, those customers were the section hands; in cattle towns, the cowboy was king. Treat the customer right and he will come back and bring his friends. No barkeep wanted to have a trail driver or track foreman put his saloon off limits to the boys or, worse still, turn them loose on a place because of some perceived insult. J. Frank Dobie related how a Texas drover once paid a visit to a Fort Worth saloon to get back the money one of his cowboys had lost there in a card game with a professional card sharp. The drover got the cowboy his money back after the saloonkeeper intervened to set things right.[34]

The successful saloon owner wore several hats. He had to be equal parts businessman, psychologist, glad-hander, and enforcer. One historian has observed that the regulars told "all their domestic difficulties and affairs of the heart" to their favorite barkeep, who acted as "counsellor in all the ways of life, recipient of confidences, disburser of advice."[35] And he was able to do all this while drawing pints and pouring shots. If necessary, he could also crack a few skulls or toss a drunk out into the street. Many proprietors referred to their customers as "gentlemen" irrespective of the actual social or economic status of the boys at the bar. This not only flattered the customer but was good for the public image of the saloon. Owners also cultivated an image as pillars of the community by contributing to charitable causes, supporting the firemen's association, and the like. As legitimate members of the business community, they even voiced the usual complaints about taxes and city government, defending themselves with the self-righteous arguments that they paid more than their fair share of taxes, kept out minors, and sent drunks home at the end of the night. Truth be told, some of them really did do those things.

They also complained about unfair competition from drug stores that dispensed alcohol illegally under the guise of "medication." Ironically, some of those same complaining saloonkeepers were adulterating their liquor, putting cheap stuff in high-priced bottles, and serving stale beer to unsuspecting customers. Such men gave the business a bad name, in the process hurting themselves and legitimate owners alike. The unsavory image of saloonkeepers among certain parts of society was why the Knights of Labor, when organizing in 1869, welcomed all "gainfully employed persons" but excluded from that category saloonkeepers.[36]

The union men's righteous condemnation was definitely a minority opinion; as a matter of fact, the saloonkeepers outlasted the Knights of Labor as a political force. Saloon men could be found on city councils in towns all over the West. Fort Worth's Martin McGrath was alderman for the Third Ward in the 1890s at the same time he ran a saloon on lower Main Street. Bill Ward of the same city sat on the council for over a decade and headed up the "Police Committee" for much of that time. From their elevated position in city government, these men could protect their personal interests and those of their fellow saloon men. Just the fact that they could be elected by the voting public was a testimony to their personal popularity *and* to the absence of women in the electorate before 1920.[37]

Those same male voters who put the saloonkeepers on city councils could be found standing at the bar of their favorite saloon night in and night out. Every saloon had its regular customers just as every drinker had his favorite establishment. Different places tended to attract a particular kind of patron, such as Irishmen, Germans, laborers, or cowboys. To a newcomer in town, the name over the door was the surest sign of what kind of clientele could be found inside: the Cowboy Saloon, the Bismarck, or the Shamrock. Saloon names were not copyrighted and there was no premium on originality; just the opposite in fact. Some popular names popped up in towns all across the West, almost like franchises: the Occidental, the Board of Trade, and the Cabinet Saloon were names as familiar to iterant gamblers as McDonald's is to travelers today. In the larger cities, saloons were neighborhood institutions, catering to the surrounding community, which was often designated "Irish town" or "Nigger town" or some such name by the locals.

There was another dynamic at work among the drinking fraternity that is described by the modern phrase, "making the rounds." It was just another part of a night on the town for men who did not see towns all that often. In cowtowns where saloons were the principal business up and down both sides of Main Street, saloon-hopping was the principal activity on a Saturday night, or any other night when the cowboys, buffalo hunters, or their like blew into town. Dedicated drinkers started at one end of the street and worked their way down to the other end during the course of a night of drinking. The evening only ended when the last saloon closed down or when they were too drunk to continue their "pilgrims' progress." In the latter case, they woke up the next morning in the gutter or sleeping it off in some back room.

Saloon-hopping could stretch a party or a feud out until it consumed a whole night. Feuds that commenced in one establishment were often concluded with gunplay in another establishment later that same evening. Any man who did not want to continue a feud made a short night of it by going home early, hoping the causes for the feud would be forgotten the next day. If he preferred to continue making the rounds, a sort of informal grapevine kept him informed of where his antagonist was drinking. It was never an accident when two men met up in some saloon to finish their business after a long night of making the rounds and issuing threats at every stop. Saloon-hopping was a practice favored by bored men with money in their pocket looking for a good time, not by dedicated gamblers looking for the "best" game in town. When the gamblers found a good game, they tended to settle down for the evening. Most saloons catered to both groups by having one or more private gambling rooms set off from the main barroom.

The distinctions between gamblers and drinkers, whites and blacks, this or that ethnic group, were well understood by any man brave

enough to walk through the swinging doors. To the casual observer, saloon culture was one of the most democratic aspects of the whole society. In particular, on the frontier where a "town" might consist of one
main street and only a handful of businesses, the saloon beckoned one
and all to step into its cool interior for a drink or a friendly game of faro.
In reality, the Western saloon was a peculiarly American institution,
egalitarian on the surface but recognizing a definite hierarchy of customers. Certain groups were systematically excluded from the majority
of establishments based on an unwritten code, often reinforced by a
small sign in the window. At the top of the excluded list were blacks, Indians, and women. George Holland's Theater in Fort Worth was typical.
"No Negroes were allowed in there or in the barroom except for a few
train porters," declared a local newspaper in the late 1800s. Most saloons
employed African Americans in a purely menial capacity to clean up and
do odd jobs around the place. These men were generally known as
"porters" just like the train variety, but saloon porters did not enjoy the
same status as train porters in Jim Crow America.[38]

With right of entry narrowed down to white males only, a rough form
of democracy took over. A man could stand anywhere he wanted at the
bar or take an empty seat at any open card game. Occasionally, a customer feeling magnanimous might "set 'em up" for the house. A man's
limit, unless he started making trouble, was determined by the amount
of money he had in his pants pocket. Running a bar tab was a rarely extended courtesy. When a man exceeded his "limit," he was unceremo-
niously tossed into the street, exiting either out the front door or the
back door, depending on the joint and whether he was a regular customer or not.

Saloons were ubiquitous across the West because they filled several
basic needs and because moral objections to them remained muted for
many years. The voice of the moral up-lifters was weak and their cause
unpopular at a time when women could not vote or even run for office.
Generally speaking, the fiery temperance reformers who bedeviled
saloonkeepers back East did not push out to the frontier in significant
numbers for many years. As a result, saloons remained "wide open" in
the West long after they were "tamed" back East. The Texas constitution of 1876 provided for "local option" among the state's towns

and counties, but few took the option of completely prohibiting liquor sales. The saloon was too much a part of frontier culture and the liquor interests too powerful. Up to 1895, only 53 of the state's 239 counties were "dry," with another 79 "partly dry" (meaning some towns in the county). Texas' first state-wide prohibition election was an 1887 referendum that went down in defeat by a margin of more than ninety thousand votes.[39]

The legislature had to content itself during these years with trying to regulate saloons rather than shutting them down. It did this with such tactics as prohibiting the sale of spirits to "habitual drunkards" or minors, licensing saloons, limiting hours of operation, and severing the ties between gambling and drinking. None of these measures had much effect however. One law that did not do anything to discourage the culture of drinking but did have a marvelous effect on state revenues was passed in the summer of 1879; it placed an 18 percent tax on every drink sold. Compliance was supposedly guaranteed by the latest in technology, the bell cash register, which recorded every sale—or at least every sale that the bartender rang up. The liquor dealers' associations squealed loudly about "unfair taxation," but it did them no good. One unforeseen effect: Once the state was financially tied to the saloon in a symbiotic relationship, statewide Prohibition became a dead letter.[40]

About the only effective brake on drinking in a frontier town was a tough city marshal willing to crack heads and haul inebriates off to the hoosegow when things got out of hand. In 1901, Texas took the belated move of granting city marshals the authority to "close any theater, barroom, ballroom, or drinking house" at their own discretion when such places became a nuisance or threat to public order.[41] The power was seldom used, and then an *ex officio* closure only lasted until the saloonkeeper and his lawyer could hie themselves down to court and get it overturned with an injunction.

In the early days, saloonkeepers preferred to handle their problems in-house rather than call in the authorities. It did not hurt that most proprietors were equally handy with fists or six-gun. They were often aided by the regular customers in taking care of troublemakers—a sort of vigilante justice in microcosm. As a general rule, the saloon man was the ultimate arbiter of justice in his place, and the law was wont to judge any actions he took as self-defense. But not always. In 1894 after Fort Worth barkeep Martin McGrath broke up a fight at his place by shooting one-armed Jim Rushing, the law gave him nine years in prison. Despite that cautionary episode, well into the twentieth century this system of self-policing still existed in communities that had begun life as frontier towns.

In 1908 a notorious gunman named Walter Hargrove entered Fort Worth's Board of Trade Saloon, had a drink (not his first of the night), then proceeded to shoot up the place until the bartender took the situation in hand, pulling out his own pistol and putting four bullets into Hargrove. That ended the problem and the bartender was exonerated in short order by the authorities.[42]

Even before the turn of the century, the better saloons employed their own security forces under the rubric "Special Policemen." These men had to apply to the local city council for their jobs, but once approved, they were given full authority to carry guns, make arrests, and do all the things regular policemen do. They only difference was they were paid by the bar owners.[43] There was always considerable competition for those jobs because they paid well and allowed a man to wear a badge while avoiding some of the more onerous chores of the regular police force, such as walking a beat or picking up dead animals in the street.

Saloon men used a variety of tried and true methods to keep the boys with the badges "in their pocket." Besides hiring off-duty officers as bouncers, they contributed liberally to policemen's charities. But the most devious way, which has gone largely overlooked by historians, was to post the bond of a man who wanted to be a law officer. By state law, all lawmen were required to post a surety bond—one thousand dollars for a city marshal and five hundred dollars for a policeman—when they took the job. Either amount was a far greater sum than any average man could pledge by himself. Enter the saloonkeepers and other well-heeled gentlemen who signed up as bondsmen. As an act of generosity, the saloon man could be reasonably assured of the officer's future good will for as long as the fellow was on the force![44]

The lines were so blurred between law enforcement and saloons that policemen often had second jobs as bartenders, dealers, or even part owners of the places they were supposed to patrol. The legendary Wyatt Earp is remembered as a lawman, but it was his "night job" that paid the bills and provided his entrée into society whenever he landed in a new town. While city marshal of Dodge City, Kansas, Earp dealt faro at the Long Branch Saloon and took his pay out of the winnings of the house. A few years later, while wearing the badge of a peace officer in Tombstone, Arizona Territory, he owned an interest in the Oriental Saloon where he earned one thousand dollars a week dealing cards.[45] Not all lawmen did that well at their night job, but not all lawmen were named Earp.

A policeman running his own bar seemed a natural thing in a society where the line between good guys and bad guys was so imprecise. In the Fort Worth Police Department, two of the most respected, longest-serving officers in the force's history, Joe Witcher and Henry P. Shiel, both ran saloons on the side in the 1880s, and no one made an issue of it, at least not before 1909. After all, a man had to make a living, and police work was known to be "damn poor pay." Shiel was also a former city marshal (1874–75). And Martin McGrath, the saloon-man-cum-alderman who shot and killed Jim Rushing at his saloon in 1894, spent several years on the Fort Worth police force prior to that.

The sort of incestuous relationship between police work and the saloon business represented by such men as Shiel, Witcher, and McGrath only occasionally brought down public censure. In 1909 a disgruntled applicant for the Fort Worth police force took the unusual step of lodging an official complaint. B. C. Baldwin wanted badly to be appointed detective, and when he was turned down he fired off an angry letter to the city commission, saying in part, "I am sure that I am not eligible [to be] a member of the force, as I was never a Bartender, or never run a saloon or gambling house."[46]

Shiel, Witcher, and McGrath were fairly typical law officers of their day who went effortlessly from hauling in drunks to pulling pints behind a bar. Rarer was the story of Alton G. Ray, a Fort Worth bartender who went the other direction, trading in his apron for a policeman's badge. Ray started out as a bartender at the Palace Hotel Saloon in the early 1890s. By 1901 he had become a "city detective" and six years later he was Chief of Detectives. Apparently, being a bartender was not considered a blemish on his record; he eventually joined the U.S. Secret Service and was assigned to protect ex–President Theodore Roosevelt![47]

Anyone, law officer or not, could open a saloon, and many men did. Barkeeps came in all shapes, sizes, and ethnic types, just like their customers. It was an equal-opportunity profession that welcomed blacks, Jews, and Hispanics, along with the more familiar Irish and Germans. Tending bar was old-fashioned free enterprise at its most unfettered. But while anyone could nail up a sign and start serving drinks, only a few men made a name for themselves in that line of work: Bill Ward in Fort Worth, Jack Harris in San Antonio, and Ben Dowell in El Paso were three of the best. They perfected the equation of male rendezvous + well-stocked bar = business success. In the process they established themselves as genial hosts who looked after the needs of their customers and maintained cordial relations with the authorities. Both of these latter elements were crucial to running a successful first-class saloon.

Below the aristocracy of the vocation were a lot of other men who simply wanted to open their own little place. Owning a saloon was practically a retirement plan or sideline for Western lawmen. It allowed them to keep their hand in things and maintain ties to friends of a lifetime. Sheriff Henry Fleming ran a successful saloon in Mobeetie, Texas, in the 1880s while wearing a badge. Old cattleman Pink Simms reminisced many years later that city marshals were "all pimps, gamblers and saloonkeepers." Chalkey McArtor ("Chalk") Beeson was a co-owner of the Long Branch Saloon in Dodge while serving two terms as sheriff of Ford County, Kansas, and U.S. Deputy Marshal Virgil Earp had his office upstairs at Tombstone's Crystal Palace Saloon in 1882.[48]

Barkeeping had an equal fascination for men on the other side of the law as well. For bad men like John King Fisher, it was an honorable if only temporary line of work between their real jobs like cattle rustling or contract killing. And they spent so much time in saloons anyway, it was only natural that when they were looking for honest work, they turned to what they knew best. For many older outlaws, opening a saloon was the only way they knew to "go straight" after a lengthy life of crime. Doc Middleton, a Nebraska cattle rustler and horse thief in the 1870s, retired to Ardmore, Oklahoma, where he ran a peaceable saloon for many years. Bob Ford, the "dirty little coward" who shot Jesse James in the back of the head in 1882, fled Missouri after laying down his guns and in the next ten years ran saloons in Chicago and in Creede, Colorado. Wild Bunch member Matt Warner, after getting out of prison in 1900, opened a bar in Green River, Utah, and made a second career for himself as a law-abiding businessman.[49]

Violence in saloons was as normal as prayer in church, and the saloon brawl was practically a scheduled event on Saturday nights. Sometimes the brawling was confined to fists and knives, but other times, when the boys got liquored up, they reached for their six-shooters. When New York newspaper editor Horace Greeley made a trip out west in 1859, he noted that saloon patrons had "a careless way, when drunk, of firing revolvers, sometimes at each other, and other times quite miscellaneously."[50] Sometimes it got personal, and sometimes the newspapermen were part of the violence. Moses C. Harris, editor-publisher of the *Fort Worth Evening Mail*, published several editorials critical of city officials in November, 1884. City Secretary Stuart Harrison took exception, and when they met up in the Opera Saloon, Harrison attacked the editor with fists. An armed Harris pulled his six-shooter as soon as he was able, and the two had to be separated before the violence escalated.[51]

Many a Western feud was born in a saloon when one drunken "hard case" decided to take the measure of another. The legendary gunfight near the OK Corral in 1881 started the night before in one of Tombstone's saloons when a drunken Ike Clanton became embroiled in a heated quarrel with Doc Holliday. The quarrel continued the next day when Clanton's and Holliday's friends got involved until it was settled with gunfire.[52] The only reason more feuds such as this one were not settled on the spot when they first arose was because even the wildest of frontier towns typically required men to check their guns at the bar when they entered a saloon. However, it was an honor system that only applied to guns carried in plain sight. Frisking customers was not part of the routine.

Blazing gunfire was never more than an insult away. Any man without a gun when a challenge was issued or insult offered could either borrow one or go get his own, according to the unofficial rules of saloon gunfights. It is safe to say there was a shooting in some saloon in Austin, San Antonio, El Paso, or Fort Worth at least once a week.[53] Veteran

saloon patrons learned to recognize when violence was about to com-
mence and clear out. Sometimes the violence could be startling in its
suddenness and ferocity. It was always newsworthy. Wild Bill Hickock
was back-shot in Deadwood's Saloon No. 10 in the Dakota Territory in
1876, and John Wesley Hardin gunned down a deputy sheriff on the
doorstep of the Jack Wright Saloon in Comanche, Texas, in 1874.
(Hardin may have been the king of the saloon brawlers.) In 1899 noted
saloon man and gambler Joseph ("Rowdy Joe") Lowe exchanged words
with former policeman Emmanuel Kimmel in Mart. H. Watrous's Denver saloon, after which Kimmel drilled Lowe three times. Both men had
been drinking heavily before their face-off, but Lowe was unarmed at
the time. The violence did not even let up in the new century. On July 6,
1900, the youngest of the legendary "Fighting Earps," forty-five-year-
old Warren Earp, was shot to death in the Headquarters Saloon in Wilcox,
Arizona. In 1913 Fort Worth gambler Tommie Lee Young wreaked havoc
in the saloon district of south Fort Worth, first blasting a city policeman
with a 12-gauge shotgun at W. L. Sallis's saloon, then shooting barman
Bob Grimes at the Brewery Exchange Bar. The affair was covered
breathlessly in newspapers all over Texas for weeks afterwards.[54]

Similar stories were repeated dozens of times all over the West. Mix
liquor, men, and firearms, add in gambling as a chaser, and the result was
an often-fatal devil's brew. It always began with two men in a saloon, at
least one of them armed. The basic scenario always included too much
"Who-hit-John" talk, bad blood or strong words between the two men,
and a final confrontation that built during the course of an evening until
it climaxed in a spasm of gunfire. In most cases the people around them
saw it coming; sometimes the bartender even tried to get them to sim-
mer down or take their dispute outside. Sometimes they did go elsewhere but returned to where it all started to finish their quarrel. Sometimes one man would send word that he was looking for the other, and
in a town with just so many saloons, it was inevitable that they ran into
each other sometime during a long evening of drinking. Even when
they could see the blowup coming, most customers took the attitude
that it was none of their business. Many times the argument arose out of
a gambling dispute: somebody had a run of bad luck or felt like he had
been cheated and blamed somebody else at the table. The names

changed but the story usually played out the same. Sometimes these things seemed to be as ritualized and inevitable as a Greek tragedy.

Unlicensed saloons were the worst disturbers of the peace. Both the state of Texas and many local communities began licensing saloons after the Civil War. Licenses brought money into the public coffers and forced establishments to maintain a certain level of decorum. But on the fringes of the business district, in areas like Hell's Half Acre, unlicensed joints operated out of the public eye—at least until trouble erupted. They existed because they paid off the authorities and because as soon as one was shut down, another sprang up nearby to take its place, sometimes under the same management. These were the joints that were branded "dens of prostitution," "moral cesspools," and "hell-holes" in the public print. The worst of the worst were the "blind tigers" or "blind pigs" that operated in dry communities. These were joints that sold liquor surreptitiously out the back door or through a trapdoor in a secluded wall. The exchange of money and product was made without either one seeing the other, thus somewhat protecting both parties against "sting" operations or subsequent legal action. After all, a witness cannot identify someone in court that he never saw. As the number of dry communities increased, so did the problem of blind tigers/pigs until in 1903 the legislature specifically outlawed the arrangement.[55]

The late nineteenth century was the heyday of the Western saloon, a time when "live-and-let-live" still outweighed law and order. Despite the era's violence and lack of refinement, there was a certain innocence to this Gilded Age of corruption and opulence that even extended to saloons. It was a time before the current widespread concern over the scourge of alcoholism. Most people looked upon a drunk as a disgrace to himself and to his family, not as a social problem. There was more concern over the level of violence in saloons than over the social cost of drunkenness. Temperance, not complete prohibition, was the realistic goal of most reformers. The Sons of Temperance, the earliest national organization to take up the cause (1826), found the going particularly tough in the Lone Star State. In the 1860s they counted at least three thousand members across the state but could make little headway against entrenched interests and long-held habits.[56] Hard-drinking Texans found the temperance folks more of a curiosity than a genuine

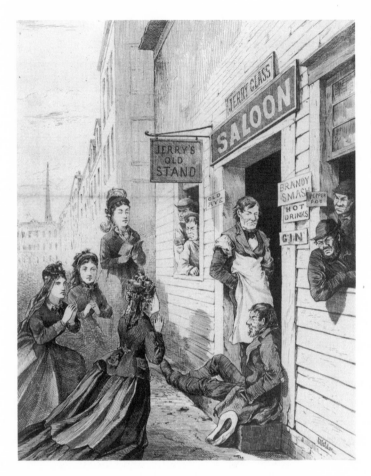

Starting in the mid-nineteenth century, the temperance movement attempted to ameliorate drunkenness without actually prohibiting drinking. The movement was led by a formidable army of women whose tactics included singing and praying at the entrances of saloons. Courtesy Library of Congress

threat. When the Woman's Christian Temperance Union (WCTU) emerged from Cleveland in 1874, they found it impossible to duplicate farther west their success in the Midwest, where they succeeded in shutting down saloons in some two hundred towns with their prayers and hymns.[57] Men on the frontier, it seemed, were not ready to be sung or prayed into "taking the pledge" by their womenfolk.

The Anti-Saloon League, a coalition of prohibitionist-minded preachers headed by the Reverend H. H. Russell also came out of Ohio's fertile reform soil. This organization called itself "The Church in Action Against the Saloon" and went national in 1895 crusading for a "saloonless nation."[58] Their strategy was to focus on the state level, securing "local option" legislation that put the decision-making in the hands of city and county voters. This approach produced a patchwork of "dry" communities across Texas and other states. The Texas chapter of the Anti-Saloon League was founded in the same year as the national organization (1895) but remained largely "ineffective" for more than a decade.[59]

The reformers' fervent prayers and appeals to conscience won few converts among the saloon crowd. On the contrary, temperance-preaching Jeremiahs were usually laughed out of town and their disciples routed at every election. Local politicians tried to have it both ways, rising to heights of self-righteous oratory at election times and promising clean-up crusades, only to turn a blind eye to the saloon business as soon as the last ballot was counted. A visitor to Amarillo in 1892 observed that "the saloon business is a great industry [here] and will continue to be so long as the saloon trust continues." He observed six saloons on a single block of the dusty Main Street, all of them doing a land-office business.[60]

The "saloon trust," as the various suppliers and dealers were known to their critics, was one of the most powerful special interests around. They generated enormous profits and counted among their ranks some of the most respected citizens of the community, including church deacons and city councilmen. In some Texas cities, members of the liquor dealers' association not only sat on the city council, but headed up the council's "Police Committee." Propriety and the apparent conflict of interest were not issues. That was simply the way business was done.

Retail and wholesale liquor dealers represented two separate heads of the same beast. The wholesalers supplied the bulk product while the retailers sold it to the public, just like today. The wholesale dealers gained strength through the 1880s by expanding into the retail side of the business. In some cases that meant taking over direct ownership of their outlets; in other cases, they forced those outlets to sign exclusive "sweetheart deals" that allowed them to sell only a single supplier's brand(s). Miller Brewery, to cite one example, had franchise arrangements with twenty-two saloons in Fort Worth in the early years of the twentieth century, referring to their partners as "lessees".[61] Thus the brewers and wholesale dealers were able to establish vertical monopolies over the manufacture, distribution, and sale of their product. The independent Western saloon was on its way to becoming just another Big Business.[62]

Another step in the evolution of the Western saloon into Big Business came in response to the attacks of temperance reformers. The nation's liquor dealers joined together in 1886 to form the National Protective Bureau (NPB), an organization aimed not at protecting them against criminals but against the law itself. That first year, the NPB spent two-third's of its budget in Texas alone fighting the enemies of the saloon.[63] In cities all over the state the various liquor dealers' associations regularly outflanked their critics at city hall and in the press. Whenever a new saloon opened, which was often, newspapers dutifully informed their readers that So-and-so "will be pleased to greet his old friends at his new place of business." Since such an occasion virtually guaranteed more than a few rounds of free drinks, a good turnout was assured. If it were a premier saloon, the occasion was treated as a grand civic event, with the mayor and city council showing up *en masse* for the festivities.[64]

One reason for the cozy relationship between saloons and city hall was that saloon licenses, granted by the city, provided an important source of income to grease the wheels of city government. A large saloon might pay as much as $650 a year for the privilege of doing business in a major city like Fort Worth or San Antonio.[65] And the saloon business was recession-proof. After the Panic of 1893 brought a national economic depression, city governments all over Texas faced a financial crisis in providing municipal services. Maintenance and repairs had to be deferred indefinitely and officials were laid off while city councils cast about for ways to meet their budgets. Citizens howled if new taxes were passed or evaluations on their property were raised. The only geese still laying golden eggs were the saloons, which were able to demand in return a more tolerant attitude from city officials. The Depression was also damaging to the prohibition/temperance crusade. Saloon owners put out none-too-subtle hints to Texas voters at election time that prohibition would be yet another blow against the state's economic base, thus casting prohibitionists as being both antifreedom *and* antibusiness. Carl

Schilder, owner of Fort Worth's Bismarck Saloon circulated this bit of doggerel prior to one of several local option elections:

> Citizens, neighbors, you and I
> What are we going to do if this town goes dry
> We may get along without our drink,
> But who'll it hurt most, do you think?[66]

For years Texans had treated reformers with the sort of undisguised contempt usually reserved for Eastern dandies and Shakespearean actors. In 1884 when the state's nascent Prohibition Party held their first convention in Fort Worth, the local newspapers gave the event barely two lines on an inside page.[67] But by the turn of the century even Texans were forced to accept that the times were changing and so must they. The WCTU finally hit on a successful antisaloon strategy with their "home protection" message, and a new wave of reformers came along calling themselves "Progressives." These well-heeled do-gooders were a nationwide movement, attacking society's ills on a broad front.[68] Another ally in the fight was the Anti-Saloon League. After twenty years of struggling to be heard, the League's Texas division reorganized itself in 1915 and launched an aggressive fight for statewide prohibition. Their newfound popularity was part of a trend that saw Governor Thomas Campbell reelected as an outspoken antisaloon candidate in 1908 and 168 counties vote themselves "dry" by 1911. Unfortunately for the Puritans in Texas, Bexar (San Antonio) and Tarrant (Fort Worth) counties were not among those dry counties, though El Paso and Matagorda (Austin) Counties were.[69]

At the same time, the saloon business itself was changing. The rise of genteel private clubs had drained away the best class of customers, leaving the second-tier saloons as the hangout of loutish and uncouth types. The saloon's public image was no longer that of a protected male resort, and a visit to the neighborhood bar was no longer accepted as a normal part of a gentleman's daily schedule. Now after a visit, a man might use a little of the new breath purifier Sen-sen to kill the scent of alcohol on his breath before going home.

Regardless of their personal feelings, public officials were forced to respond to increasing pressure from drys to "close 'em down," and for the first time reformers found they had a majority of citizens *and* business interests behind them. As the cowboy rode off into the sunset and the sporting gentleman became just another social parasite, the Western saloon went the way of the traveling circus and the Mississippi river boat as anachronisms left over from another time. All that was left were the stories—some of them even true!—of the old glory days when a gent could stroll into a saloon through the bat-wing doors with his head held high, belly up to the bar, and proceed to drown his troubles among like-minded fellows. He entered at his own peril and left when he felt like it. In between he was free from the cares of the world for at least a few hours.

People came to saloons to celebrate or to mourn, to remember or to forget. Reflecting their European roots, the best saloons had always tried to conjure up an image of refined elegance and good taste—and places like the Palace in San Francisco, the Palmer House in Chicago, and the White Elephant in Fort Worth clung to this image stubbornly. They invested heavily in fancy decorations, luxurious furnishings, carpeted floors, lots of mirrors, and well-stocked bars. But most saloons across the West took the name without bothering about all the ritzy trappings. Sticky wooden floors, weak gas lighting, and an odorous outhouse in the back alley were all they needed beyond the most basic of bar stock to satisfy their regular customers. Flies, sawdust, and a smoky haze were just part of the ambience. Overhead for such places was kept to a minimum. In 1895 when the city tax assessor of Fort Worth valued the "stock and furnishings" in C. A. Ginnochio's saloon at $1000, the owner protested vigorously that the whole lot was worth no more than $250 tops. He won his case.[70]

The saloon had started as a humble establishment whose essence was a bartender, a few bottles, and a customer with money in his pocket. Only a few visionary entrepreneurs ever aspired to elegant establishments. The best of those in the nineteenth century included the likes of Pap Wyman's saloon in Leadville, Colorado, and Milt Joyce's Oriental Saloon in Tombstone, Arizona. They were classy emporiums that boasted diamond-dust mirrors and grand staircases, whose fame extended far beyond their local environs, making them destination points for self-styled sporting men.[71]

The most successful saloons tended to be two-story structures for a good, practical reason: they could separate their customers into high rollers and hoi polloi. The high-rollers did their gambling and drinking upstairs where the surroundings were more intimate, the service more attentive, and management provided the best of everything. "You had to dress like a dude to get up there," recalled old cowpuncher Tom Blevins many years later.[72]

For everybody else, the downstairs had a certain democratic atmosphere that suited most men just fine. Most of the drinking was of the "perpendicular" variety, standing at the bar. This was out of necessity since barstools were a later custom *and* because of the shortage of table seating in the public area. Pictures of saloon interiors underscore the fact that stools were not part of the furnishings in nineteenth-century Western bars. The bar stool is a modern invention of "fern bars" and their ilk.[73] Social customs normally covering such things as spitting and swearing stopped at the bat-wing doors. All men were equal at the bar, and the dimly lit interior afforded a certain degree of anonymity. With the right connections and a good bankroll, a man could choose either the upstairs or downstairs or move back and forth between the two. Three of the four principal saloons discussed in this work—the White Elephant, the Iron Front, and the Vaudeville—were two-story operations that catered to diverse clientele.

The saloon has been an integral part of life in the Lone Star state right from the beginning. Back when we were a newly independent republic and the leaders were casting about for revenue-raising industries to support the ship of state, they quickly realized that, as Fort Worth–based author Jerry Flemmons has expressed it, "Texas had no industry aside from a little slave-produced cotton and saloons." Saloons were a ubiquitous fixture of every city, town, and hamlet. An early visitor to Mobeetie noted that "every other house is a saloon," while a Fort Concho resident stated that the nearby raw settlement soon to be known as San Angelo "seemed to have more saloons than all other businesses combined."[74] It was the same story all over Texas in the late nineteenth century.

After the Civil War, citizens of the Lone Star state seemed to turn up all over the West as barkeeps. Sometimes in Kansas cowtowns it must have seemed that there were as many Texans working behind the bar as leaning against the front of it drinking.

The state's economic base has expanded considerably since those days, but saloons are still an essential part of Texas, especially its public image. We sometimes forget that fact until something happens to remind us. A few years ago a national magazine reported in an article on "America's Hottest Cities" that Fort Worth had one saloon ("tavern") for every twenty-six residents, based on the questionable results of a local survey. The city's public relations watchdog quickly did some simple math, calculating that their figures worked out to some 16,859 saloons in a city of fewer than 450,000 people! He got busy and fired off a letter to the editor protesting, "We'll concede that a lot of us in Fort Worth like an occasional nip of bourbon, but . . . that's a few too many [saloons], even for us cowboys." The mayor's office also got in on the controversy, issuing a hasty press release to explain, "The main issue is yes, we may have a certain number [of saloons] but . . . we ought to be recognized for . . . culture *and* cowboys, not one over the other, but world class in both areas. The bars and taverns are just one part of our history." [75]

They were a part of Texas history that raised serious issues at the time of the "Texas Frontier Centennial Celebration" in 1936. While Dallas planned a dignified "official" event built around historic themes, Fort Worth leaders aimed for something more along the lines of a rootin' tootin' Wild West Show. This provoked Mrs. Anna Shelton, one of Fort Worth's grand dames, to tell a newspaper interviewer, "The idea of cowboys riding through the town shooting out the lamp posts isn't my idea of a frontier celebration. It's not my idea to have saloons on every corner either." [76] Mrs. Shelton's ideas about a proper centennial celebration lost out when the city put up the "Pioneer Palace," built to look both inside and out like an old Western saloon.

The connection between Texans and saloons, at least in the popular mind, continues to this day. When Macedonian newspaper editor Petar Lazarevski made his first trip to the United States in 1996 from his Balkan homeland, the first state he visited was Texas. He landed at Dallas–Fort Worth airport and proceeded immediately to "Cowtown." Before coming he had been convinced that he had a good handle on the Lone

Star State: "I thought life here was fairly casual, with people spending most of their time in saloons smoking cigars and drinking whiskey." He soon had his eyes opened: "The only so-called saloon I saw in downtown Fort Worth was Billy Miner's in Sundance Square, and patrons there mainly drink beer, coffee, or iced tea." This culture shock forced him to modify somewhat his preconceived notions about Texans, but only what they drank, not where they drank it.[77]

As long as there are Texans, there will be saloons, although the modern versions are pale imitations of their Western predecessors. This book celebrates some of the more notable "watering holes" in our state's past; it is not a conventional history of people or events but of places. These are places that did not just witness history; they *made* history—in the process bringing a certain notoriety to their towns. All of the saloons discussed here are gone now, but they left behind a rich legacy that deserves to be remembered just as much as the better-documented sites and landmarks that have historic markers attached to them today.

NOTES

1. Mark Edward Lender and James Kirby Martin, *Drinking in America: A History* (New York: Free Press, 1982), 99. See also Bill Bryson, *Made in America: An Informal History of the English Language in the United States* (New York: William Morrow and Co., Inc., 1994), 201.

2. Luc Sante, *Low Life: Lures and Snares of Old New York* (New York: Vintage Books, 1991), 105.

3. J. J. Dillard, *American Talk: Where Our Words Come From* (New York: Random House, 1976), 85.

4. Perry Stewart, "Whitenights . . . the White Elephant Celebrates 25 Years of Rootin'-tootin' Heritage," *Fort Worth Star-Telegram*, "Star Time," Nov. 2, 2001, 39.

5. Lender and Martin, *Drinking in America*, 103.

6. "Knights of the Green Cloth" is a name made famous by historian Robert K. DeArment in his book on the subject, *Knights of the Green Cloth: The Saga of the Frontier Gamblers* (Norman: University of Oklahoma Press, 1982). The name appeared frequently in Texas newspaper stories about gamblers, e.g., *Dallas Weekly Herald*, Sept. 17, 1885.

7. "Dig Results Show Diversity Helped Shape the West," *Fort Worth Star-Telegram*, Mar. 23, 2003, 10A.

8. For a general discussion of this point that social classes divided saloon patrons, see Thomas J. Noel, *The City and the Saloon: Denver, 1858–1916* (Niwot, Colo.: University Press of Colorado, 1996), 23–29; David Dary, *Cowboy Culture*

(New York: Alfred A. Knopf, 1981), 211; and Richard Slatta, *Comparing Cowboys and Frontiers* (Norman: University of Oklahoma Press, 1997), 112. The same point is made specifically about Fort Worth saloons in "Garish Saloons Followed the Last Chance of 1856," *Fort Worth Star-Telegram*, Centennial Edition, Oct. 30, 1949, Commerce Section, 30. For the opposing view that saloons were "great social levelers," see Robert L. Brown, *Saloons of the American West* (Silverton, Colo.: Sundance Publications, 1978), 15. All the evidence points toward the fact that Western saloons were as bigoted and class-conscious as other segments of American society in the nineteenth century.

9. Undated newspaper article in vertical files ("Saloons") of Fort Worth Public Library, Central Branch, Local History and Genealogy Dept. By the time of World War I, the tradition of the "free lunch" in saloons was ended by local ordinance, with the blessing of the saloon owners who had seen the cost of the service go up and up without a commensurate increase in business. Some of the most indignant protesters when free lunch stopped were the newspaper reporters for whom saloons had long been not only a good source of news but of sustenance. See *Fort Worth Record*, May 30, 1917. (Also quoted in *Fort Worth Star-Telegram*, "Our Growth" Section of Special Centennial Edition, Oct. 30, 1949, 2.)

10. John McIlwain, *The Pitkin Guide to English Pubs* (London: Pitkin Unichrome, Ltd., 1998), 14.

11. Robert Fleet, "The Saloons of Tyler, Texas, 1847–1901," *Chronicles of Smith County* 12, no. 1 (summer, 1973): 34.

12. Before moving to Dallas and opening a place, Gouhenant ran a saloon in Fort Worth in the town's early years. Clay Perkins, *The Fort in Fort Worth* (Keller, Tex.: Cross-Timbers Heritage Publishing Company, 2001), 175.

13. Stuart Berg Flexner, *I Hear America Talking* (New York: Simon and Schuster, 1976), 334.

14. *Fort Worth Daily Democrat*, July 1, 1877 (bears); Richard F. Selcer, *Hell's Half Acre: The Life and Legend of a Red-light District* (Fort Worth: Texas Christian University Press, 1991), 19–20 (wolf and panther).

15. Odie B. Faulk, *Dodge City: The Most Western Town of All* (New York: Oxford University Press, 1977), 89.

16. Candy Moulton, *The Writer's Guide to Everyday Life in the Wild West* (Cincinnati, Ohio: Writer's Digest Books, 1999), 131. Greeley is quoted in Sandra Dallas, *Cherry Creek Gothic* (Norman: University of Oklahoma Press, 1971), 192.

17. Rintleman is quoted without reference to date or place in oral history interviews contained in *Federal Writers' Project*, vol. 49 (Fort Worth: Fort Worth Public Library Unit, 1941), 19,448.

18. C. Robert Haywood, *Victorian West: Class and Culture in Kansas Cattle Towns* (Lawrence: University Press of Kansas, 1991), 187.

19. A. Huffmeyer, "The Daddy of All Hail Storms," *Frontier Times*, June, 1926, 32.

20. Bill O'Neal, *Encyclopedia of Western Gunfighters* (Norman: University of Oklahoma Press, 1979), 129.

Notorious outlaw John Wesley Hardin was known for his skills with a pistol, but he also fancied himself something of a bowler, which provided another excuse to wager money and intimidate opponents. He probably learned the finer points of ten-pins as a saloon habitué at an early age. See Leon Metz, *John Wesley Hardin: Dark Angel of Texas* (El Paso, Tex.: Mangan Books, 1996), 81–82.

21. For descriptions of nineteenth-century "bowling saloons" and "billiard saloons," see George G. Foster, *New York by Gas-Light, and Other Urban Sketches* (New York: N. Orr, 1850; reprint, University of California Press, 1990), 84–85; and Tyler Anbinder, *Five Points: The 19th-Century New York City Neighborhood That Invented Tap Dance, Stole Elections, and Became the World's Most Notorious Slum* (New York: Free Press, 2001), 195.

22. General Laws of the State of Texas, Passed at the Regular Session of the 19th Legislature, January 13, 1885–March 31, 1885 (Austin: State Printer, 1885), S.B. No. 126, approved March 19, 1885; and General Laws of the State of Texas, Passed at the Regular Session of the 27th Legislature, January 8, 1901–April 9, 1901 (Austin: State Printer, 1901), S.B. No. 101, approved April 17, 1901.

23. General Laws of the State of Texas, Passed at the Regular Session of the 27th Legislature, January 8, 1901–April 9, 1901 (Austin: State Printer, 1901), S.B. No. 101, approved April 17, 1901.

24. David Dary, *Red Blood and Black Ink: Journalism in the Old West* (New York: Alfred A. Knopf, 1998), 123.

25. Norman H. Clark, *Deliver Us from Evil* (New York: W. W. Norton and Co., 1976), 63–64.

26. See for instance, "Addendum to the Revised Ordinances of the City of Fort Worth," passed and accepted Mar. 3, 1917, Title XIII, Chapter 3, 126; and (for "lewd women") "Charter and Revised Ordinances of Fort Worth, Texas," 1906, Title III, Chapter V, Sec. 452, 247, both in Fort Worth Public Library, Central Branch, Local History and Genealogy Dept.

27. The practice of barring women from saloons is explained in some detail in Andrew Barr, *Drink: A Social History of America* (New York: Carroll and Graf Publishers, Inc., 1999), 138–41.

28. Mrs. Morton's recollections are cited in "In Old Fort Worth," Special edition by the *News-Tribune*, vol. 13, no. 1, July 2–4, 1976, 2. Tom Blevins' recollections are cited in J. Frank Dobie, *Cow People* (Boston: Little, Brown and Company, 1964), 109–10. For Shiel's testimony, see *Martin McGrath vs. The State*, No. 849, Court of Criminal Appeals of Texas, 35 TX. Crim. 43; 34 S.W. 127; 1896 TX. Criminal Appeals LEXIS 28.

29. No Texas variety theater could measure up to Tombstone, Arizona's legendary Bird Cage Theater (1881–92), which was the gold standard for such places in the Old West. On a good night it might take in $2,500 and have a crowd lined up outside waiting to get in. See Ben T. Traywick, "Tombstone's Bird Cage," *Wild West Magazine*, Oct., 1994, 58–64.

30. For concert saloons, see Richard Butsch, *The Making of American Audiences* (Cambridge, U.K.: Cambridge University Press, 2000), 95–103; and Douglas Gilbert, *American Vaudeville, Its Life and Times* (New York: Whittlesey House, a division of McGraw-Hill, 1940), 34–36. For a typical commentary on the protocols of the variety theaters, in this case Fort Worth's Standard Theater, see *Fort Worth Record*, Jan. 10, 1907, 3. For the end of variety theaters, see *Fort Worth Record*, Feb. 11, 1910.

31. Frances Willard, *Glimpses of Fifty Years: The Autobiography of an American Woman* (Chicago, Ill., 1889), 642.

32. J. T. Upchurch, *Black Slavery Versus White Slavery* (Arlington, Tex.: Berachah Home Printing Office, 1912), 22. Upchurch was a Baptist minister who ran a home in Arlington to redeem "erring girls." He was also a dedicated muckraker who self-published numerous tracts and books against the organized vice trade.

33. Gary L. Roberts, "Bat Masterson and the Sweetwater Shootout," *Wild West Magazine*, Oct., 2000, 46. Mollie subsequently hooked up with Billy Thompson and wound up in Sweetwater, Texas, where she worked as a "dance hall girl" and made the acquaintance of Bat Masterson. She was killed in a saloon shootout involving Bat in 1875.

34. J. Frank Dobie, *Cow People* (Boston: Little, Brown and Company, 1964), 118–19.

35. Travis Hoke, "Corner Saloon," *American Mercury*, Mar., 1931, 314.

36. The list of undesirables excluded from membership in the Knights also included lawyers and professional gamblers. See subject entry in Wayne Andrews, *Concise Dictionary of American History* (New York: Charles Scribner's Sons, 1962), 519.

37. The campaign for women's suffrage in Texas was launched in 1888 by the Women's Christian Temperance Union. Women were finally enfranchised by the legislature in March, 1918. During these years, the major issues that energized women were liquor and prostitution. See Judith N. McArthur, "Women and Politics," *The New Handbook of Texas*, ed. Ron Tyler et al., vol. 6 (Austin: Texas State Historical Association, 1996), 1053.

38. *Jim Burrus vs. the State*, Case No. 613, Court of Criminal Appeals of Texas, 34 TX Crim 387, 30 S.W. 785, 1895. Burrus, alias "Jim Toots," was an African American convicted of a murderous rampage in Fort Worth in 1895. For "colored saloon porters," see also *Fort Worth Daily Gazette*, Oct. 2, 1887.

39. K. Austin Kerr, "Prohibition," in *New Handbook of Texas*, vol. 5, 335.

40. *Fort Worth Daily Democrat*, July 16 and Nov. 8, 1879 (reprinted in *Federal Writers' Project*, vol. 9, 3,480).

41. General Laws of the State of Texas, Passed at the Regular Session of the 28th Legislature (Austin: State Printer, 1901), S.B. No. 304, approved April 19, 1901, 290.

42. For McGrath's story, see *Fort Worth Gazette*, Dec. 31, 1894, and *Dallas Morning News*, Dec. 31, 1894. For Hargrove's story, see "Bartender's Revenge," *Fort Worth Press*, Feb. 25, 1973, 1E.

43. See Fort Worth City Council Proceedings, May 4, 1900, and *passim*, vertical files transferred from Fort Worth City Secretary's Office to Fort Worth Public Library, Central Branch, Local History and Genealogy Dept.

44. For numerous examples of the saloon fraternity serving as bondsmen, see "Record of Bonds," Book A (1873–88), City of Fort Worth, Tex., Fort Worth Public Library, Central Branch, Local History and Genealogy Dept.

45. Frank C. Lockwood, *Pioneer Days in Arizona, from the Spanish Occupation to Statehood* (New York: The Macmillan Company, 1932), 282–84; Frank C. Lockwood, "They Lived in Tombstone; I Knew Them!" No. 4 in a weekly series of biographical vignettes of Tombstone pioneers, *Tombstone Epitaph*, Mar. 8, 1945.

46. Baldwin to "the Honorable Mayor and Commissioners," Fort Worth, Texas, Apr. 20, 1909, vertical files, "Fort Worth Police," originally from Fort Worth City Commission Proceedings, n.d., transferred from Fort Worth City Secretary's Office to Fort Worth Public Library, Central Branch, Local History and Genealogy Dept. The city commission replaced the city council as the governing entity after the city charter was changed in 1907.

47. Letter from Tom Seymour, Ray family descendant, to Bill Fairley, *Fort Worth Star-Telegram* columnist, Sept. 12, 2002, in author's files.

48. For Fleming, see Allen G. Hatley, "Cap Arrington, Adventurer, Ranger and Sheriff," *Wild West Magazine*, June, 2001, 55; for Beeson, see Roger Myers, "Western Lore" column, *Wild West Magazine*, Dec., 2000, 60. Pink Simms's comment comes from a 1934 letter that he wrote, quoted in Myers, "Western Lore" column, *Wild West Magazine*, Dec., 2000, 60. For Earp, see Ben T. Traywick, *The Chronicles of Tombstone*, 2d ed. (Tombstone, Ariz.: Red Marie's Bookstore, 1994), 97.

49. For Middleton, see Elizabeth Parker, "Doc Middleton, Nebraska's 'Gentleman Outlaw' . . . ," *Wild West Magazine*, Feb., 1999, 14, 66. For Fisher's checkered career, see O. C. Fisher and J. C. Dykes, *King Fisher: His Life and Times* (Norman: University of Oklahoma Press, 1966). For Ford, see Jon Kirchoff, "Bob Ford, The Man Who Killed Jesse James . . . ," *Wild West Magazine*, Oct., 1998, 20. For Matt Warner, see Gary Fitterer, "The Life and Death of Billy Thompson," Part Two, *Quarterly of the National Association for Outlaw and Lawman History, Inc.* 25, no. 2 (Apr.–May, 2001): 51.

50. Horace Greeley, *An Overland Journey from New York to San Francisco in the Summer of 1859* (New York: Saxton, Barker and Co., 1860; reprint, New York: Alfred A. Knopf, 1964), 136.

51. Reported in *Galveston Daily News*, Nov. 16, 1884, 1 ("Special to the News").

52. Neil B. Carmony, "Hello Ike! Any New War?" *Quarterly of the National Association for Outlaw and Lawman History, Inc.* 26, no. 1 (Jan.–Mar., 2002), 30–31. The so-called "gunfight at the OK Corral" actually took place in an alleyway between the OK Corral and Fly's Photographic Studio.

53. Nobody kept such statistics officially, but a perusal of each city's newspapers from around the turn of the century show the depressing regularity of

gunplay in the saloons. This subject cries out for a serious study using public records and contemporary newspaper reports.

54. For Hickock and Hardin episodes, see Bill O'Neal, *Encyclopedia of Western Gunfighters* (Norman: University of Oklahoma Press), 138–39, 130. (The Jack Wright Saloon in Comanche is still standing today.) For Joe Lowe, see Joseph G. Rosa and Waldo E. Koop, *Rowdy Joe Lowe, Gambler with a Gun* (Norman: University of Oklahoma Press, 1989), 151–54. For Earp, see Paula Mitchell Marks, *And Die in the West* (New York: William Morrow, 1989), 421. Information on Young episode from research by Sgt. Kevin Foster, historian of the Fort Worth Police Dept., contained in Bill Fairley, "The Historic Rampage and Death of Tommie Lee," *Fort Worth Star-Telegram*, Oct. 31, 2001, 6B.

55. General Laws of the State of Texas, Passed at the Regular Session of the 28th Legislature, January 13, 1903–April 1, 1903 (Austin: State Printer, 1903), S.B. No. 33, approved March 16, 1903, 57.

56. James Farber, *Fort Worth in the Civil War* (Belton, Tex.: Peer Hansbrough Bell Press, 1960), 33.

57. Wayne Andrews, ed., "Woman's Christian Temperance Union," *Concise Dictionary of American History* (New York: Charles Scribner's Sons, 1962), 1022. Other sources say the WCTU was founded in the Chicago suburb of Evanston in 1874. Either way, it was the first important national prohibition group. For success of prohibitionists in Ohio, see Norman H. Clark, *Deliver Us from Evil* (New York: W. W. Norton and Co., 1976), 71; and K. Austin Kerr, *Organized for Prohibition: A New History of the Anti-Saloon League* (New Haven, Conn.: Yale University Press, 1985), 288.

58. Andrews, "Woman's Christian Temperance Union," 41. John Allen Krout, *The Origins of Prohibition* (1925; reprint, New York: Russell and Russell, 1967), foreword.

59. Kerr, *Organized for Prohibition*, 35, 124. Some sources incorrectly use 1906 as the birth date of the Anti-Saloon League, but that is the year it was reorganized, not born.

60. Walter B. Stevens, *Through Texas* (St. Louis, Mo.: Mo., Ks., and Tx. Railway, 1893, microfilm copy in Library of Congress), 31.

61. Based on the research of Fort Worth resident Dick Ramsey, who in 1998–99 gathered material on the history of Miller Brewery in the city.

62. Madelon Powers, *Faces along the Bar: Lore and Order in the Workingman's Saloon, 1870–1920* (Chicago: The University of Chicago Press, 1998), 209.

63. Kerr, *Organized for Prohibition*, 34.

64. See *Fort Worth Daily Gazette*, Sunday, Mar. 9, 1890, 8, announcing "Grand opening at the Local Option saloon tonight from 6 to 9 pm. All are invited—Sam Kajawski, prop."

65. The fee is stated on a business card for the Panther Saloon, J. M. Williams, proprietor, n.d., in private collections of Bob Smith of Fort Worth. Quoted by permission.

66. This verse appears on the back of another saloon business card in the collections of Bob Smith, n.d. Quoted by permission.

67. See, for instance, *Dallas (Daily) Herald,* Sept. 8, 1884, 4. By comparison, note the coverage given to reunions of ex-Confederates (1885) and Mexican War veterans (1887) in the local press: *Fort Worth Daily Gazette,* Aug. 6 and 7, 1885, front page, and *Fort Worth Daily Gazette,* Sept. 26, 1887, 2.

68. Lender and Martin, *Drinking in America,* 107–108.

69. Ernest Hurst Cherrington, ed., *The Anti-Saloon League Year Book, 1915* (Westerville, Ohio: The Anti-Saloon League of America, the American Issue Press, 1915), 13, 21, 29, 200–201.

70. See Ginnochio's petition of August 3, 1896, in Fort Worth City Council Proceedings, January 19/25, 1897, vertical files transferred from Fort Worth City Secretary's Office to Fort Worth Public Library, Central Branch, Local History and Genealogy Dept.

71. Elliott West, "Saloons," in *Encyclopedia of the American West,* ed. Charles Phillips and Alan Axelrod, vol. 3 (New York: Simon and Schuster Macmillan, 1996), 1412.

72. From a speech given by Blevins in 1924 and reported in Dobie, *Cow People,* 110.

73. For an explanation of "perpendicular drinking" see Powers, *Faces along the Bar,* 127.

74. Mobeetie quote comes from R. H. Conlyn Diary, May 26, 1883; San Angelo quote comes from "Forrestine Cooper Hooker's Notes and Memoirs on Army Life in the West, 1871–1876." Both works cited in Robert Wooster, *Soldiers, Sutlers, and Settlers: Garrison Life on the Texas Frontier* (College Station: Texas A&M University Press, 1987), 79–80.

75. Jerry Flemmons, *Fort Worth Star-Telegram,* July 13, 1997, 1–8, Sec. D; and staff writers, *Fort Worth Star-Telegram,* May 23, 1989, 1-A. See also *Newsweek Magazine,* Feb. 6, 1989.

76. Undated clipping from *Fort Worth Star-Telegram* in "Texas Frontier Centennial Celebration Scrapbook, 1936–1939, Women's Division," Fort Worth Public Library, Central Branch, Local History and Genealogy Dept.

77. Petar Lazarevski, "Thank you, Texans! I'll Be Back!" *Fort Worth Star-Telegram,* Dec. 26, 1996, morning ed., 9, Sec. B.

BYRON JOHNSON

SHARON PEREGRINE JOHNSON

Chapter One

The Fine Art of Mixology

The forgotten element in the history of the Western saloon is the bartender, that fixture of every establishment who stood patiently behind the bar and blended into the woodwork. Yet good ones were held in the highest esteem and often given the respectful title of "Professor" or "Mixologist."[1] They were a migratory fraternity, just like the gamblers and cowboys they served, working for the highest bidder and traveling the "circuit" from one city to the next. The names of most have long since been forgotten. James Earp, one of the lesser members of the famous group of brothers, was not too good with a gun and walked with a bad limp, but he could produce a work of art from the myriad of bottles at his fingertips. Earp worked quietly as a bartender in Fort Worth for several years in the late 1870s. In the big cities, a few giants such as New York's Jerry Thomas and Harry Johnson and Chicago's James Malone achieved lasting fame for their skills behind the bar. They were paid princely wages and regarded as true professionals by their clientele. Like any skilled craftsman, they even had their own personal set of "tools"—custom-made silver bartending utensils worth thousands of dollars.

During the Golden Age of the Western saloon, lasting roughly from the 1870s through the 1880s, the legend of the frontier saloon was born, and a simple retail liquor establishment was transformed into an icon of American popular culture. Its swinging doors came to symbolize a nexus where good met evil. Its bar became a backdrop against which great issues were settled, sometimes with the finality of death. Today, more than a century after those glory days, no frontier institution has been as revered, maligned, misunderstood, and reinterpreted as the saloon of the Trans-Mississippi West.

The star employees were as much a part of the legend as the places where they worked. The history of the bartending fraternity is virtually a history of the Old West in microcosm, beginning with the gold strikes in California and Colorado in 1849 and 1859 respectively. Eager miners, entrepreneurs, and con men headed west in heretofore unimaginable numbers intent on making their fortunes in the shortest possible time. As soon as they arrived they sought places of easy socialization and liquid refreshment. Saloonkeepers with their liquid stock in trade were among the first to disembark from ships in San Francisco or set up their tents around the base of Pike's Peak, Colorado. They rapidly expanded their repertoire of traditional German and English bar drinks, spurred on by the spirit of experimentation and competition. Their clientele was young—mostly men in their twenties—and they constantly demanded new and novel libations to wash the dust out of their throats and ease the aches and pains of their labors. Drinks were sugared, flamed, layered, flavored, and garnished in ways unimagined by their colonial forebears. "Modern" drinks such as the martini—which began life as the less romantic sounding "Martiniz Cocktail"—were born in the rough and tumble conditions of the gold fields.[2]

The coming of the range cattle era after the Civil War brought a new influx of people—still mostly male—to the West, to be followed before the end of the century in even larger numbers by homesteaders, who were determined to put down roots. To the mining camps were now added the trail towns, railheads, and farmvilles as bustling frontier communities. The average working male spent ten to twelve hours a day hammering rock, staring at the south end of cattle, pushing plows, and laying track. Perhaps once a week or once a month these exhausted pioneers went into town to blow off a little steam and enjoy the benefits of civilization. While drinking they could observe clean, immaculately dressed, and smoothly competent "professors" overseeing a domain of walnut, brass, and crystal bars, drawing beer and mixing liquors for relatively high pay.

The unofficial "uniform" of the bartending fraternity consisted of a long-sleeved white shirt with tie (usually bow-tie), black vest, and white apron tied at the waist. Anything less in terms of attire was *déclassé*. Judging by the pictures that have survived, a handlebar mustache and slicked-back hair seem to have been standard, too. Also, based on the surviving pictures, the bartending fraternity was also exclusively white, which just indicates how the photographic record can sometimes mislead. What is true is that the photographers of the day who took pictures of bartenders posed proudly behind their bars preferred white, Anglo-Saxon subjects.

It is only natural to wonder how a person got into the business. The process was remarkably easy but hardly cheap. To begin with, the bartender rarely owned his own establishment; he was a hired hand just as much as the cowboy or railroad engineer. The business end of the saloon began with an owner-entrepreneur. The "entry-level" joints could be set up wherever somebody unhitched their wagon or staked out a tent, but the genuine entrepreneurs aimed considerably higher, thinking in terms of permanence. "Saloon outfits" could be mail ordered from one of the big companies in Chicago or St. Louis, or bought from traveling salesmen on credit. The Brunswick-Balke-Collender Company was the most famous manufacturer of fine saloon furnishings, offering a complete catalogue of walnut, oak, and mahogany bars, liquor cabinets, and screens: everything the would-be saloonkeeper needed.[3] Land or vacant buildings could be obtained through partnerships or by selling interest shares in a start-up venture. Wholesale liquor dealers and breweries—the latter sprang up all over the West to meet local demand—were glad to supply all the liquid stock saloonkeepers could move, and they could move a lot since most establishments operated on a twenty-four-hour-a-day, seven-days-a-week schedule. Manuals on how to furnish, stock, mix drinks, and in general run a successful saloon had been written by the bartending masters of the 1840s and '50s such as Jerry Thomas.[4] Since the Germans were the most prominent ethnic group in the business, some of these guidebooks were even printed in bilingual German-English text for the would-be mixologist with a poor command of English.[5]

If the whole process seemed too daunting, apprenticeship was a second route to success since there was roughly one saloon for every thirty persons out west, guaranteeing no shortage of opportunities for on-the-job training. A would-be entrepreneur could start at the bottom and work his way up from porter to bartender and ultimately to owner if he learned quickly and saved his money. As towns became more civilized, licenses became a requirement, but they were easily obtained by paying a small fee and making the right political connections.

The lure of the profession was tremendous. Although not as romanticized in American lore as the cowboy, the gambler, or the lawman, the bartender was in a highly attractive line of work where he was much less likely to get shot, trampled, or tossed in jail than any of those other, more romantic, professions. Statistics back up the appeal of the profession, revealing an all-American success story of almost Horatio Alger proportions. Between 1860 and 1900, U.S. Census records indicate that the number of bartenders and saloon owners west of the Mississippi River grew from 3,828 to 49,239. During the peak years between 1870 and 1890, 40 percent were recent immigrants of whom 25 percent traced their roots back to Germany, 11 percent to England, and 4 percent to Scotland, Ireland, or Wales. The remaining 60 percent were usually second-generation sons of the Rhineland or British Isles.[6] To a remarkable degree, the ranks of bartenders were ethnically homogeneous. Generally speaking, blacks, Hispanics, and Asians need not apply.

With competition so fierce—a dozen saloons might compete for business in a one-street town—image meant everything. Owners of "blind pigs," as the worst joints were called, were an embarrassment to their own brethren. The most successful places were clean, well-lit, and offered a wide selection of libations. They were also usually the first places in town to have gas or electric lighting, a telephone, and venues for first-rate musical entertainment.

The bartender or professor was a crucial part of the mix. He had to be not only knowledgeable of his craft but also congenial with his customers and handy with a bung-starter (mallet) on those occasions when one of the boys got a little rowdy. Research shows that the familiar im-

A group of well-dressed "mixologists" in a Kansas saloon just before Prohibition changed everything. In their white shirts and ties, these men are unabashedly proud of their profession. This unnamed saloon is obviously a busy and profitable establishment judging by the fact that it employs at least five bartenders. Note the words and date written across the picture. Courtesy *Kansas Collection, Kenneth Spencer Research Library, University of Kansas Libraries*

age of the surly bartender dispensing bad liquor and uncouth service to be largely a myth, probably created by the temperance warriors of the late nineteenth century—the same source that created the stereotype of the Mickey-Finn-mixing bartender rolling his customers for their bankroll. In truth, competition for the drinking public was stiff in established towns, and repeat business was crucial to the long-term success or failure of any saloon. Besides, those same customers that the bartender was supposed to be drugging and treating rudely were probably friends and neighbors. Bartending manuals advised mixologists not to let their patrons become falling-down drunk, but instead to send them home with memories of a good time so they would come back again and again. The same manuals admonished the conscientious bartender to prevent patrons with families from spending their last dime. Some saloon men even cashed paychecks for their regular patrons or held funds to assure that a man under the influence did not spend all his earnings.[7] The value of repeat business was a concept every saloonkeeper understood without possessing a Harvard business degree. The bottom line was, a stumblebum alcoholic who was likely to wind up in the gutter or worse very soon or a destitute patron with a starving family were liabilities to the saloon trade. Drinking in moderation had its practical proponents even in the nineteenth century.

But the title of "Mixologist" or "Professor" cannot cover up the fact that Western bartenders had to be tough hombres. In joints where fancy drinks were never requested, the bartender had to be able to act as either mediator or enforcer as the situation required. He collected customers' guns when they first came in and returned them to their owners later when they were ready to leave town. He could also be trusted to hold the bankroll of men who planned to do some serious drinking in an evening and were concerned about being robbed. He was also a one-stop tourist information office for newcomers in town. Want to find a particular fellow? Ask for directions? Get the inside dope on where the bodies are buried and the skeletons hidden? The bartender was the man to see.

In many saloons the bartender doubled as the bouncer. Some even had reputations for being as mean and lethal as any of their customers. Jerry Barton, a Phoenix bartender in 1876, was once insulted by a drunken customer. Not content just to toss the man out, Barton pushed him into the street and proceeded to pound him about the head with his fists. The man died as a result of the beating, and it was not the last time Barton assaulted a customer he took a dislike to. Bartender Luther Criswell of Santa Maria, California, dispensed whiskey and bile in equal portions at his Seventy-six Saloon. He insulted his customers and spread vicious lies about the townspeople, and threatened mayhem when called to account for his actions. It was a wonder anyone patronized his saloon. After he murdered a popular constable in 1890, a group of Santa Maria men dragged him out of jail one night and strung him up from the rafters of his own saloon, ending his reign of terror. But in general, bartenders were benign folks, well-liked and peaceable.[8]

Owners and bartenders alike were usually generous contributors to good causes. Rowdy Joe Lowe in Fort Worth was a major patron of the town's volunteer fire department in the 1870s, and when a disastrous fire occurred he was one of the first to open his wallet to get the rebuilding started. The barkeep's patrons were not only their customers but also their friends; the interests of one were the interests of the other. Every Western town had its share of schools, churches, monuments, police departments, volunteer fire companies, and destitute families, all supported by the saloon fraternity. Altruism and hard-headed business sense converged, which is why saloonkeepers did not have to always buy city officials under the table; they could win their undying gratitude by simply supporting the community in positive ways. The saloonkeeper as public benefactor!

By the end of the century the small, privately owned saloon was fast becoming a thing of the past.[9] In its place was emerging a new system of franchising where powerful breweries and distilleries bought up the best saloons and turned them into corporate entities whose stock and prices were set by a distant headquarters. In the new order profits took precedence over quality. It was the same tactics of consolidation and combination that the "robber barons" used to gain control of American industry in these same years. It was also a broad trend throughout the economy that proved irreversible.

In the saloon business, corporate ownership broke the traditional bonds that had always tied the owners and their staffs to the local community. The most obvious change was when the swank, gilded palaces of the 1880s slowly deteriorated into the shabby dives of the late 1890s. The well-paid, highly skilled bartender capable of mixing a hundred different drinks from memory was replaced by a server of dubious background and little skill. And the owner, that welcoming neighbor who knew everybody's name, was replaced by the manager, a company man who pushed the company product.

The change came on small cat's feet. The dwindling ranks of genuine mixologists who still took pride in their profession moved on to upscale hotels or one of the few remaining private bars. There was a half-hearted effort to unionize bartenders in the face of company pressure, but successful unionization was decades away. The Brunswick-Balke-Collender Company, maker of fine saloon outfits, began to simplify their bar designs, cutting corners on craftsmanship, while deleting the more grandiose outfits from the catalogues altogether. Rather than spend money maintaining the exquisite "professors' thrones" of walnut and ebony where a generation of bartenders had virtually held court for their customers, company-owned saloons covered over the fine woods with a coat of cheap paint or resurfaced them in simple-to-maintain tile and stone. The fine oil paintings which had once graced even middling establishments, often depicting languid nudes in seductive poses, were replaced by cheap, morally correct lithographs. The highly polished bars and gleaming fixtures were allowed to deteriorate, the traditional "free lunch" was eliminated, and entertainment vanished, all for the sake of the bottom line in the corporate ledger.

With the Progressive Era (ca. 1900–19) came a new mythology that painted the old saloons in the worst possible colors. One of the most persistent myths said that all a man could order in one of those places was "straight whiskey or straight beer." This was not only patently untrue but a shocking insult to the old Masters of Mixology. The Progressives helped bring on Prohibition after 1919, which was the beginning of the modern soft-drink craze. Many of the soft drinks that became popular in the early twentieth century were direct descendants of the fancy drinks and cocktails concocted in saloons of the last century. The old saloon drinks were sweet, flavored with up to a dozen ingredients, and sometimes "fizzed." If one were to take a "Dr. Pepper" (a Waco, Texas, original) today, add a shot of alcohol, and remove some of the carbonation, the results would be a fair approximation of an 1880s fancy drink or punch. The same is true of the modern Seven-Up, which is essentially an 1860s "Rocky Mountain Punch" sans the alcohol. The Old Masters knew how to tickle the taste buds of their customers and were respected for their unique skills.

Sadly, the mixologist went the way of the buffalo hunter and most other classic Western types. Their time passed. The Golden Age of the saloon will never return. Society has changed, electronic media has provided new entertainment options, a social infrastructure unknown in frontier towns is in place today, and the liquor industry is just another part of the corporate culture. However, it is important to remember that era when saloons were highly social environments, when properly run saloons were "attractive features of growing towns," and when the ordinary bartender was a professional mixologist.

NOTES

1. See, for instance, *Albuquerque Daily Democrat*, Jan. 22, 1883, 4. In less serious moments, some also called themselves "bar pilots" from sliding so many schooners of beer down the polished bar (editor's correspondence with William Holden, descendant of Bud Browne, who was proprietor of Fort Worth's Palais Royal Saloon in later years, Nov. 6, 2002).

2. Jerry Thomas, *Bar-Tender's Guide or How to Mix Drinks* (New York: Dick and Fitzgerald, 1887), 25. See also Byron A. Johnson and Sharon Peregrine Johnson, *The Wild West Bartender's Bible* (Austin: Texas Monthly Press, 1986), 158.

3. Brunswick-Balke-Collender, *Illustrated Catalog of Bar Fixtures* (Chicago: Brunswick-Balke-Collender Company, 1891, ca. 1898, 1904).

4. Jerry Thomas, *How to Mix Drinks, or, The Bon-Vivant's Companion* (New York: Dick and Fitzgerald, 1862 and 1887 eds.)

5. Harry Johnson, *Harry Johnson's New and Improved Bartender's Manual/ Practisches, Neues und Verbessertes Handbuch für Barkeeper, Salon und Hotelbesitzer, Deutsch und Englisch* (New York: Samisch and Goldman, Printers, 1882).

6. "Occupations," *U.S. Bureau of the Census Reports* (Washington, D.C.: GPO, 1870, 1880, 1900).

7. For instance, Harry Johnson, one of the profession's heroes, advised bartenders: "Show to your patrons that you are a man of sense and humanity, and endeavor to do only what is right and just by refusing to sell anything either too intoxicated or disorderly persons, or to minors. If you think a customer is about spending money for a beverage, when it is possible that he or his family needs the cash for some other, more useful purpose, it would be best to give him advice rather than the drink . . . and send him home with an extra quarter, instead of taking the dime for the drink from him." Harry Johnson, *Harry Johnson's 1882 New and Improved Bartender's Manual and a Guide for Hotels and Restaurants* (reprint, Newark, N.J.: Charles E. Graham and Co., 1934), 41.

8. For Barton, see Scott L. Nelson, "Trailing Jerry Barton," *Quarterly of the National Association for Outlaw and Lawman History, Inc.* 26, no. 1 (Jan.–Mar., 2002): 36–41. For Criswell, see Jon C. Picciuolo, "Shootout Between a Despised Bartender and a Popular Constable," *Wild West Magazine*, Apr., 2000, 64–66.

9. George Ade, *The Old-Time Saloon* (New York: Ray Long and Richard R. Smith, Inc., 1934), 155–74. Also, Thomas Noel, *The City and the Saloon, 1858–1916* (Lincoln: University of Nebraska Press, 1982), 79–118.

DAVID BOWSER

Chapter Two

Jack Harris's Vaudeville and San Antonio's "Fatal Corner"

In the old days it was known as the "Fatal Corner"—a place of bad luck, bad men, and bad endings. Everybody in San Antonio knew its reputation as far back as the 1880s. What people in those days called the "Fatal Corner" is actually the northwest corner of Soledad and Commerce Streets on Main Plaza, in the heart of old San Antonio. More than one building has occupied that site, but the most famous by far was the Jack Harris Vaudeville Saloon and Theater. "Fatal Corner" was a good name for it during the days of Jack Harris's place; the ghosts of Ben Thompson and King Fisher could have testified to that. Both men died there on the same night. If ever there existed a cursed place in old San Antonio, that corner at Soledad and Commerce was it.

It was not always so, however. In colonial times, San Antonio's old Main Plaza was a popular and charming gathering place for the citizens of Spain's largest city in Texas, indeed, in the whole Southwest. The city was founded in 1718 by an expedition commanded by Martin De Alarcon, governor of the Mexican province of Coahuila. In 1731 the first contingent of settlers arrived from the Canary Islands and were granted tracts of land on what later became Main Plaza.[1]

The land that would become the fatal corner originated as part of a grant to the Travieso family. It was given to Vicente Alvarez-Travieso by the king of Spain via the governor of Texas. Its first owner built a substantial home there. The great 1819 flood destroyed most of the house, and it had to be rebuilt.² An 1840 painting shows a strongly built rock or adobe house, but the site did not remain a family residence for long. In the years that followed several saloons were located on the site on Main Plaza as various commercial interests began to take over the area.

Sam S. Smith acquired the old Travieso property about 1850 and held onto it for more than three decades. Smith, known also by the Spanish nickname of "El Barbon" or "Big Beard," was a prominent local businessman and politician, and he was the Bexar County Clerk for several years. He managed to keep his hands clean of the worst of the shady dealings that went on at the corner of Soledad and Main Plaza, but that does not mean he was ignorant of them.³

He opened a small saloon and gambling place on the infamous corner. It consisted of a square room measuring about fourteen by fourteen feet with another, smaller room attached to the rear. The stone-and-adobe structure probably incorporated part of the old Travieso house. Many famous saloons had humble origins, starting out in store fronts, log cabins, or even tents. Smith's joint had a thatched roof and dirt floor. A few tables and chairs and probably a crude bar rounded out the "décor." Despite its modest fixtures, it soon became a favorite gambling and drinking spot.⁴ Next door to it on the west side stood the old Plaza House Hotel.

The little saloon attracted its share of hard cases. One of the worst was John Glanton, a former Texas Ranger who had served in the Mexican War. He became notorious as an Indian "scalp hunter" in Mexico and married a San Antonio girl of Hispanic heritage. Once, in 1848 near Smith's saloon, a Hispanic man accidentally spilled some water on Glanton's freshly shined boots. Glanton chased the man down the street and carved him up with a pocket knife, inflicting thirty or forty deep cuts on his head and body. The victim eventually recovered, but Glanton was typical of the kind of tough *hombres* who patronized San Antonio's saloons.⁵

On another occasion, according to the Mexican War memoirs of Sam Chamberlain, Glanton was involved in the killing of a fellow ranger over a game of cards. The two were playing in a joint known as the "Bexar Exchange" when the confrontation occurred. The ranger pulled a gun to shoot Glanton, but the pistol misfired. Glanton, whose weapon of choice was clearly the blade, slashed his opponent across the throat with a Bowie knife and killed him almost instantly. The "Bexar Exchange" was possibly Sam Smith's place.[6]

Later, in the 1850s, the corner building at Main Plaza and Soledad acquired a legitimate occupant when the drugstore of Devine and Attwater moved in. But even that did not guarantee peace and quiet on the site. On this spot Dr. J. M. Devine killed J. H. McDonald over a political dispute. Devine was almost lynched by friends of the dead man before law officers intervened and took him off to jail. He was later tried for murder but a jury acquitted him.[7]

Some years before the Civil War, the original stone or adobe building was razed and a larger, two-story structure of limestone blocks was erected on the site. The construction material was unusual for most of the American frontier because skilled stone masons were rare and working quarry sites were even rarer. But this was South Texas, not the Great Plains, and San Antonio had more than a few stone quarries nearby. Apparently, San Antonio also possessed more than its share of stone masons, because limestone-block construction predominated among the city's major buildings erected between the 1850s and 1870s. The exterior of the limestone shell was finished off with stucco and a slate roof added, making a very substantial building and one as close to "fireproof" as anything in Texas. The upstairs was finished off with wood framing, and later owners added a partial wood-frame extension to the rear to hold a theater. The whole thing could not be considered an architectural gem, but it was a solid structure that provided a comfortable home for a succession of saloons in the years to follow. Its first occupant, the Cosmopolitan, continued the tradition of having a saloon on the site. The Cosmopolitan after a few years gave way to Jack Harris's Saloon and Vaudeville Theater, which is what ultimately put the location on the map.[8]

When the Civil War began in 1861, San Antonio actually prospered thanks to illicit wartime trade with Mexico. Contraband Confederate cotton was shipped overland from the city across the Rio Grande and

The rather undistinguished two-story building at the center of the picture was the home of Jack Harris's Vaudeville Saloon and Theater. This circa 1868 photograph is obviously pre-vaudeville because there is no advertising or evidence of the business. Note Soledad Street, running down the side of the building, is still a dirt track. Courtesy *Grandjean Collection, Daughters of the Republic of Texas Library, San Antonio, Texas*

eventually to the markets of Europe. Confederate authorities kept a strong grip on local affairs, and Union forces never got far enough inland to threaten the city.

But even war and a booming economy did not prevent violence between men for more personal reasons. A famous gunfight occurred near the Fatal Corner in 1862 in front of the old Plaza House Hotel. A man named William Henry, also known as "Big Henry," was killed in a pistol duel with "Captain" Warren Adams, a notorious slave hunter on the Texas border. The duel arose over who would command a certain company of Confederate troops. Another gunfight occurred on almost the same spot between two Confederate officers named Hunter and Phillips for unknown reasons in which Phillips was killed.[9]

The end of the war brought an economic downturn when the illicit wartime trade in cotton dried up. But within two years a new economic activity brought renewed prosperity. San Antonio became the staging point for the big cattle drives going from South Texas to the cow towns of Kansas, principally Abilene, Dodge City, and Ellsworth. Soon immense herds of longhorns, and horses too, were being driven up the trail. Business was booming again in "Old San Antone"! The arrival of the railroad in 1877 completed the economic revival of the city.

On a personal level, the business boom put money in men's pockets and brought out the self-styled entrepreneurs to relieve them of that money. The principal ways to relieve a man of his liquid assets were the old standbys of gambling, liquor, and women, all of which were available in plentiful supply in the city. This is where Jack Harris and his saloon and vaudeville theater entered the picture.

There is very little known about Jack Harris himself. He was born in Connecticut about 1834, and at the age of twelve he left home to go to sea. In 1855 he joined William Walker, the "Grey-eyed Man of Destiny," in his filibustering expedition to Nicaragua. When that scheme failed he settled down in San Antonio and by 1860 he was working as a policeman. Like other frontier towns of the day, San Antonio did not have a full-time professional police force, so he must have had other sources of income—legal or otherwise. When the Civil War came he enlisted in the Second Texas Cavalry, and after four years of faithful but undistinguished service he returned to San Antonio and his former job on the police force.[10] January of 1869 found him in the saloon business when he opened a saloon on Market Street.[11] In those days, a two-way bridge connected the saloon business and law enforcement, and men regularly moved back and forth between the two lines of work with no questions asked. Harris was simply following a well-established career path when he moved from behind the badge to behind the bar.

He also had ambitions to run a first-class operation, and that required a prime location. By 1871 or 1872 at the latest, he had relocated to the old Cosmopolitan Saloon on the northwest corner of Soledad and Main Plaza.[12]

Sometime in the next two to three years, Harris made the crucial decision that he wanted his place to be more than just a saloon or gambling hall. He wanted to offer popular entertainment while serving up drinks and gambling on the side; most saloons operated on the exact opposite

Jack Harris, gimpy-armed proprietor of the Jack Harris Vaudeville Saloon and Theater. Also known as a gambler and gunman. Undated photograph, but Harris sports the sort of walrus mustache that was fashionable in the 1880s. Courtesy Western History Collections, University of Oklahoma Libraries

principle, with gambling and drinking driving the operation. Harris's approach hardly made him a trailblazer, but it did make him a different kind of entrepreneur than the White Elephant's Bill Ward (Fort Worth) or the Iron Front's John B. Neff (Austin). The problem was, Jack Harris had no experience running a variety theater. He needed a partner well versed in the ways of show business. Sometime before the end of 1874 he entered into some sort of partnership with D. G. Bronson, a well-known local variety theater man. Bronson's entrance is marked by a notice he placed in the *San Antonio Express* in December of that year informing the town's citizens that the "famous" banjo player Johnny Smith and an "Ethiopian" comedian would be playing the Vaudeville Theater December 31. This is the first known advertisement in the local press for Jack Harris's Saloon and Vaudeville Theater.[13]

The use of the word "vaudeville" in its name made Jack Harris's place practically unique among Western saloons. The term does not seem to have been in general use in the West of that period. The origins of the word go back to fifteenth-century France, where a distinctive type of ballad or "lighthearted song," the *Chanson de Vau-de-Vire* (Song of the Valley of the Vire) was named for a section of Normandy. As the term evolved, it came to mean a theatrical show composed of a variety of different performers in a series of unrelated acts. Such shows might feature female dancers, jugglers, singers, comedians, acrobats, or virtually any type of specialty act, thus a "variety show." Some sources trace it back to as early as 1827 in the United States. Vaudeville or variety shows as we understand them today, however, probably first appeared in New York City in the 1850s. They were an immediate hit with unsophisticated, lower-class urban audiences. The name and the form spread westward from there, which probably explains how Harris and company got the idea. Most Western saloons that adopted this form of entertainment called themselves "variety theaters," possibly because their customers would not know what "vaudeville" meant, much less how to pronounce it. Harris apparently wanted to add a veneer of class to the operation, although most of the acts they booked could hardly be considered "high-class." [14]

Harris was likely the first theater impresario in the Old West to describe his operation as a "vaudeville theater," although he was certainly not the first in the United States to do so. The whole concept of vaudeville on the frontier was either laughable or a shrewd business move. It certainly stood out from the other variety theaters in San Antonio. However, if Harris had any ambitions about running his joint like a first-rate vaudeville house, he kept them to himself. The business became a one-man operation after 1875 because in May of that year he purchased D. G. Bronson's half-interest. Bronson was not a saloon man, and Harris had probably learned all he needed to know from his partner about the theater business. There is no indication that they had a falling-out. It was probably at this time that the place became known by its notorious namesake, the "Jack Harris Saloon and Vaudeville Theater." However, while Harris was sole proprietor of the business, he did not own the property on which it sat. That was leased from Sam Smith, who was never a partner in the business. Harris continued to run the Vaudeville until his death in July, 1882. [15]

D. G. Bronson dropped out of the Vaudeville's story at this point. He went on to run the city's Adelphi Theater, a rival establishment that offered the same brand of entertainment, not to say legitimate theater. He apparently had other business interests as well, because his wife was hauled into Bexar County court in 1878. "Mrs. D. G. Bronson," as the judge's docket identifies her, was charged with "keeping a disorderly house," a legal euphemism of this time to describe a house of prostitution. The only surprise is that she did so under her married name, since most members of the profession preferred to adopt working names.[16]

Harris himself seems to have been a dedicated entrepreneur and sporting man. He never married but, beyond that, almost nothing is known about his personal life. There were some kinfolk back East with whom he had little contact. He was married to his saloon. Eventually he also became a prominent businessman, which represented a step up from being simply a "saloon man," as well as a power in the local Democratic Party. His circle of friends included some of the best and some of the worst people in San Antonio. The story of Jack Harris's life and times as told by himself would have made interesting reading, but he never wrote his memoirs. He did not live that long.

In his public image, Harris never outgrew his rough, frontier origins despite the gentleman's clothes and theater society he favored. He could hold his own in any company, but as a barkeep he seems to have transformed himself into a very capable businessman who knew what his customers wanted and how to provide it for them. The Vaudeville under his proprietorship had the reputation of being a rather rowdy place, but in the saloon business rowdy was better than sedate. Being sedate meant boring; customers looking for a little excitement were likely to go someplace else. To their credit, Harris and his associates always strove to maintain an orderly and basically honest operation. To most of the respectable citizens of San Antonio the Jack Harris Vaudeville Theater and Saloon was a wild and wicked den of vice, but it was still several cuts above most of its sister establishments in the city.

Any well-traveled saloon afficionados would have considered it quite tame, for instance, compared to a joint like the Gem Variety Theater in Deadwood, Dakota Territory, where hardened prostitutes not only plied their trade, but innocent girls were cruelly forced into the profession.[17] Jack Harris was a rough fellow but a fair and square one. He did

The building that housed Jack Harris's Vaudeville Saloon and Theater can be seen at the right end of the row of buildings, ca. 1868. The photographer's view is from the south side of Main Plaza, looking north. A horse and cart stand in front of the building. Note the plaza is still an unpaved expanse. Courtesy *Grandjean Collection, Daughters of the Republic of Texas Library, San Antonio, Texas*

have some scruples, a fact that was reflected in the popularity of his establishment and its long reign as the city's premier saloon and place of entertainment.

By 1880 Harris had acquired a good deal of political influence in San Antonio, a natural development for the city's most powerful saloon man. He was a prominent member of the Democratic Party, which was a good thing in a city that still identified Republicans with carpetbaggers and scalawags. He acted as sort of a middleman between San Antonio's visible political structure and its underworld controlled by the "sporting" fraternity. It was said that anyone hoping to run for office on the Democratic ticket had to first get the approval of Jack Harris. Though he never held elective office, he was the power behind the throne of city government.[18]

The source of his power as well as his base of operations was the Vaudeville. The theater-saloon complex faced south on Main Plaza. Its principal entrance was on the Main Plaza side of the building, but there were also several entrances on the Soledad Street side. Not an impres-

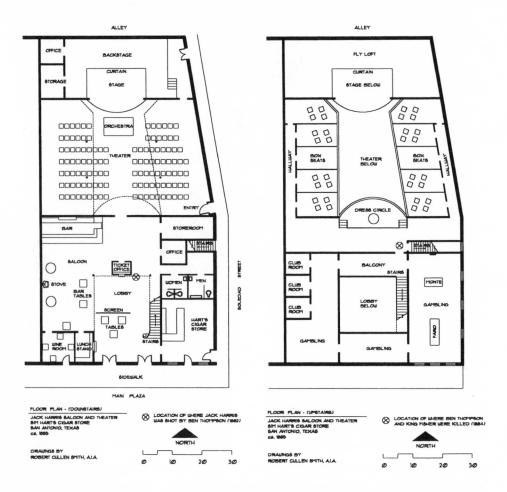

FLOOR PLAN - (DOWNSTAIRS)

JACK HARRIS SALOON AND THEATER
SIM HART'S CIGAR STORE
SAN ANTONIO, TEXAS
ca. 1883

DRAWINGS BY
ROBERT CULLEN SMITH, A.I.A.

⊗ LOCATION OF WHERE JACK HARRIS
WAS SHOT BY BEN THOMPSON (1882)

NORTH

0   10   20   30

FLOOR PLAN - (UPSTAIRS)

JACK HARRIS SALOON AND THEATER
SIM HART'S CIGAR STORE
SAN ANTONIO, TEXAS
ca. 1883

DRAWINGS BY
ROBERT CULLEN SMITH, A.I.A.

⊗ LOCATION OF WHERE BEN THOMPSON
AND KING FISHER WERE KILLED (1884)

NORTH

0   10   20   30

sive structure when it was constructed in the 1850s, the building under-
went several remodelings during the next thirty years, reflecting its
growing popularity and profitability.

In its general layout, which went virtually unchanged over the years,
the Vaudeville was a two-story, stone structure with a sixty-foot frontage
on the plaza. The building measured about 110 feet down the long side
on Soledad Street.[19] A classic Western false front covered the stonework
on about two-thirds of the Main Plaza side, stopping just short of Sim
Hart's Tobacco Shop on the corner. Hart's place was connected to the
saloon by an inner door, suggesting that the two were also connected by
business ties. A covered boardwalk supported by iron posts stretched
across the front of the building, providing a pedestrian thoroughfare

above the seasonal dust or mud of the street. At night torches flamed out front not so much to provide illumination as to attract attention like a bright light attracts moths, which was also accomplished by having the house orchestra play loud, lively tunes on the outside balcony. The music could be heard all over the plaza, pulling in customers to the best show in San Antonio.

Before 1882, the interior was illuminated not by torches but by gaslight, which produced, in addition to flickering light, such unpleasant by-products as heat, oily residue, and the ever-present danger of flash fire. All that changed in 1882. Like its sister saloons in other cities, the Vaudeville positioned itself on the cutting edge of technology. When electricity came to San Antonio early in the decade, the Vaudeville became one of the first places to install the new lighting. Customers marveled at how bright the interior of the saloon was, no matter how dark the night outside. The conversion was such a significant step that the *San Antonio Express* took more interest in it than in the evening's program or the actors when announcing on March 4, 1882, "The Vaudeville will be resplendent with electric light tonight." This was the first mention made in public print of electric lighting being used in any San Antonio theater or saloon.[20]

Entering through the double doors of the main entrance, customers had to walk around a wood latticework screen strategically placed just a few feet inside the doorway before they reached the public areas. The screen provided a modicum of privacy against the prying eyes of the very young or very proper walking by outside. The first floor's main room measured about forty by forty feet but was divided by a partition into theater and saloon areas. The theater ticket office and the traditional "free lunch" counter were up front on the left. Directly across the room to the right was the door leading to Sim Hart's Tobacco Shop. Also on that same side of the room was an open staircase leading up to the second floor where the "101" gambling rooms as well as the entrance to the theater's balcony and dress circle were located. Straight ahead from the front doors was the entryway into the theater. Also ahead but off to the left was the long bar, the heart of every Western saloon, where customers could belly up and order their favorite drink. The bar was made of solid oak, stained to a dark brown. It had fancy brass fittings including the traditional brass rail running along the bottom for customers to rest one foot on while they leaned up against the bar.

The real showpiece in the bar area was the mirrored back bar that featured ornate wood carving and paneled oak, also stained to a rich, dark brown hue. The back bar had several wooden arches in which mirrors were encased. Practically every type of whiskey imaginable was visible in corked bottles on the back bar, the glassware and amber liquids refracting the light to create a glittering display. The place offered a good selection of wine and beer, too, in keeping with the Vaudeville's reputation as a full-service establishment. When the theater was not in session, a piano in the saloon provided musical background to the conversations and clinking of glasses.

The customers of the Vaudeville were a diverse lot. On any night one might see a veritable menagerie of humanity within its walls. Cowboys, cattlemen, soldiers, tradesmen, fancy gamblers, "drummers" (traveling salesmen), general laborers, railroad men, doctors, lawyers, big and small businessmen, all comprised the crowd on a typical night. The bulk of the customers were Anglo-American males with a sprinkling of Hispanics. Management would not have allowed African Americans and Chinese inside the door in keeping with the usual Jim Crow admission policies of the day. San Antonio historian Frank Bushick says, "The saloons were in fact places of popular resort where men of all classes dropped in for social confab, to tell stories and talk politics, as much as to whet their whistles."[21] Reflecting his own upbringing and culture, when Bushick wrote about "men of all classes" he probably had in mind men who might have been rich or poor but still looked like himself: white males.

The key word is "men." San Antonio's saloons and variety theaters were resorts for men where the only women allowed were those who worked on the premises, as opposed to the "decent" variety who would not be caught dead in such places. The Vaudeville's management gave special consideration to big spenders in the form of private theater boxes, a fancy "dress circle" balcony, private clubrooms, or a reserved table in a quiet corner for a high-stakes game of poker. Special consideration might also include private time with the female performers after the show or other attractive women brought in from outside. The wealthy customer was king.

As a self-styled classy establishment, the Vaudeville also had a "wine room," which was a private area for small parties or where a gentleman could entertain a "lady" with a measure of privacy. The entrance to the wine room was to one side of the bar. Some of the Vaudeville's girls were regularly assigned to the wine room to serve the needs of special customers, meaning those with powerful connections or sizable bankrolls. The quality of that service ranged from "good hustlers" to "chair warmers." [22]

On the other side of the partition, the theater auditorium measured about sixty by sixty feet including the narrow backstage area. Rows of uncomfortable wooden chairs filled the rest of the room, divided into two sections by an aisle down the middle. Above were the balcony and dress circle. The latter was usually reserved for big-spenders and prominent guests. For even more privileged customers there was a row of red-curtained theater boxes on each side of the auditorium above the hoi polloi on the floor.

Straight ahead was the stage, the obvious focus of the room. It was semicircular, jutting out a bit into the seating area. Fancy woodwork framed the stage, painted red and gold and green. For most of its history, illumination of the performers came from gas lights. A decoratively painted curtain separated the stage from the audience. Musical accompaniment was provided by a little orchestra, of dubious talents, sitting in an enclosure at the foot of the stage. They played popular airs and show tunes, adapting their limited repertoire to every performance rather than learning new material all the time.

The Jack Harris Vaudeville Theater and Saloon actually incorporated three operations under one roof, as was customary in such places. In addition to the theater and saloon, it offered gambling facilities. A different manager ran each area, with Harris overseeing the entire operation as a sort of congenial innkeeper.[23] The tobacco room, or "apartment" as it was called, faced the corner of Main Plaza and Soledad, where it could serve both the Vaudeville's clientele and walk-in customers off the street. The popular Sim Hart ran the tobacco apartment, and it was known as a first-class shop.

The theater was the best known side of the multifaceted operation. It might also have been the most interesting, if only because of the parade of colorful performers who appeared on its stage over the years. A recitation of those actors must begin with the resident stock company. At the time the Harris-Bronson partnership took over in 1873, there was already a regular performing troupe on the payroll, consisting of the "Misses" Nellie Saroney, Mary Olive, Hattie Pierce, Hattie Harton, and sisters Annie and Mollie Sommers, plus "Messrs." Lew Ginger, Johnny Pierce, Arthur Graham, and H. Seamon, and a team billed as "Boyd and Hart." The word "Miss" in front of an actress' name could be taken in two ways: as an honorific title recognizing her professional status, or it could suggest that she was employed in the world's oldest profession. With theater performers, the two meanings often merged in the public mind until "actress" became nearly synonymous with prostitute. The fact that many actresses adopted stage names only added to the public's suspicion that they had something to hide. San Antonio's Fashion Theater employed one Belle Storms, better known by her stage name, Loa Durand.[24] And since actors were a small and close-knit fraternity, many actresses found husbands or lovers among the ranks of the actors they performed with regularly. This is why, so often on playbills, the same last name appears more than once. Ironically, sexual discrimination in Western variety theaters tended to be the opposite of what we are accustomed to today. Actresses found many more employment opportunities (so long as they were not too choosy about working conditions) than actors. The all-male audiences simply preferred their stage performers to be curvaceous and feminine.

Frank Bushick gives us a peek at some of the stage actresses and their modus operandi, calling them "the original gold-diggers." A typical show was based on old minstrel show routines, right down to black-faced performers. In the first part of the show, all the talent was on the stage, with the "gag men" in black face on the ends. The actresses formed a semicircle of "well-filled hosiery" in this part, after which they all trooped down into the all-male audience to mingle with the spectators and accept refreshments from "perfect strangers." The girls got a percentage on all the drinks served, which encouraged a lot of mingling. "Smile on them once and your money was no longer your own." When the "boys from the sticks" ran out of money or got tired of buying overpriced drinks for no more than a wink and a smile, the girls retreated to the stage. "Over-rouged and under-dressed, these stage fairies were of-the-earth earthy and did not tarry long with dead ones." [25]

The men who belonged to the stock company were probably either comics, acrobats, or jugglers, although there may have been a Shake-spearean actor in the bunch. Western audiences seemed to enjoy the occasional Shakespeare performance, so long as it did not cut into the dancing girls' time on stage.[26] In 1876, Seamon and Pierce were not only performers but also listed in the records as "proprietors" of the theater. Will C. Burton served as stage manager that year.

The regular troupe in 1878 was composed of L. W. Herty, Frank Sparrow, Sam Charles, J. G. Miller, Dave W. Douglas, J. Blechini, Augustine Gutierres, R. W. Howard, Henry and Eldon Gaylor, James C. Mulligan, the McDermott Sisters, Carrie Woods, Annie Braddon, and "Miss Gayor." Douglas was commonly referred to as "Professor" because of his elevated position as the orchestra leader, but even so, he was not the most important name on the list. That honor went to Frank Sparrow for several reasons. Besides being a member of the acting company, he functioned as the theater's business and stage manager from December 20, 1875, until 1884. His observations about those who came and went on the Vaudeville's stage over the years is an invaluable record. Sparrow was a New Yorker before landing in San Antonio. He had been born in New York City in 1846, the son of a well-known minstrel performer, and started his stage career there in the Olympic and Atheneum theaters.[27]

Horace Wambold, one of the actors in the Vaudeville's stock company for a number of years, was once involved in a real, live shoot-out in another of the city's watering holes . Wambold killed someone known as the "Pilot Point Kid" at the Silver King Saloon and Gambling House on Military Plaza, which made him a "bad actor" in an entirely different sense of the word than his fellow players used the term. It did not seem to affect his stage career, however, and may have even made him a bigger draw thereafter.[28]

Visiting actors performed with the resident troupe over the years, usually brought in to headline a show. In 1876 Sophie Rost, Charles Conrad, Marvin and Kitty Smith, Mr. and Mrs. Billy Scott, and Oscar Babel all passed through town appearing on the Vaudeville stage.[29] Some of

the more prominent visiting performers over the years included Grace
Thorne, Fannie Bloodgood, and Marie Wainwright, dramatic actresses
of some renown, and Frank Brown, a popular minstrel performer who
performed in black face. All of these actors had played the New York
stage and were well known in the American theater of their day, playing
major cities as well as backwaters like San Antonio.[30] They were the
equivalent of today's movie stars. One of the Vaudeville's visiting players shared the same name, and perhaps the same bloodline, as a famous
Hollywood stage and screen actor of the twentieth century, Lionel Barrymore.[31] In 1879 an act who came all the way from Madrid's Teatro Real
(Royal Theater) played the Vaudeville. Exactly what they did is a mystery, but anytime an act could be imported from Europe, it was a sure
sign that the theater was prospering.

Whether performing as variety acts or filling featured roles in some
production, visiting players quickly moved on. As for where they came
from before landing in San Antonio and where they went after leaving,
most such information is lost to history. And although they may have
been headliners at the Vaudeville, in the larger world of theater most
were poor rootless actors barely surviving on the fringes of their profession. Itinerant players came and went, their names and performances
quickly lost to history except for a brief mention in a newspaper ad tout-
ing the show. They might as well have been mayflies, living for a few
days in the glow of the footlights before dying when the last curtain was
rung down.

The stock company not only performed and handled the technical
and business side of the theater, they also wrote some of their own material. In 1877, a member of the troupe named Sam Charles wrote
"Mazeppa; or The Bunko of the San Pedro," which the company subsequently performed. New members to the troupe that year were banjo
player Dick Brown, Miss Ella Davis, Mr. O'Donohue and Miss Rose
Marretta.[32]

The only record we have of the Vaudeville Theater's operations
comes from Frank Sparrow. He wrote no memoirs, but he did leave behind a business ledger that he kept during his years as stage manager.
The faded old hardbound notebook with crumbling bindings measures
about fourteen by six inches and covers the years from 1875 through

1884. The information recorded on its yellowed and brittle pages offers a glimpse into the inner workings of Texas' first full-blown popular theater. Sparrow recorded such things as who was hired, what they were hired to do, and how much they were paid. He also noted the length of their booking at the theater. But what makes the old ledger especially interesting are Sparrow's sometimes caustic comments in the form of marginal notes written beside the names of the performers who came through the Vaudeville. Biographical details on most of these early show people are nonexistent, but there is something fascinating about them in their very anonymity. Just a perusal of Sparrow's notations during the years 1882–84 gives a revealing picture of a small-time, frontier theater company:

Emma De Haven, hired for 4 weeks as a ballad singer at $25 per week: "Fine form/good voice, a good hustler in the W. R. [Wine Room] when watched."

Jerry J. Dwyer, hired as a violinist and orchestra leader. "[A] fart and a booger from way back. . . . Poor Jerry. Generous to a fault. [There are] worse than him in the World."

Lulu Alberts, hired as a "chair warmer" in the wine room at $10 a week for 4 weeks.

Lizzie Haywood, Seriocomic, $20 a week for 4 "or more" weeks. "Damn bad."

Belle Sautley, hired at $20 a week for the balance of the season. A "male impersonator." Her act is "no good on earth."

George Wilson, Doorkeeper, $9 a week.

Annie Milton, Jig and song and dance at $12 a week.

Chicago Girls, for the fall season. "Chair warmers at 3 in number, ought to be slinging hash in a hotel."

Kitty Wells, Seriocomic, $30 a week. "$15 [is] too much for her. Very fresh."

Maud Walker, $30 a week. "Very good but very conceited, chair warmer and C."

Charles Frye, Comedian, booked for 12 weeks at $20 a week.

Minnie Leonard, Hustler, $10 a week. "Gone to Fort Allen. Closed May 27th." [Fort Allen was a locally famous bordello located near the Alamo. It was run by a madam named Blanche Dearwood.]

Pearl Sherwood, Hustler, $20 a week.

Gussie Robinson, Hustler, $20 a week.

Baker and Maurice, booked for 4 weeks, comedians and dancers.

McGill and Reardon, 4 weeks, Irish comedians. "Very fair but terrible boozers."

Lottie Richmond, 12 weeks, song and dance act, $30 a week. "Too many pads. Hop fiend." ["Hop fiend" meant an opium addict.]

Daisy Scott, Chair warmer, $10 per week. "Will never be killed for good looks." [33]

Like all theaters throughout history, finding fresh talent was a constant problem, as was dealing with drunken or drugged-up actors ("hop fiends") who were too addled by booze or opium to go on. Singing, dancing, and comedy were, naturally, the most desirable talents. Most of the actors who graced the Vaudeville's stage over the years were on the downhill side of their careers, or they were young newcomers hoping for a big break that would get them to the big cities and bright lights back East. The turnover among members of the regular company was rapid as actors were replaced, were fired, or moved on to other venues.

Actors were paid according to whatever they could negotiate with a tight-fisted manager or how desperate that manager was for any kind of show to put on his stage. There was no "scale" or minimum wage. Jack Harris did not concern himself with this side of the business; that is what he hired men like Sparrow or Burton to do. Sports (fashionable and admired "men about town," men who were money-makers and risk-takers) like Ben Thompson and Luke Short, not thespians, were more Jack Harris's type. The usual contract at the Vaudeville seems to have been six weeks, although some lucky acts were hired for a full "season," which literally meant fall, winter, spring, or summer.[34] Less popular acts, such as Shakespearean actors and grand opera singers, might get only a four-week contract, or less. Ethnic humor, especially in the form of Irish comics, seems to have been a hit with audiences of the day.

The revue-style variety shows were interspersed with regular two- and three-act plays. Sparrow kept the newspaper clippings about a number of plays presented at the Vaudeville, from *Lights O' London, Devils Auction, Sporting Life, Nathan Hale,* and *James Boys,* to heavier fare such as *Faust, Silver King, Cleopatra, East Lynne, Carmen,* and *Bohemian Girl.* These apparently were all special presentations because the actors and actresses in them are not mentioned otherwise in the ledger book; they may have been touring companies who were not part of the regular vaudeville circuit. At least some of the full-scale productions, however, were plays written by local talent, including one odd piece presented in 1879 entitled *The Effects of the Belt Punch*.[35]

The demise of the Vaudeville Saloon and Theater in the summer of 1884 coincides with the end of Frank Sparrow's ledger detailing the theater's operations. Like so many of the actors who had come through its doors, he moved on to other stages. And like Will Burton before him, he subsequently worked both sides of the lights, dividing his time between managing and performing. Not much is known about him outside of his eight-year association with the Vaudeville. Sparrow died in San Antonio on November 8, 1888, following a long battle with tuberculosis (called "consumption" in that day). His passing was noted on the front page of the newspaper. Residents of the city would remember him fondly not merely as the behind-the-scenes manager of the theater, but as a "versatile comedian and old favorite in San Antonio." [36]

With a little imagination, one can easily picture Frank Sparrow sitting at his desk in the manager's office backstage at the Vaudeville. His typical day is far different from the gamblers, gunmen, and sports who make up the regular clientele. For one thing, they will not show up until that evening while his workday begins early and runs late. All the doors are open to take advantage of any breezes blowing through the plaza. The band is rehearsing and workmen are moving scenery and props for the evening performance. Sparrow puffs on a cigar as he interviews people seeking a job at the Vaudeville. It is quite a menagerie of human beings from a variety of backgrounds, but he is used to that. There is a high turnover rate among both the staff and acting company. His years in the theater business have made him a pretty shrewd judge of thespian talent, and of people in general. He hires all the actors and actresses, barmaids, bouncers, and whatever other personnel are needed to run the place. He will probably be there until well after midnight. Sometimes he does not arrive back at his home at 309 Madison Street until 2:00 or 3:00 in the morning.[37] Yet he does not have the luxury of sleeping late; he usually rises at 9:00 and is back at the theater by noon.

Typically, he interviews job seekers while making arrangements for the evening's performance. His interview routine is methodical and smooth. As he asks questions, he jots down notations in his ledger.

On this day he interviews one Emma De Haven. She is good-looking, a ballad singer who has worked there before but left in good standing. He knows she is a good hustler in the wine room who can really get the gents to put down their money. He hires her right off. Next to come through his door is Lizzie Heywood. She has a comedy act that is not very good, but he has to fill that slot on the playbill; no one else is available, so he hires her with a sigh. Annie Milton follows her. She is a cute little song-and-dance girl who has played San Francisco, Tucson, Tombstone, and El Paso—an admirable resume on the frontier. She has a pleasing manner, too, so he hires her quickly.

Jack Harris and Billy Simms stop by about this time, so Sparrow introduces Miss Milton to them. They size the new girl up without the least subtlety. Jack is in a particularly good mood because the establishment has been doing great in the past few weeks, with money rolling in from all parts of the business. Good times in the saloon–variety theater business can be very good!

Jack and Billy saunter out and it is back to work. Next into his office are three giggling girls from Chicago who claim to have worked in variety theaters in Omaha, Nebraska; Dodge City, Kansas; and Austin. They are all in their late teens but have the look of having been "around the block a few times." They have no particular theatrical talents that he can detect, but are not bad lookers, which in his book makes them candidates to be drink hustlers or perhaps barmaids. He hires them as "chair warmers," albeit with some reservations noted in the ledger. Then comes one Kitty Wells. She is a serio-comic actress she says and reels off a list of theatrical credits to back up her claim. Being pretty does not hurt her chances, but she is arrogant, and he takes an instant dislike to her. Still, his business sense reminds him the show must go on, and qualified actresses do not come through his door every day, so he hires her on the spot.

The manager takes a short break in mid-afternoon and wanders out to the bar to have a whiskey. There he runs into regular customer Sim Hart who, as usual, has a joke for him. A few minutes later Sparrow is backstage again where he takes a few moments to check on the scenery painters. They have not created quite what he wants, so he gives them more specific instructions. Then it is back to his office for more interviews. He quickly hires Pearl Sherwood and Gussie Robinson. They are not bad looking although a little rough around the edges; they definitely have some mileage on them. The last of this day's hirings are a couple of Irish comedians known as McGill and Reardon; those may even be their real names. They have played the Vaudeville before, and he considers them to be a good act with plenty of "style." They are also known to drink copious quantities of whiskey, and Reardon has a reputation for being as good with his fists as he is with a joke. The last time they played the Vaudeville, Reardon paid a visit to Sallie Brewer's parlor house in the San Pedro district where he got into a fight and wrecked the joint, which earned him a trip to jail. Sparrow rounded up the Vaudeville's special policeman (bouncer), Jacob S. Coy, and together they went down to the jail to bail the brawling Irishman out. The popular manager had sufficient pull with the authorities to ensure that the case never went to trial, but it cost him more money to placate Sallie and cover her damages. It is all part of the cost of running a frontier theater. He warns McGill and Reardon to keep their noses clean this time.

After finishing his interviews for the day, Sparrow can take a break and prop his feet up on the desk, laying the ever-present ledger to one side. He leans back and lights a fresh cigar, puffing on it casually as he reflects back on the day's hires. Through the doorway, he can see old Jesse sweeping up and arranging chairs in the balcony. In a couple of hours the evening crowd will start coming in and Sparrow will get busy again. He hopes he can get home early tonight.

Although his association with the Vaudeville Theater assured Frank Sparrow's place in San Antonio history, even before the place closed in 1884 he had already faded into the background. In a diminished role, he continued to function as stage manager, overseeing the actors and shows under the direction of a higher-up. Two new managers, Sim Hart and John Martin, came in to oversee general operations. This change occurred sometime before September, 1878, when they are first mentioned in that capacity in local accounts. Little is known of John Martin prior to this time, but Sim Hart had run the little corner tobacco "apartment" on the first floor, before moving up to theater management.[38] Martin and Hart wanted to run the theater as a tonier establishment than the common variety theaters of the day. At this time, the Vaudeville was probably the best and most popular variety theater in San Antonio. The revolving door that was the performing troupe continued to go around. New members who came in at the beginning of the Martin and Hart regime included Frank Monroe, Horace Wambold, Marie Zaurine, and J. C. Murphy. The talent level of the troupe remained the same. As the Vaudeville became more popular and hence more profitable, additional members were hired to augment the regular troupe: Josie Fey, Ida Vivienne, Miss Zoe West, Melina Jones, and Blanche Nichols all made their debut on the Vaudeville's stage while Hart and Martin were in charge.

The staff of the Vaudeville included, in addition to the resident troupe of actors and house orchestra, the usual complement of skilled bartenders and burly porters. The bartenders were as tough as the customers. The Vaudeville's were not only capable at mixing drinks but kept a shooting iron close at hand and knew how to use it. At the first sign of trouble, they could reach under the bar and pull out a double-barreled shotgun, adding welcome backup to the house security force.[39] It was all part of their job description.

One member of the staff was specifically charged with keeping a lid on things, the equivalent of today's "bouncer" but wearing the more dignified title, "Special Policeman." His job was to be around whenever trouble broke out, utilizing either diplomacy or brute strength to break it up. Such officers were a normal adjunct to frontier law enforcement all over the West and operated in the gray area between private security forces and public servants. They were more than mere "bouncers," however, because they got to wear uniforms and make arrests just like regular policemen. Favored by penurious city councils that could never afford salaried policemen, they were "hired" by the city but paid by establishments like the Vaudeville where they worked exclusively. While on the premises, they enjoyed limited police powers and were considered duly appointed officers of the law. Most saloons employed one man in this capacity, who handled the usual assortment of drunks and sore losers, but in an emergency he could call for backup from the city's regular police force. The Vaudeville's special policeman in its last few years was one Jacob Coy, about whom little is known except his name and his involvement in some historic events.[40]

The San Antonio of Jack Harris's heyday was a vibrant and exciting place to be, with a full cast of colorful characters and plenty of interesting walk-ons. The federal census of 1880 showed the city's population to be 20,550. From January, 1875, to January, 1885, James H. French ruled as mayor. He was succeeded by the well-liked Bryan Callaghan, known to his constituents as "King Bryan," who occupied the mayor's office from 1885 until 1892. The city's first railroad, the Galveston, Harrisburg and San Antonio, arrived in February, 1877, and in February, 1881, the first International and Great Northern Railway train pulled into town. The town was booming in these years, with new buildings going up and old ones being razed in the name of progress. The city got an electric utility company and a telephone exchange during the decade. Little by little during the 1880s, the old Mexican provincial town that had once been San Antonio was fast being replaced by a modern city.[41]

San Antonio enjoyed the status of being not only the largest city in Texas at the time but was also the commercial center of the state. Its stores offered a wide variety of goods from boots and saddles to pistols and rifles to books and stationary. It was the fashion center of the state also, where the latest in men's and women's apparel could be seen in the store windows: hats, coats, and vests for the gents, dresses, hats, and parasols for the ladies. San Antonio had left its days as a sleepy Spanish town far behind. Many of the city's businesses occupied sites on or near the two largest public squares, Main Plaza and Military Plaza, although newer commercial districts were fast developing on Houston Street and Alamo Plaza. The cattle and horse yards were located just south of Main and Military Plazas, underscoring the fact that the city was also a livestock center.

San Antonio was also an army town. It had always been the site of a substantial military presence ever since colonial times, and the 1880s were no different, with a new U.S. Army post (later to be known as Fort Sam Houston) going up on "Government Hill." This post served as a Quartermaster Depot funneling supplies to the various frontier forts scattered across the state. Members of the garrison on Government Hill would have been quite familiar with Jack Harris's place and all it had to offer in the way of entertainment. For the visitor from out of town who was not a guest of the army, local accommodations ranged from the fancy Menger Hotel at the top end to the comfortable Pacific House, Southern and Maverick hostelries on the lower end of the scale.

For the visitor or citizen who found himself an unwilling "guest" of the city, San Antonio had a brand-new, state-of-the-art county jail in the 1880s. The lock-up had been built in 1878 by English architect Alfred Giles. It was located just off Military Plaza, on Camaron Street. The gothic-style, two-story structure was made of limestone blocks and looked distinctly castlelike. Administrative offices occupied the front, and the cells for prisoners stood in the back. A stout, fifteen-foot-high wall enclosed the jail yard, and in later years, as crime became more gender-neutral, a special women's section was added.[42] The new jail replaced the old, circa 1850 courthouse and jail on the west side of Military Plaza. The old building remained in service until 1889 as the home of the city jail and recorder's court. Some of the Vaudeville's customers at one time or another tried out the hospitality of the city's jailhouse.

The chief competition for the Vaudeville during these years came from a small handful of first-class establishments in the business district. Saloons of all types were more numerous than churches—and took in more money—but only a few stood out as rivals to the Vaudeville in terms of hospitality, quality of gambling, and how well stocked the bar was. The Tivoli and the Revolving Light, both on the east side of Main Plaza, were highly rated by aficionados of such places. But the best of the competition was the White Elephant Saloon, located on the same side of Main Plaza (the north) as the Vaudeville and just three doors down the street. It occupied a limestone building built in 1883 and had a legitimate claim to the title of San Antonio's showplace saloon and gambling emporium. Like its Fort Worth sister (no relation), the White Elephant was known for its high-class decor, which included an elegant bar, fancy marble floors, and plush gambling rooms. It lost out in competition with the Vaudeville, however, because it lacked a theater, being only a gambling emporium and saloon.[43]

There were other places in San Antonio that called themselves theaters, but none combined all the qualities of the Vaudeville. Some of the city's better-known variety theaters of the era were the Washington, the Fashion Theater, and the Bella Union. All of these featured in-house saloons and gambling rooms, just like the Vaudeville, as well as "available" women for a price, but they lacked Jack Harris's Midas touch.

The Washington Theater, on the northeast corner of Commerce and North Laredo Streets, opened in 1885 as an outgrowth of the Washington Saloon. Its owner may have been influenced to make the change by the enviable success of Jack Harris's operation. The Washington continued in operation until about 1910. For a variety theater, it had a fairly clean reputation. At least it was never the scene of any full-blown gun battles.[44]

The Fashion Theater, located on the west side of Military Plaza, opened in December, 1884. It was known for its first-class stage acts, which also featured plenty of scantily clad female performers in some of those acts. The Fashion burned down in 1891.[45]

The Bella Union, on the northeast corner of South Laredo and Dolorosa Streets, represented the worst of the lot. It was managed by Santiago Villanueva and had a reputation as a rough place that catered to a rough crowd.[46]

For one reason or another none of these places could dislodge the Vaudeville from its spot atop the city's saloon listings. The Vaudeville, in its glory days, was simply the best. No other saloon in San Antonio could match its combination of services and facilities: good variety shows, top-quality gambling, and an excellently stocked bar, all emceed by the inestimable Jack Harris.

Prostitutes were not part of the regular program at the Vaudeville although they operated in the shadows of the operation. That they were present is a given, but putting names and faces on their presence is another matter. Unlike the gamblers and gunmen of the Old West, prostitutes tended to be anonymous. Yet women of a particular type were an integral part of the saloon–variety theater business. In the world of prostitution, they occupied a niche somewhere between the lowly crib girls and the elite parlor misses. In classy joints like the Vaudeville, self-employed "tarts" were not allowed to brazenly solicit business on the premises like they did at places such as San Francisco's Bella Union, Tombstone's Bird Cage Saloon and Theater, or Deadwood's Gem Theater. Prostitution was folded into the other operations of the Vaudeville.

Some hint of where such women fit into the Vaudeville's operations is to be found in Frank Sparrow's references to "drink hustlers." These were not the same as the barmaids, who waited on tables and thereby occupied a slightly more exalted position on the staff. The drink hustlers were "good-time girls" whose only discernable talent was the ability to entice men to hang around all evening and drink. The turnover rate was high because of the nature of the job and also because this type of work did not attract the most conscientious workers. The Vaudeville dressed its serving girls in scanty outfits and red hosiery, and by all accounts, those red-stockinged lasses were one of the city's most popular attractions for visitors and locals alike.

Their uniform was part of their job, and their job was to "entertain" the male customers in the broadest meaning of that term. They kept the boys in a good mood and, just as important, kept them buying drinks at outrageous prices. According to saloon etiquette, the customer bought drinks for himself *and* his consort for the evening. If they moved upstairs to one of the curtained boxes, a privilege earned only by spending generously, he could grope the girl to his heart's content as long as he kept buying drinks. For an additional outlay of money, he could have sex with her behind the curtains. It was accepted that the house got its cut of all these extracurricular arrangements. Woe to the girl who tried to hold out by not giving the Vaudeville its cut.

Some of the girls were reputed to be charming beauties, but nineteenth-century standards of beauty were quite different from modern standards, particularly on the frontier. Most were of the plainer sort, and they all started to look alike after a few years of working long nights in saloons. Sometimes the girls would help out in the stage shows as "extras," assisting the regular troupe where needed.

The barmaids and drink hustlers made "good wages" by the standards of the time, even without the extracurricular activities. In return, they paid a heavy price by being looked down upon by the "decent folks" of the town. Those decent folks included some of the same men who patronized their services at night. When they passed on the street during daylight hours, they were strangers. That was all part of the code of the business.

The ladies who performed nightly in front of the footlights sometimes practiced the world's oldest profession on a more elevated level. They could earn a little extra income by joining a gentleman at his table after the show, and many theater owners insisted that their performers work the theater boxes after the show. There is no indication that the Vaudeville management ever forced its stage actresses to moonlight with customers. Those who did, therefore, negotiated their own terms with the gentlemen in the audience. Where things went after that was up to the gentleman and the lady, but there was good reason why "actress" was often used as a synonym for prostitute in this era. Unlike the situation with the "drink hustlers," actresses' liaisons were not orchestrated by management, and Frank Sparrow's character at least seems to have been above reproach. He was never accused of pimping.

Variety actresses tended to cut a wide swath through the local male population. This is not surprising since they tended to be the most glamorous and good-looking girls in town. Plus, they were a lot less prudish with the boys than their more genteel Victorian sisters. The fellows were drawn to them like bees to honey, and this inevitably led to jealousy, possessiveness, and frequently violence of one sort or another.

One of San Antonio's most popular actresses was Georgia Drake, who worked at the Green Front, a friendly competitor of the Vaudeville. The Green Front stood on the northwest corner of Commerce and Flores, about two blocks west of Jack Harris's place. There is no record that Georgia ever worked at the Vaudeville, although she could have had her pick of any variety theater in town. She was widely known for her beauty. The *San Antonio Express* described her as "a large, well-formed [read "buxom"] and very attractive woman. . . . the most handsome woman that ever appeared as an actress in the variety theaters of this city." Alas, Georgia's acting talent was modest; her greatest, and last, role was appearing as a scantily clad Lady Liberty in a tableau.

Georgia Drake's true claim to local fame was not her acting but her involvement in another of the city's sensational killings. It occurred at the Green Front on August 4, 1878. About eight o'clock that evening, Georgia's paramour, an actor named John Lanham, showed up at the theater in an inebriated state. He was an intensely jealous man and threatened to "fix" her if she ever had a relationship with any other man but him. Unfortunately for all concerned, Georgia had a new boyfriend, a U.S. cavalryman named Gilbert Squires who also happened to be in the building that night, having a drink in the wine room. Lanham learned of this and made his way there to confront Squires. There was little doubt he was looking for trouble because he had come armed. They exchanged heated words, and the actor pulled a pistol, whereupon the cavalryman, who was unarmed, sprinted for the door. Lanham shot him in the hip and may have fired more than once. As usual, the crowd stampeded for the exits at the first sound of gunfire. The only person who wanted to be in the same room with Lanham right then was Georgia, who had run to confront him as soon as the trouble broke out. Now he leveled the gun at his lover, shooting her in the face. She collapsed on the sawdust-covered floor, bleeding heavily through a gaping hole in her chin, with the bullet lodged in her throat. Lanham turned the gun on himself and fired again. This time he missed, and the bullet he thought to be aiming at his head instead thudded into the wall. Unwilling to try again, he ran out the back door and disappeared into the night.

Friends and customers gathered around Georgia, and somebody sent for the doctor. The police were already on the scene, searching the neighborhood for Lanham. As Georgia's life ran out, a reporter for the *Express* arrived in time to record her final moments. She died there on the saloon floor, choking on her blood and unable to make even a final statement because of her wound.

John Lanham was caught soon enough, subsequently charged with murder, and tried by a jury of San Antonio men, some of whom had probably appreciated Georgia's talents on stage. They found him guilty and sentenced him to life in the state prison at Huntsville. Typically in these sorts of crimes, the jury considered the social standing of the victim in determining the guilt of the accused. The *Express* reporter who had covered the event on the scene provided the coda to the affair, which appeared under the following headline in the next day's newspaper:

> A Murderer's Idea of Heroism
> or How John Lanham Would

Perpetuate His Memory
He Buys a Pistol to Kill the
Woman Who Jilted Him, and
Her Paramour
The Sensation Last Evening at the
Green Front Theater[47]

The close link between the variety actresses and common prostitutes is supported by the number of "actresses" who took their lives in the same manner as the so-called "soiled doves" of the street and in the write-ups in the newspaper afterwards. Both kinds of suicide were treated with similar bemusement by male newspaper reporters and editors. In a large number of cases actresses and prostitutes retreated to their solitary rooms in boarding houses, fortified themselves with drink, and then took an overdose of laudanum. Thirty-two-year-old Nellie Clemente was one of San Antonio's lesser actresses who found work in a variety theater on Laredo Street (probably either the Washington or the Bella Union) after falling on hard times and separating from her husband. Nellie Clemente was not even her real name. On the morning of July 2, 1896, perhaps after she got off work from the night before, Nellie downed an ounce of laudanum and died in the police wagon that came to carry her to the hospital. The *Express* summed up her life when it referred to "the misery of a variety show life."[48] Her death was otherwise only notable for rekindling the long-running debate among the city's respectable citizens over what to do about the variety theaters and the whole red-light district, which served as both a source of profit and a source of shame to the city.

Not all legitimate actresses who played the Vaudeville took part in extracurricular sexual activities, although the pressure to do so was enormous. The low wages for performing, the itinerant lifestyle and lack of job security, and the expectations of influential customers were hard to resist. Nor was the traditional connection between stage acting and prostitution all in the prude's mind; some girls really were less interested in practicing the thespian art than in making a fast buck. And the connection between prostitution and the theater was not always demeaning for all concerned. Marriages between "theater men" and madams or their girls were common occurrences. Typical of such matches was that between a San Antonio theater man named Volino and the notorious madam Claude Duval sometime before 1895.[49]

For those theater patrons who preferred to find their female companionship off premises, the bartenders and regulars at the Vaudeville could always refer them to a suitable establishment in the city's vice district. The major bawdy houses and madams of San Antonio were well known to the city's male population and, if human nature is any guide, were a common topic of barroom conversation.

The "oldest profession" was a major facet of San Antonio's underworld scene, and by the 1880s it was fairly well organized. At that time there was no official red-light district as there would be in the 1905 to 1941 era, but the various bawdy houses tended to be located in or near the commercial district. Most of them could be found near Main or Military Plaza and in the area west and south of the San Pedro Creek. In time, the term "West of the Creek," would become shorthand for the vice district.[50]

Blanche Dearwood ran a high-toned bawdy house known as "Fort Allen." It was a two-story adobe place with a fancy French-style mansard roof, located near the corner of Elm and Starr about three blocks northeast of the Alamo. Frank Sparrow noted in his ledger book for April of 1884 that one of the girls at the theater quit to go to work at Fort Allen.[51]

Lily Gibson's house was located on the east side of Main Avenue (formerly known as Acequia Street) between Houston and Travis Streets. In 1885 a notorious shooting occurred there. An unruly customer refused to pay his bar bill and was shot dead in a confrontation with Lily and the house "bouncer."

On the north side of Nueva Street near South Flores, close to the cattle and horse yards, stood the notorious vice den of Ignacia Cortez. The local newspapers frequently mentioned her by name in those days.[52] A lawyer from Silver City, New Mexico, Sid Stanniforth, died in a mysterious shooting at her bordello in 1885. Stanniforth was found dead in an upstairs bedroom—shot in the head. The authorities accused Ignacia Cortez of murder. The tawdry incident was well publicized in the local newspapers. A court finally ruled Stanniforth's death a suicide and acquitted Cortez of murder.[53]

Claude Duval was likely the most successful of the city's parlor house madams. She ran a large, well-appointed house near the southwest corner of Washington Square, a veritable mansion with twenty or more rooms. After marrying her theater man, Duval converted to the Methodist religion during a revival service at Travis Park Methodist Church in August, 1895. Soon after she retired from the "business" and converted the old mansion into a "rescue home" for wayward girls. This institution later became known as the Methodist Mission Home and Training School.[54]

A few blocks to the south, on the southwest corner of South Concho Street and Durango stood Sallie Brewer's "110" House. The "110" was one of those "gorgeous palaces of sin" the newspaper stories frequently mentioned. It was a two-story frame building containing some thirteen rooms, the whole place "magnificently furnished." Sallie was born in Ohio about 1835 and came to San Antonio as a young girl. She was in the city by 1857, in time to witness the killing of outlaw Bill Hart, a man she claimed to be her lover, by vigilantes at the "Brewer House." By 1880 she was running her own "female boarding house," a euphemism of the day for an urban bordello.[55]

It is impossible to say whether any of these prominent madams or their girls were ever business associates of Jack Harris, but what can be fairly stated is that there was steady traffic among their establishments. They were all part of the vice web that formed San Antonio's underworld.

Gambling was the third element in the Vaudeville's mix of red-blooded, male-oriented entertainment. The city was known as a gambler's paradise in the 1880s. In fact, it was a regular stop on the so-called "gamblers' circuit" through Texas, an unofficial trail of untamed towns across the West that were traditionally friendly to gamblers. The Texas leg of the circuit ran from Dallas through Fort Worth, south to Waco and Austin, and then San Antonio, with Laredo on the Rio Grande as the last stop.[56] The gambling crowd felt particularly at home in San Antonio thanks to the tolerant attitude of the city's authorities and the prospering local economy. Frank Bushick, who at different times was editor of the *San Antonio Express* and a politician before taking up the pen as a historian, had an insider's view of the city's workings. Years later, in his memoir *Glamorous Days,* he wrote, "Gambling was one of the leading local industries. Its apologists said it kept money in circulation. It was not necessary to sneak around through an alley. . . . The ceiling was the limit. Daybreak was closing up time. The town was wide open."[57]

Among the most notable of gamblers who graced the local scene were Harry Bennett, better known as a Dodge City resident and a notorious double-dealer; Charlie Whitman, wayward son of a minister; and Richard B. S. "Dick" Clark, one of the most cultured and successful poker players anywhere in the West. Others with a sizable reputation included Will Ford, Kid Nash, Samuel B. Berliner, and Red McDonald. San Antonio had at least one distinguished lady gambler, Lottie Deno, who got her start at the city's tables in the 1860s and practiced her craft all over the Southwest for many years.[58]

Putting aside Dick Clark's fondness for poker, the most popular games among the gambling fraternity were monte and faro, while roulette, keno, and chuckaluck also had their followings. Monte, or "Spanish monte" as it was sometimes called, seems to have been especially popular in Texas and northern Mexico.[59] It was a type of card game originating in Spain before coming to the American Southwest via Mexico. It used a deck of forty cards, and play resembled the modern casino game of "21." Players bet against a dealer who would turn up two different cards from the deck and then take bets on whether a third card, known as the "gate," would match either of the first two. After the third card was turned up, bets were paid off and the next round was dealt. Monterrey, Mexico, was known as the "Monte Capital" in the 1880s, and it was the dream of many of those who "piked" Monte (known commonly as "pikers") to take part in a major game in Monterrey where piles of silver bars and tall stacks of gold coins changed hands with every game.[60]

Even more popular than monte, however, was faro, an exciting game of chance that offered the most impressive spectacle to onlookers. The name of the game came from the fact that a picture of a "pharaoh" or Egyptian king was on the back of the cards. The game originated in France in the 1700s. According to tradition, the box that contained the Faro cards had a tiger painted on its lid, which led to the commonly used gambling term "bucking the tiger," which denotes betting against the house, known as the "faro bank." The game commenced after the cards were shuffled carefully and placed into a special box. Individual cards could then be drawn from a slit in the side of the box, with the players placing their bets on the card of their choice. The dealer paid off or collected from the players after each turn and there were twenty-five turns per game. Faro required a lot of concentration and mental quickness, especially for the dealer, who had to be vigilant as a hawk and able to remember back several turns at a time.[61]

The popularity of faro and monte is shown by the fact that whenever gamblers were hauled in by the authorities, the most common charge against them was either "dealing monte" or "dealing faro."[62] On more than one occasion between 1878 and 1881, Billy Simms and Joe Foster, both members of the Vaudeville's management team, found themselves charged with dealing either monte or faro. Arrest and even conviction was hardly a blot on their names, however; it was merely a personal inconvenience and a temporary interruption in business. Ordinarily, a gambler who ran an honest and peaceful game was as safe from official harassment as any legitimate businessman in town. Simms and Foster may have gotten crossways with city officials or violated some unwritten provision of the *modus vivendi* between the gambling fraternity and the authorities. Whatever the cause behind their problems, they did not do any time or have their pocketbooks lightened significantly.[63]

Billy Simms and Joe Foster were never much more than bit players in the cast of Western sporting types. San Antonio was their stage. Of the two, Joseph C. Foster was the more important on the local scene. Born in Missouri in 1839, he immigrated as a young man to California during the gold rush. When the Civil War came he enlisted in Confederate service in New Mexico, joining a company of partisan rangers. When his company disbanded in Houston in 1862 he opened a gambling house there, then moved to San Antonio where he signed up with another Confederate militia company. After the war he stayed on in San Antonio, opening a "gambling saloon" with two other partners. He subsequently bought them out and shrewdly parlayed the business into a fortune said to be worth "some odd hundred thousand dollars." By 1884 he owned half interest in the Vaudeville, where he ran the faro room, plus kept several racehorses and dabbled in real estate. He was forty-five years old that spring, in the prime of life and living in grand sporting style off the earnings from his horses, real estate, and the faro room at the Vaudeville. About him it was said, "To those with whom he was friendly, he was a warm and genial companion, but there was a vindictiveness in his nature which, even in his last moments, he could neither eradicate nor suppress."[64]

Foster's partner Billy Simms was another self-styled sport and a relative newcomer to San Antonio, having formerly called Austin home. Simms was a familiar face in the gambling haunts of San Antonio, Austin, Fort Worth, and Denison. In 1878 while in Denison he killed friend and fellow gambler J. V. George, but it was over a girl, not a card game. The coroner's inquest ruled self-defense, but the *Fort Worth Democrat* still labeled him a "murderer," adding that he was "a quarrelsome, troublesome young man, ambitious to shoot somebody" and that "somebody" had been a friend. It was probably Simms's first shooting scrape. Back in Austin, he became a protégé of Ben Thompson until, according to one contemporary, the two had a falling out over control of the city's keno games. Billy was overmatched and unwilling to challenge his erstwhile mentor face-to-face, so he chose to leave town, but he would not soon forget the insult (see chapter 4).[65]

Compared to the largely forgotten Foster and Simms, there were some near-legendary names associated with Jack Harris's Vaudeville Saloon and Theater—not counting Harris himself. About 1882, Wyatt Earp came to town with his lovely lady, Sarah Josephine Marcus, to partake of the city's culture, or at least that part to be found in the gambling rooms of the Vaudeville and similar establishments. Here Wyatt was joined by a longtime member of his inner circle, Bat Masterson. Wyatt, Josie, and Bat did not stay in town long but departed without causing much of a splash.[66] The same could not be said of two other Vaudeville patrons, Ben Thompson and King Fisher, who made their last stand in the theater's upstairs. Thompson was already something of a legend before the events of March 11, 1884. As a familiar face around both Austin and San Antonio, he was closely identified with two of the major Texas watering holes of this era: Austin's Iron Front Saloon and San Antonio's Vaudeville Theater and Saloon. His career is living proof of the close ties between stops on the gamblers' circuit, just as the travels of Butch Cas-

Ben Thompson, one of the most redoubtable gunmen Texas ever produced, also enjoyed careers as a gambler, lawman, and saloon proprietor. His dapper appearance here belies a nasty temper and a fondness for the bottle.
Courtesy *Western History Collections,* University of Oklahoma Libraries

sidy and the Sundance Kid between Fort Worth and San Antonio support the same thesis. Thompson, unlike Fisher, was a member of the exclusive fraternity of professional gamblers that also included men like Luke Short and Wyatt Earp. Their stories show the itinerant lifestyle of the gambling fraternity apart from its violence; even wives and families could not tie these men down in one place for very long.

"Old Ben Thompson," as he was already known even before he had turned forty, was a remarkable man. One of the most noted of Old West gunfighters, his reputation was established well before the 1880s. Bat

Masterson considered him one of the most dangerous of Western gunfighters. Thompson was quick and accurate with a pistol and not slow to fight when honor demanded. He was seemingly fearless. Masterson noted however, that it was Thompson's "intelligence" that really made him so deadly. He was a canny adversary with all the fighting instincts that helped keep a man alive if he chose to follow the gamblers' circuit or the Outlaw Trail. Though often in trouble with the law in his lifetime, he could not be called a "desperado" in the classic sense of being a murderer or a robber.[67]

Ben Thompson was born in Knottingly, England, on November 11, 1842, the oldest child of a British naval officer. The family immigrated to the United States in 1851, eventually settling down in Austin, Texas, where they had close relatives. Ben attended school in Austin and then worked for the city's newspaper as a printer's apprentice for two years. Still just a teen, he was involved in several shooting scrapes in 1858, 1859, and 1860. Young Thompson couldn't seem to stay out of trouble, thanks to a short fuse and a strong contempt for authority.

During the Civil War, Thompson served in the Confederate Army in Texas, New Mexico, and Louisiana. While off duty he passed his time drinking and gambling and was involved in several more "incidents." Probably the most serious was a shootout in a Laredo gambling hall in 1864. Ben and brother Billy got into a dispute with some Mexican American Confederates from the company of Col. Santos Benavides. Despite fighting for the same cause, the Thompsons exhibited the usual contempt Anglo Texans had for Mexican Americans and made the shootings that followed almost inevitable. Two of the soldiers were killed while the Thompson brothers escaped unscathed and uncharged with any crime. Also during the war, Ben married Catherine Moore, a member of a prominent Austin family.

Shortly after the close of the war Thompson was involved in another shooting scrape. He did some jail time but soon made his escape by bribing the guards. He fled to Mexico and enlisted at Matamoros in the forces of the Austrian-born Maximilian, Emperor of Mexico. Ben was a member of the company of fellow American Frank Mullins, rose to the rank of lieutenant, and participated in several engagements in northern Mexico.[68]

Unfortunately, he was not content to fight "Juarista" forces; he also fought in more than his share of actions against the Mexican police in Matamoros. In one incident, he killed a policeman in a dance hall fight. As Ben described it, he was provoked into the fight:

> After a time the dance ended. My partner was seated, and as is customary, I asked her what wine, confection or ices I should bring her. Before she answered, this man touched me on the shoulder and asked me to step outside the door with him . . . the devil was almost jumping out of him through his eyes. He insisted, but then stepped back a pace or two, as if he expected me to comply with his request . . . he then had his hand on his knife. He seemed to hesitate a moment, but only a moment, drew quickly and dashed at me. I was just in time; a step sideways and backwards avoided the blow. I struck him over the head with my pistol, and then, as rapidly as thought, shot him four times.[69]

When the Mexican nationalists routed the Imperialists and captured Maximillian in 1867 Thompson and the rest of the Americans headed home. He only made it as far as the port of Vera Cruz, however, before coming down with a fever that almost killed him. Eventually he recovered and returned to Texas.[70]

By the time he got back to Texas, Ben Thompson was not just a war veteran but a seasoned gunman. He had fought Indians on the frontier, Yankees in the American Civil War, and Juaristas in the Mexican Civil War. By all the rules of "probability" he should have been killed a dozen times over, but Ben Thompson's luck would hold for a few more years. His career as a gambler and occasional lawman was just beginning.

Thompson seemed to be one of those people who do not just attract trouble but who thrive on it. Not long after returning to Austin from his Mexican adventures, he was involved in a brawl on the streets of Austin over politics. He was set upon by five men with knives but chased them off with several pistol shots.[71] In September, 1868, he wounded Catherine's brother—his own brother-in-law!—in another altercation, although Thompson claimed to be defending his wife against her brother's abusive behavior. After some legal haggling Thompson served two years in the state prison at Huntsville, his only stretch of serious jail time during a long career of violence.[72]

After his release from jail he landed in Abilene, Kansas, in 1871 where he achieved a measure of respectability as co-owner of the Bull's

Head Saloon. His partner in the saloon venture was another Texan, Phil Coe, who could be just as mean-tempered and reckless as Thompson when he had a few drinks in him. Brother Billy and Ben's wife Catherine came up to join him in Abilene, and he seemed on the way to finally having a home rather than living out of saddle bags. In the saloon business Thompson finally found his true calling. The Bull's Head prospered, but Catherine was injured in a buggy accident, so the couple decided to return to Texas.

The arc of Thompson's life was set now. He could neither stay in one place very long, nor stay out of trouble. In 1873 he and Billy were in Ellsworth, Kansas, where they got into a drunken altercation with one of the town's policemen and a gambler. In the resulting shootout, Sheriff C. B. Whitney was accidentally killed by Billy Thompson.[73] Ben departed Ellsworth in something of a hurry and returned to Austin, but trouble soon found him again. On December 25, 1876, perhaps full of too much "Christmas spirits," he got into an altercation with the management of an Austin variety theater. He shot and killed Mark Wilson, the operator of the theater, and wounded the bartender, too.[74]

In 1880 he was involved in another altercation on the streets of Austin, this time with a group of drunks who took the well-dressed Thompson for a dude and thought they would have a little sport at his expense. They insulted him and even knocked his hat off before Thompson's temper took over. He pulled his pistol and traded shots with the drunks until they fled for their lives.[75]

The fact that, at the age of thirty-eight, the portly Thompson did not present a very heroic image helps explain why a party of drunks mistook him for an easy mark. Sarah Josephine Marcus Earp, upon first meeting him described him dismissively as "short, heavy-set and slightly bald." Sniffed Mrs. Earp, "I took him to be some sort of drummer or other." The man she described so witheringly was about 5 feet, 9 inches tall, weighing in at a hefty 180 pounds. He had hazel eyes, dark hair, and a dark mustache. Like his chums and fellow sports, Wyatt Earp and Bat Masterson, he dressed well and had impeccable manners—at least when sober.[76]

That meeting between Mrs. Earp and Mr. Thompson occurred in an Austin restaurant where Wyatt and Josie were dining in 1882 (or perhaps

1883). Only a year had passed since the celebrated gun battle between the Earp and Clanton factions at Tombstone's OK Corral, and Wyatt was now one of the most famous gunmen in the West. He had come to Austin not looking for trouble but only following the gamblers' circuit. Both men seemed surprised at running into each other, and Josie Earp picks up the story from there: "One day as we seated ourselves, a man called out to my husband, 'Well, I'll be jiggered if it isn't Wyatt Earp!' . . . He came over to our table. . . . [and] Wyatt introduced him as 'Mr. Thompson,' but called him 'Ben.' . . . I was a little surprised to hear that he was the town marshal. Later someone told me that he was a famous gunman and killer. I found that hard to believe. He'd impressed me as a gentleman and good company." [77]

Ben may have been "good company" in Austin, but he was bad news in San Antonio, especially for Jack Harris. On the evening of July 11, 1882, the future of the Vaudeville Saloon and its garrulous owner were changed forever. For some time there had been bad blood between Harris and Thompson over a gambling dispute. While Thompson was city marshal of Austin he made occasional gambling and drinking excursions to San Antonio. One night he suffered heavy losses playing monte at the Vaudeville, losing all his money and even his jewelry. He was drunk as usual, and this only increased his rage. Suddenly, he pulled his six-gun, leveled it at the dealer who he felt had cheated him, and ordered the man to give him back the money and jewelry. When Jack Harris learned what had happened, he put out the word that Ben Thompson was never to enter the Vaudeville again. Anyone acquainted with Ben Thompson knew he would take that as a challenge rather than a warning to stay away. There were also later reports that Harris had once threatened to kill Thompson, and the Austin gambler was only too happy to give him the chance. [78] There would be trouble, for sure, in the future between the two strong-willed men.

On July 11 Thompson was back in San Antonio and drinking heavily again. The liquor fueled his determination to settle things with Harris. Ben's friends tried to keep him occupied in his room at the Menger Hotel, but he was soon out prowling the town looking for trouble. By pure accident he did not have to go far because he ran into Harris on the street, where the two men exchanged some sharp words before a deputy sheriff happened along and intervened to avert bloodshed. Thompson was not satisfied and during the course of the evening paid several visits to the Vaudeville, asking for Harris and then leaving when the saloon proprietor did not promptly come out. The tension was building in a pattern similar to the course of events between the Earps and Clantons in Tombstone and between Luke Short and "Long-haired Jim" Courtright in Fort Worth.[79]

The final confrontation occurred about 7:15 P.M. Billy Simms ran into Jack Harris on the corner of Main and Commerce, in front of Wolfson's Dry Goods Store. He informed Harris that a very drunk and very belligerent Ben Thompson was in the barroom at the Vaudeville. Simms warned Harris not to go to the saloon, but also slipped him a pistol, realizing that a showdown was almost inevitable.[80]

Jack Harris went directly to the saloon, entering through the front entrance on Main Plaza. Ironically, now that they were both looking for each other, he had just missed Thompson by a few minutes. Harris proceeded to the theater ticket office just inside the entrance and took out a shotgun. He held the shotgun in the crook of his arm and waited. It was not a long wait.[81]

In a few minutes Thompson returned, stepping up to the main entrance but pausing before entering his enemy's lair. Charles Hoffman, who was there that night, later testified that the "electric light was burning and it was light in the saloon and it was kind of shady outside from the electric light on the inside." The wooden, latticework screen blocked a clear view of the interior, but still allowed Thompson to glimpse the shadowy form of Jack Harris standing next to the ticket office.[82] The inebriated gambler must not have been too drunk or too bleary-eyed because he reacted immediately. Pat Carney, another witness that night, recalled in court testimony that Thompson yelled to Harris, "What are you doing with that shotgun?" According to the testimony of Thomas O'Connor of Fort Worth, Harris replied rather impolitely, "Kiss my ass you son of a bitch!"[83]

This constituted the extent of the preliminary conversation. Thompson whipped out his pistol and fired two shots at Harris through the open doorway and the latticework screen. His aim was true and Harris fell mortally wounded in the chest. Thompson turned and ran off across the Plaza in the direction of the San Fernando Cathedral and eventually made his way back to the Menger Hotel.[84]

Meanwhile, Harris was taken by friends in a carriage to his residence on Soledad Street a few blocks away. As soon as the news got out, a large crowd gathered there, eager to learn the condition of one of the city's most prominent businessmen. The chest wound was examined by Drs. Adolph Herff and Thomas R. Chew, but they could do nothing to help him. He was dying. The last hours of Jack Harris were truly pitiable: "How long can I last?" he kept asking, almost delirious from pain. He died before dawn in the little house by the river.[85]

Ben Thompson returned to his room at the Menger Hotel where he was joined by Lee Tarleton, a friend and local attorney. He turned his pistol over to Tarleton and then sent word to the local authorities that he was ready to surrender to them. In a short time, Policemen Fitzhenry and Buckley arrived to take him into custody.[86]

The actors and staff of the Vaudeville were in shock over the death of their employer. Jack Harris may not have been universally loved, but he enjoyed the hearty respect of his workers. The same night as the shooting, stage manager Frank Sparrow made the following entry in his ledger: "Jack Harris, proprietor, shot and killed by Ben Thompson at 7:15 P.M. died as he lived, a true friend and kindhearted, generous gentleman. God have mercy on his soul."[87]

In death, Jack Harris proved to be more popular than in life, which is often the case. He was laid to rest in City Cemetery No. 1 out on the old Powder House Hill. His funeral procession was one of the longest ever seen up to that time, with the line of carriages going on for blocks. Harris's dog, "Skeezicks," stood by the grave during the service, and several women from the Vaudeville Theater wept on cue. The grave was covered with flowers from well-wishers.[88]

As for Thompson, he was indicted on September 6 for the killing of Jack Harris but acquitted four months later on January 20, 1883. The court ruled that both men were armed, and it was more or less a face-to-face encounter, though the victim never got off a shot. Still, public opinion seemed to be agreed that it was a private matter. In such situations, Texas courts seldom involved themselves, letting gamblers and gunmen settle their own feuds as long as everything was fair and square. Thompson returned to Austin and a hero's welcome as the town's favorite son. The crowd of people who met him at the train depot unhitched the horses from his hack and pulled it up Congress Avenue to the steps of the capitol, a public display that easily rivaled Jack Harris's funeral procession in San Antonio. The *Austin Statesman* noted this "ostentatious public demonstration," and reported at the same time a "general disapproval" of it among the populace, but without specifying precisely which elements of the populace disapproved. The *Statesman* also indicated its own feelings when it said, "The spirit which induced [the reception] was the sort of hero worship" that would have been appropriate on the return of a victorious chieftain, but was "indelicate and sadly advised" for a man who had "signalized himself in being the first to take life in private encounters." Then trying to have it both ways, the newspaper churlishly admitted that several communities owed Thompson "a debt of gratitude" for removing Harris from the scene.[89]

Although prior to this Thompson had dispatched several men without giving it a second thought, this killing seemed to have bothered him, casting a pall over the remaining days of his life, perhaps even contributing to his subsequent resignation as city marshal of Austin. There is no doubt he began to drink even more heavily than usual, and his moods became blacker. Those who knew him agreed that he was never quite the same after the death of Jack Harris.[90]

Certainly, the Vaudeville Saloon and Theater was not the same, although business went on as before. On July 15, 1882, Frank Sparrow wrote this in his ledger: "House reopened under the management of Billy Simms, Joe Foster, and John D. Dyer, company and contracts as before. But the old home ain't like it used to be."[91]

Simms, Foster, and Dyer wasted no time before remodeling the Vaudeville with an eye toward putting their own distinctive stamp on the place. They made a number of overdue improvements to the theater including new stage machinery, new chairs, repainted walls and trim, a new "dress circle" in the balcony, and a huge electric light hanging from the ceiling in the center of the auditorium. The new management even took a daring step to boost audience numbers: scheduling matinee performances for ladies and children. A fairly recent trend back East, this was something entirely new for San Antonio theaters, which had always catered to men. On September 18, 1882, following a very busy summer season, the renovated or "new" Vaudeville (no longer Jack Harris's Vaudeville) had its grand opening. The makeover was a big success. The shows continued, as popular as ever, and the establishment prospered under its new management.

The change in management did not seem to alter the booking philosophy. The theater continued to give preference to *chanteuses*, with the occasional comedy team or side-show act. And befitting the small-town audience base, bookings were short-term, usually no more than a week. Featured performers in 1882 included the team of Beeson and Fox, Mamie Merrill, May Vincent, Miss Lavascoeur, Miss Elwood, Miss Carleton, Fred Hyorth, Annie Winton, George De Haven, Miss Bosslington, and Ralston the dwarf. Meanwhile, the resident company continued to anchor the program. The sheer number of performers in the company, up to seventeen by 1884, was a sure indication of how much importance management attached to the stage side of the business. Seventeen extra employees on the payroll could only be justified if they added substantially to the bottom line. The players in 1884 were Lena Hazel, Frank Naomi, Ned Kelly, Kitty Quinn, Fred Hyorth, Josie Simmons, Burt Watson, Lizzie Robinson, Ed Sylvester, Ed Moncrief, Ida Grayson, Jennie Howard, Frank Rice, Charlie Frye, Mark Grayson, Millie Davenport, and Laura Sherrington.[92]

The Vaudeville's attendance suffered immediately after the murder of Jack Harris, but as the memory faded, business picked up—at least until early 1884 when the Fatal Corner became front-page news again. On Thursday night, February 7, 1884, at 11:00 P.M. a gunshot rang out in one of the theater boxes to the left of the stage. The dancing and music were blaring so loudly that it was another fifteen minutes or more before the tragedy was discovered. A young man named Warren Davis "from Newburo [*sic*] South Carolina" was lying dead in his theater box after shooting himself in the head. He had been drinking with a number of different theater girls that evening. "The last of his bibulous charmers," as the *San Antonio Light* described them, was Lena Hazel, "an attractive charmer of this establishment."[93]

There was the usual public outcry from the reformers. Simms, Foster, and Dyer did their best to calm things down, and if nothing else had

Outlaw-lawman King Fisher who once controlled seven Texas counties before going straight and putting on a badge. Credited by some with twenty-six kills before he himself was gunned down at the age of thirty. Saddle buddy of Ben Thompson. Courtesy Western History Collections, University of Oklahoma Libraries

happened, they probably could have weathered this latest controversy. But Ben Thompson's return to town prevented that. Thompson seemed to have a death wish, or at least a nose for trouble that frequently led him to someone more than willing to oblige. By 1884 he had become, in the words of the *San Antonio Light,* "one of the most reckless and desperate men in the State." [94] On March 11, as soon as he stepped off the "International" train from Austin, the news raced through town. Thanks to the telegraph, Simms and Foster had learned of his impending visit as soon as he left Austin.

Thompson did not come alone. By pure chance he had hooked up with an old friend and fellow firebrand, John King Fisher, who like Thompson had a reputation locally as "a very desperate character." [95] They had run into each other in Austin when the "tall, thin and dark" Fisher showed up there on business as acting sheriff of Uvalde County. When Fisher stated he was on his way to San Antonio to make his rail connection back to Uvalde, Thompson decided to tag along just for the adventure of it.[96]

King Fisher, as he is usually called, was another of those Western characters who walked both sides of the line between law enforcement and criminal activity, just like Ben Thompson and Timothy Courtright. Fisher had made a living at different times as a cattle rustler and a hired gun. By 1884 he was a living legend in southwest Texas after surviving a number of desperate encounters. He was a "dead shot," fast, accurate, and fearless, or so his reputation said. Also like Thompson, Courtright, and others of their ilk, he was a product of the tough Texas frontier where nobleness and nonaggression earned a man few points.

Fisher had been born in Collin County in North Texas in 1854, the son of Joby and Lucinda Warren Fisher. His mother died while he was still a child, leaving his father to try to raise the boy. Before the Civil War they moved to Florence in Williamson County, then to Goliad, Texas. Fisher's first foray into crime was stealing horses, followed by burglary, for which he spent some time in the state prison at Huntsville. After being pardoned, he took up ranching in southwest Texas in the notorious Nueces Strip. Fisher soon found he was more comfortable with his hand wrapped around a six-shooter than a branding iron, so he became a "Regulator" in the local wars against Indians, rustlers, and bandits. Some folks in and around Eagle Pass called him a brave and honorable man who was true to his friends, while others considered him a hell-raiser whose idea of fun was shooting the windows out of the local judge's house. The equally tough Texas Rangers who pursued him over the years developed a grudging admiration for him.[97]

There is no denying Fisher was a killer, but like all gunslingers, the number of killings attributed to him is a matter of some dispute. He himself claimed to have put away seven Anglos and an indeterminate number of Mexicans and Hispanic Americans, who, among Texas gunslingers, did not count the same as Anglos.[98]

He married Sarah Vivian in April, 1876, but it did not calm him down. She came from an important land-owning family in the Nueces Strip, and some of her male relatives acted just as wild as Fisher. In the next year and a half, he was charged with murder, accused of cattle rustling, and wanted by the Texas Rangers, none of which left much time to be a husband.[99]

Fisher may have gotten acquainted with Jack Harris in either late 1877 or early 1878 when he spent about five months in San Antonio as a "guest" in the old Bexar County jail on Military Plaza, not far from the Vaudeville. He served his time while under indictment by the state of Texas in comfortable circumstances thanks to the home-cooked meals and other luxury items brought to him by Joe Foster of the Vaudeville. Whether Foster was acting on Harris's instructions or not is hard to say, but it would not be surprising if so.[100] Such a scenario would complete the circle of Harris, Fisher, and Thompson that brought the latter two back to the Vaudeville on the night of March 11, 1884.

Eventually, Fisher was released from jail, but the experience did not have much deterrent effect on him. He was soon accused of murder again plus lesser, unspecified crimes. He settled down for a time with his wife in Eagle Pass, where he tried the saloon and the livery stable business without success, then moved to Uvalde. He was now the father of two daughters by Sarah with another on the way, which should have been reason enough to put away his guns. Although still in his twenties, he had already acquired a long list of enemies, a fact that caused him to live his life looking over his shoulder. He never went anywhere unarmed and jumped if touched unexpectedly.[101]

The fall of 1883 found him in one of his law-abiding phases, serving first as a deputy sheriff and then acting sheriff of Uvalde County. He liked it so much he decided to run for the office in the next election, and in March, 1884, he ran uncontested. That same month he made the trip to Austin where he ran into Ben Thompson. At the time, Thompson had been drinking heavily and was in high spirits when he decided to accompany his friend to San Antonio. Fisher needed to make a train connection for Uvalde there, while Thompson, besides going on a lark, may have had some thought of seeing his brother Billy, who was in San Antonio at the time.[102]

By the time the two gun-toting pals stepped off the train in San Antonio about 8:00 P.M. on March 11, 1884, Billy Simms and Joe Foster were sitting in the Vaudeville ready for whatever trouble came their way.

They had no desire to go looking for trouble, but neither would they run from it. They were determined not to end up like Jack Harris. Fisher was the joker in the hand they were playing out because he did not have a "beef" with either Simms or Foster. He was not a man who usually went looking for trouble either, but if he had come to town to back Thompson's play, he could not be ignored. There also had to be some concern about what Billy Thompson would do if trouble started. He had no beef with the Vaudeville crowd, but he was also a Thompson, with all that implied.[103]

Thompson and Fisher did not go directly to the Vaudeville. They first paid a visit to Turner's Variety Hall (southeast corner of Houston and St. Mary's Streets), where they attended a performance of *Lady Audley's Secret* starring Ada Gray. Afterwards, they commenced their evening rounds of the city's saloons, starting with Gallagher's. If they were "on the prod," looking for trouble, they seemed in no hurry to find it. But trouble found them at their next stop. About 10:00 P.M. a hack halted in front of the Vaudeville Theater and dropped off the two men.[104]

If reports of their movements are accurate, they stood outside and visited for a while before entering the saloon about 10:30 P.M. Once inside, their first stop was the bar, where each man had a drink. Simms and associates had been waiting nervously for their arrival all evening. Now, Billy Simms and Jacob Coy strolled over to greet them. After some casual conversation, the four left the bar area and proceeded upstairs to the theater balcony to watch the show. Taking their seats at a table in the "dress circle," Thompson called for another drink and Fisher, a cigar while their two hosts studied them intently trying to gauge their intentions. The conversation appeared amiable enough, and everyone seemed to be getting along at that point.[105]

Then Thompson spoiled the mood by launching into a liquor-fuelled recitation of the killing of Jack Harris, an event now two years old. Thompson's drunken reminiscences touched a raw nerve with the two San Antonio men and raised the level of tension at the table. But the situation was still under control until Joe Foster joined the group. He and Thompson immediately bristled at each other, with the latter doing most of the talking. Different witnesses later recalled different parts of the conversation, but all agreed it was incendiary. One heard Thompson call Foster "a damned thief" and other choice epithets. Another heard Thompson say he never intended to kill Jack Harris but, pointing at Foster, "That is the son of a bitch I wanted to kill." Fisher, more sober than Thompson and perhaps hoping to be a peacemaker, suggested they adjourn to the bar downstairs. All the others except Thompson promptly agreed. They stood up and walked toward the door leading to the stairs, stopping just in front of the door that led to the hallway and the stairs. Thompson, perhaps wanting to settle things, stuck out his hand to the theater man in an impulsive gesture of *bonhomie* which Foster coolly refused. This provoked another round of hard words that finally exploded into violence. Thompson was the catalyst, stepping up to Foster and slapping him across the face. He drew his revolver in almost the same motion and, as Simms told it later, pistol-whipped Foster across the mouth. This shockingly violent turn of events might have shocked the Vaudeville crew had they not already been anticipating trouble from Thompson. Rather than stunning them, it galvanized them into action. Before Thompson could do any more damage, Jacob Coy grabbed the barrel of his pistol. Almost simultaneously a shot rang out.

Whether Thompson had fired deliberately or Coy's actions caused it, the result was the same. The loud noise in the small space froze everyone in their tracks, but only for an instant. Then all hell broke loose as everybody reached for their pistol a the same time. A thunderous volley of shots rang out; some said as few as ten, others said as many as twenty-two. Down on the first floor, the stage show and music halted abruptly. The customers, who knew from experience what to do when bullets started flying, stampeded for the exits without waiting to see who was doing the shooting. Curses and screams erupted as frantic people tried to get out the door, pushing past the curious who were trying to get inside to see what was happening. In a couple of minutes the place had emptied.[106]

So much flying lead at such close quarters produced deadly results. Fisher and Thompson were riddled and went down for good. On the opposing side, Foster caught a bullet in the leg, probably fired by Thompson, but possibly by one of his own side, which took him out of the battle without killing him. Afterwards, he managed to limp out, supported by his friends but bleeding badly.

The city marshal, Phillip Shardein, picks up the thread of the story at this point. As he testified at the inquest the next day:

> I . . . was standing at Sim Hart's when I was told Thompson and Fisher had gone in there [to the Vaudeville]. In about fifteen minutes I heard a shot but thought it was fired on the stage. After this shot was fired there was a brief interval, then I heard a number of shots, about eight or ten, in very rapid succession. I saw Bob Churchill, the barkeeper at the Vaudeville, with a shotgun pointed upstairs. I passed him and went upstairs, meeting Simms and someone else helping Foster downstairs, Foster being wounded. . . . When I got to the gallery I looked into the right-hand corner and then I saw two men lying on the floor, one with his head apparently over the other. Someone said they were Ben Thompson and King Fisher.[107]

Shardein found a crime scene that looked more like a charnel house than a theater gallery. The two victims were sprawled out on the floor "weltering in their own blood," as the *San Antonio Light* described it. What had occurred was not just a simple shooting. The range was too close to miss, and nobody had been of a mind to offer quarter. There was gore on the walls near the bodies of Fisher and Thompson, and bloody footprints in the hallway and on the stairs.[108]

One of the first to arrive on the scene was Billy Thompson, who had been enjoying the hospitality of the nearby White Elephant Saloon when the uproar started. He sprinted the short distance to the Vaudeville and entered the front door right behind policeman John Chadwell. People who saw him thought he was coming to join the fight although he was not armed. Before he could go upstairs, Marshal Shardein hustled him back outside and ordered him to go somewhere else. Curiously, Billy meekly obeyed.[109]

Jesse M. Emerson, who ran a pawn shop and loan office at 12 Soledad Street, near the Vaudeville, also came running as soon as he heard the uproar, pushing his way through people running in the opposite direction. In all the confusion, he slipped upstairs to get a close-up look at the crime scene:

> I came up and went in the side door of the Vaudeville; went upstairs and saw both corpses and examined the wounds. Fisher was shot in the right leg below the knee. Thompson was shot in the right side of the abdomen, and one

shot over the left eye; Fisher also had a wound in the left breast near the heart and one in the left eye, which went through and came out under the left ear. Thompson had two shots in the forehead and one in the chin on the left side.[110]

Thompson, to his credit, died gamely, returning the fire of his assailants and possibly even firing the shot that mortally wounded Foster. His pistol was found by his side with five of the six chambers empty. In death, his eyes were open and staring wildly. Fisher, on the other hand, seemed to have been taken by complete surprise; he died instantly without ever getting his pistol out of its holster. It was ironic that a man who had made his career with a six-gun did not get off a single shot at the end. It was reported that he looked peaceful in death. The one-sided outcome surprised those who knew the principals and started the subsequent talk of ambushes and assassinations. Thompson and Fisher were both reputed to be fearless and "good with a gun," as laconic Westerners put it, but on this night they were not good enough. Such an easy explanation raised the question: Was there more to the story than that?

The lethal shootout claimed its final victim eleven days later: on March 22, a little before noon, Joe Foster died of complications from the leg wound he had received that night. He had been expected to make it, but a doctor probing the wound hit an artery, and Foster bled to death right there in bed. From beyond the grave, Fisher and Thompson had finally gotten their revenge on at least one of their assailants.

The tragedy affected more than the three lives taken by the bullets. Thompson was only forty-one years old and left behind a wife and two children. Fisher was only thirty years old and left behind a wife and three young daughters. He also left behind his one big chance to make something of himself on the right side of the law as sheriff of Uvalde County. Foster, the oldest of the three victims at forty-five, was mourned by his wife and "a large number of friends." He was buried right behind Jack Harris in San Antonio's City Cemetery No. 1.[111]

The police took away the bodies of Thompson and Fisher and laid them out at the old courthouse on Military Plaza that also served as police headquarters. The morning after the killings a coroner's jury of six citizens assembled for a hearing in the office of Justice of the Peace Anton Adam. The jury found that Fisher and Thompson were killed in justifiable self-defense by Joe Foster and Jacob Coy. The fact that Foster lay seriously wounded at the time also seemed to support the fairness of the outcome. An eye for an eye, so to speak.[112]

The body of Ben Thompson was claimed by Billy and taken home on the train the next afternoon (March 12). In Austin, an official autopsy called into doubt the first reports of Marshal Shardein and Jim Emerson, as well as the verdict of the San Antonio coroner's jury that the two men had been killed in "justifiable self-defense." The Austin autopsy stated that Thompson had been hit by eight bullets, five of them to the head, but the biggest shocker was that some of the bullets removed from his body were Winchester rifle caliber. The same report also noted that some of the bullets had hit him on the left side of his body at an angle indicating they had come from above.[113] These findings suggested something entirely different from a fair fight. Adding to the growing controversy, Thompson's Austin friends produced a pair of alleged eye-witnesses who claimed that Thompson and Fisher had been killed in cold blood while seated at their table in the balcony. The one thing that might have answered many of the claims and counter-claims, an autopsy of King Fisher's body, was never done. Instead, his corpse was taken by train back to Uvalde, accompanied by Deputy Marshal Ferd (short for Ferdinand) Niggli. The townspeople gave him a funeral on the same grand scale as the one Austin put on for Ben Thompson.[114]

The Simms-Foster-Coy version of things was the one that went into the record. Billy Simms's testimony before the coroner's jury on March 12 formed the basis of their verdict *and* of most subsequent historical accounts. Not surprisingly, the self-serving account left out several key elements that pointed to an "execution" rather than a spontaneous shoot-out. To begin with, there had been almost certainly one or more unnamed gunmen hidden behind the curtains of a theater box who fired at Thompson and Fisher. Furthermore, the evidence strongly suggests that one or more of the assailants pumped additional bullets into the victims at close range after they were already down and helpless.[115]

Forewarned is forearmed, as they say. Simms and Foster had been prepared to deal with Ben Thompson if he came calling and started trouble, and they had no reason, based on his well-known history, to expect anything else. This is not to claim that they set out to assassinate

Jack Harris's Vaudeville Saloon and Theater with a few of its well-dressed clientele posed in front, ca. 1884. The building, heavily decorated with advertising by this date, was located at San Antonio's "Fatal Corner," where Soledad Street entered Main Plaza. Courtesy *Grandjean Collection, Daughters of the Republic of Texas Library, San Antonio, Texas*

Ben and his partner; there is simply not sufficient evidence to prove such a claim, and common sense suggests otherwise. Such a vendetta could have gotten them tangled up with the law, with their victims' friends and relations, and with local reformers, a serious alliance of enemies! The two saloon owners did not need that kind of trouble.[116] If Thompson had been on his best behavior that night, he and King Fisher could have walked out of the Vaudeville unscathed.

The shooting of Ben Thompson and King Fisher stood as the most famous event ever to occur at the Vaudeville, but this was not the last that San Antonio heard of the Fatal Corner. The site continued to garner attention as the scene of violent encounters between violent men. In April, 1884, another shooting occurred; this time the scene was in the bar rather than the theater. This fight was the culmination of an encounter between Eagle Pass attorney R. H. Lombard and the unfortunate Billy Simms. The two men exchanged pistol shots, and Lombard suffered a nasty wound in the right arm. Authorities hauled both men into court, where Lombard claimed to have been a close friend of the late King Fisher, probably in a lawyer's ploy to gain the court's indul-

FRONT ELEVATION

JACK HARRIS SALOON AND THEATER   DRAWINGS BY
SIM HART'S CIGAR STORE   ROBERT CULLEN SMITH, A.I.A.
303-305 MAIN PLAZA
SAN ANTONIO, TEXAS
ca. 1885

gence. But there would be no "justifiable self-defense" pleas this time. An unsympathetic judge fined each man four hundred dollars.[117]

Another sordid incident that same year further tarnished the image of the Vaudeville, if such were possible. On March 16, a Sunday evening, twenty-three-year-old Will G. Smith took a drug overdose, or what the *San Antonio Light* called "the morphine route to the other shore." Poor Smith drank the fatal dose of morphine about 5:00 P.M. and expired by 8:15 that same night despite the best efforts of the medical profession. Smith's friends had sent for the doctor as soon as they discovered him, and the doctor pumped his stomach, but all for naught. The victim left a note explaining that his wife, an actress at the Vaudeville who went by the stage name of "Lizzie Mack," had stopped loving him. Not surprisingly, the newspaper blamed the woman, or at least her occupation, saying Smith had been the victim of "a fatal infatuation for a variety actress."[118] There was no sympathy for the widow.

The bloody events of March and April, 1884, were not the usual playbill at the Vaudeville. On a typical evening, the excitement was confined to the theater stage or the keno room and did not involve either hot words or hot lead. If we could go back in time and join a party of visiting cattlemen at Jack Harris's Saloon and Vaudeville Theater, we would experience an entertaining evening at San Antonio's premier "night spot" of the 1880s. As we accompany them, we want to view things through their eyes, even their prejudices. Such an evening might go something like this:

It is early February, 1884, and we are with a group of cattlemen from Frio County, Texas, in town on business. The whole group is staying in style at Frank Hord's Southern Hotel on Main Plaza. It is Saturday night and the men have decided to go out on the town. We change into our cowboy finest, enjoy a good dinner at the hotel restaurant (fifty cents for the works!), and head out the front door onto Main Plaza.

It has just started to get dark as the sun slips down behind the hotel. The weather is South Texas–warm tonight, but there is just the hint of a soft cooling breeze wafting over the Plaza. Saturday is just another day in the work week, so the Plaza is crowded with men on horseback and on foot, in carriages, wagons, and carts, all going about their business in that relaxed, unhurried fashion that reflects the city's Spanish heritage.

Standing in front of the hotel on Main Plaza, the first decision to be made is which direction to go. To the right, on the south side of the Plaza, we notice a number of stores and shops as well as the Central and St. Leonard Hotels. Almost all of the old Spanish-era residences on the Plaza are gone, replaced with new construction by more recent Anglo arrivals. Main Plaza is the heart of the business district. A glance across the street to the East side of the Plaza reveals a row of brick and stone buildings that include the Tivoli and the Revolving Light saloons, already doing a brisk business even though the evening has not really begun. The saloons, theaters, and restaurants will not really come to life until nine o'clock or so. On the west side of the Plaza with the Southern Hotel are the San Fernando Cathedral (dating back to 1750) and the store of Colonel T. C. Frost.[119] At Frost's you can get either "holy water" or "fire water," depending on your taste. What our group really wants to see, however, and the main purpose of this little outing, lies to the left on the north side of the Plaza. To go faster, we step off the wooden sidewalk and head up the street, being careful to step around potholes and horse droppings. Straight ahead of us, looking from west to east, we see a solid row of two-story buildings: Wolfson's fancy dry goods store is at the far left; next to it, the White Elephant Saloon and gambling house;

then two more stores, smaller than Wolfson's; and finally, our objective, Jack Harris's Saloon and Vaudeville Theater on the northeast corner of the Plaza. Customers are going in and out of Sim Hart's shop on the corner to purchase their supply of tobacco for Saturday night and Sunday. As we approach the Vaudeville, we can see through the windows and open doors that they have just lit the gas lights and turned on the electric ones to chase away the shadows. Out front, the torches have not yet been lit, but that moment cannot be far off as the dusk of winter descends rapidly. We can hear the house orchestra already warming up for the evening's first show.

There are muttered comments of, "Hot damn! Here we go." from some of our party as we step up onto the sidewalk and prepare to join the anticipated merriment inside. Through the open double doors we go and around the latticework screen to the bar area. It is time for another important decision: Where to go first. To the bar for a drink? Upstairs to check out the faro rooms? A quick turn to the right into Sim Hart's for cigars and chewing tobacco? Or maybe straight ahead to the theater box office to find out who's on stage tonight. There will be plenty of time to do it all before the evening's over. One of the boys has something else on his mind entirely and buttonholes Billy Simms as he walks by to arrange a private "party" in one of the wine rooms with one of Simms's girls. Some money changes hands furtively, and he heads off cheerfully to meet his evening's companion and pop the cork on a little bubbly.

And speaking of the ladies of the establishment, we see them around everywhere serving drinks at the tables and mingling with the throngs of male customers. They all wear short dresses that show a great deal of red-stockinged leg and are just as daringly low cut on top to reveal plenty of cleavage. This is quite a treat for male eyes, as most saloons follow the convention that prohibits women in the public areas.

The crowd tonight is the usual mixed one. Seated at the tables around the saloon or standing at the bar there are men of practically every description and class of society. Generally, if you can pay for what you order, you can get in, no questions asked. That sort of tolerant attitude does not extend to "Negroes" and "Chinamen" of course. They are never even allowed to step foot inside the front door. The Vaudeville is no different from hundreds of other saloons around Texas in this respect. Since everyone understands this unwritten rule, there is almost never any trouble from the aggrieved ethnic minorities. After all, they have their own gin joints and opium dens! Hispanics are another case altogether: the free-spending *caballeros* from South Texas and old Mexico are always welcome. San Antonio is the jumping-off place for the South Texas border country and the ethnic lines that divide society in Houston, Austin, and Fort Worth generally do not apply here.

Aside from certain unwelcome ethnic minorities, any "seedy-looking" characters seeking entrance are stopped at the door by the porter and turned back. Officially, the carrying of firearms on the premises is prohibited for everyone except officers of the law, but that rule is widely flouted. Nobody bothered to search us, or even inquire if we were "heeled" when we came in. It is a law made to be broken. The only concession to the law is that guns are carried out of sight, not strapped to the leg gunfighter-style.

We decide to step over to the ticket office and purchase tickets for the evening's first show, which will begin in a short while. Next stop is the bar to buy a round of drinks for everyone up and down the bar; after that everybody is responsible for paying their own tab. Everybody agrees, a night in town beats the hell out of another night rolled in a blanket by a cold campfire. Here we have good whiskey, plenty of women, gambling, and a show, too.

We trade banter with the bartender, a sociable sort of fellow who is not too busy yet to share the latest town gossip or give updates on long-running feuds among the sporting fraternity. He is a fountain of information and not a bit shy about sharing his knowledge. He is nattily attired in a white shirt with a black string tie. He obligingly points out Billy Simms standing watchfully over near the theater entrance. Simms looks more like a schoolteacher or an earnest young doctor, although dressed more like a dude in Prince Albert coat, vest, white shirt, and tie. Despite his "duded-up" appearance, he has a well-earned reputation as a battler who never backs down. He used to be Jack Harris's right-hand man, the bartender confides, able to run things even when Harris was not around. When Harris was killed, Simms smoothly stepped up to the top job. The bartender does not know anything about the financial arrangements that necessitated. He does, however, tell us that more trouble is expected from Ben Thompson sooner or later, and the boss has the word out around town that he is to be notified the minute Thompson comes back to town. Nobody doubts that he will. Billy and his partner Joe Foster do not intend to end up like old Jack did, gunned down in cold blood by the crazed Thompson. He takes advantage of our rapt attention to his story by pointing out the exact spot where Jack Harris was felled: "It's over there by the ticket office, just inside the main entrance," he says grimly.

Suddenly his story is superceded by something even more exciting: loud voices at one of the tables tell us that some kind of a row is going on. Two red-faced fellows sitting at a table lunge to their feet, knocking over glasses and a mostly empty whiskey bottle. They are arguing and shouting at each other—something about a bottom deal *and* a girl sitting next to one of them. Jacob Coy, the longtime special policeman, a Mexican fellow, comes running, accompanied by the doorman, to break things up before they get out of hand. Coy expertly calms everyone down, sends the girl away, orders a new deck of cards, and in general gets the situation under control. If need be, he could have cracked some skulls and had the troublemakers tossed out into the street. They know Coy can be a "tough customer" and decide not to tangle with him.

With that little "fire" put out and all the excitement over, we return our attentions to the bartender and his dime novel–sounding stories. Instead, his endless patter has switched to another subject: He proudly points out the "classical" paintings on the walls, telling us how they were done by some of those Old World artists and shipped in from back East somewhere. Almost all of them show beautiful women in various stages of undress, the kind of women we can only dream about as we survey the hardened, mostly homely women about the room. We all agree that no saloon would be complete without some good "art" to admire, even if the comparisons to the real things all around us can be depressing. Another round or two of whiskey will change all that, however.

The piano player tickling the ivories on an old upright piano against one wall stops his playing. Generally ignored by the customers while playing, in silence he attracts immediate attention. Suddenly, there is a loud blast of music coming from the orchestra in the theater auditorium, telling everyone it is showtime! Some of the boys have never been to a variety theater before and are eager to view this spectacle. We down our drinks and head over to the theater entrance. A doorman takes our tickets and tells us to have a seat anywhere; there is no reserved seating at the Vaudeville except for the private boxes.

We take our seats in the fourth row on the right side of the central aisle. The auditorium quickly fills. It is going to be a full house tonight. While waiting, we admire the decorative, painted curtain that will rise as soon as the last customer is seated. The gaslights around the stage burn brightly like our curiosity. Craning our necks, we can also admire the electric chandelier hanging from the ceiling over our heads. The little orchestra in an enclosure at the foot of the stage is really going at it, and the impatient crowd around us is loud and boisterous, ready for the show. Above us in a theater box to the left sit two well-dressed gentlemen and three of the barmaids. One of the women is obviously drunk and is leaning out of the box laughing hysterically at nothing we can see. One of our group points out Texas Ranger Captain Lee Hall sitting with friends on the other side of the auditorium. The orchestra breaks into "Dixie," a guaranteed crowd-pleaser, and the audience goes wild right on cue with cheers and "rebel yells." The song ends and the orchestra falls silent for a moment; then there is a slightly off-key blare of trumpets and a drum roll. An employee comes out and turns the gas lights down, casting the theater into darkness as soon as the electric light is turned off. The curtain rises and the audience grows quiet in anticipation.

The band strikes up the music again, and the small stage is filled with a chorus line of seven—or is it eight?—good-looking "actresses" dancing, mostly in synch, to a lively tune. We order some more drinks from the barmaid while eagerly taking in the spectacle of all of those scantily clad women cavorting in front of a roomful of men. The audience goes wild again, signaling their approval with more cheers and rebel yells.

Next on the program is a pair of Irish comedians. The two men walk out center stage, dressed in green suits with vests and black string ties, each sporting a black top hat. The audience loves them. "O'Shea and O'Brien" they call themselves.

Next up is "Mademoiselle Marguerite," who charms us with a truly touching song-and-dance routine. She is very beautiful and sings so sweetly that some of the men do not even wait for her to finish but begin cheering and throwing coins onto the stage at her feet in the middle of her act. She soldiers on resolutely to the conclusion. We hear from the fellas sitting in front of us that she was once engaged to a wealthy Mexican general who was living in exile hereabouts due to some political dispute south of the border. He was called "Don Gregorio." As the boys in front of us tell it, one night he and his staff left town on the midnight train bound for Laredo and just never returned. It was rumored they crossed the Rio Grande into Mexico to gather forces for a revolution against the central government. Poor old "Don Gregorio" got himself killed in the first—and last—battle of his revolution, and Miss Marguerite lost her chance to marry a rich man. We have to agree, it is a true love story, sad enough to bring tears to an *hombre*'s eye.

After Miss Marguerite exits the stage, the orchestra plays some sprightly incidental music until the next act comes out. This one is a juggling act, then he is followed by a song-and-dance act composed of three girls from Chicago. At this point, after too many drinks to count and the pleasant memories of Miss Marguerite, all the acts start to run together in a blur of entrances and exits. An old actor delivers a recitation of famous Shakespearean pieces that the boys do not pay much attention to. He is followed by another female ballad singer, which perks the boys up, another comedy act, and then a grand finale with the chorus line again. The employee turns the lights up and the show is over. The whole thing probably lasted a couple of hours.

The audience straggles out to the saloon. The night is still young. Some men wander off down the street to check out the scene at some of the other saloons nearby. Saloons, like high society parties, are judged at least in part by the quality of the guests. The more "big names" there are in the joint, the more of a crowd they will attract. We decide to stay at the Vaudeville. About midnight, we go upstairs to try our luck in the gambling rooms. Since it is Saturday night, the rooms are packed with people, locals and out-of-towners alike. Men are just standing around waiting for a place to open up at one of the tables so they can join a game. We see Billy Simms dealing faro at one of the tables. After one look around, we decide to save our money and come back another night. Back downstairs for one more drink and a little more ogling of the barmaids and actresses—who keep getting better and better looking as the night goes on!—then we start thinking of calling it a night. But before leaving, all that drinking calls for a quick visit to the fancy "water closet" tucked away on one side of the saloon. We bid adios to the Jack Harris Vaudeville Theater and Saloon. The last thing we can hear as we go into the night is the sound of the piano player listlessly playing the same song for the umpteenth time. Whenever we hear that song from now on, we will think of our night at the Vaudeville. We have seen some wonderful things and had a good old time, and are still able to walk out under our own power. Some men after an evening such as this wake up the next morning in an alley behind a bar that they cannot remember going into in the first place, their pocketbook and any other valuables they had cleaned out.

Before heading back to the hotel, we decide to stroll over to old Military Plaza and stop for a bite to eat at the chili stands that are open all night just for customers like us. Being in San Antonio on a Saturday night is not the time or place to sleep! The cool, winter air sobers everybody up a little. The weather is remarkably mild, and there is a full moon in the sky lighting up the plaza. We can see plenty of men still on the streets, still looking for a little action in one form or another. It has been a memorable night in "Old San Antone." Who knows when we will get back again, but everybody agrees we ought to someday.

The Vaudeville Saloon and Theater continued in business until the end of June, 1884. At that point, Simms and his partners decided to close the operation. The reasons are unclear. The economic climate in San Antonio was still good, and the saloon business was always "bullish." Plus, theaters had always had their ups and downs dependent upon the popularity of the latest show, so there must be other reasons. The most likely reason is the negative publicity from the series of killings in 1882 and 1884. Quasi-respectable places like the Vaudeville always operated on the edge of the law. As long as their shady activities were conducted with a degree of discretion and attention to public relations, such places were tolerated by the local authorities. But when they started to attract the close attentions of respectable folks, leading to, first, awkward questions and then public outcry, their days were numbered. Historian Charles Ramsdell said, "The Vaudeville Theater never emerged from the shadow cast upon it by these last killings," and that is why it closed its doors.[120] Unfortunately, the specific thinking behind that decision by the final owners is not part of the historical record, just the outcome. In July, the furniture and equipment were sold for $1,753.25. In August, a Mr. Bianchini leased the building for use as a restaurant. By the time the latest edition of the Sanborn fire maps had come out the next year, the Vaudeville's saloon and theater complex had been converted into space for a much smaller saloon, several offices, and two barber shops. In March, 1886, the building was completely gutted in a mysterious fire, leaving only the stone walls standing.[121]

The site did not remain empty long. It was too valuable for that. One thing that did not change was the nature of business at that particular location. The popular Elite Hotel, Restaurant and Saloon went up next on the site. Then tradition was broken: In 1914 the Elite Hotel was razed and replaced by a twelve-story office building on that corner of Soledad and Main Plaza.[122] That same building with many modern additions and improvements still stands today.

Old Main Plaza in general has changed a lot since Jack Harris, Billy Simms, and the rest held sway there, but there yet remain five or six buildings from those days. They remain as relics of that wild and woolly "Old San Antonio" of Western lore and legend.

Today, no historical marker identifies the "Fatal Corner," which is a shame because so much history occurred there. Nothing on the site advises the curious tourist or the casual passerby that the Jack Harris Vaudeville Saloon and Theater once stood there in all its tawdry splendor. While there is no marker to tell the story, what is gone is not completely forgotten. It may even be true, as superstitious types believe, that the site is watched over by the ghosts of Jack Harris, Ben Thompson, King Fisher, and the others who died violently there so long ago. Every day, thousands of people walk by that busy downtown corner of Main Plaza, most of them blissfully unaware of its bloody past. Perhaps, if they knew all the facts, they would walk on the other side of the street.

Jack Harris's Vaudeville Theater and Saloon is long gone, as are all the people connected with it who went to their graves taking their secrets with them. But echoes of actors and gunshots still waft on the breeze on a warm summer night. It is not too hard to imagine one of those nights when the place was in its heyday as one of the stock play-ers stepped up to the front of the stage in the glare of the footlights and delivered these famous lines from Shakespeare's "The Tempest" (act 4, scene 1):

> Our revels now are ended. These our actors, as I foretold you, were all spir-its, and are melted into air, into thin air; and like the base-less fabric of this vision, the cloud-capped towers, the gorgeous palaces, the solemn temples, the great globe itself, yea, all which we inherit, shall dissolve and, like this insubstantial pageant faded, leave not a rack behind. We are such stuff as dreams are made of and our little life is rounded with a sleep.

Shakespeare provides a fitting valedictory for the old Vaudeville The-ater and Saloon, where the drama was not always on the stage, and the actors did not always return for another performance. Dim the lights and bring down the curtain!

NOTES

1. Charles Ramsdell, *San Antonio: A Historical and Pictorial Guide* (Austin, Tex.: University of Texas Press, 1959), 23.

2. Information provided by San Antonio historian and former Bexar County archivist John Ogden Leal. Letter from Leal to Bowser, Jan. 29, 1997, in author's files.

3. Charles Merritt Barnes, *Combats and Conquests of Immortal Heroes* (San An-tonio: privately printed, 1910), 198. See also *San Antonio Light*, Aug. 7, 1910, 1.

4. *San Antonio Express*, Mar. 6, 1886, 1.

5. Ibid.

6. Sam Chamberlain, *My Confession*, ed. Roger Butterfield (New York: Harper Brothers, 1959), 39–40.

7. *San Antonio Light*, Aug. 7, 1910, 1.

8. For structural information on the Vaudeville, see 1877 and 1886 Sanborn Fire Maps of San Antonio (New York: Sanborn Map and Publishing Company, Ltd.), Center for American History, University of Texas, Austin; also, *San Anto-nio Light*, Aug. 7, 1910, 1.

9. *San Antonio Express*, Mar. 6, 1886, 1.

10. Robert K. DeArment, *Knights of the Green Cloth: The Saga of the Frontier Gamblers* (Norman: University of Oklahoma Press, 1982), 93.

11. Charles B. Myler, "A History of the English-Speaking Theater in San Antonio before 1900" (Ph.D. diss., University of Texas at Austin, 1969), 154.

12. Ibid.

13. Ibid., 155.

14. Modern vaudeville, with its tight, rapidly paced format, dates from the opening of Tony Pastor's Theater in New York City in October, 1881. Pastor, a

dynamic promoter of the theatrical, could be called the "Father of Vaudeville" in this country. By the early 1900s, vaudeville was a major form of American theatrical entertainment with a "circuit" that played big Eastern cities like New York and smaller Western communities like San Antonio. Little by little, its popularity began to be undercut by the advent of motion pictures until by 1932 vaudeville theaters and performers were fast disappearing from the American scene. Anthony Slide, *The Vaudevillians: A Dictionary of Vaudeville Performers* (Westport, Conn.: Arlington House, 1981), introduction. See also *Webster's Word Histories* (Springfield, Mass.: Merriam-Webster Co., 1980); William and Mary Morris, *Morris Dictionary of Word and Phrase Origins* (New York: Harper and Row, 1977), 586–87; and Stuart Flexner and Anne H. Soukhanov, *Speaking Freely: A Guided Tour of American English from Plymouth Rock to Silicon Valley* (New York: Oxford University Press, 1997), 335.

15. Myler, "History of the English-Speaking Theater," 157. The *San Antonio Light* of August 7, 1910, says Harris did not become the sole owner until the fall of 1876. For ownership of the property, as opposed to the business, see Bexar County Deed Records, Reverse Index to Deeds, 1837–1884, vol. H–K, 1335; and Direct Index to Deeds, 1837–1884, 2,089.

16. See "Judge's Criminal Docket . . . From 1876, County Court, Bexar County," for January, 1878, Case Nos. 40 and 53, San Antonio Justice Center, Criminal Central Filing, Bexar County (hereafter referred to as Judge's Criminal Docket, County Court).

17. Estelline Bennett, *Old Deadwood Days* (New York: J. H. Sears and Co., 1928), 109–19.

18. *San Antonio Light*, July 12, 1882, 1. See also J. Marvin Hunter and Noah H. Rose, *The Album of Gunfighters* (Bandera, Tex.: privately printed, 1951).

19. Description and dimensions of the Saloon and Theater come from the 1885 Sanborn Fire Insurance Maps for San Antonio, San Antonio Main Public Library, Texana Dept.

20. Elton Cude, *The Free and Wild Dukedom of Bexar* (San Antonio: privately printed, 1978), 107; Myler, "History of the English-Speaking Theater," 162.

21. Frank H. Bushick, *Glamorous Days* (San Antonio: Naylor Company, 1934), 53.

22. Both Emma DeHaven and Lulu Alberts were considered "chair warmers" by Sparrow. See "Ledger Book of Frank Sparrow, business and stage manager of the Vaudeville Theater, 1875–1884," in San Antonio Main Public Library, Texana Collection, Texana Dept., 62 (hereafter referred to as Sparrow Ledger).

23. Cude, *Free and Wild Dukedom*, 97.

24. *San Antonio Light*, Apr. 18, 1889.

25. Bushick, *Glamorous Days*, 205.

26. Myler, "History of the English-Speaking Theater," 155.

27. There seems to be some confusion about the Vaudeville Theater's management over the years. Frank Sparrow in his "Ledger Book" says that he was business *and* stage manager from December 20, 1875, until May 1, 1879,

although he continued to make entries until April, 1884. His exact job title after 1879 is not specified, but there is no doubt he was in charge of stage operations until April, 1884. Charles B. Myler, the leading scholar of San Antonio's early theater, states that Will C. Burton was stage manager in 1876 (p. 157). It also appears that John Martin and Sim Hart were "general managers" of the theater for a time, but the dates and lines of authority for that arrangement are likewise unclear from the record. For Sparrow's background, see obituary in *San Antonio Light*, Nov. 9, 1888, 1.

28. There is a Dave Wambold mentioned numerous times in George C. D. O'Dell, *Annals of the New York Stage*, 14 vols. (New York: Columbia University Press, 1938). It is possible that the two may have been the same man, or, if two different men, blood relations. There is no record that Dave Wambold ever shot anyone in New York City. See O'Dell, *Annals of the New York Stage*, vols. 10, 11, and 12.

29. Myler, "History of the English-Speaking Theater," 157.

30. O'Dell, *Annals of the New York Stage:* for Grace Thorne, see vols. 11 and 13; for Fannie Bloodgood, see vols. 7 and 13; for Marie Wainwright, see vols. 11, 12, and 13; for Frank Brown, see vol. 7. *Annals* contains lists of productions and players but no biographical information on the actors listed. For photographs of Marie Wainwright (also known as Mary Wainwright), see Daniel Blum, *A Pictorial History of the American Theater, 1860–1970* (New York: Crown Publishers, 1969), 28, 33; for a photograph of Frank Brown, see Blum, *Pictorial History*, 24.

31. A "Lionel Barrymore" appears on one of the playbills in Frank Sparrow's ledger book, playing the role of a cavalry officer in a production entitled *Arizona*. The Barrymores were one of the most famous acting families of the American stage, but since the Lionel Barrymore of stage and screen fame was not born until 1878, he could not have played Jack Harris's Vaudeville Theater in the 1880s. See Robert A. Juran, *Old Familiar Faces: The Great Character Actors and Actresses of Hollywood's Golden Era* (Sarasota, Fla.: Movie Memories Publishing, 1995), 14–15; also James Kotsilibas-Davis, *The Barrymores: The Royal Family in Hollywood* (New York: Crown Publishers, 1981); and Margot Peters, *The House of Barrymore* (New York: A. A. Knopf, 1990).

32. Myler, "History of the English-Speaking Theater," 158.

33. Sparrow Ledger, 62, 64, 66, 88, 94, and 96.

34. Myler, "History of the English-Speaking Theater," 160–61.

35. Sparrow Ledger. See also Myler, "History of the English-Speaking Theater."

36. "Frank Sparrow Dead," *San Antonio Light*, Nov. 9, 1888, 1.

37. The yard is still there today, but a different house sits on the lot where Frank Sparrow once lived in the old King William district.

The imagining of this day was constructed by the author, based in part on information in Sparrow's ledger.

38. Cude, *Free and Wild Dukedom*, 97.

39. *San Antonio Light*, Mar. 12, 1884, 1.

40. Jacob S. Coy's only claim to fame seems to have been his association with the Vaudeville, where he worked for several years. He was born January 2, 1841, in Zaragoza, Coahuila, Mexico; his date of death is unknown. Coy's name appears in all the detailed accounts about the killings of Ben Thompson and King Fisher in 1884. Surprisingly little is known about him otherwise. Reynaldo Esparza, a San Antonio historian, maintains that Coy was a distant kinsman of Gregorio Esparza who was killed at the Alamo on March 6, 1836. Some of the descendants of Jacob Coy still live in San Antonio and South Texas. From author's interview with Reynaldo Esparza, Nov. 22, 1991, in author's files; and Frederick C. Chabot, *With the Makers of San Antonio* (San Antonio: Artes Graficas, 1937), 77.

41. Edward W. Heusinger, *A Chronology of Events in San Antonio* (San Antonio: privately printed, 1951), 36, 40–43.

42. See Sanborn Fire insurance Maps, San Antonio, Texas, 1892. See also Mary Carolyn Hollers George, *Alfred Giles: An English Architect in Texas and Mexico* (San Antonio: Trinity University Press, 1972).

43. The White Elephant closed its doors about 1886, and was subsequently incorporated into Wolfson's Dry Goods Store. The limestone shell of the building is still standing today. Albert Curtis, *Fabulous San Antonio* (San Antonio: Naylor Company, 1955), 31–32.

44. Charles B. Myler, "History of the English-Speaking Theater," 183–86.

45. Ibid., 168–69.

46. Bushick, *Glamorous Days*, 127.

47. *San Antonio Express*, Aug. 4, 1878, 1.

48. *San Antonio Express*, July 2, 1896, 1.

49. *San Antonio Express*, Feb. 22, 1897.

50. Bushick, *Glamorous Days*, 121–31.

51. Sparrow Ledger, 97. The place was still standing on Elm Street as late as the 1930s.

52. See, for instance, *San Antonio Light*, Apr. 2, 1881; Oct. 3, 5, 6, and 8, 1885; and *San Antonio Express*, Oct. 8, 1885.

53. *San Antonio Light*, Oct. 8, 1885; and *San Antonio Express*, Oct. 8, 1885. Cortez later married a prominent local man and lived comfortably the rest of her life, dying in 1915. Ignacia Cortez-Stevens is buried in San Fernando No. 1 Cemetery.

54. Ted Richardson, *The Mission Home Story* (San Antonio: privately printed by Methodist Mission Home, 1988). The later life of madam Claude Duval Volino is unknown; she just seemed to vanish into the past.

55. *San Antonio Light*, Feb. 26, 1883. See also U.S. Census for Bexar County, 1880.

56. DeArment, *Knights of the Green Cloth*, 113.

57. Bushick, *Glamorous Days*, 107.

58. DeArment, *Knights of the Green Cloth*, 139–40, 257–67.

59. J. Frank Dobie, *A Vaquero of the Brush Country* (Dallas, Tex.: Southwest Press, 1929), 268–69.

60. Ibid.

61. Richard Erdoes, *Saloons of the Old West* (New York: Gramercy Books, 1997), 159–60.

62. Judge's Criminal Docket, County Court, 1878–81. See various gamblers' cases: Hiram Mitchell (nos. 421, 726, 342); Bud Cotton (nos. 425, 337); Dixie Land, alias A. Jordan (no. 1126); Antonio Salinas (nos. 570, 340); Kavanaugh (no. 334); Sam Dunlap (no. 718); Wally Mitchell (nos. 1034, 1115, 716); Sam Trimble (no. 329); Billy Simms (nos. 1113, 1032, 725); Joe Foster (nos. 730, 427, 1106, 349, 369); Ed Stevens, Jr. (nos. 574, 728); Juan Lujan (no. 328); and Bone Anderson (no. 713).

63. Ibid.

64. *Austin Daily Statesman*, Mar. 23 and Mar. 28, 1884.

65. Newspaper editor B. B. Paddock was no fan of Billy Simms (spelled "Sims" in the *Democrat*), and leveled an editorial broadside at him. *Fort Worth Daily Democrat*, Feb. 17, 1878. For "contemporary," see James B. Gillett, "Ben Thompson and Billy Simms," *Frontier Times Magazine* 12, no. 1 (Oct., 1934): 1–3.

66. Josephine Sarah Marcus Earp, *I Married Wyatt Earp*, ed. Glenn G. Boyer (Tucson: University of Arizona Press, 1994), 124. At the time of this writing an unfortunate controversy is raging in Western history circles regarding the book, *I Married Wyatt Earp*, edited by Glenn Boyer. It has long been a favorite of many Western enthusiasts and historians alike, based on the memoirs of Josephine Marcus Earp, the third and last wife of the legendary Wyatt Earp. Certain respected historians have raised questions about the authenticity of the version published over Boyer's name. It is to be hoped that in the future a new edition will be issued by Boyer addressing the editorial problems. In the meantime, the material quoted in this chapter from *I Married Wyatt Earp*, in the opinion of this author, has the ring of authenticity so it is being cited here with this caveat.

67. William Barclay Masterson, *Human Life Magazine* 4 (Jan., 1907). This is one of a series of articles for this magazine written by Masterson on various famous gunfighters of the West that he had known or been acquainted with personally. For a more objective, historian's view, see James D. Horan, *The Gunfighters* (New York: Gramercy Books, 1994), 142.

68. Bill O'Neal, *Encyclopedia of Western Gunfighters* (Norman: University of Oklahoma Press, 1979), 315. See also Eugene Cunningham, *Triggernometry: A Gallery of Gunfighters* (Norman: University of Oklahoma Press, 1996), 66–68.

69. W. M. Walton, *Life and Adventures of Ben Thompson* (Austin, Tex: privately published by author, 1884), 76–77.

70. Walton, *Life and Adventures of Ben Thompson*, 74–75.

71. O'Neal, *Encyclopedia*, 318.

72. Ibid.

73. Ibid., 318–19.

74. Ibid., 319. See also Colonel Charles Askins, *Texans, Guns and History* (New York: Bonanza Books, 1970), 80–81.

75. O'Neal, *Encyclopedia*, 319.

76. Earp, *I Married Wyatt Earp*, 124. Bushick, *Glamorous Days*, 195.

77. Earp, *I Married Wyatt Earp*.

78. Bushick, *Glamorous Days*, 183. See also *San Antonio Express*, July 20, 1882, 1; and *Austin Statesman*, Jan. 23, 1883.

79. Cunningham, *Triggernometry*, 80–81. See also Bushick, *Glamorous Days*, 183–84.

80. Statement of W. H. "Billy" Simms. Quoted in Cude, *Free and Wild Dukedom*, 109.

81. Bushick, *Glamorous Days*, 183–84.

82. Cude, *Free and Wild Dukedom*, 107.

83. Statements of Hoffman, Carney, and O'Connor all made at the coroner's inquest the next day. Cude, *Free and Wild Dukedom*, 105–107.

84. *San Antonio Express*, July 12, 1882, 1.

85. Ibid. The newspaper misspells Dr. Chew's name as "Cheu." See also Dr. Pat Ireland Nixon, *A Century of Medicine in San Antonio* (Lancaster, Pa.: Lancaster Press, 1936), 154.

86. Bushick, *Glamorous Days*, 184.

87. Sparrow Ledger, 65.

88. O. C. Fisher and J. C. Dykes, *King Fisher: His Life and Times* (Norman: University of Oklahoma Press, 1966), 124.

89. Bushick, *Glamorous Days*, 184. Also the *Statesman*, Jan. 23, 1883.

90. O'Neal, *Encyclopedia*, 316; and Fisher and Dykes, *King Fisher*, 119, 125–26.

91. Sparrow Ledger, 65.

92. Myler, "History of the English-Speaking Theater," 163–64, 166.

93. *San Antonio Light*, Feb. 8, 1884, 1.

94. *San Antonio Light*, Mar. 12, 1884, 1.

95. Ibid.

96. Description of Fisher is by Jane Maury Maverick, from Fisher and Dykes, *King Fisher*, 113–14; also quoted in Mrs. Albert Maverick, Sr., "Ranch Life in Bandera County in 1878," *Frontier Times*, Apr., 1928, 270 (reprinted Dec., 1940, 144). For brief description of Fisher's career, see O'Neal, *Encyclopedia*, 107–108.

97. For Fisher, see O'Neal, *Encyclopedia*, 107–108. For shooting out windows, see Ben Pingenot, ed., *Paso del Aguila: A Chronicle of Frontier Days on the Texas Border as Recorded in the Memoirs of Jesse Sumpter* (Austin, Tex.: Encino Press, 1969), 99–100. For Rangers, see Fisher and Dykes, *King Fisher*, 91; and Vinton Lee James, *Frontier and Pioneer Recollections of Early Days in San Antonio and West Texas* (San Antonio: privately printed, 1938).

98. O'Neal, *Encyclopedia*, 108.

99. Fisher and Dykes, *King Fisher*, 14–15, 65, and 76–80. See also George Durham, *Taming the Nueces Strip* (Austin: University of Texas Press, 1975), 138–47.

100. Fisher and Dykes, *King Fisher*, 96–97. See also Eugene Cunningham, *Triggernometry*, 85.

101. Fisher and Dykes, *King Fisher*, 96–97, 108–109. For jumpiness, see

first-person account of Mrs. (Jane) Maverick, describing a visit by Fisher to her husband's ranch in 1878, in Fisher and Dykes, *King Fisher*, 113–14; see also Maverick, "Ranch Life in Bandera County in 1878," 270.

102. Fisher and Dykes, *King Fisher*, 117–18. See also Leon Metz, *The Shooters* (El Paso, Tex.: Mangan Books, 1976), 115–16.

103. Fisher and Dykes, *King Fisher*, 127.

104. Bushick, *Glamorous Days*, 184–85. See also O'Neal, *Encyclopedia*, 108.

105. Fisher and Dykes, *King Fisher*, 128–29. See also Bushick, *Glamorous Days*, 185.

106. A variety of witnesses are quoted in the *San Antonio Light*, Mar. 12, 1884, 1, and no two witnesses recalled the exact same chain of events. What must not be forgotten, however, is that the nearest eyewitnesses all had their own reasons for recalling things a certain way, and without a proper forensics investigation, survivors' accounts, even those given under oath, must be taken with a grain of salt.

107. Ibid.

108. Ibid.

109. Gary Fitterer, "The Life and Death of Billy Thompson (1845–1897)," part 2, *Quarterly of the National Association for Outlaw and Lawman History* 25, no. 2 (Apr.–May, 2001): 16–18.

110. For inquest testimony of J. M. Emerson, see *San Antonio Express*, Mar. 13, 1884, 1. Also quoted in Cude, *Free and Wild Dukedom*, 122.

111. *Austin Daily Statesman*, Mar. 23, 1884; Fisher and Dykes, *King Fisher*, 130–31.

112. Fisher and Dykes, *King Fisher*, 130–32.

113. Ibid., 138–39, 142–43.

114. Ibid., 134–36, 144. Fisher's grave can still be seen in the old Frontier Cemetery in Uvalde, Texas, across the street from the John Nance Garner House and Museum. Even today, visitors still come to pay their respects to the legendary gunman.

115. This is also the considered opinion of the two men who authored the principal biography of Fisher, O. C. Fisher and J. C. Dykes (*King Fisher*, 130–31, 141–42).

116. The possibility of a blood feud did indeed come up when San Antonio residents read in the *Light* three days later that there was a "conspiracy" afoot to kill Jacob Coy. According to the report, two so-called conspirators were arrested at the Washington Variety Theater (corner of Laredo and Commerce Streets). They were described as "Mexicans" but no names were given and no additional information on why they wished to assassinate Coy. Residents of San Antonio nodded knowingly, and filled in the reasons that the paper did not provide: that this was the work of unnamed friends of the two dead men. However, no one ever specifically identified the two Mexicans as "hit men." See "Rumored Conspiracy by Two Mexicans to Kill Policeman Coy," *San Antonio Light*, Mar. 14, 1884.

117. *Austin Daily Statesman*, Apr. 25, 1884, 1.

118. *San Antonio Light*, Mar. 17, 1884, 1.

119. The cornerstone of the San Fernando Cathedral was laid in 1738, and the building was completed in either 1749 or 1750. A large addition was made to the front portion of the church in 1873.

120. Charles Ramsdell, *San Antonio Express (Sunday) Magazine*, Jan. 4, 1948, 4–5.

121. Myler, "History of the English-Speaking Theater," 166–68. See also Sanborn Fire Insurance Maps for San Antonio, 1885 edition in the series; and Ramsdell, *San Antonio Express Magazine*, Jan. 4, 1948, 4–5.

122. *San Antonio Express*, Nov. 15, 1914, 1.

Chapter Three

Ben Dowell's Saloon and the "Monte Carlo of the West" (El Paso)

W. W. Mills, a newcomer to El Paso in 1858, entered Ben Dowell's saloon one evening just in time to become witness to a fight between local citizens Samuel Schutz and Tom Massie. Alarmed, he appealed to the other spectators to stop the fisticuffs: "Gentlemen, would you see the man murdered?" There was no response from the crowd, and the fight ran its course. The next day, when Mills returned to the saloon, Dowell gave him this bit of advice: "My young friend, when you see anything of that kind going on in El Paso, don't interfere. It is not considered good manners here." [1]

Benjamin Shacklett Dowell knew from experience what was and was not good manners in El Paso. Not only did he run the most popular watering hole in town, he was also a local celebrity in his own right. An unexcitable, live-and-let-live style allowed Dowell to deal with every problem that came his way during thirty years in El Paso as a saloon owner, public official, grocer, rancher, and businessman. His fellow citizens affectionately dubbed him "Uncle Ben."

Early on he recognized the synergy between saloonkeeping and politics. His saloon served a variety of civic functions over the years: post office when he was postmaster, polling place at election time, and haven for countless traders and military officers who stopped in for billiards and all-night card games. He even served as a hostler and stagecoach stand operator at various times. The saloon was a landmark on the road from San Antonio to San Diego.

Dowell's place occupied the south end of a long, low adobe building fronting on the Alameda (now South El Paso Street), which led to the Rio Grande where a ferry boat was available to take passengers across the river to El Paso del Norte (now Ciudad Juárez). This building was one of several that had been part of Ponce's Rancho, named for Juan María Ponce de León, and located on the site of what is now downtown El Paso.[2] It was built in the traditional regional architecture, with thick mud brick walls plastered white on the outside and ceiling vigas inside. The dirt floors, tamped down and carefully swept, were covered with wool carpets. Family rooms occupied the rear, and a stable out back was enclosed by high walls to protect against marauding Indians.

Like saloons elsewhere on the frontier, Dowell's adapted itself to the local conditions and available space. In the early years, the town's only other businesses occupied the same building, where Dowell's neighbors operated a grocery store and a meat market.

Dowell's Saloon, dating from his arrival in El Paso in 1850, was the first bar in town and served as the model for those that followed. It was a center of activity around which grew up in later years the Gem Saloon, the Wigwam, and the Coliseum (the town's first combination variety hall–saloon), all located within a two-block area. Dowell's, the Gem, and the Coliseum fronted on El Paso Street, with the Wigwam a half-block away on San Antonio Street. But the story properly begins with Ben Dowell, when El Paso was little more than a wide place in the road in the far western corner of Texas.

A visitor to El Paso in 1859, A. D. Richardson, found about four hundred residents, mostly Mexicans, living there. He reported that "gambling was universal, with huge piles of silver dollars staked at the monte tables in the great saloons." One hundred thousand dollars might change hands in a single night, he stated.[3] Dowell's Saloon, lubricated by a well-stocked bar, was one of the prime locales for such exchanges.

Aside from the convivial pursuits of gambling and drinking, the saloon also saw its share of violence. Like most Western saloons, Ben

Dowell's place attracted its share of confrontations, some indoors and others just outside the *portales*, the roofed front porch. A latter-day plaque in the courtyard of today's Camino Real Hotel marks the site of one of the town's most infamous gun battles—the "four dead in five seconds" incident of 1881, which took place on the Alameda near the saloon.

El Paso was not much of a town when Ben Dowell arrived in 1850, a veteran of the recent war with Mexico. A volunteer in the Kentucky cavalry, he had been taken prisoner in January, 1847. Held for nearly eight months in Mexico City, he was freed in September, just a few weeks short of his twenty-ninth birthday. Two by-products of that experience would affect him in later life: his hair turned white, giving him an air of authority that he used to advantage as a respected public figure, and he learned to speak Spanish, a highly useful skill in a border town.

When he returned from the war to his Kentucky home on the Ohio River, his taste for adventure remained strong. He and his wife divorced, and he struck out for the West, likely joining one of the many wagon trains heading for the California gold fields. Many of those trains started in San Antonio and then followed the military road laid out by the U.S. Army westward. Once they reached far West Texas, they followed the valley of El Paso del Norte, the Pass of the North, past a series of military posts. The post at El Paso had been established in September, 1849, using the ranch buildings of Juan María Ponce de León, who had extensive holdings on both sides of the Rio Grande.

Dowell came as far as El Paso and found employment on Ponce's Rancho, where he tended vineyards that grew in the vicinity of the city's present-day complex of federal and county buildings at San Antonio and Campbell Streets. Locally produced wines and brandies became legendary among the travelers and soldiers who sampled them.

The ranch had several structures. One at the head of the Alameda became the Central (later Grand Central) Hotel, and the long one with adobe-pillared portales occupied the block below. In the south end of the long building, Dowell launched the town's first saloon.[4]

In 1853, a year after Ponce's death, his heirs sold the rancho to William T. Smith, a Missouri-born freighter. Four years later, Smith sold out to Dowell for $450, transferring possession of the 128-by-60-foot lot plus the building that became the billiard saloon and grocery store. A year later Dowell and a partner paid $1,200 for the next lot to the north. Then Dowell bought out his partner, gaining sole title to more than half the block plus the building on it.[5]

As early as 1855 the saloon was the site of a shooting, an event that could only be read about in regional newspapers since El Paso had no journals of its own as yet. A robbery had occurred in the town's customs house, with $2,300 taken, part of it government money and the rest being held for private citizens. A break-in at the saloon around the same time netted the thieves, believed to be the same men, three guns along with all but one of Dowell's horses, which were taken from his stable behind the saloon. Barking dogs wakened him just in time to discover his loss.

Being sought for the customs house theft were William McElroy (also known as William Blair), William Miller, Edward Russell, and Jack Gordon. Fleeing El Paso, they raced northward toward Las Cruces in New Mexico Territory. Dowell blamed McElroy for his personal losses and put out the word that he wanted to settle accounts with the outlaw.

In August, 1856, McElroy and Gordon turned up in San Elizario, a farming town on the river southeast of El Paso. They took refreshments in the bar of Bill Ford, to whom they bragged that they planned to return to El Paso the next day for the purpose of robbing and killing Ben Dowell. Since saloon clients regarded barmen as father-confessors, the pair explained their plan in detail to Ford. One of them would wait outside Dowell's place while the other went in and ordered a drink. When Dowell turned his back to get the liquor, the two would close in on him.

What they did not know was that Ford was one of Dowell's closest friends and had earlier been his business partner in El Paso. Ford sent a fast rider upriver to give the warning. When the two unsuspecting outlaws arrived at Dowell's Saloon the next morning, a group of well-armed men awaited them, carefully hidden behind the bar and a cracker barrel. As McElroy came through the door, Dowell felled him, and Albert Kuhn polished him off with a fatal shot to the head. The San Antonio newspapers reported that McElroy was the third safe robber to have been killed in El Paso in recent months. Although Gordon managed to flee, Dowell was able to recover his missing livestock except for two prize horses.[6]

Violence visited Dowell's on another occasion when a gunslinger started taking potshots at El Paso legislator Jeff Hall on the street in front of the saloon. A crowd gathered, started after the gunman, and cornered him behind the Central Hotel. After he had been administered a generous dose of bullets, an argument began among the vigilantes over who deserved credit for putting him away.

"Gentlemen," admonished Uncle Ben, "some day some judge or other may come along and be holding court, and some of us may have trouble about this business."

The men reconsidered and quickly convened a coroner's jury, which delivered its verdict: the deceased had come to his end "by gunshot wounds from the hands of parties unknown."[7]

When the Civil War came, Dowell was the first to fly a Confederate flag over El Paso. His blatant personal bias did not deter the state from scheduling an election on the secession issue at the saloon, which had been a regular polling place for years. Although the 1860 census had counted a population of just 428, more than twice that number cast ballots on voting day—a characteristic of El Paso elections that would continue for many years. Only two votes favored the Union. In their autobiographies, brothers Anson and W. W. Mills made it clear that those ballots were theirs.[8]

Texas voters approved secession in early 1861, and El Paso's Fort Bliss surrendered to the Confederates on March 31. When H. H. Sibley's Confederate invasion army was defeated in battle in northern New Mexico in 1862, they retreated to San Antonio via El Paso and burned the fort to keep it out of the hands of pursuing Unionists. Several local families fled, some relocating as far away as San Antonio and St. Louis, but many just crossed the river to sit out the war. In the fall of 1862 Ben took his Tigua Indian wife, Juana, their six-year-old daughter, Mary, and their new baby, Juan, to El Paso del Norte (now Ciudad Juárez), where their friend Juan Ruíz, for whom the baby had been named, helped them get settled. Then Dowell left for the Texas coast where, as a Confederate captain, he worked as a recruiter and blockade runner.

The fixtures from his saloon, including billiard tables, were taken to El Paso del Norte by one of Dowell's Masonic brothers, Rufus Doane, who used them to set up his own bar on the Mexican side of the river. The main customers were Union soldiers, who paid in greenbacks, worth thirty cents on the dollar in Mexico.[9]

After its wartime hiatus, Dowell's place was reincarnated in its original location, although not without some difficulty. The property of Confederates had been declared forfeit during the war and confiscated whenever possible. It took years for some former Rebels to get their possessions back, if they got them back at all. Dowell was more fortunate. W. W. Mills had been appointed El Paso's collector of customs, with authority over goods smuggled into El Paso County. A federal judge extended that authority to cover property confiscated from the Confederates. Mills's approval was vital in resolving all property cases. Fortunately for Dowell, he was a brother Mason. Through personal diplomacy and friendship, Dowell was able to recover his holdings. By 1869 he had bought new furnishings for his bar from John Woods, operator of the Franklin House hotel and bar. Dowell paid $163 for mirrors, pictures, chairs, tables, and tumblers, and his restored bar was once again El Paso's social center.[10]

Business was slow in the postwar years on both sides of the border. The French were finally ousted from Mexico in 1867 by Benito Juárez (for whom El Paso del Norte would be renamed in 1888) after a bitter ten-year ordeal. New Mexico, where several Civil War battles had taken place, and El Paso, which had changed hands repeatedly between the Confederate and Union forces, remained devastated for several years. Yet travelers and traders continued to move through the pass. Dowell knew that railroads were starting their march across the West and predicted that the town's face would change dramatically once the trains arrived.[11]

The unstable political climate of Reconstruction led to one of the most notorious shooting incidents at Dowell's Saloon. This time a district judge and his killer were the victims.

Although El Paso lies six hundred miles from Austin—nearer the capitals of New Mexico and Arizona than its own—the political intrigues of the post–Civil War years had an impact even in the far western reaches of the state. Two factions had developed in the Texas Republican Party, Conservatives and Radicals. Customs collector W. W. Mills participated in the 1868 constitutional convention in Austin as a Conservative. At that time, he married the daughter of former governor A. J. Hamilton, also a Conservative, which created a powerful political alliance. During Mills's absence, Albert Fountain took command of Republican interests in El Paso. With a state election set for November, 1869, the Conservatives put up Mills for representative and Hamilton for governor. On the Radicals' side Fountain was the nominee for state senator and Edmund Davis for governor. When the Radical candidates won, Mills not only lost the race but was subsequently removed from his lucrative customs post after a former employee complained about him to Washington.

Fountain tried to heal the party differences by appointing two of Mills's friends to choice jobs: Gaylord Clarke as district judge and A. H. French, former county judge, as state police lieutenant for the El Paso district. This merely complicated things further. Benjamin Franklin "Frank" Williams, a local lawyer and friend of Mills, who had his eye on the judgeship, now found himself passed over when the appointment went to Clarke. Williams took to drinking heavily and ranting about injustices but did not stop at that. When pleading cases in district court, he did not show proper respect to Judge Clarke.

On the evening of December 6, 1870, Williams was imbibing in Dowell's Saloon, calling for vengeance against Fountain. The next morning he saw Clarke on the street, warned him he would not be judge much longer, and drew a gun. He backed off when the unarmed Clarke advanced toward him. The judge quickly informed Fountain about the incident. Fountain offered to speak to Williams and found him at Dowell's again, drinking heavily and still armed. In response to Fountain's admonishment, Williams pulled out his pistol and fired five shots at him, three of which hit their intended target. One caused a scalp wound, the second a wound in the left arm, and the third was deflected from his heart by a pocket watch. Williams fled to his nearby rooming house, while Fountain went home to get his own gun. The Fountain and Clarke families lived in the Overland Building about a block south at El Paso and Overland Streets.

Seeing Clarke, Fountain urged him to gather a posse, with French heading it. The men advanced on Williams's quarters, where they started beating the door down. Williams emerged, holding a double-barreled shotgun. He aimed at Clarke and shot him dead. French, several yards away, raised his rifle and killed the assassin with one shot, ending the incident.[12]

Saloons in small towns like El Paso became centers of political decision making in the West. According to historian Thomas J. Noel, "Before city halls, county courthouses, and statehouses were built in frontier capitals . . . , settlers commonly met in saloonhalls to create and conduct their first governments. As the first, largest, and most ubiquitous public meeting places, saloonhalls were birthplaces of self-government and housed city councils, courts, and legislatures in their early years. Government not only found a home in the liquor houses but also developed close ties with the liquor men during the territorial period." [13]

In 1872, when the census counted 764 residents, El Pasoans decided they needed a city government. The Texas Legislature authorized the incorporation on May 17, 1873, and in August an election was held. Ben Dowell was chosen the first mayor by the 105 qualified voters and served with six aldermen. Since there were no funds to construct public buildings, Dowell's Saloon followed the pattern found in many other Western cities and became the city hall. Citizens squabbled over such issues as paying taxes, cleaning the *acequia* that brought the water supply through town, and controlling loose dogs.[14]

At one point his proximity to Mexico brought Mayor Dowell a chance to settle with a handshake a problem that might have saved his nation $45 million nearly a century later when the Chamizal Convention was finalized.

The Rio Grande had been designated as the international boundary between the United States and Mexico first by the Congress of the Texas Republic in 1936 and again in the 1848 Treaty of Guadalupe Hidalgo. The river had changed its course between El Paso del Norte, Mexico, and El Paso, Texas, several times between 1853 and 1863, then moved farther south after a severe flood in 1864. Mexico claimed some three hundred acres of land that now lay north of the river.

Ben Dowell heard in 1874 that the Mexican collector of customs was proposing to the U.S. collector, Colbert Coldwell, that a Mexican Custom House officer be stationed on the road leading from El Paso to El Paso del Norte, two or three hundred yards north of the river and not far from Dowell's Saloon. Coldwell surmised that such a move would give the Mexicans a claim to the land that had once been on their side of the boundary and turned down the proposal.

Failing in that effort, the Mexicans pursued another plan. When Dowell got wind of it, he wrote to the *prefecto* of El Paso del Norte, José María Uranga, about it. He advised his fellow mayor that he had learned Uranga planned "to meet some parties in consultation, with a view of entering into some arrangement tending to the changing of the natural channel of the Rio Grande River against which I do most earnestly protest." In his capacity as El Paso's mayor and a property-owning citizen, said Dowell, he felt it would be unlawful for the two city officials to effect a change in the international boundary. That was, he stressed, the prerogative of "the sovereign governments of the Republic of Mexico and the United States of America, and then only by treaty stipulations entered into in the proper form and manner." Some three hundred acres of land were involved. Dowell further pointed out that any proposed artificial changing of the channel by placing dams or canals would be in violation of the treaty between the two governments.[15]

Nearly a century later this problem—which Dowell and Uranga might have settled with a handshake—was resolved through action taken by Presidents John F. Kennedy and Adolfo López Mateos in 1962. The Chamizal Convention, named for the area in question, straightened the river channel, which placed 630 acres from the El Paso side in Mexico and transferred 193 acres from Mexico to the United States. As a result, 5,500 El Pasoans were relocated to other parts of the city.[16]

Ben Dowell's public career did not end with his one term as mayor. He was elected a county commissioner in 1878 and a city alderman in 1880, all while continuing to run his saloon, operate a ranch north of town, and hold high office in the Masonic fraternity. Uncle Ben died unexpectedly on November 8, 1880, three weeks short of his sixty-second birthday and six months short of the arrival of the railroad he had predicted would make El Paso a real city. His fellow Masons buried him with honors in their cemetery.[17]

The 100 block of South El Paso Street looked much the same as before in the early 1880s, except for poles installed to carry electric transmission lines in 1883 and telephone lines in 1884. After Ben Dowell's death, his saloon at the far end of the business block was leased by the Manning Brothers. Courtesy *El Paso County Historical Society*

The saloon continued to operate under new management. Dowell's widow, Juana, leased it for $185 a month to Frank Manning, who retained the billiards and gambling operations and continued to serve up alcoholic refreshments.[18] Frank Manning and his two brothers, James (Jim) and John, had arrived in El Paso in 1880 and would achieve notoriety as bar owners and gunfighters. Frank first had built a saloon about five miles west of town. It was successful, but Dowell's had a better location and was larger, so when it became available he relocated.[19] Meanwhile, his brother Jim and a partner opened the Gem just down the block from the former Dowell's. That partnership ended in a few months and

FRONT ELEVATION

DOWELL'S SALOON - 1858
CORNER OF EL PASO AND SONORA STREETS
EL PASO, TEXAS
ca. 1858

DRAWINGS BY
ROBERT CULLEN SMITH, A.I.A.

Jim, joined by brother John Manning and James A. McDaniels, established the Coliseum a few doors south at the rear of the El Paso Hotel. The two-story barnlike structure was a combination variety theater and saloon, complete with show girls who solicited drinks. McDaniels left in 1882, and the Mannings controlled the enterprise through 1883.[20]

Through the 1880s, Western gamblers followed a circuit, focusing on "wide-open new communities where money was plentiful and 'true-blue sports' abounded who were willing to take a risk on the turn of a card."[21] The Mannings's Coliseum early earned repute as a choice spot on the circuit, which took men to northern mining camps in the summer and southern towns in the winter.

Newcomers arrived by the carload with the coming of the railroads in 1881, which linked El Paso to east-west and north-south points throughout the United States and Mexico. Two daily newspapers started in April and advertised some of the popular spots for men seeking an evening out: the Tivoli Beer Hall on San Francisco Street, saloons of George W. Thomas and Paul Keating on El Paso Street, S. J. Obenchain's place on the north side of the main plaza, and across the river in El Paso, Mexico, the El Paso Brewery and the International Saloon Beer Garden. The Central Hotel was planning the addition of a third floor to take care of the influx of visitors.[22]

The first in a series of major shooting incidents to be covered in the new journals occurred in front of Manning's saloon and became known as the "Four Men Dead in Five Seconds" incident of April 14, 1881. It is remembered in a historic marker on the site, now the Camino Real Hotel.

El Paso's city council had been hard put to find a competent marshal. In early April, Dallas Stoudenmire, six-foot-two, 185 pounds, applied for the job and won it. He succeeded George Campbell, whose assistant had been Bill Johnson, a man with a well-known weakness for liquor. One of Stoudenmire's first acts in office was to relieve Johnson of the keys to the jail and oust him from the premises.

Ten days after Stoudenmire became marshal, a posse headed by Gus Krempkau rode ten miles upriver to a *bosque* where two men from Mexico had been killed in a cattle smuggling incident. The bodies were brought to the office of Julius A. Buckler, at that time city attorney and later county judge, a few doors down from Manning's place.

Constable Krempkau, a former Texas ranger, was serving as translator as the inquest proceedings got under way. A large crowd had gathered, then dispersed at noon for dinner. When Krempkau reached the street, he was accosted first by George Campbell, the deposed city marshal, then by Johnny Hale, who had a ranch in the upper valley and managed the next one to it for the Manning brothers. Hale was a suspect in the killings of the two Mexican men. He quickly fired his .45 at Krempkau, hitting him near the heart. Marshal Stoudenmire, who was across the street, heard the gunfire and readied his guns for action. He was followed outside by his sister Virginia's husband, Samuel M. "Doc" Cummings, who carried a shotgun.[23]

Stoudenmire's first shot wounded a bystander named Ochoa, who died the next day. The second one hit Hale in the head. Campbell then entered the street, waving his pistol around. As he did so, the dying Krempkau held up his revolver and began firing at Campbell, getting him in the hand and the foot, then releasing two more wild shots. Stoudenmire also targeted Campbell, killing him.

Zach White, who operated a grocery store nearby, stepped out to see what was happening and was sent back inside by a profane outburst from Stoudenmire. (White later was to become the owner of the Manning saloon and adjacent property on which he built the Hotel Paso del Norte, today's Camino Real.)

A coroner's jury was summoned to rule on the killings: Krempkau died of a pistol shot fired by John Hale; Campbell and Hale died of pistol shots fired by Stoudenmire in executing his duties. No mention was made of Ochoa's death.[24]

Three days after the big shootout, Bill Johnson was encouraged by friends of Campbell to ambush Stoudenmire as he made his rounds. His courage fortified by a bottle, Johnson hid behind a pile of bricks at San Antonio Street where it dead-ended at Manning's saloon. As the marshal approached from the Acme Saloon down the block, his assailant raised a double-barrel shotgun and fired over the head of his prey. Stoudenmire pulled a pistol and repeatedly hit Johnson with deadly accuracy. Campbell's friends, hiding across the street, opened fire on the marshal, wounding him in the foot. Undaunted, he charged them and they could not get away fast enough. This incident passed into folklore of the period, and by 1910 there was a version that said at least a hundred men had fired at Stoudenmire from behind the portal columns of the Manning saloon building, but "he was not even scathed." The next morning, went the tale, at least two hundred men left town by train, horseback, and even on foot, so fearful were they of the marshal's retaliation.[25]

As the town began an unprecedented period of growth and economic success thanks to the railroads, Marshal Stoudenmire built on his reputation as a threat to gunmen looking for trouble. The Manning brothers, however, were not enthusiastic about his peacekeeping abilities. Johnny Hale had been not only their Canutillo ranch manager, but their friend. On the other hand, Stoudenmire and Cummings, Hale's opponents in the gunfight, believed that when Johnson came after the marshal he was egged on by the Mannings. The extra shots had come, after all, from the direction of their saloon.

Not quite a year after the celebrated shootouts, another incident occurred in February, 1882, while Stoudenmire was away getting married; his brother-in-law, "Doc" Cummings, proprietor of the Globe Restaurant, was killed by Jim Manning. For weeks Cummings had been opining that Jim Manning needed killing. One night, after he had been imbibing heavily, he spotted Manning at the corner of Overland and El Paso Streets and invited him into the Coliseum for a drink, all the while telling him what a rotten person he was. Manning ordered seltzer water, which Doc knocked to the floor as they argued. Witnesses were not clear about how the guns came into play or who fired first, but Cummings was felled by two bullets. Only one had been fired from Manning's pistol. Stoudenmire's deputy marshal, James B. Gillett, a former Texas Ranger, believed that the other shot had been fired by the bartender, a Manning employee, but no action was taken against him. Ranger Capt. George W. Baylor held Jim Manning briefly, but he was not charged with the slaying. There was an unwritten code that when armed enemies met in circumstances like these, and the aggressor ended up dead, his slayer was more to be congratulated than denigrated.[26]

After a period of hard feelings, the Stoudenmire and Manning factions called a truce dated April 16 and published it in a local newspaper:

> We the undersigned parties having this day settled all differences and unfriendly feelings existing between us, hereby agree that we will hereafter meet and pass each other on friendly terms, and that bygones shall be bygones, and that we shall never allude in the future to any past animosities that have existed between us.

Witness	Signed
R. F. Campbell	Dallas Stoudenmire
J. F. Harrison	J. Manning
F. V. Hogan	G. F. Manning
J. Hague	Frank Manning[27]

As Stoudenmire's reputation had grown, so had his penchant for heavy drinking. Around the time of the truce, he was asked to resign. He did so and almost immediately became a U.S. deputy marshal for the Western District of Texas. Gillett succeeded him as city marshal. Despite the promises made in the truce, Stoudenmire remained a target of the Mannings's animosity. He had been a married man for only six months when he met his fate in a saloon—not theirs, but at their hands—in September, 1882. He had been having words with various of the brothers over a period of several days. Finally the oldest, Dr. G. F. "Doc" Manning, a respected physician, confronted him and both men drew their guns almost simultaneously. Stoudenmire shot the doctor in his surgeon's hand, but took bullets near the heart and in the left arm and breast in return. He backed out the door, where Jim Manning saw him and shot him in the head. No one was charged with Stoudenmire's death at the inquest, echoing the verdict of that earlier coroner's jury after the slaying of Doc Cummings.[28]

Meanwhile, as a result of the rail lines linking El Paso with other cities in all directions, the population zoomed from 736 in 1880 to 10,336 in 1890. Saloons became a major factor in the expanding economy, with railroads vying for their trade. In December, 1881, for example, a carload of beer could be brought from St. Louis to El Paso via the Santa Fe railroad at a cost of $500, but the Texas and Pacific's competitive price was only $254. Likewise, the charge for a carload of whiskey on the Santa Fe was $450, but half that much on the newer T&P.[29]

Owen White, the town's first historian, described the changes of that period as "quick and startling. . . . Brick buildings began to replace adobe ones, ornate bar fixtures and fancy gambling tables ousted the makeshift equipment formerly in use; pine boards took the place of Mother Earth on the floors in the dance halls. At the same time a new element in the life of El Paso, a blondined, hand-decorated female element, recruited in the East and Middle West and shipped in by the carload, arrived to compete with the brown-skinned, black-eyed señoritas of the earlier day." [30]

These improvements were remarked upon by a news reporter who in 1882 described his sojourn down El Paso Street to look in on gambling saloons in the area where the Mannings held forth. He started at the head of the street, the Central Hotel, where he saw "an immense pile of Mexican dollars arranged in stacks. . . . One player had a pile of gold pieces and greenbacks in front of him."

As he meandered down the block, the writer "turned into an elegant saloon for a game of billiards," which though not identified by name was undoubtedly Frank Manning's place. "Here was a large crowd drinking at the bar and observing the games." In a club room were a half dozen persons seated at two tables, trying their luck at casino and draw poker. Down the street, apparently at the Coliseum, identified as "the variety theatre," crowds were large and noisy. Ten gambling games were in progress. The writer philosophized about the losers:

> Who can fathom the emotions of a gambler's breast? Bitter hard luck and unexpected good fortune come to him, apparently unappreciated, and one can not help thinking that the fluctuating emotions of a tyro whose money is sweating in his palm, is preferable to the cold, unimpassioned demonstration of the gambler. But the most miserable of men is he who cannot resist the fascination, and is devoured by conflicting emotion, and is by turns flushed with exaltation and eaten by remorse.[31]

At the time of this saloon report, population estimates were seven thousand for the Mexican side of the river and five thousand for the Texas side, including the towns of El Paso through San Elizario.[32]

Later the same year, a visitor from the East observed that saloons were flourishing in a community that had gained four-fifths of its 2,500 citizens in only the past eighteen months, "with the goal of making money." He found the population principally Americans or American-ized Germans, Mexicans, and Chinese, with a sprinkling of other na-tionalities. Upon visiting one of the prospering saloons, he saw a "young gentleman from the city with watch and fob, Derby hat, short coat, tight pants and large cravat; almond-eyed Mongolian with simple blue jeans trousers, flowing white shirt and long, well-plaited cue, ornamented just after leaving the head with a Chinese fan; well-to-do Mexican, with his highly ornamented sombrero, and lastly the poorer and plainer day la-borer. The motley crowd drink and carouse with a congeniality that is rather singular, but withal, sobriety and good will seems to prevail. . . . Strangers are treated with more civility here than they are in eastern towns." [33]

The influx of new people caused the merchants along El Paso Street, heart of the business district, to reconsider their quarters. The old adobe building that had been part of Ponce's ranch gradually gave way to new facilities, a section at a time. One of them was a two-story brick build-ing with basement. It was erected in 1883 by the Dowell heirs and "was regarded at that time as the most splendid and imposing business struc-ture in the city." [34] Zachary White, who later would buy the site for his hotel, operated a grocery store in that block.

Several Western towns of this period, Denver among them, had rules against allowing women in saloons, either as patrons or as bartenders. Not long after incorporation in 1873, El Paso had drawn up a city char-ter dedicated to suppressing and restraining "disorderly houses, houses of prostitution or assignation, gambling houses, lotteries and all fraudu-lent devices and practices, and all kinds of indecencies." As put into practice, the charter provisions confined prostitution to a section of Utah Street (now South Mesa), and women were not normally found in the popular saloons along El Paso and San Antonio streets.[35]

Although the city charter aimed at preventing the operation of "houses of prostitution" within the city limits, its wording provided that the government could "adopt summary measures for the removal or suppression or regulation and inspection of all such establishments." From the 1880s until 1941, a "zone of tolerance" existed, with periodic interruptions or boundary changes in response to moralist crusades or military demands. The arrangement offered two important advantages: venereal diseases could be controlled by regular medical inspections of the prostitutes, and the monthly "fines" that they and their employers paid kept the city treasury afloat. Early on, the city fathers discovered that it was costly and time-consuming to try to prosecute individual girls from the zone; the pre-1881 fine for violating vice laws was one dollar plus court costs of $4.50. In 1882, with the railroads delivering newcomers by the hundreds, the council established, along with fines for breaking the law, a monthly fee system—five dollars per girl—that was, in effect, a license to practice.[36]

When the fee was doubled in 1886, the women protested as a group to the city council, which responded by taking them to court individually, taking another twenty-eight dollars from each of them. The girls quickly complied with the new rate until an economic recession in 1894 reduced their income, and a similar appeal to the council brought a temporary reduction to five dollars. Fees were also collected from gambling houses, dance halls, and saloons, an arrangement that supported the police department into the 1920s.[37]

The classic bordellos with their elegant bars were located just a few blocks south and east of the busy saloon district. The boundaries of the zone of tolerance were set in a recommendation made by the Police Committee, chaired by former mayor Joseph Magoffin. Under the Reservation Ordinance of 1890, the area was bounded by the south side of East Overland from Oregon to Utah, south on Utah to Third Street, including the east half of Utah to the alley, west on Third to Oregon, and north on Oregon to East Overland. From time to time the boundaries were redefined, usually pushed southward, and the girls were run out of town in periods of severe enforcement, but this always brought the same set of headaches; the city government lost revenue and sexually transmitted diseases increased.[38]

As a side benefit of their fee arrangement, proprietors of brothels were issued whistles with which to summon police, who were always within calling distance in the red light district. The quick response of armed officers helped deter brawls and gunfights in the area.

Fatal incidents were minimal there, at least in comparison to those in standard saloons, but history recorded some memorable confrontations. The most celebrated gunshot was fired by one madam who was being attacked by another.

In the summer of 1881 Madam Alice Abbott brought her girls down from Louisville, Kentucky, and opened her business in a two-story frame house at 19 South Utah Street. She was lacking in personal beauty, a sturdy six feet tall, weighing nearly two hundred pounds, with her hair drawn back in a bun from a plain face. But she knew how to entertain her clients by creating posh surroundings and employing enticing young ladies.

The next pioneer of the trade to arrive in town was Etta Clark, a tempestuous French-Canadian redhead, who set up shop near Alice on Utah Street in a rented six-room, one-story house. Etta was opposite Alice not only in location, but in looks, a petite five feet tall with a good figure. She imported girls from San Francisco. By the end of 1881, four more brothels had opened in the neighborhood.[39]

The competitive spirit of Alice Abbott and Etta Clark was challenged in 1886 in an incident immortalized by a newspaper "typo." Alice Abbott two years earlier had hired a beauty, Bessie Colvin, who immediately became the most popular girl of Alice's coterie. As an industrious money-maker, Bessie won Alice's favor in the form of shopping sprees for finery that would be paid off in work. Their amity did not last, however; Alice accused Bessie of taking customers in secret and not paying what was due her boss. Their arguments over money and cheating grew more heated, and Bessie took refuge in alcohol. Her decision to resolve the situation came on April 18, 1886, when she mumbled drunken insults at Alice's customers and crossed the street to Etta Clark's place, where she asked for a job. Knowing Bessie's reputation for attracting business, Etta eagerly agreed to hire her.

When Bessie returned for her personal effects, Alice found her packing her trunk and confronted her angrily. News of her plan to leave enraged Alice, who tried to stop her. Bessie fled to Etta's front porch, rang the bell, and was admitted with "Fat Alice" bellowing at her heels. The door slammed behind Bessie. Alice attacked it with her fists and finally Etta opened it, armed with a curious defensive weapon: a thin tube used for lighting gas fixtures. With Bessie pleading in the background, Etta ordered Alice to leave. Alice instead barreled her way into the hallway, was hit by the lighter, and responded by socking Etta in the face. While Alice scolded Bessie, Etta retrieved a .44-caliber bone-handled revolver from her room. Again she ordered Alice to go. As Alice approached her, the petite madam fired a shot that hit her adversary in the nether regions, sending her reeling out the door to collapse in the street. After Etta's second shot missed the target, she went back inside.

Three of Alice's girls carried her to her room and called a doctor. He found the bullet had gone through her body to the right of the pubic arch, and while no vital organs were hit, there was a possibility of blood poisoning. The news account in the *Herald* the next day headlined the story with its classic typo: Alice had been hit in "The Public Arch."

Etta was charged with attempted first-degree murder, but at the trial in May she was found not guilty on grounds of self-defense. Fat Alice, who recovered readily from her wound, soon persuaded Bessie Colvin to return to work for her. Two years later, Alice was accused of hiring three men to set fire to Etta's place of business, but the case was dismissed for lack of evidence.[40]

While most saloons in the West put a ceiling on winnings available to gamblers—$2,500 in San Francisco in midcentury, for example—El Paso had no limits from 1888 to the fall of 1894, according to newspaperman J. D. Ponder. The Gem, the Wigwam, and the Cactus frequently "lifted the roof," and gamblers came from as far away as Mexico City to take advantage of the chance to make a fortune at the gaming tables. The phenomenon took on new life during the early December observance of the Fiesta of Our Lady of Guadalupe in Ciudad Juárez and El Paso. Bullfights and other diversions soon lost their appeal as gamblers on the Mexican side of the river crossed to the promise of open-ended rewards in El Paso's gambling houses.

The Gem had opened as a variety hall on September 5, 1885, two doors down from the original Dowell Saloon, and offered dog fights, boxing matches, and vaudeville. In 1887 it changed its focus to that of a saloon with more lucrative gambling facilities. A disastrous fire in 1894 ruined the place, but it was soon rebuilt.[41]

"In each of the three largest houses," recalled Ponder, "was one table upon which was stacked bankrolls ranging from $10,000 to $20,000 each, and a player who could show $10,000 and asked for the limit to be raised, was usually informed that the roof was off and he could go to it. Such privilege, however, was not accorded the men with only $500 to play. Gamblers are superstitious about the luck of a man with a small bankroll." [42]

Roulette and faro appealed to men who came from other parts of the country, but the ranchers from Texas and nearby New Mexico preferred poker. They had some control over the contents of their hands, as well as proficiency in running bluffs. A man's "poker face" could allow him to win a round with a pair of deuces, outsmarting the holder of three queens.[43]

Among celebrated patrons of the Gem was Luis Terrazas, Jr., son of the noted Mexican general, who in a few minutes could win or lose impressive thousands of dollars. He had a reputation for fearlessness at the gaming tables.[44]

Like the other saloons along El Paso Street, the Gem had its share of shooting incidents. On April 15, 1885, a fancy dresser named Billy Raynor, attired in a Prince Albert coat with a white Stetson hat, and his friend Charles M. "Buck" Linn, a former lawyer, entered the saloon. They were far from sober, and Bob Cahill, who worked the faro table, tried to send them home. But Raynor was primed for a fight. He was looking for Harry Williams, a noted gambler, against whom he held a grudge of some sort. Failing to find Williams, Raynor approached a stranger, R. B. Rennick, who was at the time planning a holdup, although he did not have a gun on him. Raynor challenged him, asking if he were a fighter; when he received a negative answer, he pressed the subject, calling Rennick a name, and then stalked out of the room.

Rennick knew that a drawer in the faro table held a pistol. He retrieved it and went after Raynor, who drew his own gun, fired, and missed his target. Rennick hit him with a fatal bullet.

Meanwhile, Buck Linn went after Cahill, the faro dealer who had made it possible for Rennick to get the gun with which Raynor was killed. Linn fired five times but missed as Cahill fled to the refuge of the nearby Ranch Saloon. After a few minutes, Cahill returned to the Gem, Linn having moved on to another saloon, bragging that he would kill Cahill. Warned of the threat, Cahill took a .45 from the well-stocked faro drawer and awaited Linn's return. When Linn stepped in the door, Cahill blasted him twice in the heart—instant death. Among the witnesses who testified at the hearing into the incident was Wyatt Earp.[45]

Rudolph Eikemeyer, a successful inventor and businessman from Yonkers, New York, spent the spring of 1893 in El Paso taking copious notes about what he saw and reporting them in a book published the following year. He was much taken with the opulence of the major watering holes. He changed their names in print—"Tepee" for "Wigwam" and "Jewel" for "Gem"—but otherwise his descriptions were accurate. The Gem ("Jewel") extended about forty feet back from the entrance and was adorned on the left side of the room with statuary "lacking the conventional fig-leaf." At the end of the bar was a black walnut partition "carved in the highest style of art." He described one visit this way: "We passed through the door, and entered a room filled with a promiscuous crowd. There were Chinamen, Mexicans (real 'Greasers'), Negroes of all shades and colors, a few cowboys, and some business men."[46] The Gem's attractions were extolled in more detail by a writer for the *El Paso Times:*

> Upon entering the wide doors the stranger cannot but view the fixtures of the saloon. They are all of solid black walnut, and the ornaments are of the finest. Back of the bar are three immense solid French plate glass mirrors. These are relieved by three beautiful solid walnut cornices. In these cornices are the famous "Nathan" vases of solid bronze, weighing 150 lbs. each. The vases have quite a history. They were purchased in Paris by a rich New Yorker named Nathan for $2,200. Mr. Nathan was mysteriously murdered in his office. His works of art were sold at public auction. The rooms were sold to Sam Schutz of this city, who in turn sold them to George Look and J. J. Taylor.[47]

From the saloon section of the Gem, one passed through swinging doors into a large room with "gaming tables of every description," including faro, roulette, monte—whatever the gambler might want. The writer described the room as "the Monte Carlo of the West," a nickname often applied to the entire community during this period. The club

One of the premier watering holes of El Paso in the late nineteenth century, the Senate Saloon counted more "gentlemen" among its clientele than did Ben Dowell's place. The Senate Saloon is shown here as it appeared in 1881, with City Marshal James B. Gillett (seated) second from left and looking right at home. Courtesy *Western History Collections, University of Oklahoma Libraries*

rooms led to the Gem Theater where patrons could be seated to watch a variety show while partaking of a meal and some shots of choice W. H. McBrayer whiskey.[48]

Good food was a specialty at El Paso's popular saloons, as well as at the barrooms of the downtown hotels. Lunch offerings ranged from raw oysters at twenty-five cents each to a hot lunch for fifteen cents, or more modest fare at the free lunch table. The Senate Saloon boasted of Blue Point and Saddle Rock oysters on the half shell, while St. Julian's featured imported Swiss, Kummel Hand, and Limburger cheeses, Melcher Holland herring, and European wines.

One of the most intriguing menus was that of the Old Cabinet, also known as Miller's Place, whose hot merchant lunch was served daily from eleven to two. Among cold dishes were pickled lamb's tongue, imported sausage, pigs' feet in *gelée*, boiled Eastern ham, hard-boiled eggs, pickled herrings, imported Swiss cheese, caviar, and sardines. To wash it down there were Lemps beer and fine wines, topped off with a fine cigar. If a businessman preferred lunch at home to visiting the saloon,

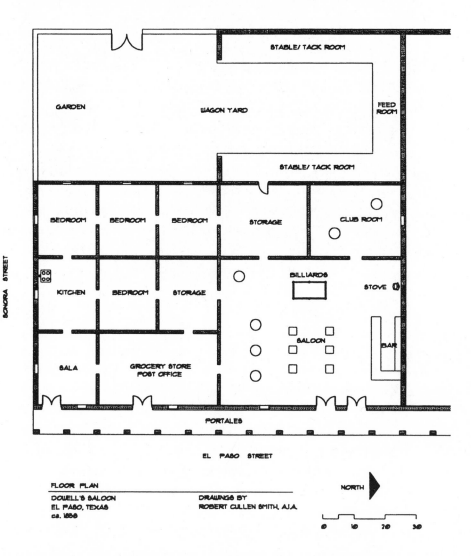

FLOOR PLAN

DOWELL'S SALOON
EL PASO, TEXAS
ca. 1888

DRAWINGS BY
ROBERT CULLEN SMITH, A.I.A.

NORTH

he could send a servant to pick up a pail of beer and the specialties of the day.[49]

In the early 1890s, Houck and Dieter, wholesalers of domestic and imported wines and liquors, were sole agents for the William J. Lemps Brewing Company of St. Louis and Pabst Brewing Company of Milwaukee. The Anheuser-Busch Brewing Association agent was R. F. Johnson. Beers were shipped in kegs, and bars served them in glasses or steins.[50]

A custom of closing saloons on election day was started by Mayor

Joseph Magoffin on November 4, 1884, and continued for several years. A count taken in 1886 disclosed that there was one saloon for every 232 inhabitants of the town.[51]

El Paso's saloon scene was the backdrop for the early education of a man who later was to serve as a prominent Texas university president. Louis H. Hubbard, known to his young friends as "Jack," became a delivery boy for the *El Paso Times* as a small boy, after the death of his father. He quickly developed a steady clientele among saloon customers when he learned they were more than generous with their tips. One who especially impressed him was the notorious John Wesley Hardin, who spent only four months in El Paso but was celebrated for dying there in a saloon gunfight.[52]

Eleven-year-old Jack, who regularly sold newspapers to Hardin, had acquired a new job by the summer of 1895, delivering telegrams for Western Union for wages of $3.60 per week. Whenever he had a message for Hardin, he knew he would find him at either the Acme or the Wigwam, both on San Antonio Street. One early afternoon, he delivered a telegram to Hardin at the Acme, passing through the swinging doors. "I saw him standing at the bar," he related, "and reached him just as he was lifting a big tumbler, not a small glass, of whiskey to his lips. When I accosted him and told him I had a telegram for him he looked at me, lowered his glass to the bar, put his hand on my head and said, 'Son, don't ever do this.' Then he reached into his trousers pocket and took out a dime and gave it to me." The boy said, "I won't, sir; thank you," and left.

He next saw Hardin the following morning, laid out in a casket at the undertaker's. The feared killer had himself been killed August 19, 1895, by Constable John Selman; Selman in turn would be gunned down by Deputy Marshal George Scarborough the following April near the Wigwam Saloon. Hubbard, who recorded his story many years later, had a distinguished career as an educator, serving as president of Texas State College for Women (now Texas Woman's University) from 1926 until his retirement in 1950. But he never forgot his friendship with the famous gunfighter.[53]

At the time forty-two-year-old John Wesley Hardin made El Paso his home, in April, 1895, he had been dubbed "the fastest gun in Texas" with somewhere between thirty and fifty killings to his credit. His other "baggage" included a twenty-year marriage to Jane Bowen, who died in 1892, three children, fifteen years behind bars, a governor's pardon, and a second marriage. Six weeks after the pardon, with his citizenship restored, he capitalized on his study of law while a prisoner and in July, 1894, was licensed to practice in Texas courts. He hung out his shingle briefly in Gonzales, then in Junction, where he married fifteen-year-old Callie Lewis, whom he was said to have won in a card game. They were together less than a week and never divorced.[54]

Drinking, gambling, and prostitution flourished in the town Hardin knew as "the Monte Carlo of the West." He opened a law office on the second floor of the Wells Fargo Building (which is still standing) at 200½ South El Paso Street, opposite the Gem Saloon and the site of the former Dowell Saloon. He roomed at the Herndon Lodging House on Overland Street, where another tenant, Mrs. Beulah Mróz, sought his legal services for her husband, Martin. The Silesian-born Martin Mróz had left San Antonio for the Pecos River Valley of New Mexico and far west Texas where, with three fellow Poles, he had switched from herding cattle to rustling them. When a reward was offered for him in early 1895 by the cattlemen's association, he fled to Juárez and was arrested and jailed there. He could not return to El Paso because of the reward offer but, concerned about rumors of an affair between his wife and Hardin, he was persuaded to cross the railroad bridge to El Paso by U.S. Marshal George Scarborough and was killed by persons unknown.[55]

Local speculation was that Hardin had arranged the killing of Mróz, who had left considerable cash with his wife before departing for Mexico. That cash, it was said, was subsequently used by Hardin to buy a half-interest in the Wigwam. The saloon faced on San Antonio Street just around the corner from his law office.[56]

In May, Hardin began a series of scrapes with the law, charged variously with carrying a gun illegally, gambling, and robbing the Gem Saloon at the point of a gun. He was found guilty and fined twenty-five dollars on the Gem charge, paid a ten-dollar fine on a guilty plea to gambling, and was granted a continuance on the robbery charge, which was never tried because of his untimely death. Both before and after the death of Mróz, Hardin was in fear of the fugitive's confederates because of his not-so-secret romance with Beulah. He stepped up his already heavy habits of gambling and drinking and was developing serious financial and health problems. He sold his interest in the Wigwam in late June. He and Beulah, who was also drinking to excess, fought mightily, and she left town. Before she left, however, she had a drunken run-in with John Selman, Jr., a police officer and son of the constable, which led to her arrest for threatening to shoot young Selman.[57]

Hardin had been complaining about the young police officer for some time, and on August 18, 1895, he was confronted by Selman senior, who challenged him to a shootout. Hardin agreed to go after his gun, but nothing came of the incident. The next evening, about ten o'clock, Hardin, who had been drinking most of the day, found his way to the Acme Saloon (near the corner of San Antonio and Utah Streets). Constable Selman, whose proposed duel the night before had failed to develop, showed up at the Acme with a friend and, while keeping an eye on Hardin, entered and left the premises several times, even at one point playing cards with his opponent. The constable finally got up and exited the saloon by the front door, remaining outside for a while. Then, on his friend's signal, he stormed back into the building and fired three shots into Hardin, the first bullet to the back of the head being the fatal one.[58]

Although John Selman claimed that he did it out of fear for his son's life, Hardin biographer Leon Metz believes the incident grew out of the Mróz shooting. Hardin had admitted that he had hired four men—one of them John Selman, Sr.—to kill Beulah's husband. Selman had not yet been paid for the deed, which led him to commit the "most noted killing in El Paso's history." John Selman, Jr., poised at the time on a stack of boxes across the street from the Acme with a rifle in his hands, heard the shots, ran to his father, and took his gun. This account by an eyewitness strongly suggests that he was part of a murder conspiracy, and that, had Selman Sr. failed, Selman Jr. was prepared to do the job.[59]

The elder Selman was tried for murder in February, 1896. The jury could not agree on a verdict, however, and the case was postponed until the next term of court, which proved too late to decide anything in a court of law; John Selman was already dead.[60]

In April, 1896, Selman's son was jailed in Juárez, Mexico, after trying to elope with the daughter of a prominent Mexican family. His father tried to enlist the help of George Scarborough, deputy U.S. marshal, to free young John. Early on Easter morning, April 5, Scarborough descended the stairs from the gambling rooms above the Wigwam and met Selman in the alley next to the saloon. Whatever the two gun-toting men said to each other was not heard by anyone else, but four shots pierced the Sunday silence, and Selman fell to the ground. He died in surgery a few hours later. Scarborough maintained that Selman had threatened him after a brief argument, and he shot in self-defense. A jury acquitted him of a murder charge, and he left town. Saloon owner George Look, however, opined that Selman was killed over the Mróz matter; as he saw it, Scarborough and Selman were co-conspirators hired by Hardin to murder the unwanted husband. Instead of paying Selman his share of the contract fee, however, Scarborough gunned down the constable. If it all seemed unnecessarily complicated, at least it put an end to the cycle of murders.[61]

An odd footnote to the Hardin-Selman killings was the failure of Hardin's cousin to successfully carry out two attempts on the life of a lawyer who had been involved in the defense of Selman in the Hardin slaying. Owen White speculated that the administration of Warren G. Harding might have been free of scandal had the bullets found their target.

The would-be assassin was Emanuel "Mannen" Clements III (1868–1908). He wanted to kill Albert Bacon Fall, prominent attorney and political figure in El Paso and southern New Mexico. As White had it, Clements confronted Fall one evening in the wine room of the Coney Island Saloon, "stuck a gun in his face, and didn't pull the trigger!" The reason was the appearance of Justice of the Peace Charles Pollock, who stepped into the room at an opportune moment for Fall.[62]

The situation was repeated in the same saloon some time later when the attorney was drinking with friends at the bar. Clements came in the door a little tipsy, pulled his gun, and was quickly disarmed and thrown out into the street.

Fall, who maintained a home in El Paso and a ranch in New Mexico, was to become the secretary of the interior in the Harding administration (1921–23) and won notoriety in the Teapot Dome scandal. He served prison time for bribery, although the man who allegedly bribed him was acquitted. Thus, had Clements's saloon shooting succeeded, it would have deprived Americans of some interesting political history.[63]

By 1899 El Paso had become "a rip-roaring town of 16,000 population," recalled J. Marvin Hunter, longtime publisher of *Frontier Times* magazine, of his brief sojourn there. "Saloons and gambling houses were numerous, and some of them kept open twenty-four hours a day, Sunday included. The red-light district was a hell-hole of crime, being located on Utah Street from Overland Street south, where there were dives, honkatonks, dance halls, saloons, and gambling houses. . . . Criminals from the East and from the west made El Paso their stopping place." [64]

The appeal of saloons was not limited to food and drink and the gambling opportunities they offered, according to Owen White. The individuals who operated them were singular characters. "The most interesting type of bartender," he wrote in 1942, "the type that stands out more prominently in my memory than any other, . . . is the type that was prevalent along the Texas-Mexican border from twenty-five to thirty-five years ago. In those days, and in that section of the country, if a man wasn't a strong character who could say to the porter, after a gun battle: 'Sweep him out, John, and mop up the floor,' and then, without changing his tone, turn to his customers with 'What'll it be, gentlemen,' he couldn't long hold down a job." White also recalled that patrons of El Paso bars would fight over nothing.

> [They would] kill each other with a nonchalance that was amazing to behold and, either in celebration of some happy event or that they might forget the sufferings occasioned by unrequited love, would indulge in the pastime of wrecking one saloon after another. But no matter what happened, no matter what the occasion of the bombardment or the proportions that it assumed, the bartender had to stick. All others could leave the place if they wanted to—and they generally did as soon as the first gun was fired—but not so the bartender. It was his duty to stay with the ship and, again speaking from personal experience gained from having participated in several wrecking parties, I can say that I never saw one fail to fulfill it.

Besides being gifted with tenacity, contended White, the bartender in the Southwest was "the living depository of the confidences of men" and knew all the secrets of the community. He could sense trouble brewing and knew instinctively those who would become victims and those who would be survivors.[65]

Although the Texas Legislature in 1881 had enacted a law against gambling, El Paso's officials had routinely looked the other way. They chose not to enforce the fines of ten to twenty-five dollars for a gambler and twenty-five to one hundred dollars for a person allowing use of his premises for public gaming. During the 1880s and 1890s, local politics often revolved around pro- or antigambling sentiments.

Citizens who did not enjoy the town's reputation as a "sin city" joined forces in the Law and Order League in 1889. They did not go so far as to insist upon closing down the gaming halls. Instead, they pressed the city council to take measures that, while not exactly making the operations legal, would realize some benefit for the city treasury. As a result, an ordinance was passed December 30, 1889, requiring a license fee to be paid in advance, with appropriate fines and imprisonment for failure to comply. The first saloon to be licensed was the Wigwam, just a half-block from the site of the old Dowell Saloon.[66]

No significant changes had occurred by 1893, when the *Herald* complained in a January 26 editorial that the city was collecting fees from three classes of gambling houses. "First class" saloons were notably the Wigwam, the Gem, and the Mint. Identified as second-class places were the Chief on lower El Paso Street, the Monte Carlo on South Oregon, and Charlie Townsend's on East Overland. Their clientele was described as the laboring classes, Mexicans, and Negroes. Three "Chinese joints" were counted in the third-class group, serving the local population of four hundred Chinese. The $800 per year per gambling house was denounced by the editor as indirectly taking hard-earned money from the pockets of local wage-earners.

A minor step toward reform came later that year when the council ruled that gambling would no longer be allowed on the ground floor of any building. Where two-story buildings were available, the proprietors simply moved the tables upstairs. Others relocated downriver in Ysleta, where a shaky town government was unable to run them off.[67]

Mayor R. F. Johnson tried to shut down the gambling halls in 1894 and again in 1895, but the lights were out for only a few weeks each time. The reformers, however, were gaining strength, not entirely based on moral grounds. Storekeepers and professional businessmen realized that money they could be taking in was being siphoned into the pockets of gamblers.

The 1895 action against gambling inspired an editorial in the *Herald* of September 19, speculating that the Chinese population would start sending money home to the old country instead of wagering it. "Chinese are great gamblers," wrote the editor, "but are so slick in that line that they seldom make any heavy losses." The Chinese population at that time was about five hundred.[68]

Loss of Sunday business in the saloons became an economic hazard for their proprietors, who petitioned the mayor to reconsider the shutdown. He did, and by June 18 the Sunday closing requirement was limited only to 9 A.M. to 4 P.M.[69]

The church-going ladies of the community boarded the reform bandwagon in 1896, when they counted twenty-five saloons for fifteen thousand people. They organized a local chapter of the Women's Christian Temperance Union (WCTU), but their protests failed to persuade local government leaders to alter the traditional drinking patterns of the town.[70]

One of the popular pubs on Overland Street was Si Ryan's Astor House where "General Stoneman" hung out. The "general" was a statue carved from the remains of a tree in the Petrified Forest. His promoters touted him to the public as a petrified man who had been found buried in Mexico. At one point they considered a promotion that would involve taking the figure into Mexico to authenticate its origin and make a few dollars exhibiting it, but import duty on its great weight would have eaten up the profits, so they abandoned the project. After that failed venture, Ryan obtained the statue and set it up at his place. His customers would accost their friends around town, suggesting that they had heard calumnies about them from a "General Stoneman" down at Ryan's. Soon a regular parade of men headed for the bar, ready to take on the offender. Once they discovered the trick, they joined in spreading the word. Ryan prospered enough from their business to relocate to the 100 block of San Antonio Street, just a few yards from the site of the original Dowell Saloon.[71]

The antigambling cause finally blossomed in 1902 when a new reform campaign was trumpeted by the *Times* on May 1. Mayor B. F. Hammett planned to start "an experiment in reform" that would have two phases: 1) saloons must close all day Sunday; and 2) all gaming must be removed from saloons, although it could be as near as the basement or the second floor of the same building. At the time, El Paso's gambling houses and their employees were still paying fees to the city (as did the brothels). Elsewhere in Texas, news of the mayor's experimental reform brought hoots of derision, since there was still a state law against gambling on the books that should have made any regulatory ordinance a moot point. The *Fort Worth Telegram* asked how El Paso's mayor could make rules about gambling when it was already illegal, to which the *El Paso Times* responded: "The difference between El Paso and Fort Worth . . . is that while gambling is going on in both places, with the knowledge of officials, the mayor of El Paso compels the gamblers to share with the taxpayers the cost of running the city, while in Fort Worth the people have to submit to the evil without any compensation." [72] The mayor proceeded with his regulatory measure.

The recurring reform drives demonstrated that the legal status of saloons bore little relationship to their popularity among the general male population. The two most vociferous foes of saloons at the end of the nineteenth century were the WCTU, who opposed them for encouraging a culture of drinking, and the state legislature in Austin, who took a more tolerant view of drinking but opposed the organized gambling activities that went on behind the bat-wing doors. Unfortunately, these two groups found it nearly impossible to work together in furthering their cause.

In 1903 the town boasted ninety-six saloons all "going full-blast twenty-four hours a day to service a population estimated at 33,000—more than triple the 1890 figure of 10,000. There were nineteen churches in town, not nearly as well attended as the saloons, where gambling was the main attraction." [73]

That spring, the election of Charles R. Morehead as mayor heralded a new move to clean up the saloons, reflecting a nationwide trend that would continue for nearly two decades. The following year the Citizens' League for Reform gathered 1,320 names on a petition asking Sheriff J. H. Boone to shut down gambling in El Paso County. A *Times* editorial of November 11 pointed out that the move would cost the city $30,000, but the City Council was at work on a new tax to compensate for the canceled fees. The town risked the loss of its reputation as "the Monte Carlo of the United States."

Sheriff Boone then announced his intention to enforce the state's "blue laws" that called for store closings on Sunday. By the end of November, gamblers had relocated across the border in Ciudad Juárez, and the "ladies" of the Utah Street red-light district were leaving town in all directions, mainly crossing the river or moving west to Arizona.[74]

A saloonkeeper, Max Miller, figured he would test the sheriff's action in court, sensing that a jury likely would not uphold Sunday closings. He was right. He opened his Legal Tender Saloon on a Sunday in December and was tried in justice of the peace court. After six hours of deliberation, the jury returned a "not guilty" verdict. This led seven more saloons to open the following Sunday. By Christmas Day the gamblers were back in town, and business went on as usual. No jury would convict them or the bar owners. The Wigwam and the Astor House, just to play it safe, moved their gambling operations upstairs, recalling an earlier local rule that allowed that kind of separation from the first-floor saloon.[75]

To pacify the Citizens' League, the annoyed Sheriff Boone arrested several gamblers. Some of them paid fines, but most demanded trials in which they were acquitted. At the League's insistence, a state law was drawn up that passed on April 14, 1905, preventing by injunction the use of any building for gambling purposes. A test case was filed in Waco in November and worked its way up to the Court of Criminal Appeals. Since the law provided that an injunction must be issued against a gambling house, the argument was made that it was invalid because operating a gambling house was already a crime on the books. The appeals court upheld the new law. As a direct result, open gambling finally vanished from El Paso.[76] The *Herald* noted on August 14, 1905, that the Wigwam was the first saloon to succumb to the new rules.

From that point on, recalled Owen White, "El Paso was a changed town." As he described the situation mournfully, "It was no longer my town. Of course it still had Utah Street and two or three saloons to every block, but with no gamblers around, and with the fiddles in Louis Vidal's dance hall, and Jim Burns' joint, and the Crystal Palace forever silent, it seemed so pure that I began to lose interest in it." [77]

He looked back with feelings of nostalgia on his experience as a lad of thirteen in 1892, when he worked for jeweler W. T. Hixson on San Antonio Street, in the heart of the downtown saloon district. A service window in the jewelry store had been cut through to the back room of the saloon next door. "The gals and gamblers who were in the market for diamonds," he related, "would assemble therein, and at a signal from the boss I would begin to supply them with drinks at the predetermined rate of 'one every three minutes until I tell you to stop.'" Sales resistance was broken down at a predictable pace. White said Hixson's competitors could not understand why his sales so far outstripped their own.[78] Just a little over ten years later, the picture had changed drastically and other thirteen-year-olds would never have the chance to replicate White's record.

As late as 1911 the neighborhood surrounding the historic El Paso Street saloons continued to attract shooting incidents. Henry C. Bernauer entered the Eastern Grill, an oriental cafe a door away from the Gem, and found his wife there with another man. He fired his gun five times at Frank Richard, was taken before a judge, pleaded not guilty to the charge of murder, and was acquitted by a jury in just four hours.[79]

Within a few weeks, Zach T. White, who had been a storekeeper on El Paso Street, was meeting with a group of entrepreneurs to plan the demise of the block that had housed the original saloon—Dowell's—to be replaced by a splendid new hotel. The Gem, the Vogue Department Store, and the Eastern Grill were in the section that was opened to extend Sonora Street (now West San Antonio) westward from El Paso Street. The part of the block that had belonged to Dowell now housed the Happy Hour Theater and several other businesses, all marked for demolition.

The Hotel Paso del Norte took its name from the former appellation of Ciudad Juárez, changed in 1888 to honor the onetime Mexican president, Benito Juárez. Joining White as incorporators of the El Paso Hotel Company were J. J. Mundy, Félix Martínez, J. G. McNary, C. M. Newman, W. L. Tooley, and G. R. Benton. Chief architects were Trost and Trost of El Paso. Fred Jones Building Company was the contractor.

The hotel was originally nine stories, with a tenth-floor ballroom added by Trost in 1922. On the West San Antonio Street side, a natural light shaft begins at the third floor above the two-story lobby. Stained glass windows also face on that street. The spectacular feature of the lobby is a stained glass dome, twenty-five feet in diameter, attributed to Louis Tiffany.

Zach White had visited San Francisco after its disastrous 1906 earthquake and insisted that his hotel be designed for safety against both earthquakes and fires. Interior partitions utilized fireproof gypsum from the nearby White Sands of New Mexico.[80]

From the time of its gala dedication on December 6, 1912, the Del Norte, as locals called it, was a center of social life for the community and its visitors. Orchestras played for dancing on the weekends. Magnificent banquets were served for wedding receptions, club celebrations, conventions, and the like. Celebrated guests from the worlds of entertainment and politics signed the register. And while the hotel was indeed built to withstand earthquakes and fires, the designers did not consider revolution. During various battles of the Mexican Revolution that took place in Juárez, El Pasoans would gather at the Del Norte to watch the action. Occasional stray bullets imbedded themselves in the hotel facade.

The revolution had started in 1910 and would continue through a decade that found El Paso businessmen and suppliers of services (such as medical care) involved in dealings with the various military leaders. Periodically, groups of refugees would cross the river, carrying their household goods, depositing their money in El Paso banks. Many of them took up permanent residence in El Paso, especially those who were relatively well off and could afford to purchase homes. Many others were less fortunate; a camp was set up at Fort Bliss to house some of them.

The Del Norte was affected by the refugee problems. "The hotels were packed and, according to the *Times,* 'unescorted women with children and babies wandered from hotel to hotel in vain attempts to secure accommodations.' El Paso assumed the appearance of an armed camp."[81]

The Del Norte served as headquarters for Gen. Álvaro Obregón when he arrived in late 1915 to take command in Ciudad Juárez after

Venustiano Carranza's troops took over from Francisco "Pancho" Villa, who had held the city for a brief time. Obregón entered the city on December 31. He returned to the hotel for a conference held in response to the Villista invasion of Columbus, New Mexico, in March, 1916, and Gen. John J. Pershing's expedition into Mexico seeking Villa. Obregón was then the secretary of war for President Carranza. An American mining official, A. J. McQuatters, who knew both Obregón and Gen. Hugh Scott, U.S. Army chief of staff, rented a large room at the hotel and persuaded the two men to meet there on May 2. Their goal was a resolution of the problem affecting both their nations: the crossing of borders with armed troops. After a marathon session, they reached an agreement that fell short of what either side had hoped for. The United States agreed to gradual withdrawal of its troops—not completed until the following February—and Mexico promised to keep invaders south of the border. Had the agreement not been reached at this meeting, the U.S.-Mexican confrontation could have reached disastrous proportions.[82]

The sending of Fort Bliss troops into Mexico was not the only concern of the U.S. Army during this period. The coming of the Great War in Europe in 1914 led to a nationwide mobilization effort, with El Paso's post among those scheduled for expansion. The city's reputation for sinful activities, however, was of concern to Secretary of War Newton D. Baker. He proclaimed on June 2, 1917: "El Paso must clean up. I am in receipt of daily reports showing social conditions to which our soldiers are subjected which can no longer be tolerated." He threatened not only to withhold future assignment of troops but perhaps even to take away all those already at Fort Bliss if illegal sales of alcohol to soldiers and open prostitution were not ended.[83]

An estimated seven hundred prostitutes were doing business in the city, plus numerous "liquor clubs" and illegal bars. The police swung into action and drove about half the prostitutes out of town—most of them only moving across the river to Ciudad Juárez. Clergymen preached sermons in praise of the clean-up. Police raids on suspect liquor clubs revealed that six deputy sheriffs were running illegal bars. Other officials were found to have close ties with bootleggers and prostitutes. Police reports on arrests routinely disappeared. The half-hearted reform effort was not enough to please the military commander, who placed the vice district around Utah Street in South El Paso off limits to soldiers.[84]

In late 1917, State Senator Claude B. Hudspeth advised El Pasoans that if only they would clean up the vices, a cantonment of thirty thousand men would be sent to Fort Bliss by the federal government. The city council responded quickly by making it illegal to sell liquor to soldiers. The county shut down roadhouses that catered to the military. The army provided undercover soldiers to spot bootleggers. And the ministers cooperated in demanding a local-option election on the issue of alcohol.[85]

After a bitter three-week campaign, the county prohibition election was held on January 30, 1918. Influencing the "dry" cause was the national pressure for a prohibition amendment to the Constitution. Residents of the city voted down the proposal by 2,421 to 2,207; in the county the totals were 2,668 against prohibition and 2,497 for. "In the end," concludes historian Shawn Lay, "the Pass's social heritage had asserted itself." [86]

The secretary of war found the latest cleanup efforts and the election did not meet his expectations of a community destined for more troops. Meanwhile, the Texas Legislature was at work again on the question of prohibition.

Texans had been concerned about liquor—either too much or too little—for years. The 1876 Constitution provided that counties and their subdivisions could vote local option on liquor sales. Prohibition amendments to the constitution were rejected in state elections in 1887 and 1911. A special legislative session was called in February, 1918, to consider the question anew. The resulting actions would render El Paso effectively dry. Not only did the legislature ratify the Eighteenth Amendment to the U.S. Constitution (to be finally adopted nationwide in December, 1919), but a new law prohibited the sale of liquor within ten miles of any military base in Texas. The proximity to Fort Bliss spelled doom for El Paso's saloons, with closing day set for April 15.[87]

Zach White reportedly bought out the stock of Hotel Paso del Norte for his private use. Liquor dealers and saloonkeepers either sold what they had or moved across the river to Juárez. On the eve of the April deadline, more than two hundred saloons were emptying their shelves.

The Gem, successor to the original of that name, drew the largest crowd, so large that in the last few hours the barkeeps simply placed the liquors, beers, and mixes on the bar and let customers serve themselves. The lights went out at 10:30 P.M. and barricades were placed at the doors.[88]

The Great War was over after the armistice on November 11, ending the likelihood of additional troops for Fort Bliss. At the same time, the city was fighting a new war against Spanish influenza, with five thousand cases and four hundred deaths reported in October. Soldiers were not allowed to patronize local restaurants or other possible sources of infection unless certificates from the board of health proclaimed them to be safe.[89]

Ciudad Juárez over the years has served as a barometer for the liquor laws in the United States. As early as 1900, some 23 percent of Americans lived in "dry" areas. Liquor vendors soon learned that they could relocate from dry regions of the United States to the Mexican border towns that were easily accessible to patrons from the north. Whenever El Paso's reformers rolled up their sleeves, the prostitutes and bartenders simply moved across the river to Ciudad Juárez. The economies of the two cities became entwined as a result. "Regardless of their origin," writes historian Oscar J. Martínez, "evidence indicates that Americans made substantial investments in Juárez's race-track, restaurant, gambling, and bar operations." Even before the enactment of the Eighteenth Amendment, some twenty-nine states, Texas among them, had prohibition legislation, which impacted the drift southward of saloonkeepers and their clientele. When Texas went dry in 1918, Martínez relates, El Paso's 250 drinking clubs and open saloons, 50 liquor stores, and related establishments were put out of business.[90]

One reaction to the ban was the springing up of illicit spots along the border, such as the Hole in the Wall, a large frame structure in the Cordova Island area, a neck of Mexican territory that had been left north of the Rio Grande in El Paso by a change in the river's flow. Thirsty customers would proceed south on Eucalyptus Street to the International Boundary, slip through the fence that marked it, and cross a ramp over a dry channel about three feet deep. Hoodlums hung out there; the El Paso police were frequently called by Americans who had been robbed as they approached the boundary. The popular bar was torn down on January 1, 1931. Another Hole in the Wall operated downriver at the farming town of Fabens, reached by crossing a drainage ditch. It featured an orchestra and a large dance floor.[91]

Meanwhile, in Ciudad Juárez a cluster of new saloons prospered under the auspices of former El Paso proprietors, some bearing the same names as their earlier counterparts in El Paso, such as the Lobby and the Mint. Tourism became a vital element of the economy. For El Pasoans, the habit of having a drink with a fine dinner was simply transplanted south. For a few years, slot machines and other gambling diversions were popular. Prohibition worked negligible hardship on those tipplers who chose to take a trolley or drive across the bridge.

El Paso's Roman Catholic bishop, A. J. Schuler, celebrated the thirty-second anniversary of his ordination as a priest on June 27, 1933, with a statement in favor of repeal and gambling, reflecting the attitudes of a good many townspeople. "The bishop took the stand," reported the *El Paso Times*, "that no word against drink, betting or boxing appears in the Holy Bible."[92]

The sixteen-year-old constitutional ban on liquor was ended with an election on August 24, 1935, and a new liquor control law for Texas was enacted the following November. Four sales options were now available to local jurisdictions: 1) no alcohol; 2) only 4.0 percent or less alcohol content; 3) wine and beer with no more than 14 percent alcohol content; or 4) all alcohol sold to be limited to 14 percent or less. For those localities that took the "all alcohol" route, liquor could be sold only in full bottles with no consumption allowed on the premises.[93]

In El Paso, where bottled liquor was legalized, there was still the inconvenience of being unable to drink it in a club or with dinner. Thus Juárez bars and restaurants continued to prosper. By the 1950s several night clubs in Juárez offered top American entertainers such as Wayne Newton and gourmet dining, the most glamorous of them La Fiesta. They drew the tourist trade in large numbers, including celebrities seeking quickie Mexican divorces.

During the prohibition years, El Paso's notorious red-light district had continued its quiet operations from Ninth and Mesa Streets southward. The women were required to have weekly health examinations and regularly greased the palms of various public officials and lawmen.

Gambling could be found in that area and other locations around town, although officially it did not exist. The arrest of a young prostitute on December 23, 1937, and her subsequent death would bring about a new reform at the direction of Mayor M. A. Harlan. The young woman became ill in jail, was hospitalized, and quickly died of hepatitis. A news report of the incident stirred the ambitions of some political candidates, notably a judge who wanted to become district attorney and the mayor who sought re-election. Harlan ordered a vice raid of South Mesa Street brothels on December 29. The prostitutes and others arrested became the subjects of legal arguments among several judges and lawyers, and the court proceedings were sensationalized in the press. The police chief was forced to resign, a court of inquiry into the police department was initiated, and by February the town had had its fill of the squabbling; Mayor Harlan suffered a humiliating defeat in his election bid.[94]

In 1939, with an epidemic of venereal disease reported after the red-light district's demise, Mayor J. E. Anderson and Police Chief L. T. Robey considered restoring it with its health check safeguards. The ministers got wind of the idea, however, and rallied enough protests to quash it. A campaign against venereal diseases was all officials could come up with at the time. The advent of World War II and increased military activity at Fort Bliss renewed the issue. City councilmen in 1940 restored the zone of tolerance at Utah and Ninth. Although from time to time the military forbade soldiers to cross the river, they had the option of visiting the flourishing brothels in Juárez.[95]

Besides being adjacent to Mexico, where liquor had remained available during the long dry spell, El Paso was immediately next door to New Mexico, which offered mixed drinks. The popular Tom Burchell's bar was on a road that weaves in and out of El Paso along the state boundary line, a popular hangout of students at the Texas College of Mines and Metallurgy (now the University of Texas at El Paso). The bright neon lights of three other clubs were reflected in the Rio Grande just north of the Mexican border on McNutt Road in New Mexico.

Texans soon figured out a way around the liquor-by-the-drink ban. They established private clubs where members paid a liquor-pool fee that enabled the bar to be stocked. The showing of a membership card entitled a customer to buy mixed drinks. Veterans' organizations and others with clubhouses were able to take advantage of this plan. Hotels with clubs would issue membership cards to patrons as they registered.

Beer-and-wine bars sprang up, and package stores offered the hard stuff. By the early 1950s El Paso had seventy-one liquor stores within the city limits, twenty-five of them on one street alone. There were 185 bars, more than a dozen liquor distributors, and sixteen beer distributors, plus the Harry Mitchell brewery. Numerous eating establishments served beer and wine with meals, in compliance with the state law. Among them was the Hotel Paso del Norte, sustaining the historic tradition of having some form of spirits available at that spot on El Paso Street since the earliest days of the town.[96] Texas enacted yet another amendment to the state constitution in 1970 and, with subsequent legislation, legalized liquor by the drink after more than fifty years. Local option elections could still keep an area dry. El Paso County was one of 174 where distilled spirits were legal in 1985.[97]

Zach White's heirs kept the Del Norte property until 1971 when they sold it to TGK Investment Corporation, which in turn sold it in 1975 to the Paso del Norte Corporation; a year later it went briefly to Ed Vásquez, then was reclaimed by the previous owner. After the lobby was remodeled in 1978, the dining room was dubbed "The Union Depot," with the slogan "Your railway ticket to fine food." Recordings of train sounds were played in the background, and service was patterned after that of railway dining cars. Menu selections were named with an eye to travel: "Santa Fe Omelet," "Sunset Limited" (chopped sirloin with cheese and green chili), "Switch Engine" (a fruit plate), and "Rio Grande Burgers." On the opposite side of the lobby, at approximately the same site as the original, was instituted a reincarnation: the Ben Dowell Saloon, est. 1978, with a logo featuring the only known photograph of El Paso's first mayor and white-bearded "First Citizen," Benjamin Shacklett Dowell. Ben's great-granddaughter, Aurelia "Chella" Phillips, paid it a visit one afternoon and found, to her amazement, that the waitresses were garbed as can-can girls, a form of entertainment unknown to the early-day patrons of the saloon.

The National Register of Historic Places recognized the hotel in

1979 with an official plaque and listing, but this bolstering of its fame was not enough to keep it solvent. The hotel closed, a victim of the malaise affecting major city downtowns all over the country. Then in 1982 Franklin Land and Resources, Inc., a venture of El Paso Electric Company, began its major efforts to revive the downtown area with purchases of the Del Norte and another defunct hotel, the Cortez, facing on San Jacinto Plaza. To the Del Norte's original ten-story building with 195 rooms was added a seventeen-story tower at the north end of the block, bringing the total to 383 rooms. The new main entrance was from San Francisco Street, also leading to a multilevel parking garage for 250 vehicles. During the excavations at this site and the Civic Center in the next block to the west, archaeologists found numerous bottles that had contained beers and liquors from the period of the Dowell and Manning saloons. The hotel reopened with a gala celebration in May, 1986, as the Westin Paso del Norte. It was subsequently renamed the Camino Real Hotel when a group of Mexican investors purchased it; then in 2001, under a franchise agreement with the Hilton Corporation, it became for several months the Hilton Camino Real of El Paso.

The rejuvenated hotel today includes one significant improvement in consideration of the fact that it sits on historic ground: beneath the spectacular Tiffany dome that was the centerpiece of the original hotel lobby, the new corporate owners placed a circular bar. They christened it the Dome Bar and gave it an appropriate advertising slogan to reflect its historic roots: "A journey back in time." The past is on display elsewhere in the hotel as well. Adjacent to the lobby are a posh dining room and a less ornate coffee shop leading to a courtyard where historic plaques are displayed tracing memorable events related to the site.[98]

The hotel's present clientele in their business suits and vacation leisure clothes know nothing of the long heritage of the ground beneath their feet. But they are not so very far removed from the cowboys and rough types who once passed the time there leaning up against another bar. Through national prohibition, local option, two world wars, and seismic changes in the city's ethnic composition, El Paso has never lost its fondness for a good drink or three and a congenial place to enjoy those libations. The Dome Bar of the Camino Real Hotel today sits almost on top of the site where old Ben Dowell once presided over the best saloon in El Paso.

NOTES

1. W. W. Mills, *Forty Years at El Paso, 1848–1898,* ed. Rex W. Strickland (1901; reprint, El Paso: Carl Hertzog, 1962), 18.

2. Juan María Ponce de León in 1827 purchased a tract of land across the river from El Paso del Norte (now Ciudad Juárez) on which he built a house and a canal for the water supply from the Rio Grande. He planted corn and wheat fields and an extensive orchard. Called Ponce's Rancho, it became the site of the downtown business district of El Paso, Texas. J. J. Bowden, *The Ponce de León Land Grant* (El Paso: Texas Western Press, 1969), 3, 4.

3. Robert K. DeArment, *Knights of the Green Cloth: The Saga of the Frontier Gamblers* (Norman: University of Oklahoma Press, 1982), 135–36.

4. Nancy Hamilton, *Ben Dowell: El Paso's First Mayor* (El Paso: Texas Western Press, 1976), 9–11.

5. El Paso County Deed Records, book 3, 171, 324. After Dowell's death in 1880, his heirs sold the land over several years for a total of $24,050. By 1912, when Hotel Paso del Norte was built there, the land was said to be worth $1,500 to $2,500 per front foot. Deed Records, book 3, 297, 311, 582; book 9, 407; book 19, 366; book 23, 263. Dowell included Lot 87 Block 16 with other property in his homestead declaration of 1872.

6. Hamilton, *Ben Dowell,* 19–21.

7. Mills, *Forty Years at El Paso,* 32–33.

8. Ibid., 37; Anson Mills, *My Story* (Washington, D.C.: Byron S. Adams, 1818), 60.

9. Mills, *My Story,* 29–32.

10. Mills, *Forty Years at El Paso,* 134; El Paso County Deed Records, book B, 370.

11. Hamilton, *Ben Dowell,* 6, 35–37.

12. Ibid., 23, 26, 27.

13. Thomas J. Noel, *The City and the Saloon: Denver 1858–1916* (Lincoln: University of Nebraska Press, 1982), 33.

14. Hamilton, *Ben Dowell,* 47, 48.

15. Letter, B. S. Dowell to José María Uranga, Jan. 21, 1875, University of Texas at El Paso Microfilm Archives, MF 495, r. 70, dates 1872–1876. Thanks to W. H. Timmons for this information.

16. An appropriation of $44.9 million was authorized in Public Law 88-300, signed April 29, 1964, to facilitate compliance with the convention. This enabled the federal government to acquire 186 commercial and industrial buildings, 14 public buildings, and other public facilities including school land and sewage treatment facilities. Some 596 single- and multiple-family dwellings and 65 tenements were acquired. Franklin G. Smith, "The Chamizal Since 1963," in

Robert M. Utley, *Changing Course: The International Boundary, United States and Mexico, 1848–1963* (Tucson: Southwest Parks and Monuments Assn., 1996), 112–17.

17. Hamilton, *Ben Dowell*, 57–58.

18. El Paso County Deed Records, book 5, 31, 102; Eugene Cunningham, *Triggernometry, A Gallery of Gunfighters* (Caldwell, Idaho: Caxton Printers, 1975), 175.

19. Leon C. Metz, *Dallas Stoudenmire: El Paso Marshal* (Norman: University of Oklahoma Press, 1979), 95–97.

20. Donald V. Brady, *The Theatre in Early El Paso, 1881–1905* (El Paso: Texas Western College Press, 1966), 7–9.

21. DeArment, *Knights of the Green Cloth*, 113, 136.

22. *El Paso Herald*, various dates in April, 1881.

23. Metz, *Dallas Stoudenmire*, 59.

24. Ibid., 40–46; James B. Gillett, *Six Years with the Texas Rangers, 1875 to 1881*, ed. M. M. Quaife (1921; reprint, Lincoln: University of Nebraska Press, 1976), 234–37; George Wythe Baylor, *Into the Far, Wild Country* (El Paso: Texas Western Press, 1996), 323; J. Morgan Broaddus, *The Legal Heritage of El Paso* (El Paso: Texas Western Press, 1963), 132–33.

25. Baylor, *Into the Far, Wild Country*, 236.

26. Ibid.; C. L. Sonnichsen, *Pass of the North*, vol. 1 (El Paso: Texas Western Press, 1968), 238–39.

27. Baylor, *Into the Far, Wild Country*, 323–26; Metz, *Dallas Stoudenmire*, 90, 99; *El Paso Herald*, Sept. 20, 1882, quoted in Metz.

28. Gillett, *Six Years with the Texas Rangers*, 237; Sonnichsen, *Pass of the North*, 244–45.

29. *El Paso Herald*, Dec. 7, 1881.

30. Owen White, *The Autobiography of a Durable Sinner* (New York: Putnam's, 1942), 42.

31. *El Paso Herald*, Jan. 11, 1882.

32. *El Paso Herald*, Jan. 25, 1882.

33. *El Paso Herald*, Aug. 2, 1882.

34. *El Paso Herald*, July 5, 1928.

35. *Lone Star*, June 9, 1882.

36. G. Gordon Frost, *The Gentlemen's Club* (El Paso: Mangan Books, 1983), 18.

37. Ibid., 22, 23, 35.

38. Ibid., 77.

39. Ibid., 21–22.

40. Ibid., 26–41; Sonnichsen, *Pass of the North*, 287–90.

41. Brady, *The Theatre in Early El Paso*, 17.

42. J. D. Ponder, "Gambling in El Paso," *Password* 12, no. 1 (spring, 1967): 21–26.

43. Ibid., 23.

44. Ibid. The Terrazas economic empire has been described as "unequaled in prerevolutionary Mexico or nineteenth-century Latin America." Headed by

General Luis Terrazas, the family owned over 15 million acres in the state of Chihuahua on which they grazed 400,000 cattle, 100,000 sheep, and 25,000 horses. The extended family, including children and in-laws, owned another 15 million acres and controlled banks, commerce, transport, industry, and livestock in the region. Luis Terrazas was governor of the state for an extended period (1860–73, 1879–84, 1903–1907). In 1912 he supported the failed revolt of Pascual Orozco, and the family was forced into exile. He spent seven years in El Paso, a brief period in Los Angeles, and returned to Chihuahua where he died in 1923. Mark Wasserman, *Capitalists, Caciques, and Revolution: The Native Elite and Foreign Enterprise in Chihuahua, Mexico, 1854–1911* (Chapel Hill and London: University of North Carolina Press, 1984), 27, 31, 43, 48, 165.

45. Sonnichsen, *Pass of the North*, 281–82.

46. Emilia Gay Griffith Means, "'Pen Pictures' of El Paso: The Letters of Rudolph Eickemeyer, 1893," *Password* 33, no. 3 (fall, 1988): 131; Rudolph Eickemeyer, *Letters from the Southwest* (New York: 1894), 11, quoted in Helen Whitner Somerville, "The World Was Their Oyster—Fine Eating in Early El Paso," *Password* 2, no. 2 (May, 1957): 48.

47. *El Paso Times*, Jan. 27, 1991, quoted in Somerville, "The World Was Their Oyster," 48.

48. Somerville, "The World Was Their Oyster," 48, 49.

49. Ibid., 46, 47.

50. Ibid., 47.

51. *El Paso Times*, Nov. 3, 1884; Leon C. Metz, *El Paso Chronicles* (El Paso: Mangan Books, 1993), 101.

52. Leon C. Metz, *John Wesley Hardin, Dark Angel of Texas* (El Paso: Mangan Books, 1996), 287–93.

53. Louis H. Hubbard, "A Boy's Impression of El Paso in the 1890's," *Password* 11, no. 3 (fall, 1966): 94–99; Metz, *El Paso Chronicles*, 129, 131.

54. Metz, *John Wesley Hardin*, 284, 206, 208, 215–16, 323n 17; Sonnichsen, *Pass of the North*, 324–25.

55. Richard C. Marohn, *The Last Gunfighter: John Wesley Hardin* (College Station, Tex.: Creative Publishing Co., 1995), 214–15, 217, 267; T. Lindsay Baker, *The Polish Texans* (San Antonio: University of Texas Institute of Texan Cultures, 1982), 83. Baker gives the name as Mróz; newspaper and other sources spell it variously as Marose, M'Rose, and McRose.

56. Sonnichsen, *Pass of the North*, 330; Metz, *John Wesley Hardin*, 241.

57. Metz, *John Wesley Hardin*, 242, 256–57, 259.

58. Ibid., 264–65.

59. Ibid., 269–72.

60. Leon C. Metz, *John Selman, Gunfighter* (Norman: University of Oklahoma Press, 1980), 187–88; Sonnichsen, *Pass of the North*, 333.

61. Sonnichsen, *Pass of the North*, 335–36; Metz, *John Wesley Hardin*, 278–79.

62. White, *Autobiography*, 102.

63. Owen White, *Lead and Likker* (New York: Minton, Balch and Co., 1932), 20–22. Clements, often confused with his father because of their similar names,

met his own end in a shooting in the Coney Island Saloon, December 29, 1908. Metz, *John Wesley Hardin,* 279, 313. Hardin biographer Richard C. Marohn doubts that Fall's role in the legal defense of Selman was as great as White contended, although news reports indicated he was part of the legal team. Marohn, 273–74. Efforts by Fall's family to clear his name continued for some years after Fall's death in 1944. Herman B. Weisner, *The Politics of Justice: A. B. Fall and the Teapot Dome Scandal, A New Perspective* (Albuquerque: Creative Designs, 1988).

64. *Frontier Times* 18, no. 8 (May, 1941): 377–81.

65. Owen White, *Them Was the Days: From El Paso to Prohibition* (New York: Minton, Balch and Co., 1925), 194–96.

66. J. F. Hulse, *Texas Lawyer: The Life of W. H. Burges* (El Paso: Mangan Books, 1982), 39, 40.

67. Sonnichsen, *Pass of the North,* 353; Frost, *The Gentleman's Club,* 93, 94.

68. Nancy Farrar, *The Chinese in El Paso* (El Paso: Texas Western Press, 1972), 9, 35.

69. John J. Middagh, *Frontier Newspaper: The El Paso Times* (El Paso: Texas Western Press, 1958), 98–101.

70. Cleofas Calleros, *El Paso Then and Now,* vol. 7 (El Paso: American Printing Co., 1954), 31. During the early 1920s, when Prohibition had answered the WCTU's demands, a national field agent of the organization visited El Paso, with a side trip to Ciudad Juárez. "The El Paso newspapers cryptically quoted the W.C.T.U. lady as saying that she had never enjoyed an experience so much as her trip to Juarez, but left it to the reader to determine what she meant by that," reported Duncan Aikman in *The Home Town Mind* (New York: Minton, Balch and Co., 1926), 259.

71. Samuel J. Freudenthal, *El Paso Merchant and Civic Leader from the 1880's through the Mexican Revolution* (El Paso: Texas Western Press, 1965), 20–22.

72. *El Paso Times,* May 4, 1902.

73. Bryan W. Brown, "Boyhood in Early El Paso," *Password* 15, no. 2 (summer, 1970): 54–55.

74. Middagh, *Frontier Newspaper,* 107–108.

75. Ibid., 111–12.

76. Ibid., 113–14.

77. White, *Autobiography,* 90.

78. Ibid., 52–53.

79. *El Paso Herald,* Mar. 12 and 22, 1911.

80. Lloyd C. Engelbrecht and June-Marie F. Engelbrecht, *Henry Trost, Architect of the Southwest* (El Paso: El Paso Public Library Assn., 1981), 63; Evan Haywood Antone, ed., *Portals at the Pass: El Paso Area Architecture to 1930* (El Paso: El Paso Chapter, American Institute of Architects, 1984), 39–41.

81. Mardee Belding deWetter, "Revolutionary El Paso, 1910–1917," pt. 1, *Password* 3, no. 2 (Apr., 1958): 108–109.

82. DeWetter, "Revolutionary," pt. 3, *Password* 3, no. 4 (Oct., 1958): 152; Herbert Molloy Mason, Jr., *The Great Pursuit: Pershing's Expedition to Destroy Pancho Villa* (New York: Smithmark, 1995), 154–57.

83. Shawn Lay, *War, Revolution and the Ku Klux Klan* (El Paso: Texas Western Press, 1985), 38.

84. Ibid., 38, 39.

85. Ibid., 39, 40.

86. Ibid., 41–43.

87. Ibid., 42, 45.

88. W. H. Timmons, *El Paso: A Borderlands History* (El Paso: Texas Western Press, 1990), 225–26.

89. Bradford Luckingham, *Epidemic in the Southwest, 1918–1919* (El Paso: Texas Western Press, 1984), 13, 14.

90. Oscar J. Martínez, *Border Boom Town: Ciudad Juárez Since 1848* (Austin: University of Texas Press, 1978), 31, 52.

91. *El Paso Herald-Post,* May 15, 1985.

92. *El Paso Times,* June 28, 1933.

93. Jeanne Bozzell McCarty, *The Struggle for Sobriety: Protestants and Prohibition in Texas, 1919–1935* (El Paso: Texas Western Press, 1980), 49.

94. Frost, *The Gentlemen's Club,* 220–25.

95. Ibid., 228–35.

96. Calleros, *El Paso Then and Now,* 31.

97. Mike Kingston, ed., *1986–87 Texas Almanac and State Industrial Guide* (Dallas: Dallas Morning News, 1985), 691.

98. Sandra Lyon Collins, ed., *Under the Dome—Footsteps Through History* (El Paso: SL&G Publication, 1989), 48 ff.

Chapter Four

The "Free-Hearted Fellows"
of the Iron Front (Austin)

In July, 1909, Austin old-timers had good reason to feel a little nostalgic about a group of decayed, old buildings on the northeast corner of Sixth (formerly Pecan) Street and Congress Avenue; they were all slated to be demolished very soon in the name of progress.[1] The unsightly structures were to be replaced by a brand-new skyscraper, the nine-story American National Bank. One of the landmarks scheduled for demolition was the venerable Iron Front Saloon, a familiar sight for nearly forty years, but it was neither the first building nor even the first saloon at that location. In fact, between the Iron Front and its predecessors, a saloon had occupied that site for sixty years under one name or another. The man behind the bank building was George W. Littlefield, who represented an unlikely link between the saloon and the skyscraper, between Austin's frontier past and its glass-and-steel future.

Littlefield had come to banking late in a very exciting life; before that he was one of the biggest cattle kings in Texas, and before that he had tried a little bit of everything. As one of a breed of men who once patronized the Iron Front on a regular basis, Littlefield had probably spent his share of hours drinking, shooting pool, and playing cards there, especially if it were true what one cowboy said of him: "He could look in your eye and tell you what you was up to." That kind of fellow just naturally had to be successful at the poker table!

How he came to be a regular at the Iron Front and much later a power broker in the city's board rooms is a tale worth telling. Born in Panola County, Mississippi, in 1842, Littlefield had come to Texas as a boy with his family in 1850, settling near Belmont. When the Civil War came, the nineteen-year-old lad enlisted in the famed band known as Terry's Texas Rangers, seeing action in the battles of Shiloh, Perryville, and Chickamauga. At Chickamauga, an exploding cannon shot put an end to his soldiering days and left him with a game leg the rest of his life. Returning home to Gonzales County he began developing plantations and farms and launched a career in the cattle industry with little more than grit and a few head of wild longhorns. Within a few years he established the LIT Ranch on the Canadian River in the Panhandle, which he eventually sold in 1881 for $248,000, using the profits to add to his growing land and cattle holdings. In 1883 he moved to Austin and accepted a position on the board of the State National Bank. Seven years later he organized the American National Bank and served as its president until 1918. The skyscraper that he built in 1909 was soon dubbed the "Littlefield Building" by locals, and the old buildings it replaced passed into history, to be forgotten in the public consciousness.

George Littlefield was only seven years old when Jobe's Saloon (predecessor of the Iron Front) opened on the Congress Avenue site. By the time it became the Iron Front, the boy had become a young man, graduating from peeking in through the front doors to ordering at the big bar. In a sense, the saloon and the man became local institutions together. He could trace the twists and turns of his own life in every scar and ding on the polished oak bar top. He had watched the face that looked back at him in the mirror behind the bar age over the years. But sentimentality has no place in business, so when the opportunity came along to cash out the old place, Littlefield gave it scarcely a second thought before ordering the demolition of the granddaddy of all Austin saloons.[2]

The Iron Front and another of the old cowboy watering holes, the Crystal Saloon, were the last of their kind still standing in the city, defying the wrecking ball. In their day, the Iron Front and the Crystal Saloon had shared the same block as friendly rivals. They were a large part

For years this intersection was a contender for most notorious corner in Texas: Congress Avenue and Pecan Street (now 6th Street), where the Crystal Saloon and two doors to the right, at 605 Congress, the Iron Front Saloon stood. The Iron Front name can be clearly seen at the second-floor level, to the right of the large Reno and Reasonover building sign. Original photo attributed to Jordan-Ellison Photographers, Austin. Courtesy *Austin History Center, Austin Public Library, HB C00044*

of the reason why Congress Avenue had a wild and woolly reputation in those days. Both had livened the heart of the capital in scandalous fashion, attracting a diverse clientele that included the sporting crowd, callow students, and probably more than a few off-duty legislators. Now, the Crystal was scheduled to come down at the same time as the Iron Front. Although there may have been feelings of loss and regret by some Austinites over their fate, nothing indicates that there were any protests or organized efforts to halt the work of destruction. The inexorable march of progress was all that mattered.

On January 1, 1910, workmen began the job of tearing them down, which finally prompted some belated recognition of their historic importance, in the form of representatives of the Fourth Estate who showed up to cover the occasion. The editors of the Austin's leading

FRONT ELEVATION
IRON FRONT SALOON
605 CONGRESS AVE.
AUSTIN, TEXAS
ca. 1849 - 1910

DRAWINGS BY
ROBERT CULLEN SMITH, A.I.A.

newspaper, the *Statesman*, which in the past had been practically a house organ for the Iron Front, sent a reporter who may himself have been a habitué of the place. The fellow described the setting in elegiac terms as among "the most famous old buildings in the south," although this was certainly more journalistic hyperbole than fact. He went on to say that after opening their doors "many years before" the Civil War, the Crystal Saloon and the Iron Front Saloon had been both "playground and battlefield [of men] in whose breasts throbbed the spirit of the frontier." No fewer than thirty men, he claimed, were killed "in and around that block" over the years, but he did not give their names.[3] Probably he did not know them; it is doubtful if anyone did.

This is a remarkably high number of homicides in such a small area, even for a wild, unincorporated cow town like Fort Worth or Dodge City, let alone for the capital city of a state, leading to the suspicion that the reporter may have been the victim of a boozy interviewee, or perhaps he let his own imagination run away with him, because that many killings were never reported in the local newspapers. Although there was gunplay in the vicinity on numerous occasions, some of which probably started with harsh words exchanged across the tables or at the bar of the Iron Front or the Crystal Saloon, there is no verifiable account of a killing ever taking place inside either place. Just how wide an area "around the block" covered was something only the *Statesman*'s reporter knew, and he did not bother to explain. As the more famous of the two saloons, the Iron Front would have been more likely to have its name attached to any dimly remembered killings over the years. Although un-credited with any recorded fatalities in its long history, it did not lack for high jinks among both the high-born and low who patronized the place. The place was a haven for men who welcomed challenges and took their risks in the smoke-filled rooms, surrounded by other men in stovepipe chaps and clanking spurs alongside fancy-dressed gamblers ready to bet a dollar or a thousand dollars on the turn of the card. Perhaps every man felt equal with a heavy six-shooter dangling from his waist, or more likely hidden out of sight under a coat. The professional gambler, or self-styled "sport," probably carried such a "hideaway gun" in a leather-lined pocket plus a knife hidden in his sleeve or boot. The rich and influential, as well as men of more modest means, all enjoyed the con-genial atmosphere of the Iron Front Saloon and its companion places up and down Congress Avenue.

Most of those men were armed and for good reason. When Phillip Jobe opened the first saloon on the site a dozen years before the Civil War, Austin was on the edge of the Texas frontier. The western half of the state was still considered "Indian Territory," and Austin was in the gray area between civilization and the lands where the Indian still reigned supreme. William Martin "Buck" Walton, a local lawyer and longtime resident, recalled years later that in the early days Austin was, "a small village—a few thousand inhabitants—a frontier town." He added that the "whole country to the west of Austin, divided by a line north and south, was a frontier. The Indians made frequent incursions and often killed men, women and children, and drove the stock away."[4]

The origins of the Iron Front Saloon go back to 1849 when Phillip W. Jobe, a twenty-nine-year-old from Kentucky, bought an empty lot from the state of Texas. Jobe had served as a private in the Mexican War un-der Capt. Samuel Highsmith in the First Texas Mounted Volunteers, a unit of Jack Hays's Texas Cavalry. A year after that war ended, the would-be entrepreneur was in Austin aiming to build himself a saloon.[5] He paid $150 for the land, which represented a sizable investment in those days, and proceeded to construct a two-story frame building with a gallery running the full width of the front side. On the ground floor Jobe put in a saloon, and the second story was reserved for gambling, which was the conventional layout for such places. One unusual feature of the saloon was its basement. Excavating a below-ground space on the Texas plains where there was always plenty of room to build out and up was an added expense that most saloon owners saw no reason to incur. Besides, most saloons moved into already existing buildings when they opened for business.

The establishment's second-floor gambling facilities soon became famous statewide, particularly among members of the footloose sporting fraternity that traveled the Southwest.[6] It became part of the lore of the place that the most desperate men of the times gathered there to spend their money, and thousands of dollars could pass over the green cloth every night. Among men who earned their living working with cattle, poker and faro were the preferred games. Sizable pots changed hands, made up of dollars that had been earned branding mavericks on 'the range.[7] Poker was perhaps the favorite game of the period but other games such as keno and monte were also popular. Cards were not the only games of chance for those with talent, steely nerves, and a few dollars in their pocket. Men talented with a cue stick could win or lose sizable sums playing pool or billiards, while others could take their chances shooting "craps" at the dice tables. There were plenty of ways to increase a bankroll—or lose one.

Jobe's shrewd—or lucky—$150 investment grew over the decades into a nice little fortune. In the 1870 Travis County census he was identified as a fifty-year-old, single white male whose occupation was quaintly described as "Keeping [a] Liquor Saloon."[8] The former Kentuckian's real estate was valued at $8,000, but since he also had an interest in the popular hotel known as the Raymond House, it is impossible to say how much of this $8,000 was represented by the saloon and how much by his other holdings. A decade later Jobe gave his occupation to another census taker as "Capitalist," suggesting that he now considered himself a far more solid citizen than the saloonkeeper of a decade before! Curiously, he had aged only three years (from fifty to fifty-three) in the preceding decade, and his birthplace had been moved to Indiana, contradictions that could be attributed either to careless recording or a faulty memory since there was no reason to lie about such mundane matters.[9] Jobe remained an important Austin businessman for many years. His grave marker in Austin's Oakwood Cemetery shows he lived from March 6, 1820, to January 27, 1905, and he achieved an enviable reputation as a frontier entrepreneur during more than eight decades. His considerable business acumen was probably acquired on the job, as any schooling he might have received would have been minimal at best, from growing up in Kentucky before going off to war in 1846. Phillip Jobe was a classic example of that American archetype, the self-made man who got everything as a result of simple hard work and native intelligence.

Whatever the source of his success, Phillip Jobe was the first man to put his stamp on the Iron Front, although in the early years it was known not by its more famous later name but simply as "Jobe's Saloon." That original building was an unprepossessing wooden structure that was hardly the stuff of later legends, but saloon and proprietor grew together, just not during the Civil War.

Like every other form of business, the saloon industry suffered mightily during the Civil War, the result of wartime shortages of good booze, male customers, and spending money. Even long-standing saloons were forced to operate on more modest budgets, dispensing with such luxuries as exotic liquors and stage shows for the duration. The games tended to be penny-ante affairs. Some places were even forced to close their doors, not for lack of customers but because the owner/proprietor was himself off soldiering.

There is virtually nothing in the local wartime newspapers about the Iron Front or the other most popular saloons in Austin. In fact there is virtually nothing documenting the existence of any business in the city during the war; military operations seemed to be the only activities going on, or at least the only ones reported in the newspapers. That the Iron Front would simply shut down during the war is possible but unlikely. However, when George Southernwood took over as proprietor about 1894 his advertising stated that the Iron Front had been in business since 1866, not 1849 when Phillip Jobe first began operating a saloon on the site. The address given in Southernwood's advertisement was also 606 Congress Avenue, indicating the business had either moved across the street, or else a different building now carried the same name.[10] In either case, the Iron Front Saloon would not long be at the 606 Congress Avenue address; in succeeding city directories it was consistently located at 605 Congress. Was the pre-1866 establishment so different from what Southernwood advertised that he considered his business a totally new endeavor?

The Iron Front came into its own after the Civil War when the cattleman became "King" in Texas, and cowboying was the occupation of choice for a generation of young, footloose men. No one knows exactly how long Jobe remained sole owner of his namesake saloon, but by the early 1870s he had taken on John H. Robinson as a partner to help run things. The two men were first listed as co-owners in the 1872–73 city directory. The Robinson half of Jobe and Robinson was an Englishman in his early fifties, only slightly older than Jobe. At the time they formed their partnership, he was already a successful merchant with assets valued in the 1870 census at $16,000 worth of real estate and $1,500 worth of personal estate.[11] Just when and where the two men became acquainted or when Robinson first arrived in Austin is undetermined. What is known is that through some magic combination of business acumen and winning personalities, they soon had the bar on the first floor doing the same kind of "land office" business as the gambling hall above. They had discovered the classic symbiosis between drinking and gambling that made the Western saloon an institution. When business became good enough, they tore down the old wooden structure and put up a brick and iron structure that they named the "Iron Front." To the regular clientele of the old place was now added a brand-new crowd attracted by its upgraded facilities.

Aside from the identity of those original proprietors, little is known today of the saloon's early history. One incident from those early years stands out. Around 1870 it nearly fell victim to one of the frequent fires that plagued Western communities constructed mostly of wood and tar paper. A three-story brick building just north of the saloon caught fire, and its walls collapsed. Two men passing between the two buildings at this inopportune moment were almost killed when the wall fell on them. Fortunately, they were dragged to safety and saved. It was shortly after this mishap that the original Jobe saloon building was torn down and the more substantial Iron Front put up in its place. Damage caused by the fire may have necessitated the reconstruction. In any case, it proved to be a turning point in the saloon's history, transforming an un-pretentious little joint into a true Texas legend.[12]

The saloon was never again threatened by the urban nightmare of fire. By the mid-1870s, Austin had a relatively well-equipped fire de-partment, although it was strictly a volunteer outfit. The city's popula-tion of 18,000 was guarded by two steam fire engines drawn by hand and carrying three thousand feet of hose, a large Babcock fire extinguisher, two hook-and-ladder trucks, and 180 men ready to spring to action at the first sound of the fire bell. No frontier community could rest too lightly as long as flimsy wooden construction and part-time, underfunded fire departments were the rule.

The new bar attracted men from all stations in life, but it became es-pecially a favorite resort of the "blue bloods," both the locals and those who came to Austin to conduct business. The businessmen of Austin went there to spend leisurely hours socializing with their friends, and travelers found the hospitality first-rate. The proprietors made their cus-tomers feel welcome not just on account of the money they spent, but as persons. While in recent times the consumption of copious amounts of alcohol, particularly in a barroom setting, has come to be considered disgraceful, such was hardly the attitude among the majority of men and even women in the American West of the last century. The saloon was considered an entirely proper social setting for men. It was not consid-ered so for the fairer sex, but they generally tolerated this prerogative for their menfolk.

By the 1880s the Iron Front had acquired an enviable reputation that did not even stop at the borders of the Lone Star state. The process whereby it was transformed from merely a popular local watering hole into a famous establishment is as much about the sociology of American gambling as it is the drinking habits of thirsty men. Most Westerners gambled to one degree or another, and the professional gambler was considered a respectable member of the community. The horde of "ar-gonauts" who descended on the California gold fields after 1848 were by nature gamblers, risking first their lives and health working a claim, then risking whatever precious mineral they took out of the earth in games of chance with fellow argonauts. In other locales, cattlemen gambled on their herds surviving drought, deadly winters, and stampedes. All over the West, brave and sometimes foolhardy men lived life on the edge, which is really what the frontier was to begin with: the edge of civilization. In all aspects, life out west almost dictated that a person had to be a gambler to even justify his existence. Historian Robert K. DeArment expressed the phenomenon capably in his study of the frontier gambler:

> In that historical time and place everyone was to some extent a gambler. All who sought fortunes in the West were betting on the land, the future, and themselves. It was a period of great enthusiasm and optimism, for all were convinced that huge rewards awaited those with nerve enough to take a risk. For those too impatient to wait for the claim to produce a bonanza in gold, the cattle to multiply, or the town to develop, the gambler's table offered an opportunity for instant riches.[13]

During the course of westward expansion, gambling became an integral part of everyday life wherever men spent a few hours together in pleasant camaraderie—in cow towns, mining camps, and frontier villages stretching from the Great Plains to the Golden Gate.

Austin was no exception to this phenomenon. By the time Jobe and Robinson hung out their sign on Congress Avenue, gambling was more than a mere pastime; it was a recognized profession, and more than that, it was big business! Attorney William Walton was only one of a great number of men, and even women, who considered gambling a reasonable livelihood for supporting not only one's self but one's family as well. He spoke from first-hand experience when he described the "advent" on the local scene of men possessing "large means and great skill in manipulating the history of the four Kings."[14] The various forms of wagering included practically any game that could be played with cards, ball, or dice, beginning with but not limited to keno, faro, monte, roulette, A.B.C., Rouge et Noir, Boston, seven-up, euchre, old poker, and draw poker. The names were as creative as the rules, but each had its devotees.

All of these games were to be found in Austin's saloons, although whether all of them were played at the Iron Front Walton does not say. However, the well-chronicled popularity of the place with gamblers from all over suggests that it offered a wide variety of games for discriminating players. And if the conventional games played with cards and dice were not to one's fancy, there were other diversions available in

A rare gambling device used in the Iron Front. This French-made device, a monkey dressed as a magician, allowed the dice to be shaken by mechanical means rather than by a human hand. Courtesy *Robert K. De Arment*

the Iron Front, such as pool, dominoes, and billiards, as well as the most popular beverages.

We are on shakier ground speculating about whether the Iron Front offered prostitution on its "menu" of activities. Although the record is very dim on this question due to the shadowy nature of the profession, prostitutes certainly were a presence in the city while the Iron Front was in its heyday. During the Civil War their numbers may have been so few that they were not considered a public nuisance. That picture changed following the war with the return of young men, now hardened and worldly-wise, from the battlefields. With the arrival of U.S. Army occupation troops during Reconstruction (1865–74), the military became a major presence in Austin, and it is an unwritten rule of war that wherever troops settle in, the painted women follow.

By 1870 Congress Avenue was the city's main thoroughfare, but there was nothing glamorous about the street. Cattle drives went up the avenue on the way to Kansas markets; hogs roamed the street along with dogs and occasional loose horses or mules. Paved streets, municipal garbage collection, and sewers were all in the future. Gun play occasionally took place as many men carried a weapon and were willing with little provocation to use it. With the prospect of the railroad and the state's first public university coming to town, the citizens had to take a concerned look at vice.

In June of 1870, the city council took up the problem officially for the first time, voting later that same year to completely "suppress bawdy houses." There were but a few bawdy houses in town at the time, so there were not many special interests willing to come to their defense, but this was still a change from a decade earlier when there had been no bawdy houses in the city. One could blame the change on the Civil War and Reconstruction, but the problem was more than just a few bawdy houses. A full-blown vice district was taking shape, and it was not far from the location of the Iron Front.[15]

Two blocks west of Congress Avenue was the area that became the unofficial center of vice activities in Austin. It had various nicknames but was best known as "Guy Town." It was not a set-aside district; it was simply a neighborhood where vice operators seemed to flock together, and for the most part police and officialdom left it alone. By the 1880s, there were more than two score bawds, blacks and whites, working in Austin. John Cardwell, the conscience of the *Statesman*, railed against prostitutes appearing in the city's business district proper, but was curiously silent on their presence a couple of blocks away in Guy Town. Meanwhile, the idea of completely eliminating prostitution was not even an issue among Austin officials, only its control.[16]

Control was best done by having an ordinance on the books prohibiting it but only occasionally enforcing it by arresting the *filles de joie*. Of course, paying a small fine satisfied the legal necessity of "punishing" lawbreakers, but in reality the fines were actually licensing fees.

The few dollars that a violator was fined in the 1870s grew to $10 plus court costs by the mid-1880s. If the girls were pressured to tell who their customers were, they did not violate their professional code of silence about such things; therefore, no names ever got into print. The *Statesman*, however, did not hesitate to print the names of the girls who were arrested, and since that was a regular occurrence, some of the girls acquired a sort of perverse celebrity status. For instance, in March, 1884, the newspaper recorded the names of forty-seven prostitutes who had been brought before the recorder's court and who paid a fine of $10 each plus court costs of $5.30. Not only were their names listed but their color as well.[17] The growing attention that prostitution rated in the newspaper indicates what a problem it was becoming. As in other frontier towns, city fathers found it hard to live with prostitution, impossible to live without it.

Why the profession was such a thorn in the side of officials who theoretically had the power to eliminate it is simple: the bawds held their customers' public reputations hostage. On more than one occasion, prostitutes who felt too much pressure to pack up and leave town threatened to name names. As early as 1876, and probably not for the first time, two madams charged with keeping a "disreputable house" threatened to tell who their most frequent visitors were. Cardwell noted smugly that "several high-toned gentlemen are trembling in their boots."[18] There was more than a little irony in this situation. The reformers' penchant for viewing prostitutes as victims of society conveniently ignored the fact that those so-called victims possessed considerable leverage in being able to "out" respectable city fathers.

Prostitution could not exist in a vacuum; it was just one head of a three-headed monster, gambling and saloons being the other two. Wherever one was found, the other two were always nearby. They did not always arouse the same level of righteous indignation, however. During John Cardwell's tenure as editor of the *Statesman*, gambling and the saloons usually received kid-glove treatment, but in 1884 that cozy arrangement began to unravel. A lengthy editorial headlined "Will Gambling Dens Be Suppressed in Austin?" reflected an admirable change in attitude by both the newspaper and the authorities, yet fell far short of declaring a war on vice. Still, it was better than the old "live-

and-let-live" approach. The tenor was set by City Attorney Dudley Goodall Wooten who was quoted as saying that the gamblers had to go and asked for the "active co-operation and moral support of all good citizens." [19]

The vice operators were subjected to additional public scrutiny at this time because of a highly publicized search to find a home for the new state university. Opponents of Austin's bid to become the educational as well as the political capital of Texas pointed out that "the vices of gambling and prostitution prevailed to an alarming extent [in the city], rendering it an unfit place for the location" of the state's first public university. City fathers responded to the accusations sometimes with flat-out denials and sometimes by admitting such vices existed but that they were no worse than in any other large city. The city's dark side did not seem to unduly worry the legislature, however, and Austin was awarded the university. But that did not stop the criticism. Even after one wing of the university building had gone up and it was well on the way to completion, the *Statesman*'s editor complained that nothing had been done about the most egregious vices: "Gambling houses and houses of prostitution continue as heretofore to ply their damnable vocations openly and conspicuously on the principal streets in the heart of the city, and the support of the proprietors and patrons of these dens of infamy is eagerly and openly solicited by candidates for office." [20]

These denunciations were the clearest indications yet of a turnaround in both the editorial policy of the *Statesman* and the attitude of city fathers. Such a turnaround did not portend well for places like the Iron Front. During the John Cardwell–Ben Thompson era, gambling and saloons had always been treated as respectable businesses in the city's commercial mix. By 1886, however, the city's respectable community had finally mustered a measure of indignation about the presence of open vice operations in their city. And for the first time, city fathers evidenced some willingness to consider it a public problem. In January, Mayor J. W. Robertson presented a petition to the city council from Austin citizens asking them to "suspend at once all gambling houses and bawdy houses, and pass and enforce such an ordinance as will be required to control the saloons and drinking places in the city." The petition was accepted and turned over to the ordinance committee for study.

They reported (without a hint of irony) that there was already an ordinance on the books for the suppression of gambling and other games of chance. Likewise, existing ordinances prohibited the sale of liquor to minors, habitual drunkards, or anyone of school age; defined and prohibited "disorderly houses"; and even classified gamblers and prostitutes as "vagrants" subject to arrest and fine.[21] All the legal weapons the authorities needed to crack down on vice were already available in the city ordinances; the problem was they were not being enforced either energetically or consistently. It was an age-old tale of politics and power. Gambling, saloons, and prostitution would continue to operate right out in the open in spite of calls for reform and city council hand-wringing.

Most of the city's saloons could hook up a lonely customer with a good-time girl, if not on the premises then in nearby cribs or parlor houses to which they had ties. It was a given that female companionship for a price was high on the agenda of the average, red-blooded sport, cattle drover, or drummer. The Iron Front held the line on its "males only" policy, meaning its customers had to leave the premises to pick up a girl, which was only a minor inconvenience. This allowed the place to maintain at least a facade of rugged respectability. The "boys only" policy would have been impossible to enforce had the place included a theater under the same roof like Jack Harris's Vaudeville Saloon in San Antonio or employed female drink servers. But the Iron Front was an old-fashioned stag club that discriminated proudly against the fairer sex. Its name was never linked in public print with the local sex trade, nor in the saloon's long history was it ever labeled a "disorderly house," the favorite legal euphemism for bordellos in Western vernacular. Instead, prostitution Austin style seemed to be a problem not in the haven of the saloon, but on the main streets of the town where "so-called respectable young men and old married men" rode around in carriages after dark accompanied by "notorious prostitutes" on the way to who-knew-where.[22]

From the street, the Iron Front looked like most other saloons in Austin, or in dozens of other frontier towns across the West for that matter. It was hardly an architectural masterpiece, but then it was built to be a business address, not a historic landmark. Commercial structures in Austin and most other cities were generally plain and unprepossessing, at least from the exterior. Few owners or builders were concerned with architectural flourishes or the beauty of a line. Form followed function. During what is known as the "frontier period" most buildings were constructed of wood, with brick and stone coming in a distant second and third. The more expensive ones stopped at two stories topped with a flat roof. The standard frontage followed the three-windows rule of thumb, that is, as wide across the front as three windows, and some added a false front to this, making the building appear grander than it really was.

The earliest image of the building at 605 Congress Avenue, from 1877, shows a thoroughly conventional structure two stories high and approximately twenty-five feet wide, just enough for three windows. At the rear of the saloon, on the second floor level, was a porch where gamblers might go to stretch their legs and take in some fresh air without having to mix with the downstairs crowd. On the south side of the building was a fifteen-foot-long wall extending into the alley, its purpose unknown. This sketchy information comes from a fire insurance map prepared by the Sanborn Company of New York, which provided similar maps for cities of all sizes all over the country from the 1870s on. The maps were updated every few years, thus showing the evolution of the urban heart of American cities in "snapshot" form. They were not actually intended for historians but to help insurance carriers and fire fighters by showing the building materials and general layout, location of all doors and windows, and other pertinent information. Sometime before 1885, the Iron Front building was enlarged to include the addition of a second staircase leading up to the second floor.[23]

None of this is particularly remarkable. Photographs of Congress Avenue from the same time period show other buildings on the street with the standard second-floor trio of windows and an awning extending outward from that level supported by two or more posts. (The awning supports served an additional function as hitching posts.) The Iron Front had all of these conventional features plus something else that made it stand out from its neighbors. The saloon derived its name quite literally from the ferrous material that adorned its facade at least as early as 1866. The iron-trimmed facade was well known in Eastern cities but represented something unique in Austin if not all of Texas for many years. According to one expert, "Until the railroad came, the extremely popular and common iron front of the East was an unnecessary luxury in Austin." Iron construction was used "more effectively" for framing than for exterior decoration of commercial buildings. The use of iron girders or trusses allowed builders during the frontier period to increase the usual three-window width. By the late 1870s, however, iron had "left its mark" on the Austin business district as builders "copied in limestone the iron imitations of stone palaces once popular in the East." [24] But the Iron Front did it first and thus made history just by its mere existence.

Contemporary shutterbugs seem to have completely overlooked the historical significance of the Iron Front in its heyday. There are any number of photographs showing various street scenes on Congress Avenue over the years, including some with the Iron Front in the background, but there are no known photographs showing a full exterior view of the place. It appears only in part, with the saloon itself never the actual subject of the photograph, just background. This represents a genuine loss for historians. One unidentified photographer, around the turn of the century, placed his camera at the center of the intersection of Congress and Sixth Street and directed the lens towards the northeast corner. The resulting image shows both sides of the Crystal Saloon on the corner, with its name in tall letters at a diagonal on the roof above the second floor. To the right, facing Sixth Street is a huge billboard advertising Tom Moore's cigars at only ten cents each. To the left, or facing Congress, is another huge sign advertising a rival ten-cent cigar, this one the General Arthur. Unfortunately the huge General Arthur sign almost completely blocks the view of the Iron Front above the first floor, except for the name, "Iron Front Saloon," at the very top. On street level, close to the edge of the sidewalk, is another small sign identifying the place. The scene is dressed with hacks, saddle horses, and pedestrians all going about their business, blissfully unaware that they would be an object of historical study nearly a hundred years later.

Other existing photographs provide some additional albeit sketchy visual information: the front entrance was well protected from the sun and elements by the awning, and entry was gained not through the swinging "bat-wing" doors that so many Western movies have depicted as being an essential part of the Western saloon, but through a regular doorway. If there were any bat wings they were inside the building, not at the entrance. The Iron Front's patrons did not know that, according to the best Hollywood tradition, they were supposed to enter the place through swinging bat-wing doors.[25]

Sadly, no photographer brought his camera into the interior of the Iron Front to capture its appearance for posterity. Getting customers to pose might have been a problem even had a would-be photographer been so inclined, and if, like most saloons of the day, it was open around the clock, trying to capture images of an empty room would have been practically impossible.

To get an idea what the interior of the Iron Front looked like, we must look somewhere else besides the Sanborn fire maps and the photographic record. Almost all drinking and gambling establishments started out with the same basic floor plan before adding a unique touch or two that reflected the owner's personal tastes: a front foyer, the main barroom, billiard rooms in the back, and an upstairs devoted to serious gambling. Standing in the front door of the Iron Front, the most welcome sight to a thirsty man was the bar, which ran along the left side of the room, at least half the length of the building. The wall behind the bar was most certainly taken up by a mirror that probably extended very nearly the entire length of the bar. Spittoons were placed on the floor at convenient intervals along the foot rail for plug-chewing and snuff-dipping customers. So far these items were as essential as a stove and a sink in a kitchen. But then the Iron Front added an exotic touch in the form of stuffed animal heads on the walls. An 1894 Board of Trade publication stressed this masculine decorative scheme, with its variety of "natural history specimens and hunting trophies." Most saloons were content with a large painting or two on the walls, whose subject matter was guaranteed to offend moral sensibilities in this age of Queen Victoria. Some of the most popular works included a scantily clad Mazeppa on horseback or some other captivating lovely in a revealing pose. The Iron Front had its share of paintings on the walls in the front "parlor," but inside the barroom it aimed at the red-blooded sportsman with its wall decorations.[26]

In the rear was the billiard room, plus tables for refreshments, dominoes, and other friendly games. If inclined to test his luck and his bank roll against the big boys, the customer could take either of the two staircases leading upstairs where the second floor was specifically designated as the gambling area. At some point in the Iron Front's history one of those stairways was boarded up and forgotten, only to be "discovered" years later when the building was being torn down. It was imaginatively if inaccurately dubbed a "secret stairway" by its discoverers, giving rise to rampant speculation about its original purpose and users.

Over the years, the interior was remodeled a few times, probably whenever a new proprietor came on board, but it could not have strayed far from the prototypical Western saloon. Making improvements and adding the latest amenities was necessary to keep up with the competition, whether it was the Crystal Saloon, on the corner of Sixth and Congress, or any one of half a dozen other fancy places up and down the street.

The entire saloon, upstairs and downstairs, received a face-lift starting in late 1878, with special attention lavished on the game rooms, where the clientele had expectations of first-class treatment in return for spending generously. By late January the results were on display as the word went out that the new billiard parlor "just thrown open to the public" was a "perfect gem." Players could choose from among three new Brunswick, Balke and Company tables of the swank pattern called "Monarch." These were "the finest made, the likes of which was never before seen in Texas." The entry parlor was also new and improved, "fitted up in superb style—unapproached by anything in the city" with decorations that catered to a cultured clientele. The "elegant paintings, steel engravings, and other useful ornaments" provided an ambiance that was "cozy and secluded." The owners expressed the hope that their establishment would "become a favorite resort for 'the boys.'" The high-class amenities did not stop with the billiard tables and decorative arts. Customers with a hankering for a smoke or a drink could enjoy the "purest of wines, liquors, cigars, etc." for sale on the main floor.[27]

It obviously took a considerable investment of time and money to create a "fashionable resort" for gentlemen "of all types," and this was not a one-shot deal. Upgrading the facilities was an ongoing process that required both a commitment to excellence and deep pockets. As much as anything, this shows the healthy profits that could be made in the upscale saloon business.

By its third decade, the Iron Front was one of the snazziest drinking-gambling establishments in the capital city if not the entire state of Texas. In 1882 the *Statesman* did a special write-up on the occasion of its being recently "renovated and beautifully embellished by some modern improvements." A reporter was sent to check out the changes. The most noteworthy improvement he saw was the new billiard table, which brought the house's total number of tables to four. The latest addition was a state-of-the-art "combination table, ready for billiards, pin and ball pool."

The entire bar had also been repainted and "elegantly ornamented," so that "it will now class [*sic*], in appearance and appointment, with any saloon in the state." And in the highly competitive local saloon business, the Iron Front was unofficially crowned "chief place of entertainment in the city." An exclamation point was put on that statement on January 3, 1884, when the first electric light fixture in the entire city was installed in the Iron Front. At the time it was more of a novelty than a practical source of light, but it shows just how quick saloons were to latch on to the "latest thing." The Iron Front may not have had the first telephone in Austin, but it certainly had *one* of the first. That meant that by 1894 a customer with his own phone could ring up the operator and ask to be connected to #49 and before they knew it be talking to the bartender at the Iron Front! [28]

One thing that did not need to be improved at the Iron Front during the periodic remodelings was the service. From the polite porters at the front door to the well-dressed bartenders behind the bar, everything was first class. The bar was kept stocked with the best goods money could buy, and the visitor was treated with "every consideration and courtesy." [29]

The Iron Front's interior decorations ran from the merely curious to the downright bizarre. Among the latter must be included the stalactite presented to the owner on July 9, 1883. It was a "peculiar specimen of stalactite from a cave on the Colorado River [which runs through Austin], . . . brought by a gentleman who explored the cave . . . [and] about 8 feet long," reported the obviously impressed *Statesman*. [30]

Later that same month F. M. Gandsor presented a lightning rod fixture to the proprietor. It was "a silver-plated weather vane having gold tips on the rods indicating direction." It was also adorned with a gold-plated ball above and a silver-plated one below the directional rods. The *Statesman* did not state whether the lightning rod was to be attached to the roof or merely put on display inside the saloon, but it did say that the object was "one of the most beautiful ornaments a *Statesman* reporter has ever seen in Austin for many a day—and what a *Statesman* reporter does not see is not worth seeing." [31]

One of the oddest items ever put on display at the Iron Front was an uncarved tombstone that rested against one wall of the upstairs gambling rooms for a while. The stone marker belonged to the man who presided over the gambling rooms, Ben Thompson, who had won it in a card game. It occupied a place of honor until the novelty wore off, and Thompson had it removed.[32]

All of these curiosities were useful not only as conversation starters among the customers but as drawing cards to bring in more customers. After all, what other saloon in Austin could boast a stalactite, a silver-and-gold-plated lightning rod, and a tombstone? While John B. Neff was proprietor (ca. 1878–94), he seemed to have a special affinity for such novelties, which is why people who came into possession of them always brought them to the Iron Front first.

Management over the years was fairly stable, not surprising for an operation with such a successful track record in the tough saloon business. Exactly when founder Philip W. Jobe turned over the reins, and whether he sold out willingly or was forced out, is unknown. But the place did not miss a beat when he took in John H. Robinson as a partner in the early 1870s. The Austin city directory shows that by 1872 "Jobe & Robinson" were calling the shots, and they continued to do so until at least 1877. Sometime before 1879, however, Harry H. Duff and John B. Neff replaced Jobe and Robinson. Neff was a native Texan, having come to Austin in 1872 from his birthplace at La Grange in Fayette County. He made his home in Austin and his career in the saloon business for the rest of his life. By 1881 Neff was the sole proprietor, and an able proprietor he was, too. The *Statesman* applauded him in 1882 as "a man of great taste," whatever that means, but it was obviously a great compliment because this was the same article that described the Iron Front as "the chief place of entertainment in the city." [33]

Neff was more than a mere saloonkeeper; he was also very active in the community, which was good for the Iron Front's public relations as well as for his own image. In 1882, when the directors of the Capital State Fair were talking about canceling the popular steer roping contest due to a lack of steer entries and suitable prizes, Neff got things back on track by offering to provide a fine saddle "with complete fittings and of the handsomest finish," presumably for first prize. Subsequently, the local cattlemen promised to provide as many steers as necessary "to assure fine sport for those who enter the lists." Neff received the thanks of a grateful community "for his display of public spirit in connection with the Capital State Fair." The *Statesman* said that his generous contribution guaranteed "a complete success of the [steer roping] contest," one of the most popular parts of the program. The ultimate compliment, however, may have been that the *Statesman* during these years referred to it as "John Neff's Iron Front Saloon" frequently in its pages.[34]

Despite his personal popularity and apparently successful management, Neff reestablished the partnership with Duff, probably in 1884. The *Austin Statesman* apparently considered theirs a good partnership because it called them a "strong team," but this was a town steeped in politics, so how much of that praise was simple admiration and how much was calculated politics is something to be considered.[35]

Neff by this time was already well known throughout the state as the proprietor of Austin's finest saloon. Nor was Duff a greenhorn in the business. He was just "as well and as widely known" to locals as the proprietor of the Star Saloon just across the street from the Iron Front. Duff was also considered a "genial, gentlemanly" member of the saloon proprietors' fraternity. Obviously, the two men decided there was more to be gained by joining forces than by continuing on as rivals. The *Statesman* predicted that they would undoubtedly build on their individual records of success and make their joint venture "a golden success." The new partnership promptly promised that all customers would be treated well and could always get "some of whatever you want of the very best." The *Statesman*, regarding itself as the best judge of such things, unhesitatingly declared that "no stronger or better firm could be found in Austin."[36]

Duff and Neff were quite conscious of the value of the public's good will to the success of their enterprise. Not content just to act as purveyors of cigars and booze, they made a special effort to show their appreciation to the community. An opportunity presented itself on January 2, 1880, when they prepared a banquet at Isaac S. Simon's restaurant for all the major cattlemen of the surrounding area. The result was described as an "enjoyable affair," with about thirty people present, among whom were several of the most prominent citizens of Austin. A reporter from the *Statesman* was invited, apparently with the hope of getting favorable press coverage of the event. He got a free banquet meal and the Iron Front got its free advertising, so everyone was happy.

After partaking of everything a "thorough epicure could desire" in the way of food, the guests were treated to sparkling champagne in the "aid of already brilliant wit." Numerous toasts were given and answered by party-goers in the "happiest moods of these proverbially jolly men." Duff and Neff were praised effusively for their tasteful and liberal hospitality. The two hosts secured the "everlasting good will of many old friends [and] made many new ones."[37] It was certainly a night Austin would remember for a long time.

The proprietors also invested in other measures to keep their regular clientele while at the same time attracting new customers to their establishment. Frequently, public raffles were held outside the front doors, suggesting that the Iron Front wanted to attract ordinary citizens in addition to the well-heeled sporting crowd. Every man could be a "gambler" with the right opportunity and for the right price, and for those leery of stepping into the disreputable interior of a saloon, these outdoor raffles could help break down negative stereotypes. Players bought chances for prizes ranging from saddles and bridles to a gold watch and chain or music box. If a man chose to come in after the raffle to slake his thirst or play friendly games with cards, dice, or cues, so much the better. The raffle held on January 16, 1880, provided a gold watch and chain to the lucky winner.[38] On February 28 of the same year, chances to win a horse and buggy were being sold for $2.50 at the day's raffle, but one had to be present to win. The popular tradition of the Iron Front's outdoor raffle continued for some time. Obviously, good weather was as important as good prizes, and the saloon seemed to have plenty of both. On January 20, 1883, a "fine music box" was the winning raffle prize.[39]

In spite of their highly successful partnership, the Duff and Neff combination lasted only three years. Duff was a volatile man who got into a few scrapes with the law. On January 22, 1884, he was arrested for assault, although the details of the incident were not explained in the newspaper. Such scrapes were to be expected among members of the sporting fraternity but were an embarrassment for respectable business-men. Assaulting someone who might be a potential customer was not only bad for business but definitely contradicted the "genial and gen-tlemanly" tag that the *Statesman* would soon bestow on Duff.[40]

By 1887 Duff had been replaced by Oscar Rohde for reasons un-known, although Duff's reputation for beating up enemies might have something to do with it. Neff and Rohde did not last long, however, and two years later Neff was again calling the shots as sole proprietor. This arrangement lasted another five years, until 1894, at which point he sold his interest to a new pair of owners, Frank C. Wedig and George South-ernwood. In a statement more notable for its encomiums than its syntax, the Austin Board of Trade publication endorsed the latest change: "These gentlemen, by their experience and character, are both able and willing to continue and enhance the old-time reputation of the place, and there is every reason to predict, therefore, a continuance of the pros-perity and appreciation [the Iron Front] has always enjoyed." Elsewhere in the same story, the writer went even further, stating that the Iron Front was "entitled" to all the "prosperity and support" it had received over the years.[41] Clearly, the venerable saloon was first in the hearts of the city's chamber of commerce forerunner.

Even in retirement, John Neff continued his association with the establishment he had presided over for so many years, maintaining an office at 605 Congress Avenue. He stayed out of the spotlight and lived quietly with his family until his death in 1896. On February 10, while cleaning a pistol, he accidentally shot himself, dying almost immediately.[42]

Another former owner did not fare so well after leaving the Iron Front. Frank C. Wedig, former partner with George Southernwood, opened his own saloon down the block at 701 Congress Avenue in 1898. After two years as a rival, Wedig was back at the Iron Front in 1900, only this time working as a bartender with Southernwood now as his employer. The proprietorship of Southernwood lasted until 1904 when Thomas Alonzo "Lon" Martin took over. Southernwood subsequently moved on to the Avenue Hotel to take over bartending duties at its bar, seemingly a step down in the saloon hierarchy from the Iron Front.[43] Meanwhile, the Iron Front continued under Martin's proprietorship for another six years (1904–10) until the doors were closed for the last time.

John Neff and Lon Martin belong on the same select list of storied saloon owners in Texas history as Fort Worth's Bill Ward, El Paso's Ben Dowell, and San Antonio's Jack Harris. All of these men made their mark on both their communities and the saloon business. And like the "robber barons" of the nineteenth century, they were not always the most admirable of men, but there is no denying their impact on history.

At some point around the turn of the century, the Iron Front added a first-class restaurant and divided up management responsibilities between the restaurant and the bar proper. Both places operated under the familiar name. This arrangement did not last long, however, and the Iron Front never became recognized for its food service, unlike Fort Worth's White Elephant. In 1907 Lon Martin was running the saloon while China-born Wing Lung managed the restaurant. How they divided the profits up is unknown, but one suspects that Martin claimed the lion's share of the proceeds of the combined business, which is not to say that Lung worked for Martin.[44]

As a saloon, the Iron Front could not avoid being the scene of a certain amount of what was termed "riotous behavior" from time to time; it was expected. Yet there was always a "gentlemen's agreement" among the regular customers about the acceptable limits of such behavior. The back room, where the billiard tables were located, was designated as "strictly a gentleman's resort and there never was any rioting there," which suggests that there was a firm, if unwritten, code of conduct. Arguments that began indoors might end up on the street with someone being shot or knifed or roughed up, but inside the saloon everything was kept orderly. One unidentified Austin resident, interviewed at the time the building was being razed, recalled that almost the entire block of

Congress Avenue where the Iron Front stood had been occupied by gambling houses. "Austin," he said with more than a hint of hyperbole, "was then the center of as lawless a class as ever lived. But in the back room of the Iron Front we used to gather and hold our kangaroo court, drink good liquor and have some of the best times men ever had." Any man was welcome in the Iron Front, be he an army officer, cattleman, businessman, or church-goer, "for there was no harm in drinking your toddies in those days, and we all had a good time." There were times when some real "bad men" would pay a visit, but "they generally behaved in the Iron Front and despite their bad blood they were a bunch of free-hearted fellows."[45] Thus, the Iron Front's regulars always looked upon themselves as "a bunch of free-hearted fellows."

Although most of the so-called "bad men" who tried the hospitality of the Iron Front are long since forgotten, legends still survive today that during the 1870s some of the most notorious characters of the Wild West came through the doors. Those were bad times in Texas history, just after the Civil War, when the passions and lawlessness of Reconstruction turned many men into outlaws. Among those who made a name for themselves with their gun were Ben Thompson, the four Younger brothers (Cole, John, James, and Bob), and John Wesley Hardin, all of whom had their names associated with the Iron Front at one time or another.[46]

The most likely visitor among that group of hard-boiled killers was the Texas-born Hardin, although hard documentation is lacking to back up the popular lore. Wes Hardin, considered by many to have been the "greatest killer of them all," began his outlaw career in 1868 at the tender age of fifteen, motivated as much by the politics of Reconstruction as by sociopathic tendencies. He would continue his outlaw ways unabated until arrested in Pensacola, Florida, in 1877. Hardin's candidacy as an Iron Front patron is based on the fact that he was friends with Austin resident Ben Thompson, quite fond of gambling, and crisscrossed Texas numerous times during a ten-year career on the outlaw trail. Hardin and Thompson had become acquainted in the Kansas cattle towns during the days of the "long drives," and although they did not become bosom friends, they never had a falling out, which was remarkable considering the notoriously short fuses of both men. Hardin could have passed through Austin and visited any number of saloons on his peregrinations through the state, but he never mentions the Iron Front by name in his autobiography, written in semiretirement late in life and published posthumously.[47]

The notorious Younger brothers, who rode with Jesse and Frank James and were shot up in the bloody Northfield, Minnesota, raid of 1876, may also have been Iron Front customers. There were four of them: John, Cole, Bob, and Jim. They definitely spent time in Texas; this much the record shows. Cole and John made numerous forays to the Lone Star state after the Civil War, and John in particular had a criminal record in Texas before his death in 1874. At the end of 1875 the remaining three were in Dallas, and in May, 1876, they held up a stage coach on the road between Austin and San Antonio. But no solid evidence has been found placing them in Austin. If indeed they ever got into Austin, they surely tried the well-known hospitality of the Iron Front, but as in the case of Wes Hardin, we are dependent upon local lore and educated guesses to place them there.[48]

Every legendary watering hole could boast at least one celebrated patron possessing a reputation on the same larger-than-life scale as the saloon itself, the two being joined together in the historic record. The Iron Front's most celebrated patron was the English-born gunfighter-gambler Benjamin F. Thompson. He was born November 2, 1843, in Knottingley, England, as was younger brother Billy, who would be a frequent source of problems for his better-known sibling. The Thompson family moved from England to America when the children were still young. Ben saw action as a Confederate during the War of the Rebellion, although his war record was not exemplary. Following the war he and brother Billy roamed around Mexico and Texas, then established themselves as gamblers in Austin where they had spent their boyhood. Throughout the 1870s they followed their gambling passion over much of the West, mostly from Texas to Kansas in the cow towns where boisterous cowboys blew off steam and spent their trail wages. Ben later participated in the so-called Royal Gorge War in Colorado, the conflict between the Atchison, Topeka and Santa Fe and the Denver and Rio Grande railroads.[49]

Following the conclusion of the railroad war, for which Thompson received $5,000, he invested in various properties in Austin.[50] Thinking

Phillip W. Jobe, a Mexican War veteran, established a saloon in 1849 near the corner of Congress and Pecan Street. It became notorious as the Iron Front. Jobe's establishment flourished from 1849 until 1910, when it and other corner establishments were razed and then replaced by the nine story Littlefield Building. Courtesy *Austin History Center, Austin Public Library, PIC BO 4600*

not only of himself but of his family as well, he purchased a fine home near the present University of Texas for his wife and children, expensive guns for his collection, and still had enough money left over to establish gambling rooms in various places. He purchased the "gambling concession" over the Iron Front, which meant he had the exclusive right to run the games, splitting the profits with the saloon's owner(s). And here, at the Iron Front, he maintained his headquarters in grand style, like Luke Short at Fort Worth's White Elephant, or numerous other distinguished sports in countless towns across the West.

Most if not all of the second floor was devoted to gambling of various types, with keno and faro attracting the largest crowds. Thompson himself, as part owner, would have sat in occasionally as a dealer and the rest of the time simply circulating between the rooms keeping an eye on things and chatting up the regular customers. Officially, guns were barred from the premises, but it is unlikely that prohibition was strictly enforced, especially since Thompson himself never went anywhere unarmed. Thompson was not a big fan of keno, but he tolerated it because it was such a money-maker for management.

As co-owner/manager of the gambling rooms, Thompson established a reputation for running an honest place. One Austin resident said, "Ben never run a crooked game in the house." [51] This was an essential character issue for a man in his position. Crooked operators were soon found out, and customers took their business elsewhere—to any one of several other popular saloons and gambling halls up and down the street. In one way, Thompson's notoriously violent temper aided his cause: Even the slightest hint of a crooked game was enough to spark a gun-waving outburst on his part that usually ended with bullet holes in the walls, the equipment, and occasionally some of the players!

Since the Iron Front provided their own enforcers, the same as other major saloons, the Austin police tended to steer clear of it. Only when they were specifically called in to quell some knock-down-drag-out brawl did they make an appearance, and even then things were usually settled up quietly. Ironically, Thompson himself was the cause of more police calls to his own establishment than any other member of the sporting fraternity that patronized the place. The police, through pay-offs, friendly connections, or simple lenience, allowed large operations like the Iron Front to conduct business with a minimum of interference. So long as they ran honest games and kept a lid on the violence, the city's "finest" adopted an attitude of live and let live. The problem was, men like Ben Thompson could not avoid violence for any sustained period.

Nor was running a large gambling concession and being one of the most successful gamblers in the Southwest enough for Ben Thompson; he craved more tangible measures of success and approval. In October, 1879, he announced as a candidate for the position of Austin city marshal, running against popular incumbent Edward Creary, who still used his wartime rank of "Captain" with his name. [52] Supporters immediately lined up to support Thompson, who was also entitled to use the title "Captain" if that was what voters wanted. "Mr. Ben Thompson," commented the *Statesman* in announcing its endorsement, "is well and favorably known to every man in the city, and is in every way worthy of the confidence and support of the people. Mr. Thompson is a formida-

ble competitor for the office, and if elected will serve the people faith-
fully." In spite of the backing of the *Statesman* Austinites showed their
preference for Captain Creary by giving him 1,174 votes to Thompson's
744. But Creary quit before serving his full term, and Thompson made
the most of his second chance at the office. He won a special election in
December, 1880, to serve out the unexpired portion of the term and
beat his only competition, John Kelly, by 227 votes. Once in office,
Thompson proved to be an effective marshal, and he decided to run for
a full term at the next election. He had apparently won over the city's
voters because he was reelected by a comfortable margin of 1,173 votes
to J. R. Kirk's 933.[53]

Wearing the marshal's badge did not stop Thompson from frequent-
ing the tables at the Iron Front. Marshalling was only his part-time job;
gambling was his true calling. Because of his name and position in the
city's power structure, he had many opportunities to participate in big
games against some of the slickest sports in the Southwest. Some of
those games achieved legendary status, to be spoken of in awe many
years later.

During the demolition of the Iron Front in 1910, the *Statesman* interviewed one Austin old-timer who told of a big game he had participated in at that popular saloon many years prior. The newspaper did not
identify the man, and the time period was given only as "one night in
the late '70s", but there was no doubt about the place: "upstairs over the
Iron Front." Sitting in on the game were seven men: Ben Thompson,
Bute Robinson, three nameless fellows who may have been unidentified
in the newspaper because they were highly respectable citizens, another
gent who was only referred to as "the Westerner," and the old-timer
himself.

The stakes were high and the situation was volatile with so much
riding on each hand. The men had been playing all afternoon and "Old-
timer" had lost all but about $300 of the $760 bankroll that he started
with. One particular pot had been "building up for half an hour, about
fifteen rounds," but no one had managed to bring in the Jacks. Following another deal, the "Westerner" picked up his hand and, contrary to
conventional poker-playing behavior, "grinned a little," then pushed
$50 worth of chips into the center of the table as his opener. The other

players looked at him warily, wondering if he actually had intended to "ante up" that amount, and seeing that he was serious, they all folded except Ben Thompson and Old-timer. Thompson accused the Westerner of running a "garl darn" bluff and declared he would see the fellow "packed in ice before he'd get bluffed out of that pot." Thompson backed up his brave words with $50 of his own money without missing a beat, then it was the turn of Old-timer. As the interviewee told the newspaper reporter, "I was sitting back there behind a little pair of sixes, a queen, a nine and a two spot," and it looked "mighty tough," but after a little hesitation he shoved in his $50 to stay in the game. In the draw that followed, Thompson took one card, the Westerner took two, and Old-timer took three. He was hoping for another six in the best scenario, "but figured if I caught that, maybe there would be something doing for I thought the other fellows were bluffing," in which case a trio of threes would win the pot.

Old-timer realized that the other two players were interested in their own hands and had almost forgotten about him; thus when he picked up his cards and found two more sixes plus the ace of spades he tried hard not to show any change of expression. He was afraid his face might have betrayed his good fortune, but apparently the others failed to pick up any warning signs. Westerner came back with a $100 bet, which was "covered by Ben mighty quick with a raise of $50. Then my time came and I went in for the whole thing with the balance of my pot on a raise." Thompson and Westerner "eyed" him suspiciously, Ben even warning him that bluffing wouldn't work. Both men however "came in," bringing the pot up to a grand total of $900.

The men showed their hands: Westerner held three aces; Thompson had filled on a queen high straight. Then the old-timer dropped the hammer on them: "You ought to have seen them when I showed those four little sixes. Everybody in the room yelled but Ben and the Westerner, and they both said about the same time, 'Well, I'll be damned,' and looked like two sick hound pups."[54] What the unidentified old-timer had described was a classic confrontation across the "green cloth table." Sometimes, such confrontations resulted in bloodshed when the losers did not take kindly to being cleaned out, but on this occasion everybody left the Iron Front still upright to test their skills another day.

Another encounter across the card table also deserves the designation "Big Game," but for entirely different reasons. This time it was not the size of the pot but what was put into the pot that made it memorable: a tombstone. The night that Ben Thompson won a tombstone in a poker game at the Iron Front was recalled in 1910 when the building was being torn down and such a marker showed up on the site. The exact date of the game had long since been forgotten—sometime in the early 1880s was about as close as anybody could get—but the people involved and the course of events were still vivid. The story came up again fourteen years later when an Austin old-timer, John Long, was interviewed by the press.[55]

The whole thing started with a tombstone peddler named Luke Watts who was working the Texas Hill Country on a one-horse wagon. He carried a few sample tombstones with him, and as he traveled from community to community he took orders for copies of his samples. Salesman Watts was also "a pretty good sculptor," and if a buyer of a stone wanted an inscription put on it, Watts would do the work right there on the spot.

In those days every man gambled and Watts was no exception. He arrived in Austin with a pocket full of orders from San Antonio, New Braunfels, and San Marcos, and a hankering to try the hospitality of the city's premier watering hole. He stabled his horse and wagon in Deats's stables and headed for the Iron Front, where he bought a round of drinks for the bar customers, then headed up stairs to try a little gambling. He purchased some poker chips and sat down to play with the big boss himself, Ben Thompson.

Thompson found it humorous to be playing against a tombstone peddler and "jollied" Watts about making his living off dead people. Watts knew the nasty reputation of his opponent but refused to be intimidated and responded with like jocularity, "Ben, you will be took off sudden one of these days and I may not be around just at the time to sell a tombstone to ornament your grave. You had better order one from me now." Thompson took the needling good-naturedly, saying that a wooden marker was all he would need to mark his grave when the time came.

The game ran on for hours with Watts getting the worst of it. By midnight he was "cleaned out," but Thompson was not ready to see the game end yet. He was thoroughly enjoying himself and eager to find a way to keep his opponent in the game. "Hold on there. How much are those tombstones of yours worth?" he asked. Watts replied that the price depended on what sort of stone was desired. "I don't want any cheap monument," declared Ben. "Have you got any that is made out of marble?"

Watts bragged that he had a marble stone with him as fine as any slab to be found south of St. Louis, valued at two hundred dollars, which was "cheap considering it's a long ways from the quarries." That sly enticement was all it took to make up Thompson's mind. He put up two hundred dollars of his winnings against the tombstone, more to keep the game going than because he had any real desire to win the thing. Still, he wanted to see his opponent's collateral before they proceeded, so Watts went to the stable, hitched up his horse and brought the polished headstone right to the entrance of the Iron Front. Porters helped him wrestle it upstairs and present it for Thompson's inspection.

With the gambler's approval, the game continued. Before long Thompson had taken the tombstone the same way he took the peddler's bankroll. Watts took his losses with equanimity, even suggesting that he carve an inscription on the stone for its new owner. Thompson, however, rejected this notion, saying, "No, you can wait until I have done something that will give you the subject for a fitting epitaph."

The tombstone peddler soon left town, but the tombstone occupied the center of the gambling room for a while until it was removed on orders from Thompson. It was then forgotten about until that day during the razing of the building when it saw the light of day for the first time in three decades.

The mystery of the Iron Front's tombstone does not end there. The authoritative version of the story, by John Long, makes no mention of any inscription being put on the stone at the time Thompson took possession, or later while it was on public display. However, the 1910 *Austin Statesman* offered a version different in several key particulars. According to the newspaper, what was discovered on the second floor of the building on January 8 of that year was a "remarkable fine obelisk tombstone" with the name of a lady inscribed on it. And the discovery was made not by workmen but by "several prominent citizens" poking around in the "ruins." The stone was approximately four feet high and of "proportionate width." Although the name on the stone was not divulged, the newspaper did say that the deceased was eighty-three years old at the time of her death.

The discovery created a great deal of excitement, causing the same "prominent citizens" who had found it, plus others, to drop everything and start searching for a grave inside the crumbling shell. Tappings were made on the remaining walls to determine if there were any hollow places where a corpse may have been stashed. Nothing was found, of course, but that was not to satisfy the searchers. They brought in picks, and the high-born, with their "hands as tender as a babe's," joined forces with the low-born to begin digging up the ground. Still, nothing appeared after hours of work except blisters on the hands of those unused to such work.

Finally, in an effort to find a solution to the mystery, the last proprietor of the Iron Front, Thomas Alonzo Martin, was called on. Martin refused to join in on the madness, and his nonchalant explanation cast no light on matters either. All he knew was that a traveling tombstone salesman had left it behind after a visit to the Iron Front, recalling neither how it came to be left or who left it. The *Statesman* reported sadly that "[t]he mystery bubble was busted and the disappointed grave hunters left the scene in silence." Long's story and the *Statesman*'s are too similar to assume there were two tombstones; the mystery is in the details. Thompson never got around to writing his own epitaph, and when he was buried in Oakwood Cemetery in March, 1884, contemporary accounts say nothing about what kind of marker he was given. The famous Iron Front tombstone was apparently never used for anything but a wager in a poker game.[56]

Not surprisingly, the same names often popped up again and again in stories about big games and angry face-offs. On another occasion there was a killing in one of the gambling houses on Congress Avenue during a game that also involved Ben Thompson and Bute Robinson. That pair plus a man named Jim Jackson and an unidentified man were playing cards when harsh words erupted. Robinson lunged across the table and stabbed Jackson in the breast, then ran from the building waving a pistol in the air. Apparently he got out of town ahead of the law, only to fall victim to a different sort of justice meted out by members of the gambling fraternity. Some time later when Robinson was in San Antonio standing on the street talking to friends, an unidentified man from across the street shot him dead.[57]

While hosting its share of "big games" and "bad characters" over the years, the Iron Front managed to avoid any shoot-outs across the card table or on the front steps. The game described above by the old-timer was unusual because of the size of the pot involved, not because it ended peaceably. The stakes in most of the games were not what Hollywood movie makers and nineteenth-century dime novelists have made them out to be. The average player was probably a cowboy, a homesteader, or a drummer, not a big-time sport, and he did not have hundreds of dollars in his bankroll. Typically, games had a one or two dollar limit, with most bets ranging from twenty-five cents to a dollar. Roulette allowed a ten-cent chip, and dice could be played for as little as a nickel a throw. When one considers that the typical wage for a cowboy, or even a Texas Ranger, in the 1870s was one or two dollars a day, it is easy to understand why the professional gambler made his living not by winning a single high-stakes hand but by collecting a large number of small pots.

Ben Thompson considered himself a major player and participated in enough big games to be a "card-carrying" member of the exclusive gambling fraternity who practically lived at the tables in places like the Iron Front. Unfortunately, as Thompson's fortunes rose, so did the frequency of his drinking. While in San Antonio on a pleasure trip with his family, Thompson visited the notorious gambling establishment of Jack Harris's Vaudeville Saloon and Theater. As a dedicated gambler, he could hardly have done otherwise, family or no family. The chance to match skills with the big boys in the high-class emporiums was something no sporting man could pass up.

Ironically, one of Harrris's partners, William H. "Billy" Simms, was a former Austin resident whose father, James M. Simms, Sr., had served on the police force during the city's turbulent Creary-Thompson years. According to Texas Ranger James B. Gillett, who knew the entire Simms family well, Ben had earlier forced Simms to leave Austin after the two men feuded over control of keno operations. Simms became a bitter enemy of Thompson ever after and moved to San Antonio, where he became a partner of Jack Harris in San Antonio's notorious Vaudeville Saloon and Theater. Harris was no admirer of Thompson either.[58]

This in itself was not unusual, that in a frontier setting forceful men had little toleration for a rival seeking a larger share of gambling profits, although there may have been more than a difference over keno to set the two volatile characters against each other. The fact that Thompson was a frequent visitor to San Antonio and a regular at the gaming tables there did not help the situation. The bad blood between Thompson and the Vaudeville proprietors could not be resolved peacefully. Harris was shot and killed by Thompson in his own theater, and the latter was subsequently killed in a conspiracy involving Billy Simms, Joe Foster, and others. (See chapter 2, "Jack Harris's Vaudeville and San Antonio's 'Fatal Corner'.")

Thompson's killing of Jack Harris cost him a little jail time, but more importantly, it cost him his position as City Marshal. Even as popular a figure as Ben Thompson was in Austin, public pressure, led primarily by the *Statesman*, caused him to rightfully conclude that the position was no longer compatible with his gunfighter-gambler lifestyle. To his credit, he resigned without making further trouble.

The accompanying loss of the city marshal's salary was hardly a meaningful sacrifice; he continued to earn most of his money in other, more dubious ways. Although would-be desperadoes now had to have a higher degree of respect and fear for Thompson's skills as a shootist, the loss of status and public respect were considerably more troubling. Giving up the marshal's badge was a blow to the proud gambler who considered himself the "boss-king" of the Texas gambling fraternity. Nevertheless, Thompson continued to live life the only way he knew how: drinking, gambling, and fighting. During his increasing bouts of drunkenness, he became ever more destructive, causing public opinion to turn against him more and more. The Fourth Estate did not let up on their criticism of the ex-marshal, and in early February, 1884, the *Statesman* found itself the latest object of Thompson's wrath. On February 1 Thompson had an altercation with W. A. Bowen, the Austin correspondent of the *San Antonio Express* in front of the opera house. Whatever caused his rage is unknown, but Thompson struck at the newspaperman and attempted to kick him, too. During this physical assault, as the newspaper reported it, he "made use of language that ought not to be tolerated at such a time by any man." Making matters worse, all this occurred at a time when the sidewalk was "crowded with ladies," which brought down the righteous indignation of the *Statesman*. The newspaper found Thompson's actions inexcusable and suggested that the police force was incapable of putting a stop to the former marshal's shenanigans. The newspaper concluded its report by suggesting a convoluted solution that was more sarcastic than serious: "If the [city] council can do no better, for shame [*sic*] sake, appoint Ben Thompson himself to get somebody who will not be afraid to wink when Ben frowns." [59]

Thompson felt the newspaper had no right to criticize his language or behavior and barged into the *Statesman* offices to exact some type of vengeance or apology. He threatened and waved a pistol in the face of several employees who, upon his departure, promptly swore out complaints against the man. W. Gaines charged Thompson with carrying a pistol, threatening to take his life, malicious mischief, rudely displaying a pistol in a public place, and, for good measure, disorderly conduct and disturbing the peace. J. Q. Wing charged him with threatening to take his life, and H. R. Debarlehan charged him with committing assault and battery on his person.

The once-respected city marshal was a thoroughly dangerous individual to ordinary citizens by 1884. He had already been arrested on January 7 for discharging a pistol; a week after that he was arrested for disturbing the peace; on February 5 he was arrested on the various charges resulting from his assault on the *Statesman* offices; again on February 23 he was arrested for discharging a pistol; and yet again on February 25 for the same crime. Since Thompson spent so much time at the Iron Front, it is likely that at least some of these incidents had their origins at the saloon's bar. Drinking had surpassed gambling as Thompson's chief vocation; the only reason the Iron Front's management tolerated his behavior was because he had a monetary interest in the place through his control of the gambling concession. Whatever his faults, Ben Thompson made the Iron Front gambling rooms the most popular in town.

The ultimate result of Thompson's chosen lifestyle was predictable enough. He could not continue to buffalo or browbeat into submission everyone who crossed him, and the string of blood feuds of which he was a part grew longer every year. On March 11, 1884, the Iron Front's most famous patron was killed in ambush in San Antonio's Vaudeville Saloon and Theater, the same establishment where he had not long before killed Jack Harris. He was in the company of a friend, former outlaw John King Fisher, who at the time was a deputy sheriff of Uvalde County, Texas. Fisher also was killed in the same ambush. The wonder is that it did not happen at the Iron Front; instead he played out his last hand at the Vaudeville.

Just a few days before he was gunned down at the Vaudeville, Thompson may have had a premonition about his death. He had received a special invitation from Joseph C. Foster of San Antonio to come and visit the Vaudeville. The bearer of the invitation found Thompson in his usual Austin haunt, the Iron Front, but was promptly brushed off with this remonstrance: "They do not catch me in that trap. I know if I were to go into that place it would be my grave yard." Nobody thought much about it until later, on the day of Thompson's funeral (March 13), when his fateful words were widely reported by the *Austin Statesman*. "Notwithstanding, he went, and his own prophecy proved literally true," said the newspaper.[60]

Reaction to Thompson's death was mixed, with some claiming the city could breathe easier now that a killer no longer walked the streets, while others mourned his death because he had over the years supported numerous widows and orphans and shown himself a valuable friend to many men. There was also his record as city marshal to consider. During his tenure in that office he had held crime to an all-time low in the city. Although his unofficial "rap sheet" offered little to be proud of, he had provided much good copy for the public press, having often served as the favorite whipping boy for the *Statesman*. In a posthumous editorial entitled "Judgment," the newspaper offered a highly equivocal eulogy, admitting that, although his killing would "bring sorrow to many a breast," the officers of law and order as well as peaceful citizens who hate "blood and disorder" would feel a sense of relief more than sorrow. The "quiet people in the city," who had for years "dreaded the evil genius of Ben Thompson," may have pitied the man but "will weep not that he is at last deprived of the power to kill and to terrorize Austin, as he has done for many years."[61]

History has been a little kinder to Ben Thompson. He is remembered as one of the most fascinating gambler-gunfighters of the Old West and a man who, during his day, was considered one of the leading members of the state's exclusive sporting fraternity.

Thompson's life provides a case study in the exciting yet ultimately tragic life of the gambler-gunfighter, a type whose natural habitat was the saloon. His contemporary and earliest biographer, William Martin Walton, described the life of the professional gambler as more of an addiction than a vocation, using Thompson's life as an example. "The Famous Texan," as Walton dubbed him, began his career as a gambler "promptly" and with some success had continued it, making just one "notable effort to change the current of his life and engage in other pursuits." But the circumstances were not "propitious," and Thompson quickly fell back onto his old habits. Thus it was "doubly confirmed, that the wild[,] dangerous, enchanting, bitter, adventurous, blissful, damned career of a gambler was his lot." [62]

During his tenure as manager of the gambling concession over the Iron Front, Thompson seems to have had only a single partner, John A. Loraine, a man who is otherwise a cipher in the city's history. Loraine also happens to be one of the most obscure of Thompson's associates, one of those itinerant gamblers who left virtually no paper trail. In 1877 he boarded over 710 Congress Avenue. Three years later he was a business partner with Ben Thompson in the Iron Front. Even being a gambling associate (friend?) of Ben Thompson, however, could not save Loraine from the latter's drunken wrath on occasion. Wednesday night, April 21, 1880, was one of those nights when Thompson had indulged himself in one of his favorite libations and gone looking for trouble. Perhaps he was celebrating San Jacinto Day, the date of the historic victory over Santa Anna's Mexican army in 1836 that marked the victorious end of the Texas War for Independence. What followed was the only remembered instance of gunplay inside the Iron Front during all its years of operation. Two versions of the event have come down to us, one by Thompson's worshipful biographer, William Walton, and the other by the highly critical *Austin Statesman*.

Both agree that it began with a drunken Ben Thompson. Feeling the effects of too much champagne and "consequently in humor to catch fun on the wing," he and a friend named Bill Johnson decided to visit the Iron Front gambling rooms. Johnson was another one of those "reckless, brave, open-hearted, loud-talking, generous gamblers" who was so beloved of Western mythmakers for the broad swath they cut through Western history. He and Thompson were two of a kind. At the time of their visit, according to Walton, Loraine was sitting at one of the tables dealing faro. Walton says the two men had already had some sort of falling out so that they "were not exactly in good humor with one another, Ben deeming himself the aggrieved." Thompson got it in his head that his partner was running a less-than-square game as he watched one after another players drop out due to their heavy losses. He decided to correct the situation the only way he knew how—with his revolver.

Bill Johnson had expected some type of trouble from his friend and sought to head it off at the pass by searching him for weapons. Finding none, he went off to another room, leaving Thompson to work himself up into a towering rage. No sooner had Johnson stepped out than he heard the unmistakable crack of a pistol that Thompson had somehow produced either out of thin air or some secret hiding place. He fired into the stack of chips, scattering them in every direction, and also shot up the dealer's box. Then, still not satisfied, he fired a shot or two into the chandelier, breaking it into many pieces. Loraine remained unruffled, either hoping Thompson would confine his shooting to inanimate objects or knowing that Thompson would not intentionally shoot his business partner. When Johnson rushed back into the room demanding to know what had happened, Thompson replied, "I don't think that set of tools is altogether honest, and I want to help Mr. Loraine buy another." He then turned to Loraine and said, "You can buy another set of tools and charge them to me; I don't like the ones you had."

Thompson was not finished for the night however. Here, the newspaper picks up the story. The inebriated gambler moved to the keno rooms and continued to fire indiscriminately, using a "festive little pistol." One of his targets was the poor "goose" as the device is called where the numbered balls are kept until released by the keno dealer. He "knocked the goose off her roost," then began looking about for new targets, finding one in Bob Holman, whom he "assaulted" but did not shoot. With Thompson shooting up his own establishment, the gamblers "suddenly remembered it was time to go home, and got out of that keno room in short order."

According to the *Statesman,* Thompson was apparently satisfied and wandered out to rejoin the celebration in the streets. He joined members of the Austin fire department in their celebrations, but before long one of the city's police officers came and told him that complaints had been made against him. Thompson promised he would settle up by paying the fines but otherwise continued his partying. Perhaps he felt since it was his own place that he had shot up, he could not be in that much trouble.

But Ben Thompson was never one to do things in small measure; he preferred the grand gesture and the loud statement. He returned to the scene of the crime and continued his assault on the gambling operation, focusing his special attentions on the keno room. Apparently, after Thompson had left the first time, most of the sports had drifted back in to resume their games. Big mistake. When Thompson returned to the upstairs rooms and found keno going "full blast" again, he vowed to wipe it out "if it took all summer." At the sight of Ben with pistol in hand again, the sports hightailed it for the exits one more time. Both the *Statesman* and Walton agree that one particular young man stood out from the fast disappearing crowd by dint of his extraordinary path of egress. He went out the window and "glided down the awning post" in front of the saloon, "[doing] it up brown" before landing in the water tank. At this point, Thompson considered his evening's work done and departed the premises for the last time. Fortunately, no one had suffered any physical injuries in this escapade, proving that Thompson was either the best shot in the West or the worst. The *Statesman* suggests that Thompson was lucky he was not arrested for murder or at least attempted murder. During the course of his second rampage, he aimed his pistol at Isaac S. Simon, owner of the Imperial Restaurant, and fired a shot. If another customer, cited only as "Mr. Hines," had not knocked Thompson's arm up in the air just as he fired, the shot might well have struck Hines, or some other innocent bystander. Instead, the only fatality that night was the keno "goose." [63]

Complaints were indeed made against Thompson. The two most serious ones were sworn out in county court before Judge J. T. W. Lee: one

charged him with assaulting Holman, the other with "assaulting with intent to kill I[saac] S. Simon." Four additional complaints were filed
against him by irate patrons in the mayor's court. The *Statesman* observed somewhat glibly that taken altogether, the "cheerful Ben succeeded admirably in getting himself into a fix that is likely to give him
much trouble."[64]

However, what started out looking like "much trouble" soon blew
over as all the principals evinced a willingness to settle things out of
court. By December, 1880, all was forgiven if not entirely forgotten
when the voters trooped to the polls to elect Ben Thompson city marshal on his third run (counting the special election) for the post. On December 27, he assumed possession of the office, although he continued
to maintain his unofficial headquarters at the Iron Front.[65]

While the *Statesman* supported his latest run for office, it had evinced
a strangely ambivalent attitude toward the San Jacinto Day "hoorah"
back in April when it occurred. It was less critical of the man who had
shot up the Iron Front than of the police officers who had been called to
the scene to quell the disturbance! In the days that followed, the newspaper shrugged off the incident itself as relatively harmless while using
it as an opportunity to condemn the lack of moral courage of the Austin
police department. The *Statesman* said that Thompson, "single-handed
and alone," had accomplished what the city authorities had so long
failed to do, which was to shut down the gambling operations at the Iron
Front. As the newspaper reported things, Thompson, his "conscience,
apparently becoming quickened," had determined that his own keno
operation should be demolished. What followed was an exceedingly
perfunctory account of the events by a reporter who proceeded to use
the rest of the space to launch into a diatribe against gambling. He was
happy the place had been destroyed, he said. He expressed gladness for
the mothers and fathers of all the young men who nightly spent their
hard earned money on the game, and for the wives and children of the
husbands who spent money that should rightfully go to feed and clothe
their children. "[We are] glad that the game so enticing, yet so ruinous
and demoralizing, has been abolished."

Turning to the man who single-handedly destroyed the gambling
rooms of the Iron Front, the reporter paradoxically condemned Ben

Thompson's behavior, calling it "inexcusable," on the grounds that the rights of property were as sacred as those of human life. This was a very mixed message, but the reporter pursued it to its questionable conclusion: If the authorities were willing "to permit the establishment to be run in open defiance of law," then the Iron Front's owners had a right to expect protection from such "lawless assault and wanton destruction."[66] The logic of praising the destruction of the gambling operation while condemning the destroyer must have left some readers scratching their heads in puzzlement.

Whether or not Ben Thompson had the entire Austin police force bulldozed, as the *Statesman* charged, it is certainly true that the city's finest gave him *and* his gambling operation a wide berth. No officer seemed willing to beard the lion in his lair by arresting either Thompson or his customers while they were going about their business. Whether the police force were indeed a bunch of "craven cowards" or merely observing the usual accord between gamblers and law enforcement officials that was standard operating procedure all over the West is something that cannot be judged here. In any event the *Statesman* had its own opinion, which was expressed in an 1880 editorial where it suggested that there were "brave and true" members of the city force who would arrest Thompson like he was a "petty offender from the country" were they only given the chance.[67]

The relationship between police and gamblers was sometimes more than just a working alliance; sometimes it was a blood relationship, and a complicated one at that. Respected Austin policeman James M. Simms was the father of notorious sport William H. "Billy" Simms. When Thompson ran the younger Simms out of Austin for operating a crooked keno game, Billy landed in San Antonio where he went into partnership with Jack Harris at the Vaudeville Saloon. Another Simms son, James M., Jr., also preferred to make a living with the cards rather than a badge and was killed in a quarrel over a game in one of Austin's gambling halls (not the Iron Front) on March 10, 1880. His opponent in that card game, and the man who shot him, was Blanco County constable "Frenchy" Shubert.[68] Ben Thompson was hardly the first man to discover the natural symbiosis between gambling and law enforcement.

Further evidence supporting the charge that a cozy relationship existed between Austin's police and gamblers came up in the aftermath of the San Jacinto Day affair. Officer Sublett, who filed the original complaints against Thompson on the night of April 21, was pressured to withdraw them. The reason given publicly was that Thompson had settled his difficulties with Holman and Simon, thus removing the need for further legal action. Officer Sublett, however, refused to go along with sweeping everything under the carpet, and to its credit, the city supported him. Commenting on this latest turn in affairs, the *Statesman* said, "If the complaints in question [i.e., Holman's and Simon's] were not based upon facts, and if the officer had reasons to believe that his information was inaccurate he had no business making the complaints in the first place." Conversely, if he made his complaints in good faith, then they should be resolved in a court of law. The city authorities refused to permit the complaints to be withdrawn, and as the *Statesman* reported, "Ben will have to answer." [69]

But Ben did not have to answer, and the reasons are not hard to deduce. Breaking up the games caused only a temporary halt in business and represented only a momentary inconvenience for the players and dealers involved. That same night, after Ben's first rampage through the gambling rooms, most of the patrons were back at the tables almost as soon as the gunfire stopped and the smoke cleared. Indeed, it was the persistence of the keno players that had provoked Ben's second rampage. Everybody seemed to agree that Ben Thompson ran the best games in town, and the quicker things could get back to normal, the better as far as most of his patrons were concerned. As long as no one was really hurt and the damage was to the gambling manager's own premises, where was the harm?

Gunplay aside, over the years, the Iron Front saw its share of violent and criminal activity. Fists and knives were the usual weapons when violence broke out, gambling disagreements were often the provocation, and liquor usually fueled it. On December 23, 1880, a customer named Henry Handly, an auctioneer by trade "supposed to be from the rural districts," got into a row with John Robinson, one of the porters. Sharp words from Handly were quickly followed up by a "still sharper knife" and Handly "made demonstration as if he intended to carve up Jim after the most approved style in vogue in the Cannibal Islands." Officer

Patrick Conly was sent for and took Handly into custody. The next day in mayor's court the now penitent auctioneer was fined five dollars for "committing a nuisance," and since he could not pay it, he was sentenced to "work it out." [70]

Sometimes the violence spilled over outside the saloon to become bloody "street theater" that attracted sizable crowds. On November 25, 1880, there was a "disgraceful row on the Avenue" just in front of the Iron Front. Policemen soon arrived on the scene and separated the "warlike persons," but this did not end it. One of the pair began cursing the officers while the other one defied them to arrest him. The three officers present, Chenneville, Simms, and Conly, quelled the disturbance and cleared the sidewalk, but their tough method of handling things got them "severely condemned" by the crowd who had gathered.[71] Such affairs, inside or outside the saloon, were bad for the public image of the place, providing fresh ammunition for those who called for a crackdown.

On two occasions, the Iron Front itself was the "victim" of the crime. In the early morning hours of November 5, 1881, a man was caught trying to steal a box of cigars. He was arrested by Officer L. C. Look and deposited in the city jail. He gave his name as Charles A. Smith, and from other remarks he made it was suspected that "Smith" had a confederate in crime. Marshal Thompson sent an officer to pull in a second shady character off the street. It turned out the two men were wanted for a recent robbery in Hearne, Texas, and "Smith's" real name was Morgan. Thompson and the Austin police were praised for their quick action and sharp detective work, at least until it came out that they had gotten their information out of Morgan by using a little old-fashioned "third-degree" methods, or as the *Statesman* put it, "a little judicious [lead?] 'piping' secured the truth." [72]

On December 28, 1883, the Iron Front was again the target of criminals, who burglarized the place and got away with an undisclosed amount of money. The efficient Austin police force swung into action again and within two weeks Officer John Chenneville had identified two suspects and taken them into custody. As it turned out they had not only burglarized the Iron Front but another Austin saloon, the Black Elephant, as well. Everyone agreed, it had taken "a skillful piece of detective work" to solve the case.[73]

For most of its history, the Iron Front enjoyed a cozy relationship not just with the local authorities but also with the *Statesman*. Both the police and the newspaper were essential allies if the saloon's owners hoped to keep up a good public image. The *Statesman* carried news about the Iron Front regularly in its pages and for the most part the reports were positive: management was praised, gambling represented business as usual, and the occasional violence was treated waggishly. Even the vile-tempered Ben Thompson received kid-glove treatment, perhaps because he had once worked as a typesetter for a newspaper in his youth; more likely, they feared his legendary wrath. Founded in the early 1870s when the Iron Front was just reaching its stride, the *Statesman* gave more type space to this one saloon than to all of its competitors combined. They also supported Ben Thompson's two runs for city marshal with fulsome praise for the candidate. That praise may have set new standards for partisanship on November 6, 1881, when the newspaper carried the following one-liners in boldface type:

"Everything has been quiet for a year past and will continue also if Ben Thompson is re-elected city marshal."
"The best people in Austin elected Ben Thompson city marshal, and they will do it again on Monday." [74]

The newspaper even carried such prosaic items as the report that a gold watch, valued at $150, was raffled off at the saloon on Saturday, January 12, 1884, and was "won by Bill Phillips for John E. Williams." [75]

When he was proprietor, John Neff made it a special point to keep his bridges mended with the members of the Fourth Estate. One way to do that was to include the editor and staff of the *Statesman* in special holiday festivities. As 1882 wound down, he invited editor John Cardwell and reporters Wing, Scott, and Gaines to help "smile out the old year and grin in the new" at the Iron Front. Cardwell declined regretfully explaining that because he had resolved to quit drinking, "the kind invitation could not be accepted at that time." Because true sports never passed up a chance to wager on anything, no matter how trivial, it was reported that "swear-off bets" on how long the editor could hold out were heavy. But that did not keep the other three from RSVPing in the positive.[76]

The Iron Front's famous hospitality, of course, did not extend to women or people of color. In 1881, when the *Statesman* crowned the Iron Front "the chief place of entertainment in the city," it was only for the white, male population of Austin. The pointed snub of women and blacks in particular did not need to be explained; it was understood as one of the social conventions of the day. The only "coloreds" allowed in the front door were the porters who stood ready to lend a hand with the heavy lifting or keep out the riff-raff as the situation demanded. The city's African American population was not even welcome to stand *outside* the saloon on the public street. In January, 1883, the *Statesman* sniffed that "[o]n the northeast corner of the Avenue and Pecan [Sixth] street there is generally a crowd of negroes and others who seem to have no occupation except to blockade the walk and make it impossible for people, especially ladies, to pass without elbowing through the mob." The newspaper's recommendation: "It should be broken up." [77] Eighteen months later, Police Officer Howe ordered a "colored woman" to "leave a crowd of blacks" on Congress Avenue, presumably because she was breaking the peace. Howe was white. When she resisted, a public row resulted that was blamed entirely on the African Americans. [78]

As for the women of Austin, no self-respecting lady would have ventured into the Iron Front for a drink, much less sought to invade the male preserve of the gambling fraternity upstairs. If there were any women in the Iron Front, they were performing on stage for the benefit of the male clientele.

Over the years, the Iron Front was more than just a drinking and gambling emporium. It was one of the city's principal meeting halls when public decisions were to be made. Its spacious interior, well-stocked bar, and familiarity made it a natural for political gatherings. On July 13, 1880, members of the Greenback Party and conservative Republicans met together at 605 Congress Avenue. The two groups had to try to work together to oppose the state's entrenched Democratic Party. According to the *Statesman*, the "disconsolate Greenpublicans and the gaseous Stalwartbacks had a real love feast over at the Iron Front Saloon." But the newspaper had to settle for second-hand accounts because the attendees at the meeting refused the reporter admittance; he was "not permitted to even poke his nose into the room." That fact, however, did not prevent the newspaper from reporting that there was a great deal of "weeping and clinging to necks after which a collection was taken up and the brethren purchased a mug of beer and wet their whistles, and tried to look happy and couldn't, and taking a parting weep and embrace mournfully dispersed." [79]

Despite the importance of the public saloon to the frontier community and in particular of the Iron Front to the community of Austin, there were still vociferous critics of the saloon business. The antisaloon movement and the antigamblers found common cause and a big, fat target in the Iron Front. Prohibitionists, as opposed to temperance advocates, believed that "a sober America was attainable only under laws that declared illegal the manufacture and sale of liquor." As early as 1843 laws were on the books dealing with liquor, and in 1845 a law was passed by the state legislature banning saloons altogether, but it was never enforced and it was repealed in 1856. The United Friends of Temperance organized in Texas around 1870, and by 1883 a state branch of the Women's Christian Temperance Union was operating. Three years later the Prohibition Party offered candidates for office, and by 1895 fifty-three of 239 counties in the state were dry.[80]

In Austin, the *Statesman* was much harder on gambling than on drinking, and the most despicable form of gambling was deemed to be keno. Towards the end of 1881 the newspaper took a public stand against this very popular game. "The keno boys are doing a rattling business and scoop in no end of ducats. The business should be squelched." [81] This was relatively mild compared to what they were soon saying. The game was called "a snare and delusion" for the city's young men.

No doubt about it, keno made a convenient target for reformers. Although frequently compared to the harmless game of bingo, the similarities are more superficial than real. In bingo the game continues until there is a winner. There was not necessarily a winner in keno. The player chose whatever numbers he wished between 1 and 80 and placed his bet(s). The conductor of the game, or "roller" as he was called, controlled the "goose" holding the numbered balls by means of a lever. If the player's numbers matched those thrown from the goose then that player won. The amount won depended on how much the player had bet and how many others had chosen the same number. Although there were winners in keno to be sure, the odds were definitely in favor of the house. The *Statesman* sarcastically headlined one editorial, "Innocent Keno," and stated that if there was "a game of chance on earth that ought to be throttled by the officers of the law and forever [closed]" it was the game of keno. The game was "most disastrous to the effects [*sic*] upon young men and the poor laboring classes of the large cities." Whether Austin fit into the latter category is debatable, but as the newspaper noted, the game flourished in Austin "right under the noses of the officers of the law."

So popular was keno in the state capital that the rooms devoted to it were thronged with old and young alike who were "scooped without stint and relieved of their small earnings." The patrons of keno were, "as a clan . . . poor men who cannot afford to indulge in the ordinary games conducted by the gambling fraternity." Working men and young clerks who frequented the keno rooms on a Saturday night typically lost all, or nearly all, of their week's earnings. Worse, many of the laboring men had families who suffered "for the necessities of life, their earnings having been raked into the capacious craw of the 'keno goose.'"

And why was the game worse than any other? "Keno is a one-sided game," the newspaper explained, "entirely destitute of the favorable chances of winning common to other banking games, and not one man in ten thousand ever leaves the keno table a winner of any considerable sum of money." The *Statesman* pulled out all the stops in making its case against keno:

> There is no excuse for permitting keno to run in this or any other city, and it is the duty of the officers to close the rooms. They know where they are, and they know who patronizes them. It is their duty to attend to this matter, for many young men in this city, allured by the attractiveness of the game, are gradually being drawn into its vortex, from which, if they escape at all, it will be with marred reputations and as outcasts from respectable, decent society. The keno rooms . . . should be closed.[82]

An official campaign to wipe out saloons and their attendant evils began in late 1881 but made little headway against the Forces of Darkness. It was not that the authorities lacked the necessary legal weapons; the laws were on the books, including one city ordinance specifically prohibiting the display of any gaming table as well as "betting, winning or losing any money, property or other valuable, at any game of chance."

Plain wording like that left no room for misunderstanding, or so it would seem. Another ordinance prohibited the carrying of handguns within city limits, and that, too, was widely flouted.[83] The problem was not in the law but in the law enforcement. The police only selectively enforced the laws and courts refused to convict influential and well-connected perpetrators; meanwhile, ordinary citizens shrugged at blatant examples of law-breaking. The result, according to the *Statesman*, was that Austin had "a reputation for lawlessness not only in Texas but throughout the nation," a statement that surely went a little overboard but nonetheless indicated the seriousness of the problem.[84]

The lack of commitment to serious law enforcement was reflected in the size of the city's police force. After midnight only three men were typically on duty, and sometimes only one was available to patrol and answer calls because the others were sick or otherwise absent from the posts.

By the summer of 1882, nothing had changed. The gaming rooms of the city were still being "run with doors wide open and no effort at concealment." As the *Statesman* pointed out, "The officers know this and yet do not do their duty under the law."[85] Prostitutes continued to ply their trade openly, and the young men of Austin "habitually carry deadly weapons" as always. The newspaper pointed to an unnamed saloon visited by one of its reporters on the night of July 30 where "no less than eight pocket pistols were exhibited."[86]

The *Statesman* at least was ready to do its part, perhaps in the hope of shaming the authorities into action. The newspaper threatened to print the names of all "so-called respectable" men caught in the company of prostitutes. The fact that this violated any one of several constitutional protections against guilt by association, innocent until proven guilty, etc., did not seem to have been an issue.[87]

All this crusading zeal had the least effect on genteel, well-connected establishments like the Iron Front, which seemed to operate under a different set of laws than those applied to workingmen's joints and soiled doves on the streets. That was the way things had always been, but those days were coming to an end. What men like John B. Neff and H. H. Duff did not realize was that great changes were in the winds. The saloon as a social center of urban life had seen its heyday by the end of the century. Frances Taylor Love lived in Austin during those years and recalled the city at the turn-of-the-century as glittering "with some of Texas' most fabulous characters." Yet even with cattle barons such as George Littlefield erecting "gaudy Victorian architectural monuments for homes" and such cultured individuals as author O. Henry and artist Elizabet Ney making the city "interesting," there was still the fact that "ladies" never strolled along the east side of Congress Avenue because of the "insults that hurled from saloon row." [88] The difference between this time and twenty years earlier was that now the public outrage was being listened to at city hall, and the level of tolerance was far lower than in former days.

One of a new breed of reformers determined to change things was City Attorney Dudley Goodall Wooten, who began practicing law in Austin in 1880 and vigorously prosecuted the city's bad guys for most of the decade. By mid-1884 he was making some inroads into the gambling problem, prompting the *Statesman* to commend him for his efforts.[89]

One of Wooten's early victories in the war on gamblers came against Richard Herndon, who was arrested for wagering on pool, an extremely minor violation of the antigambling ordinance. Nonetheless, he was charged with violating the law and scheduled for trial. Herndon demanded a jury trial in hopes of getting a sympathetic jury of his peers, but after hearing Wooten present the evidence against him he settled for a guilty plea and a twenty-five dollar fine plus court costs. This was the highest penalty permissible under the law. What was more important, it was the first case brought to trial since the antigambling crusade had begun, and it was "so strongly contested." Ironically Herndon was not a "bad actor" or even a sporting type but a young man who had come to Austin to enter law school at the state university! His conviction was hardly a signal victory by the forces of law and order since he was the smallest of the small fish. But County Attorney Wooten had made an example of him and, according to the *Statesman*, was "making an unflinching fight on gambling" backed by "the best sentiment of this community." [90]

But Wooten's efforts were not as significant as the *Statesman* made them out to be. Before long the newspaper found other crusades, and the citizens of Austin went on with more pressing concerns. It took far

Looking east on Congress Avenue from Sixth Street, ca. 1908. The Iron Front is just two years away from being demolished and becoming "history." The streets are paved with bricks, and the visible pedestrians are society ladies and white-shirted businessmen rather than cowboys and bawds. Another sign of progress: streetcars and horseless carriages have largely replaced four-footed transportation. Streetlights and crosswalks are still in the future. Courtesy *Austin History Center Association, Austin, Texas*

bigger forces to bring down the curtain on Austin's saloon avenue. Changing times rather than a single hero were responsible for the new moral climate. However, the years when the second floor of so many buildings along Congress Avenue were gambling rooms were clearly numbered by the time Dudley Wooten left town. Soon, there would no longer be a need for hitching rails, trolley tracks would replace hoof prints on the Avenue, and other business interests would move in to replace the saloons and gambling establishments that first defined the street. The most significant change came when cattle-king George W. Littlefield began looking for a site on which to establish his new bank. Littlefield's decision to erect the American National Bank on the corner of Sixth Street and Congress Avenue punctuated the end of the era for the Iron Front and places like it.

When the grand old Iron Front closed its doors for the last time in 1910, proprietor Thomas Martin either understood the modern concept of "brand-name recognition" or maybe he had a genuine sense of his-

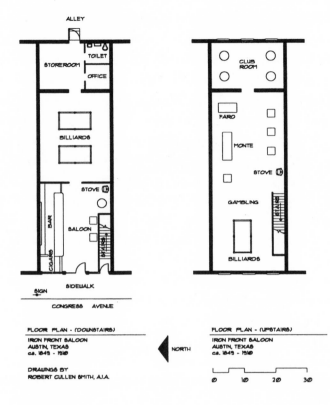

ALLEY

STOREROOM

TOILET

OFFICE

BILLIARDS

STOVE

BAR

CIGARS

SALOON

SIGN   SIDEWALK

CONGRESS   AVENUE

CLUB ROOM

FARO

MONTE

STOVE

GAMBLING

STAIRS

BILLIARDS

FLOOR PLAN - (DOWNSTAIRS)

IRON FRONT SALOON
AUSTIN, TEXAS
ca. 1849 - 1910

DRAWINGS BY
ROBERT CULLEN SMITH, A.I.A.

NORTH

FLOOR PLAN - (UPSTAIRS)

IRON FRONT SALOON
AUSTIN, TEXAS
ca. 1849 - 1910

0   10   20   30

tory. Whichever the case, he refused to retire the legendary name, instead taking it with him when he moved around the corner to 106 West Sixth and opened a new, considerably more modest place under the "Iron Front" moniker. But longtime customers were not fooled, and the "new" Iron Front never measured up to the name as a premier drinking emporium.[91]

The original Iron Front lived on in local lore and in the form of countless saloon tokens handed out by John Neff and Thomas Martin to their customers over the years. Those tokens were not the usual cheap bar tokens of brass or pot metal; they were genuine silver, reflecting the pedigree of the saloon itself. They were squirreled away as mementos by former customers until eventually they became valuable collectors' items, bought and sold like rare coins today.

With the destruction of the corner buildings at Sixth and Congress to make way for the American National Bank, the ghosts of the old Iron Front came forth to remind Austinites of their wild and woolly past. Besides the discovery of the "secret" stairway on January 15, workmen engaged in the demolition discovered a skull imbedded in the walls. It had evidently been there a great many years and was believed to be the skull of an Indian, "a good Indian now, no matter what he was when alive," commented the *Statesman*. Close examination by expert or experts unknown determined it to be a Native American skull based on the shape, the even teeth, "and other indications of a savage nature." No trace was ever found of the rest of the mysterious Indian who belonged to the disembodied skull. The most likely explanation was that an Iron Front customer had brought it in following a violent encounter that the Indian got the worst of. Some old-timers recalled that it had been kept for a while on a pole in front of the saloon, "to warn other Redskins what would be their fate if they were not good, and then imbedded in the wall at some time when the buildings were being remodeled." [92] With modern racial sensibilities considerably different from the old days, and with no threatening "Redskins" to warn off in 1910, the skull was at long last given a decent burial, and that chapter of the Iron Front's history was closed.

And when George Littlefield died in 1920 he received a much more respectful send-off than the poor, unknown Indian. Littlefield was buried in Austin's Oakwood Cemetery, the final resting place for such other Iron Front notables as Benjamin Thompson, John B. Neff, Phillip W. Jobe, policeman James M. Simms, Sr., and police captain Edward Creary. All at one time or another had played a key role in creating the legend of Austin's most famous watering hole.

NOTES

1. Most of the east-west streets in Austin were once named after trees. Then between 1886 and 1887 and 1889 and 1890 the city decided to change them to numbered streets so that firemen, policemen, and others on official business could more easily find a given public road. Thus, Pecan Street became Sixth after the first phase of renamings.

2. David B. Gracy II, "George Washington Littlefield," *The New Handbook of Texas*, ed. by Ron Tyler et al., vol. 4 (Austin: Texas State Historical Assoc., 1996), 230–31.

3. The *Austin Daily Statesman*, "Historic Buildings," July 5, 1909. (Hereafter, the *Austin Daily Statesman*, the *Austin Democratic Statesman*, and the *Daily Democratic Statesman* will all be abbreviated as *Statesman*.)

4. William M. Walton, *Life and Adventures of Ben Thompson The Famous Texan* (Austin: The Steck Co., 1956; facsimile of 1884 edition, privately printed by Edwards and Church of Austin), 8.

5. "Historic Buildings," *Statesman*, July 5, 1909; "Texas Volunteer Units in the Mexican War 1846–1848," *Austin Genealogical Society*, vol. 21, no. 3, part 7, 97.

6. "Historic Buildings," *Statesman*, July 5, 1909.

7. Ibid.

8. Census of Travis County, Texas, enumerated June [?], 1870, 272.

9. Census of Travis County, Texas, enumerated June 1, 1880, 278.

10. David C. Humphrey, *Austin: An Illustrated History* (Northridge, Calif.: Windsor Publications, 1985), 114. *General Directory of the City of Austin, 1891–92* (Galveston, Tex.: Morrison and Fourny), 197.

11. *Mercantile and General City Directory of Austin, Texas, 1872–1873* (Austin: Gray and Moore, 1872), 65. Census of Travis County, Texas, enumerated June [?], 1870, 283.

12. "Historic Buildings," *Statesman*, July 5, 1909.

13. Robert K. DeArment, *Knights of the Green Cloth: The Saga of the Frontier Gamblers* (Norman: University of Oklahoma Press, 1982), 4.

14. Walton, *Life and Adventures of Ben Thompson*, 19.

15. David C. Humphrey, "Prostitution and Public Policy in Austin, Texas, 1870–1915," *Southwestern Historical Quarterly*, 86, no. 4 (Apr., 1983): 473–516.

16. John Fisher, "Where Grand[d]ad Wasted His Youth," *Free and Easy Magazine* 2, no. 3 (July 15–Aug. 15, 1975): 7.

17. *Statesman*, Mar. 25, 1884.

18. Ibid., May 21, 1876.

19. Ibid., Aug. 24, 1884.

20. Ibid.

21. Milton Morris, *Official Record, Austin City Council Proceedings, 1885–88*, vol. 2, no. 3 (Jan. 11 and 25, 1886), Austin History Center, Austin Public Library.

22. "Disreputable," *Statesman*, Aug. 1, 1882.

23. *Sanborn Fire Insurance Maps* for Austin, Texas, were prepared in 1877, 1885, and 1889. Although extremely useful, the maps reveal practically nothing of interior details. Originals and microfilm copies of all three editions of the maps are in the Center for American History, University of Texas at Austin.

24. Roxanne Williamson, *Austin, Texas: An American Architectural History* (San Antonio, Tex.: Trinity University Press, 1973), 54.

25. Personal correspondence with Jens Kiecksee, June 13, 1997, in this author's files.

26. Austin Board of Trade, *The Industrial Advantages of Austin, Texas or Austin Up to Date. Compiled Under the Auspices of the Austin Board of Trade* (Austin: Akehurst Publishing Co., 1894), 85.

27. *Statesman*, Jan. 26, 1879.

28. Humphrey, *Austin: An Illustrated History*, 114.

29. *Statesman*, Aug. 13, 1882.

30. Ibid., July 10, 1883.

31. Ibid.

32. "Ben Thompson Wins A Tombstone," *Frontier Times* 2, no. 6 (Mar., 1925): 1–3. (Reprinted from *Houston Chronicle*, Dec. 21, 1924.)

33. "The Iron Front," *Statesman*, Aug. 13, 1882.

34. "The Steer Roping," *Statesman*, Oct. 20, 1882. For "John Neff's Iron Front," see *Statesman*, Jan. 3 and 20, 1883.

35. *Statesman*, July 4, 1884.

36. Ibid.

37. Ibid., Jan. 3, 1880.

38. Ibid., Jan. 16, 1880.

39. Ibid., Jan. 20, 1883.

40. *Record of Arrests Made by the Police Force, City of Austin*, vol. from Jan. 1, 1876–Jan. 1, 1879. Original in the Austin History Center, Austin Public Library. Compare Duff's reputation as a (genial and gentlemanly) businessman, as reported in the *Statesman*, July 4, 1884.

41. Austin Board of Trade, *The Industrial Advantages of Austin*, 85.

42. "Mr. John Neff," *Statesman*, Feb. 11, 1896.

43. *Morrison and Fourny's General Directory of the City of Austin, 1898–99* (Galveston, Tex.: Morrison and Fourny, 1898), 313; *Morrison and Fourny's General Directory of the City of Austin, 1900* (Galveston, Tex.: Morrison and Fourny, 1900), 203; *1905–06 City Directory of Austin with Street Directory of Residents* (Austin: J. B. Stephenson, 1905), 163; *1905–06 City Directory*, 244.

44. *1905–06 City Directory*, 244; *1906–07 City Directory of Austin with Street Directory* (Austin: J. B. Stephenson, 1907), 175.

45. "Historic Buildings," *Statesman*, July 5, 1909.

46. When describing the destruction of the building in 1909, the *Austin Statesman* mentions several noted outlaws of the day, "such as Ben Thompson, Henry Younger, Bob Younger, Wesley Hardin and others" who reputedly patronized the Iron Front but without giving any specifics or providing any creditable sources. The inclusion here of Henry Younger, undistinguished father of the more famous outlaw brothers, suggests that this list is pure journalese since the Younger sire was never known to have set foot in Texas. See "Historic Buildings," *Statesman*, July 5, 1909.

47. "Historic Buildings," *Statesman*, July 5, 1909. For Hardin's reputation as "the greatest killer of them all," see Richard Maxwell Brown's entry in Howard R. Lamar, ed., *The Reader's Encyclopedia of the American West* (New York: Thomas Y. Crowell, 1977), 483–85. John Wesley Hardin, *The Life of John Wesley Hardin as Written by Himself* (1896; reprint, Norman: University of Oklahoma Press, 1961).

48. Authoritative opinion on possible visit(s) by the Youngers to Austin comes from author's correspondence with Western historian Marley Brant of Marietta, Georgia, April 16, 1997, in this author's files.

49. "A Sketch of the Career of Thompson Who Met His Death in San Antonio," *Statesman*, Mar. 13, 1884.

50. Ibid.

51. Lafayette Rogers, quoted in Patrick Cox, "Thompson, Ben," *The New Handbook of Texas*, vol. 6, 468–69.

52. During his long career in public office, Edward Creary served at various times as city marshal, police chief, and street commissioner of Austin, sheriff of Travis County, and sergeant-at-arms of the Twelfth Legislature of Texas. Being born in 1840 he was old enough to have received the rank of "Captain" in the Civil War, but whether it was fairly earned or bestowed as an honor at some point is unknown.

53. For "formidable competitor," see *Statesman*, Oct. 2, 1879. For 1879 vote totals, see *Statesman*, Nov. 4, 1879. For 1881 vote totals, see *Statesman*, Nov. 8, 1881.

54. "Historic Buildings," *Statesman*, July 5, 1909.

55. The most complete accounting of this strange poker game appeared in the *Houston Chronicle* in 1924 on the occasion of the *Austin Statesman* and *Austin American* merging into one newspaper. The merger reminded people of John Cardwell, the first editor of the *Statesman*, provoking other memories to flow. One such memory recalled when the Iron Front was being torn down and a tombstone was discovered in the building. Jim Long, a longtime resident of Austin, was interviewed and related what he recalled of the incident. The story that follows is his story. See *Houston Chronicle*, Dec. 21, 1924. Reprinted in "Ben Thompson Wins a Tombstone," *Frontier Times Magazine*, Mar., 1925, vol. 2, no. 6, 1–3.

56. "City marshal reduced crime after killing 32," *Statesman*, June 13, 1980. See also J. M. Owens, "Ceremonies at the restoration of the Austin City Marshal Ben Thompson headstone in Oakwood Cemetery Austin, Texas, June 17th, 1980," in Audrey Bateman, "Waterloo Scrapbook," transcript from recording of program by Mulkey Owens, Travis County Historical Commission (Austin: Austin History Center, Austin Public Library).

57. "Historic Buildings," *Statesman*, July 5, 1909.

58. James B. Gillett, "Ben Thompson and Billy Sim[m]s, *Frontier Times* 12, no. 1 (Oct., 1934): 1–3.

59. "Historic Buildings," *Statesman*, July 5, 1909.

60. For Foster's invitation to Thompson, see *Statesman*, Mar. 13, 1884. For other information on Thompson's funeral, see "Round about Town," *Statesman*, Mar. 13, 1884.

61. "Judgment," *Statesman*, Mar. 13, 1884.

62. Walton, *Life and Adventures of Ben Thompson*, 19.

63. Ibid., 19; "Ben Thompson on Warpath," *Statesman*, Apr. 23, 1880; and "Ben Thompson Kills Keno," *Statesman*, Apr. 25, 1880.

64. "Thompson on Warpath," *Statesman*, Apr. 23, 1880.

65. *Morrison and Fourny's General Directory of the City of Austin, 1881–1882* (Austin: E. W. Swindells, Printer, 1881), 161.

66. Walton, *Life and Adventures of Ben Thompson*, 87, 151. See also *Statesman*, Apr. 25, 1880.

67. Ibid., Apr. 25, 1880.

68. Ibid., Mar. 11, 1880.

69. Ibid., Apr. 24, 1880.

70. Ibid., Dec. 24, 1880. (In the *Statesman* Handly is incorrectly identified as "Hanley.") Compare to "The Record of Arrests Made by the Police Force of Austin, under Supervision of Ed Creary, City Marshal." Arrest Entry No. 9802 shows that on December 24, 1880, Officer Pat Conly arrested H. Handly (occupation, auctioneer). Handly was fined five dollars by the court, which he "worked out."

71. *Statesman*, Nov. 26, 1880.

72. "Thieves Arrested," *Statesman*, Nov. 6, 1881.

73. *Statesman*, Jan. 17, 1884.

74. Ibid., Nov. 6, 1881.

75. Ibid., Jan. 15, 1884.

76. Ibid., Jan. 3, 1883.

77. "City Matters in Brief," *Statesman*, Jan. 16, 1883.

78. *Statesman*, July 17, 1884, 4.

79. Ibid., Aug. 14, 1880.

80. K. Austin Kerr, "Prohibition," in *The New Handbook of Texas*, vol. 5, 355.

81. *Statesman*, Nov. 17, 1881.

82. "Innocent Keno," *Statesman*, Nov. 18, 1881.

83. William G. Thomas, *A Digest of the General Ordinances of the City of Austin* (Austin: Caldwell and Waller, Printers, 1874), 101.

84. *Statesman*, July 17, 1884.

85. Ibid., Aug. 1, 1882.

86. Ibid.

87. "Disreputable," *Statesman*, Aug. 1, 1882.

88. Frances Taylor Love, *My Home Is Austin, Texas* (Lafayette, La.: privately printed, 1958), 66.

89. In 1889, Wooten relocated to Dallas where he was elected county judge and later to the Texas Legislature. He had a long, exemplary career in public service, but he got his start fighting crime in Austin. See "Wooten, Dudley Goodhall," *The Handbook of Texas*, vol. 6, 1074. For "commend," see "Gambling," *Statesman*, Aug. 9, 1884.

90. "Gambling," *Statesman*, Aug. 9, 1884.

91. *Directory of the City of Austin, 1910–1911* (Galveston, Tex.: Morrison and Fourny, 1910), 168.

92. "Old Skull Discovered," *Statesman*, Jan. 16, 1910.

Chapter Five

The White Elephant:
Fort Worth's Saloon *par Excellence*

In 1887 one of the most famous shootouts in all of Western history occurred on Fort Worth's Main Street, just outside the twin frosted-glass
doors of the White Elephant Saloon. The fight between Timothy Isaiah
Courtright and Luke Short was a classic confrontation between a couple
of "hard cases" where neither was willing to back down an inch in protecting what he felt was rightfully his. Courtright, known to history
as "Longhair Jim," was a former city marshal of Fort Worth, self-
proclaimed private detective, and full-time drunk at the time he was
gunned down by Luke Short, a professional gambler, sometime gunman, and pal of the rich and famous.

The Short-Courtright duel put this small-town bar on the map the
same way another deadly gun battle in Tombstone, Arizona, in 1881
transformed an ordinary horse corral into a legend. But the White Elephant was more than just the site of a legendary gunfight. For years it
was the premier restaurant and gambling emporium in North Texas,
perhaps in all of the state. But you would never have predicted this
when it opened for business in 1883.

When the White Elephant first opened its doors, Fort Worth was still
struggling to put its frontier origins behind it. It was only a few years

removed from being a trail town and before that a military outpost. The twin vices of drinking and gambling were still the definition of "Big Business" in town. When the 1880s began, nine churches were fighting it out with more than sixty saloons for customers, and the ratio only grew in favor of the saloons as the decade progressed. The city seemed to be completely given over to drinking and gambling establishments, and they were certainly more prevalent than at any other time in its history.[1]

The saloon as an institution made life on the North Texas frontier more livable and had done so ever since Fort Worth was an army post (1849–53). After the army moved, Ed Terrell took over one of the fort's abandoned buildings and opened up the First and Last Chance Saloon, Fort Worth's first dedicated drinking establishment. It was described as "a small, dingy room with a few shelves . . . a plain bar counter on one side . . . a bench for customers on the other, and a box stove in the center of the room."[2] It might have been a hole-in-the-wall, but it looked like a little piece of heaven-on-earth to thirsty customers. Ed's place enjoyed a local monopoly only until other entrepreneurs could hammer together a shack or throw up a tent and hang out a sign. Frenchman Adolphus Gouhenant (sometimes spelled "Gounah"), who had taught music and language lessons to Maj. Ripley Arnold's children, was one of those who also opened a place on the public square, and the customers who sauntered in were not looking for French lessons.

In the years that followed, the town grew but the number of saloons grew faster, which was to be expected in any town favored by buffalo hunters and cowboys. The favorite joints had names like the Silver Dollar, the Dixie, and the Cotton Boll. A faded picture of Courthouse Square taken in the 1860s shows two saloon signs (the Alamo Sample Room and the Farmer's Saloon) on the south side of the square, sandwiched between a couple of grocery stores and a hardware store. A sign reading "free lunch from 10–12" above the entrance to the Farmer's Saloon represents an early example of the modern advertising arts on the frontier.[3]

It took Hell's Half Acre to put Fort Worth on the map. The "Acre" as it was commonly called, was a wide-open vice district on the south end of town below Eighth Street that transformed Fort Worth from just another trail town into the "Gambler's Mecca" of Texas and a popular stop on the Western "gamblers' circuit" that stretched from the Rocky Mountains through the Plains states all the way to the Gulf coast.[4] Money of the free and easy variety flowed into the town on the rails and in the pockets of the cowboys who drove their herds up the Eastern Trail. Men with a month's wages in their jeans were eager to test their skills against professional gamblers and to try their luck at the roulette wheel and faro table. There was some type of game for every taste, and they all operated right out in the open.[5]

The importance of the saloon to the city's development in these early years can be gauged by three seemingly insignificant things: The home of the federal district court for North Texas during its first six years of existence was Gouhenant's Saloon. Brothers Chris and Gus Rintle-man's Local Option Saloon, at the foot of Main Street when it opened in 1876, was the first brick building south of Courthouse Square. And the town's second telephone line, installed in May, 1880, connected the Club Room Saloon with the offices of the *Fort Worth Democrat* because editor B. B. Paddock believed the saloon to be the most "prolific news source of the period."[6]

The 1880s continued the trend begun in the 1870s of Fort Worth being a wide-open town. The *Democrat-Advance* proclaimed it "the liveliest city in Texas." When C. W. Wilson arrived in town in 1880 as an eleven-year-old boy, "There was a saloon in nearly every block and they did a thriving business."[7]

All of them combined drinking and gambling but they tended to fall into one of two categories: ordinary beer joints and what might be called "full-service establishments." The former dotted the south end of town and were not too choosy about their clientele. The full-service places were mostly on the north end of town and catered to starch-shirted gentlemen. They served a greater variety and a better quality of libations, offered such perks as shoeshines and newspapers, and cleaned out their spittoons more often. They also preferred to be known as "clubs" rather than saloons.

The difference in the two classes of saloons is striking. One scholar has called the Western saloon "the great social leveler" of frontier male society, but they were not all created equal.[8] Lines were drawn between the races, the sexes, ethnic groups, and even social classes. There was a gulf separating places like the White Elephant Saloon in the 300 block of Main from joints like My Office Saloon in the 1100 block—and the distance was measured in more than just city blocks. Fort Worth had a good, representative cross section, from ethnic saloons like the Bismarck and the Black Elephant for ethnic minorities, to humble joints like the Farmer's and Mechanic's Bar or My Option for the working man, to the White Elephant and Cattle Exchange for the high and the mighty.

The name over the front door defined the place and sometimes the clientele. Saloon names all over the West seemed to have been taken from a short list. Certain names, such as the White Elephant, the Oriental, and the Last Chance were repeated in towns large and small. Denison, Texas, had a White Elephant; so did San Antonio, Wichita Falls, El Paso, and Fredericksburg. San Antonio's White Elephant was both a saloon *and* a variety theater, so ornate that a local newspaper reported the citizens were "in ecstasy about its beauty" when it opened in 1883.[9] Even such backwaters as Butte, Montana; Bingham Canyon, Utah; and Eagle City, Idaho, had establishments operating under the sign of the pale pachyderm.[10]

The sheer familiarity of the name, just like with fast food franchises today, was a selling point with thirsty travelers looking for a friendly watering hole, but the exact origins of the "White Elephant" name are elusive. Two possible explanations suggest themselves: "white elephant" was already a well-known term in the nineteenth century to describe a worthless investment—something that required much upkeep and expense while yielding little or no profits, or by the same token, something that the owner could not afford to keep but was unable to sell. In other words, a "White Elephant" of a saloon might have been what we call a "money pit" today.[11]

Another explanation derives from the nineteenth-century expression, "seeing the elephant," which meant to have a life-altering experience, usually in the form of one's first time in combat or some other sort of high adventure. Such an adventure might include a risqué encounter involving wild women and copious amounts of alcohol. Many a callow farm lad "saw the elephant" on his first trip to the big city. One scholar has called "seeing the elephant" a virtual synonym for "raising hell," defining it as a "a siege of carousing and drinking in celebration of reaching trail's end or some similar purpose." Whatever its exact meaning, "seeing the elephant" seems to have originated during the California gold rush and spread from there. In the years that followed, Westerners were more likely to talk about "seeing the elephant" than Easterners, so it was only natural that a frontier saloon incorporate this icon of adventure and excitement in its name.[12]

There are also a number of possible explanations for why it was a *white* elephant and not some other color. A white elephant was a more exotic image than the standard gray variety. For another, it simplified the unpleasant chore of sign painting since whitewash was never hard to come by and getting the right shade was not a problem (consider the challenge facing J. W. Schueber with his Red Lion Saloon). It also sent a clear message to African Americans to stay out, no minor consideration since Fort Worth was a typically race-conscious community in those days. Segregation was strictly enforced on every level of city life, from the all-white police force to the bigoted editorial policies of the leading newspapers. The segregated races were symbolized by the existence of a "Black Elephant Saloon" on the south end of town for African Americans. So hard and fast was the racial line that African Americans were not even allowed in the front door of the White Elephant unless they were shoeshine boys or porters.[13]

At least the choice of the elephant, from among all the creatures of the animal kingdom, was far less offensive than the oversexed bull that advertised the Bull's Head Saloon in Abilene, Kansas. Owners Ben Thompson and Phil Coe ordered their sign painters to depict the bull in all his "full amorous glory" so that anyone passing by on First Street got an eyeful. When some of Abilene's good citizens complained about the sign and their protests were ignored, Marshal "Wild Bill" Hickock ordered the painting touched up. Fortunately for Fort Worth's morals, the good citizens making their way up and down Main Street only had to confront a benign-looking, asexual pachyderm.[14]

The White Elephant began life in early 1883 as an unprepossessing restaurant under the ownership of Frenchman F. A. Borodino. At that time the best eateries in Fort Worth were the Planter's House at the corner of Taylor and Third Streets ("Everything cooked in the best style") and the Commercial Restaurant ("all the delicacies of home and foreign markets served to order").[15] The quality of Borodino's cuisine is unknown, but the fact that he was closed "by attachment" within a year may be a clue. Among his creditors was hardware dealer Will F. Lake, who charged him with embezzlement after the restaurant owner tried to remove some expensive silverware while the court-ordered lien was in effect. The case took a strange turn when Borodino was jailed for failure to make bond, and Mrs. Borodino, a "very handsome French lady," threatened to "kill Lake at sight [sic]."[16] Altogether, it was an inauspicious beginning for the good name of the White Elephant, but this was still "Cowtown," and people were not too shocked by such goings-on.

The White Elephant was resurrected as a modest saloon in 1884 by a trio of Jewish newcomers to Fort Worth, Gabriel Burgower, Nathaniel Bornstein, and Samuel Berliner, with Burgower as the principal owner. It appeared under the "Saloon" listings in the city directory for the first time that year, under the owners' names ("G. Burgower & Co.") rather than the saloon's name. It was described as a "saloon *and* billiard parlor."

Two of the three, Burgower and Bornstein, were members of a very small Jewish community in the city. In the late 1880s this community included between fifteen and twenty Jewish families with "about seven business houses run by Israelites." There was a cluster of those Jewish businesses within a block or two of the White Elephant.[17] Gabriel Burgower had arrived in town as a bachelor some two years earlier and opened a jewelry and watch-making business at 300 Main Street. He specialized in "watches, clocks, jewelry, silver and plated wares, and diamonds," and lived at the El Paso Hotel, allowing him to observe one of the city's most popular bars as he came and went. Nathaniel Bornstein's place in Fort Worth history is a cipher even among the city's modern Jewish historians.

Samuel Berliner had been a Fort Worth resident a few years earlier before he found the local business opportunities limited and moved to San Antonio in 1880. There he established himself as a "stockman and capitalist" of some note. Among other enterprises he became co-owner of that city's White Elephant Saloon while continuing to maintain some financial ties with Fort Worth. He was nothing more than an investor in

Fort Worth's White Elephant, though he seemed to be the only one of the three partners with any real interest in the saloon business.[18]

With one absentee member and two novices, the three-way partnership was a chummy albeit impractical arrangement. Burgower oversaw the saloon operation, Bornstein ran the restaurant, and Berliner (see chapter 2) was the silent partner. They seemed to have experienced no overt prejudice from Fort Worth's Christian community, but there were no helping hands extended either. While Fort Worth was a tolerant town in some ways, ethnic minorities were still not fully accepted members of the community.

As a barkeep, Burgower did not keep too close an eye on the saloon but split his time between it and his jewelry and watch-making business just two doors up the block.[19] He treated the White Elephant as purely a business venture, not a career move. In any event, he was shrewd enough to realize that a saloon was always a worthwhile investment in a Western town.

At this point, the White Elephant was a far cry from the legendary establishment it would later become, but hardly a hole-in-the-wall either. It covered three lots in the middle of block 42 on the original city plat from 306 to 310 Main. Corner lots were the preferred location for saloons, in order to catch the traffic from four directions, but being in the heart of the business district so near to Courthouse Square was a prime location nonetheless.

This was before the era of brick and mortar in Fort Worth, so the White Elephant was standard "balloon frame" construction with a classic Western false front. The floor space covered roughly 8,460 square feet, including the public rooms and the kitchen. The interior was filled by several billiard tables, a partitioned gambling section, a bar, and lunch counter, all ventilated by whatever breeze passed through the large front doors and windows on the east (Main Street) and west (alley) sides. The eastern exposure caught the early morning rays through the front windows, but by late afternoon when most customers started rolling in, the interior was in shadows and several degrees cooler than places across the street.

Ownership of the White Elephant was more complicated than who had the key to the cash box. There was the question of who owned the land, who owned the building that sat on the land, and who owned the business that occupied the building that sat on the land. For a town struggling with its image, each of those parties was more or less guilty of corrupting the morals of good people—and some not-so-good people, too.

The man who had held the deed to lot 13, block 42, since 1881 was the esteemed John D. Templeton, a lawyer by training, Civil War veteran, former editor of the *Fort Worth Democrat*, candidate for mayor in 1877, and at different times secretary of state and attorney general for Texas. Templeton was a pillar of the community who happened to own a piece of property with a saloon sitting on it.[20] However, Templeton's connection to the White Elephant was closer than that. He also was half owner of the building sitting on lot 13, with businessman W. H. Nanny holding the other half of the deed. Nanny had overseen the construction of the building and the leasing of the space to the White Elephant. Templeton was the silent partner, and for good reason.

In the mid-1880s John D. Templeton was attorney general of Texas, living in Austin. His position placed him at the forefront of the forces of law and order, which put him at odds with the saloon bosses. In 1884, when there was grumbling in Fort Worth about ethical conflicts between Templeton's public office versus his private interests, Nanny leaped to his partner's defense, writing this in a letter to the *Fort Worth Gazette:* "I doubt if Mr. Templeton knows the names of the tenants of the house. He had nothing to do with leasing it, nor has he had anything to do with collecting the rents. I have controlled it from the time the first brick was laid, and I am controlling it now." In the same letter, Nanny reminded the moral watchdogs that "the saloon business is licensed by the laws of the state," thus neatly shifting any moral opprobrium to the legislature![21]

For most of the Templeton's constituents in Fort Worth, Burgower & Co. was the public face of the White Elephant. It was they who bore responsibility for what went on there, both good and bad. Any effort to pin responsibility for immoral and illegal activities on absentee landlords was an exercise in futility. Most citizens simply did not make the connection.

The interior layout of the White Elephant is something of a mystery today because no blueprints or detailed descriptions survive, just tidbits

of information from newspaper accounts and local lore. It is possible to
fill in a few more details with the help of the Sanborn series of fire
insurance maps plus a little generic knowledge of Western saloons
and some educated guesses.[22] The problem of getting a clear picture of
the place is complicated by the fact that the White Elephant evolved
through three separate owners—the Jewish partners, Bill Ward, and
Winfield Scott—and two different locations—the 300 block of Main
and the 600 block of Main. There is also the fact that old-timers remi-
niscing years later sometimes confused the two different sites.

In the ruthless world of saloon operations, Burgower & Co.'s White
Elephant was not a threat to steal away business from the most popular
drinking establishments that dotted the business district. To do that, it
would have to win over the gentlemen of Fort Worth by offering first-
class gambling, drinking, and food service. Most regular drinkers tend
to be loyal to a favorite establishment, and any new place hoping to
build a regular clientele had to provide exemplary service.

One service was so popular with customers that no barkeep could
disdain it: the "free bar lunch." It came compliments of the house with
the purchase of a beer or other drink. Fort Worth drinkers got their first
taste of free lunch in 1877 at Herman Kussatz's Tivoli Beer Hall, and
when every other saloon jumped on the bandwagon soon thereafter, it
became standard practice.[23] The food put out for the free bar lunch was
undistinguished but usually edible. The fancy places served a more extensive menu, but they all worked from the assumption that nobody
came to a saloon to eat. For the hungry customer there were not many
alternatives. Public eating-places were not yet an important part of city
life. Most folks ate at home, or if they had to be out at mealtime, carried
homemade lunches wrapped in waxed paper. A few cafes and hotel dining rooms met the needs of the rest. No saloon in Fort Worth up through
the mid-1880s advertised itself as a drinking and dining place.

The White Elephant's owners introduced seated dining in a shrewd
move to lure business away from competitors. Their dining room was
backed by a commodious kitchen in the rear of the 306 address, but this
was no frontier Delmonico's (the legendary New York City eatery of the
same era). The heart of the operation was a single sink and gas stove
run by a "short-order" cook. There was nothing fancy about it, but the

White Elephant's commitment to serving both an extensive food menu *and* libations made it unusual, especially for a town where sidewalks were still a rarity and residents could legally keep hogs within city limits. It was also a step up from the typical free-lunch spread, which might consist of anything from a full turkey—carve your own—to suspicious-looking hash.

Aside from drinking, the main business for Burgower & Co. was not dining but billiards. Entering the front doors at 308 or 310 Main, the gambling rooms were on the left side, the bar and billiard tables to the right. Diners, gamblers, and billiard players were only separated by a curtain or thin partition running the length of the room. This makeshift arrangement confirmed the fact that the White Elephant was nowise a first-class saloon even by frontier standards. Indeed, even having "billiard parlor" in the name (the White Elephant Saloon *and* Billiard Parlor) did not help the image of a place trying to compete with the likes of the Occidental (Second and Main) or the Bank Exchange (Houston and Third). It was clear that Burgower & Co. had a lot to learn about the saloon business.

One of the men who helped keep the customers happy was thirty-two-year-old John L. Ward, who operated as an independent contractor running the cigar stand near the front door where he sold a variety of "cigars, tobacco, and smokers' articles." This was a familiar business arrangement in the larger saloons and hotels. The owners leased the "concessions" for the cigar stand and gambling operation, among other activities, to independent contractors. Most of the historical attention has focused on the "gambling concession" whereby a saloon owner and a professional gambler negotiated an equitable split of the gaming profits according to the reputation of the gambler and the size of the crowd the house usually drew. Wyatt Earp owned the concession at Tombstone's Oriental Saloon from 1879 until 1881 when he got crossways with the law. Other concessions received less attention than gambling but could also be cash cows. Thus a saloon like the Oriental or the White Elephant was practically a conglomerate, with the proprietor acting as CEO.

Standing behind his counter near the entrance, John Ward got to know the regular customers and, more than that, saw an enormous untapped potential for the place. The White Elephant had a loyal clientele, a well-known name, and that most valuable of real estate commodities, "location, location, location." In 1884 he approached his thirty-one-year-old brother, William, about going into partnership to buy out the current owners. Both Wards were relative newcomers to Fort Worth. John had come from Denison, Texas, in 1883, and Bill arrived the next year. They were attracted by the city's budding business opportunities and cultural ambitions: Fort Worth was not content to remain a "cowtown" forever. Many men were coming to the "Paris of the Plains" at this time, full of dreams and get-rich-quick schemes. John arrived first, took the job at the White Elephant, and then sent for his brother. Bill Ward was just another newcomer when he got off the train at Union Station, but he aimed to change that. How he supported himself for the next year is unknown, although there was no shortage of jobs available for a bright young man with railroading experience, which Ward had in abundance. Prior to landing in Fort Worth, Ward had worked out of Denison as a conductor for the Missouri, Kansas and Texas Railroad (M-K-T or "KATY"). Half a dozen new lines had come into town since the first one in 1876, and local business groups were filing charters of incorporation for new lines all the time. While looking for his niche, Bill Ward moved into the same boarding house as John at Crump and Bluff Streets, not far from the courthouse.

The Ward brothers had both been born in Galena, Illinois, John in 1851 and William in 1853. Galena's most famous son in later years was Civil War general and U.S. president, Ulysses S. Grant, and like Grant, they got out of Galena as soon as they could, going to work for the railroad while still young men. Bill was the more gregarious and ambitious of the two. He worked five years for the Illinois Central before signing on with the M-K-T as a conductor. This brought him to Denison, where he spent the next ten years laboring for the railroad Texans knew as the "KATY." In 1883 he decided to go out on his own, a decision that dovetailed nicely with John's subsequent proposal that they go into the saloon business together.[24]

When Burgower and company decided to sell out after little more than a year, the Ward brothers were there with an offer. Based on market value at that time, they probably did not pay more than three to four thousand dollars for the White Elephant, which was a bargain but not a steal. The price did not include either the building or the land it sat on.[25] Despite the fact that it was John's idea to begin with, Bill Ward put up most of the financial wherewithal to underwrite the venture and quickly assumed the role of front man.

The first thing the new owners did was to stage a grand opening the likes of which Fort Worth had never seen before. Fancy invitations were sent out to all the leading citizens and elected officials, and almost to a man they came. For three hours, from six to nine P.M., politicians and peace officers rubbed elbows with gamblers and cattlemen. There was plenty of food and drink to go around and plenty of toasts to future success. Bill Ward delivered the welcoming speech and climaxed the festivities by ceremonially throwing out the front door key into the street. This was a traditional act done whenever a new saloon opened, thereby announcing to the world that the doors would never close. But no one could recall ever attending one with such "great splendor and ceremony" on display.[26]

To the well-dressed gentlemen who attended the grand opening, the White Elephant was more than just another saloon. It was the uptown gentry's answer to all the downtown dives and joints in Hell's Half Acre that had become a growing embarrassment to the city. This would be a place where a man could go for a drink without keeping one hand on his wallet or expecting a brawl break out. A first-class saloon, like an opera house or public library, could be a credit to the entire community.

Thus the White Elephant Saloon began a new life under its third ownership in just two years. In the next three decades the transformation of the place from a modest bar-and-billiards operation into one of the premier establishments of its kind in the Southwest was mainly due to the managerial skills of Bill Ward. Brother John was co-proprietor for only the first two years, until the partnership was dissolved around November, 1886.[27] The saloon business was never a passion with him; he chased the money wherever it led him. In 1888 he moved to Thurber, Texas, a coal-mining town seventy-five miles west of Fort Worth, where he leased a saloon. When Thurber was bought by the Texas and Pacific Coal Company, he sold out for $2,700 and moved back to Fort Worth. He worked as a druggist, then dropped out of sight for a couple of years be-

W. H. "Bill" Ward was the "face" of the White Elephant. But he was much more than a saloon proprietor. He was also a pillar of the community, seen here in 1901 when he headed up the City Council's Police Committee as a First Ward Alderman. Courtesy *Special Collections Division, University of Texas at Arlington Libraries*

fore resurfacing as "The Popular Price Shoe Man" at a Main Street address in 1897. Unlike Bill he could be content not running the show.

Both brothers got in on the ground floor of Texas League baseball, with Bill making much the bigger splash, as usual. In 1888 he organized and sponsored Fort Worth's entry in the league, the Panthers (also known as the "Cats"), and stayed active in their operation until 1910. John served three terms as league president starting in 1896, during which time the Fort Worth Cats won a championship and a first-place finish in league play in successive years, but Bill is the one remembered in the team's colorful history.[28]

The White Elephant was just the beginning for Bill Ward. He was a risk taker, but only after carefully calculating the odds. Like many men in Fort Worth at this time, he dabbled in real estate because these were bullish years in the local market. He knew a bargain when he saw one, too. In November, 1885, when a piece of bankrupt property came up for auction, he bought it for a mere twenty-five dollars (but only after his first offer of ten dollars had been turned down).[29] He also did a little box-

WHITE ELEPHANT
SALOON AND RESTAURANT

W. H. WARD, Proprietor.

THE MOST COMPLETE RESTAURANT AND SALOON IN THE CITY.

COMMUTATION TICKETS GOOD FOR $6.00 IN MEALS, SOLD FOR $5.00 IN CASH.

OYSTERS SERVED TO ORDER IN ANY STYLE.

TRANSIENT CUSTOM SOLICITED.

OPEN DAY AND NIGHT.

FRESH FISH, OYSTERS AND GAME
AND EVERYTHING ELSE IN SEASON. THE FINEST THE MARKET AFFORDS.

THE CHOICEST WINES, LIQUORS AND CIGARS.

308 AND 310 MAIN STREET.

LOUIS MAAS, Proprietor.   JNO. H. TILLER, Manager.   WM. K. MAAS, Ass't Manager.

Not content to depend on word of mouth to bring in business, Bill Ward had very modern ideas about advertising—from passing out business cards and tokens to having letterhead printed up and taking out ads in the City Directory, like this one from 1891. White Elephant advertising promoted both the restaurant and the saloon. From the author's collection

ing promotion and later, after deciding to get out of baseball, he entered the theatrical business, operating vaudeville venues first and then movie houses well into the 1920s.[30]

But his main focus in the beginning was the saloon business. The money was good, and the job brought with it a certain status that few other lines of work in a Western town enjoyed. "Saloon-keepers rode the best horses, drove the fanciest rigs, wore the best clothes, and were elected to public office," said one journalist, and that description certainly fit Bill Ward.[31]

In 1892 he added the Board of Trade Saloon at 316 Main to his holdings. He could easily shuttle back and forth between his two saloons since they were only a few doors apart. Both places catered to a gentlemen clientele by offering fine wines and liquors and high-stakes gambling, all in refined surroundings. The biggest difference was that the Board of Trade did not include a restaurant. He ran the two saloons conjointly for the next several years.

As a saloonkeeper, Bill Ward was a natural host with a special fondness for sporting types. He spoke their language, understood their basic needs, and offered their favorite games at the White Elephant. More than that, he was tight with all the big players in the local gambling fraternity, men like Jake Johnson, Bill Atterbury, Jim Brown, and John Sheehan. They sometimes made the rounds together, stopping in places like John Leer's Comique Theater and Saloon and engaging in horseplay.[32]

Ward had a "genial nature" and a garrulousness that made entry into politics a logical step in an age when owning or operating a saloon was considered a respectable occupation.[33] He parlayed his popularity and sporting connections into winning his first political office in 1892 as alderman for the First Ward. He kept that seat until 1907 when the commission form of government replaced the old ward system.[34]

Sitting on the city council all those years made him one of the power brokers in the city and allowed him to head off any antisaloon drive mounted by the prohibitionist crowd. Even better, he got himself appointed to the Police Committee early in his tenure, which gave him oversight over Fort Worth's Finest. Some saloon owners got crossways with the law and suffered nothing but trouble at their establishments as a result. Bill Ward, by contrast, not only got along with the law, he *was* the law! Among other responsibilities, the Police Committee was in charge of the hiring and firing of police officers, although their immediate boss, the city marshal, was an elected position.[35]

Beneath all the hoopla of the grand opening, the White Elephant had an image problem when the Wards took over that was in need of immediate fixing. Occasionally, the shenanigans down in Hell's Half Acre had overflowed the vice district and washed uptown, leaving a bad stench in the nostrils of respectable men. On the night of November 29, 1884, police officers Thomas and Brandon had followed up a tip that led them to the White Elephant looking for Tom Cheshire, a notorious cattle rustler with a one-thousand-dollar reward on his head. Sure enough, they found Cheshire and hauled him off to jail. The incident was noted as far away as Dallas, where the *Herald* sniffed that the unregenerate patrons of the White Elephant were blocking progress and corrupting the morals of the better citizens of Fort Worth.[36]

Now, with Bill Ward at the helm, the White Elephant received a makeover in terms of both image and operations. On the image side, he set out to create a safe, congenial environment for his "uptown" customers. The measure of his success can be found in an editorial that appeared in the *Fort Worth Mail* in March, 1886, not much more than a year after the new ownership took over. The *Mail* praised the Wards in 1886 for "the perfect order maintained" on the premises.[37] With a couple of notable exceptions, Bill Ward managed to keep a tight lid on things over the years and served as a model for other saloon men in Fort Worth.

On the operations side, Ward aimed to serve the best food and drink in Fort Worth, bar none. He began his campaign to remake the White Elephant by changing the saloon's layout in ways both cosmetic and significant. One of his first moves was to partition off the front to create a "cigar apartment." This larger version of the stand that John Ward had manned under the former management served as a "package store" and tobacconist shop for customers. Next, Ward moved the billiard tables into a back room, making the bar the focus of the main room.

And that bar was a wonder to behold. The standard bar area in a Western saloon was an ensemble piece consisting of two or three parts: the front counter where the customers were served and the workboard and liquor case behind the bar. The workboard held the glassware, and the liquor case held a variety of bottled merchandise, a sure sign of a better establishment. In the humbler sort of joints that bought their whiskey in barrels and transferred it to bottles on the premises, the bottles were kept under the counter. The workboard and liquor case were known as the "back-bar," and in some fancy saloons included a mirror that allowed a man standing at the bar to survey the room behind him without appearing to stare.

The expanse of mirror, the amount of crystal or cut glass on the workboard, and the ornateness of the woodwork distinguished the first-class saloons from the rest. If the mirror stretched the length of the bar, if glassware and neat rows of bottles were stacked up on glass shelves, if the woodwork was of fine wood and richly carved, then a man knew he was in saloon heaven.

The White Elephant's front counter and mirrored back-bar were finely crafted pieces of furniture, made of solid mahogany filigreed to a fare-thee-well and with a polished brass foot rail down the length of the bar. (Western bars never had stools in front of them; sitting customers would have clogged up traffic and obstructed the bartender's view of

The legendary Luke Short bar and back-bar combination, restored to their former glory, albeit in considerably different surroundings. At the time this picture was taken in 1949, then-owner O. L. Shipman had them occupying one wall of his El Paso candy shop. The two pieces have subsequently changed hands several more times, and this author has lost track of them. From the author's collection

the room.) Onyx columns and built-in gas lighting fixtures flanked the back-bar. Stacked against the back-bar were tiers of high-grade, cut glassware, polished to a high sheen that reflected the lights like a chandelier. The liquor case held "an immense display" of bottled wines, liquors, brandies, and cordials, most with labels that testified to the fact that they had not been poured out of the same barrel in a back room. Beer taps up front connected to kegs under the bar counter.

Legend has it this magnificent bar was installed at Luke Short's insistence when he set up shop at the White Elephant. Some even say he brought it down from Dodge City with him. After his death in 1893 and the saloon's relocation down the street, the "Luke Short back-bar" embarked on a strange odyssey that saw it change hands several times and turn up in some strange places.[38]

Another nice Ward touch was the "cigar factory" he installed at the back of the building, where workers rolled the stogies that were sold in the tobacco apartment up front. The house brand was known as "Billy Ward's Choice" and was advertised in the *Fort Worth Gazette* as "the only

FRONT ELEVATION
WHITE ELEPHANT SALOON - CLUB ROOMS
308 - 310 MAIN STREET
FORT WORTH, TEXAS
ca. 1889

DRAWINGS BY
ROBERT CULLEN SMITH, A.I.A.

five-cent cigar containing Havana tobaccos."[39] Unlike whiskey, a house brand of cigar bespoke quality. It was also another way of getting the White Elephant's name before the public, just like the tokens and business cards that Ward handed out liberally.

Bill Ward's most questionable innovation was installing a cockfighting arena on the second floor. His position as a city councilman after 1892 provided the legal cover for what was a misdemeanor crime. Cockfighting had been a staple of Fort Worth gambling since at least the late 1870s, even on Main Street, although it was customarily done in backyards in the Acre, not uptown saloons. Bill Ward brought it inside and elevated it into a sporting event where "gentlemen" could rub elbows with cowboys.[40]

The regularly staged fights at the White Elephant were not exactly hush-hush affairs either; they brought in contestants from as far away as Kansas City and were advertised in the Austin newspapers. The fighting arena or "pit" was even labeled on the Sanborn fire maps. A "main event" in 1893 featured twenty-one pairs of birds with a purse of two thousand dollars. On another occasion, one of the fights was attended by legendary boxer John L. Sullivan, who placed a "rather stiff bet" and managed to rile some of the cowboys in attendance. Sullivan later admitted leaving town in a hurry that night to avoid the drovers' murderous wrath.[41]

The cock-pit was just one small part of a greatly expanded gambling operation that Bill Ward put in place. He wasted no time because he rightly recognized gambling as the engine that drove the train. His dream was to establish a new gambling headquarters for Fort Worth that would leave the competition in the dust, and he succeeded. Soon the White Elephant was being described in awed terms as "an elegant place of resort . . . with a reputation second to no place of the kind in the south"— a far cry from its former days as a mere saloon *cum* billiard parlor.[42]

The 300 block of Main Street was Bill Ward's kingdom. The whole operation at 308–310 Main, from cigar apartment to cock-pit, totaled some 4,458 square feet under one roof. It shared common walls with its two nearest neighbors, a restaurant to the north and a barber shop to the south. He had plans to bring both of those businesses under the White Elephant umbrella. Why should a man have to leave his place and go somewhere else to get a good meal or a hair cut? For a time, the White Elephant held bragging rights to being the biggest saloon in the city. Equally important, it was just a few minutes walk from such downtown gathering places as the Pickwick and Mansion Hotels, Greenwall's Opera House, the Knights of Pythias Hall, and the Natatorium.

The one missing piece necessary to transform the White Elephant into a premier gambling emporium was a big-name sporting man to oversee the games, someone who could attract the high rollers. Gambling, Ward knew, was a lot like baseball: people came to see the stars play. So he set out to find himself some "stars." In 1886, he took on a pair of partners, both of whom had impeccable credentials among the Southwest gambling fraternity.

Thirty-six-year-old Jacob G. "Jake" Johnson was a former cattleman who had found it more profitable and less gritty work to invest in other people's promising business ventures and to race horses on the side. In 1882 he described himself as a "capitalist"; by 1886 he preferred the title "turfman," an inflated term for anyone who kept a string of race horses. That he made good choices in both horses and business partners was demonstrated by the fact that the *Fort Worth Gazette* a few years later listed his personal worth as $59,400, making him one of the wealthiest men in Fort Worth.[43] He made a worthy partner to Bill Ward because he was well connected to the city's gambling fraternity, and he had estab-

Luke Short, as always dressed to the nines with hair neatly combed, appears suitably attired for either a high-stakes card game or a Sunday church service! Courtesy *Kansas State Historical Society, Topeka, Kansas*

lished his *bona fides* by running the club room at the exclusive Cattle Exchange Saloon in 1883–84.

Luke Short became the third member of the partnership. He brought both flash and cash to the partnership. Short had been the Gambling King of Dodge City before jealous rivals ran him out of town in 1883, forcing "Little Luke" to look for a new place to set himself up. He landed in Fort Worth in late 1883 (the same year as John Ward), carrying a satchel full of money and looking for a place to invest it.[44]

The local gambling fraternity was more than a little in awe of their latest addition. Short, as described by a Kansas newspaper, was a polished gentleman: " . . . a regular dandy, quite handsome, and a perfect ladies man. He dresses fashionably, is particular as to his appearance, and always takes pains to look as neat as possible.[45]

He was not as impressed with them. Luke found no fancy saloons that measured up to his standards but decided to stay anyway. Having previously pitched his tent in Dodge City, and before that in Tombstone, Fort Worth was still his kind of place: a frontier town with wide-open gambling and a casual attitude about law and order. The lack of a saloon comparable to the Oriental (Tombstone) or the Long Branch (Dodge City) did not bother him unduly; he planned to change that as soon as he found a home base for himself.[46]

Most professional gamblers liked to establish a home base as soon as possible after settling down in a new town. Luke put himself and wife Hettie up in an apartment at the Lindell Hotel on Bluff Street when they first arrived in Fort Worth. Then for more than a year he was a "floating gambler," making the rounds and getting to know the owners and barkeeps. He eventually connected with Bill Ward and Jake Johnson, and the three men struck up a partnership that allowed Short a free hand running the upstairs gambling while Ward handled the downstairs, and Johnson was content to glad-hand the customers and occasionally count the till.

Luke Short wasted no time putting his stamp on the White Elephant's upstairs. He launched a complete redecoration of the public area and the private rooms that included importing fancy fixtures from back east. The new "club rooms" were as nice as any hotel luxury suite that most customers were likely to have ever seen. They had mahogany, felt-covered playing tables, rich draperies covering the windows, thick carpets on the floors, and waiters on call to bring drinks from the bar. In the public area there were more felt-covered tables for the so-called "bank" games: faro, monte, and roulette. Luke was an old faro dealer himself, so he gave special attention to the faro tables with their painted, oilcloth layouts, dealers' boxes, and abacus-like cases. The boxes that held the cards were made of finest rosewood, as were the frames of the cases that held ivory counters showing how many cards had been played. The pieces were described as "works of art," probably by those who never lost their bankroll there.[47]

It was the fanciest gambling operation Cowtown had ever seen! But there was more. Luke was a believer in hands-on management so he wanted his living quarters right next door to his workplace. After his carpenters finished remodeling the gambling rooms, he ordered them to build a two-bedroom apartment for himself and Hettie, separated from the gaming area by a soundproof wall and with a private outside staircase leading to the alley behind the saloon. A dumbwaiter connecting to the restaurant downstairs even allowed the Shorts to take their meals privately. It was the perfect hideaway for the gambler who had everything.[48]

By early 1887 Luke was the proud manager (the newspapers called him "proprietor") of the White Elephant's casino and, more importantly, had established himself as "King of the Fort Worth Gamblers."[49] Since the Ward brothers knew nothing about running a big-time gambling operation, and Jake Johnson's reputation was strictly local, Luke's expertise and connections to the elite gambling fraternity were invaluable in transforming the White Elephant into the kind of palace that Bill Ward had imagined. Every saloon with any pretensions to class had a resident gambler cum "pit boss" to oversee the gaming operations, and Luke Short filled that role perfectly.

The dapper little gambler made the saloon his home and his castle. Bill Ward later stated under oath that Short spent three-fourths of his time on the premises.[50] That helped him out-hustle any and all rivals for the gentlemen's gambling business in town. It was no coincidence that the upstairs rooms over 308–310 Main were the playground of Fort Worth's money men and a magnet for sporting men from all over the Southwest. Luke's formula was a simple one: There would be no "brace games" (crooked games) run at the White Elephant like those uncovered by police at the Occidental's gambling rooms in the summer of 1889; all games run by house dealers at the White Elephant would be square.[51] Secondly, men who wanted a little more privacy were always able to rent a clubroom for their parties and invitation-only games. The White Elephant provided the food and drinks, while "party girls" could be procured on request from well-known madams in town. Discretion, of course, was guaranteed, as was protection from the embarrassment of police raids.

In fact, the police did not raid the White Elephant even once while "Little Luke" ruled the roost. Nor did they nab any wanted men on the premises. The White Elephant's clientele was strictly high class. The best citizens of Fort Worth could be found here on any given evening, dressed in their expensive finery and flashing a jewelry-display case worth of diamonds in their rings, shirt studs, and "watch charms."[52] They also carried large bankrolls or sometimes just signed markers to

"Jim" Courtright (right), *one of the principals in the most famous gunfight in Fort Worth history, is shown here with saddle buddy and fellow gunman Jim McIntyre* (left), *with whom he got into a scrape in New Mexico in 1883. His marshalling days behind him when this photograph was taken, Courtright still looks every inch the gunman.* Courtesy *Fort Worth Public Library, Local History and Genealogy Department*

cover their bets. Luke was not averse to extending credit to such customers. After all, it was their presence and their continued good will that kept him open.

Part of Luke Short's secret of success was knowing his clientele. He knew that men loved to gamble, even if they were not top-drawer players, particularly when the surroundings were congenial and they had a reasonable chance of winning. Keno was the ideal game for such men—and their ladies—because it did not require any card smarts to play and the potential winnings were high. Unlike poker, it depended more on luck than skill, and also unlike poker it was not known to provoke murderous confrontations between winners and losers. The customers played against the house, not each other.

Within a year after setting up shop in the White Elephant, Short had sparked a "keno craze" among Fort Worth's well-scrubbed classes. The upstairs was packed every night with eager players of both sexes who practically threw their money down in their eagerness to play. In fact, the keno take became so big it provoked grumbling among leading citizens who considered it nothing more than a con game and Luke Short the biggest "con" of all.

While all the grumbling targeted Short, contrary to later lore, he does not deserve the blame (or the credit) for introducing keno to Fort Worth; it had been played in the city's better gambling parlors for years. In fact, six years before Short hit town, John C. Morris was the reigning keno king of Fort Worth, and the Cattle Exchange Saloon was keno headquarters. In an ominous portent of the future in 1880, Morris and Jim Courtright came to blows over control of the game. That feud had been defused long before Short showed up in Fort Worth, but another keno feud was soon brewing after Little Luke made the White Elephant the new keno headquarters. Short's appointed role in this Cowtown gambling drama was to encourage the craze and hitch his wagon to it. Meanwhile, Jim Courtright was shoved aside, losing the keno "franchise" just as he had lost the marshal's office to an upstart challenger.[53]

Meanwhile, the cliquish fraternity of professional gamblers turned up their noses at keno, preferring games that could be played with a deck of fifty-two. The White Elephant catered to them, too. Among the more famous Western characters who tried their luck at the White Elephant were Richard B. S. "Dick" Clark, Wyatt Earp, and Bat Masterson. All three men were drawn to Fort Worth not only by the White Elephant's distinguished pedigree but by their friendship with Luke Short. Clark has been overshadowed in history by the more flamboyant Earp and Masterson, but he was considered one of the very best in his day. He was known as "the King of the Tombstone [Arizona] Gamblers" and was not afraid to test his skills in Fort Worth's best clubrooms.[54]

Masterson, who saw the inside of more than a few saloons in his day, was so impressed with the White Elephant that, writing more than two decades later, he still described it in awed terms as "one of the largest and costliest establishments of its kind in the entire Southwest."[55] He was on the premises the night Short and Courtright had their dust-up, and according to his fanciful recollections, spent the night in the same jail cell with Short, armed and ready in case a lynch mob showed up.[56]

Earp was a familiar face around town from the late 1870s through the mid-1880s. No one ever knew when he was going to show up, not even his brother James who worked at the Cattle Exchange Saloon on Houston Street. In the mid-eighties Wyatt brought along his lady friend, Josephine Sarah Marcus. He and "Josie" would have supper in the White Elephant's restaurant before he parked her in the Mansion Hotel and returned to the saloon to spend all night playing high-stakes poker. After a few days enjoying the hospitality of the White Elephant, Earp would move on, as always, following the gamblers' circuit, which guaranteed a return visit sooner or later.[57]

Gamblers lived for the "Big Game," and one of the biggest in the history of the West occurred at the White Elephant in August, 1885, when Burgower and company were still the owners. Luke Short, Bat Masterson, Wyatt Earp, Timothy Courtright, and Charlie Coe were assembled around the same table, with Short joining the little group as another "friend of the house." All had big reputations and equally large bankrolls that day. Masterson's alone was more than nine thousand dollars when the game began. Several hours later they were all cleaned out except Charlie Coe. Short, the last to cash in, lost the hand holding a full house to Coe's four kings. It was the pinnacle of Coe's gambling career and helped win him the reputation of being "the most successful and also the most feared gambler of them all." [58]

The main value of men like Earp, Masterson, and Clark to the White Elephant was not as paying customers, since their games tended to be private affairs, but as drawing cards for the public. Night in and night out, it was the ordinary customers eating and drinking in the White Elephant and testing their gaming skills against the house that swelled the receipts. It had always been thus. In 1884 Dallasite Henry Edgar had made a rather costly visit to Fort Worth where, over the course of a long night's gambling at the White Elephant, he dropped "some $510 or $560" at the tables. There is no doubt he would have returned for another go at it if he had not been murdered in Dallas soon thereafter.[59]

Keno was a house favorite because it was a bigger money-maker even than high-stakes poker. The substantial profits being made off the game and the grip it had on bush-league gamblers roused a storm of condemnation that targeted the White Elephant. A group of irate Fort Worth citizens in 1887 called for it to be shut down, citing the "suffering and distress" it caused the city's mothers, wives, children. They called themselves the "Law and Order Society" but sounded more like a bunch of sore losers when they said keno was a game "where men have no equal chance." The criticism was deserved, if smugly self-righteous. As everyone knew, keno was easy to rig. All the house had to do was plant a confederate in the audience with the winning game card, and then have the keno "goose" operator pull the preselected winning numbers at intervals and announce them until the lucky "winner" sprang up in faux surprise. He received his winnings and the rest of the crowd anted up for the next game. It was laughably easy.[60]

The Law and Order Society demanded that the White Elephant stop running keno altogether and backed up their demand with a brazen threat to burn the place down if the games continued. But as long as keno drew big crowds and produced fat profits for Bill Ward and Company, it would continue to be the game du jour.[61]

The nightly crowds and the easy camaraderie with members of Fort Worth's upper crust were a deceptive measure of Luke Short's popularity. While the *Fort Worth Gazette* considered him "a man of quiet and gentlemanly manners . . . generous to a fault . . . and unobtrusive in demeanor," members of Fort Worth's Law and Order Society took a much dimmer view. They called him a drunkard, a woman-beater, and a whore-monger, and those were just for starters. They also called him "a black-hearted murderer" and "a low-down dog." None of these accusations became public until after the shootout with Timothy Courtright, but they had been building for months before February 8, 1887. In the winter of 1886–87, Short's life was threatened if he did not leave town, and his business partners were warned to disassociate themselves from him or face dire consequences.[62]

Luke Short, even more than Bill Ward, came to personify the White Elephant, which was part of the problem. There was only room for one Prince of the Realm. The upstairs was Short's personal fief, keno was his game, and many of the steely-eyed, gun-toting strangers who dropped in to play high-stakes poker in the clubrooms were his longtime friends.

Wearing a gun was against both state law and city ordinance, but Short and his friends acted as if the laws were suspended at the White Elephant. To the dime novelists and their readers, such men may have been "legends of the West," but to too many decent citizens they were nothing more than "outlaws, desperadoes, and murderers."[63]

Ward saw himself being eclipsed by Short and was also uncomfortably aware of Little Luke's history of violent confrontation. Trouble seemed to follow Short wherever he went. So in November, 1886, Ward bought out the gambler's interest, thereby dissolving the partnership of the Ward brothers and Luke Short. It was not a complete break, however, because while Ward wore the proprietor's hat, Short stayed on to run the gambling operation upstairs just as before only now at the pleasure of Bill Ward. Reducing Short's role to independent contractor, however, also meant that Ward now had to pay all taxes and fines (due to, for example, violations of the Sunday closing law) out of his own pocket.[64]

Completely terminating the association of Luke Short with the White Elephant proved to be as messy as ending a marriage where valuable community property is involved. When the "divorce" finally came, it was not through any action of Bill Ward, but rather the result of a long-simmering feud between Short and one of his own kind, ex-marshal and hired gun Timothy Courtright.

Courtright had called Fort Worth home for nearly a decade when Short arrived in town. He was both popular and feared by the citizens, having done some good work as city marshal but also intimidating anyone who did not dance to his tune. By the mid-1880s Courtright was running a slick protection racket as a private detective that did not require him to do much more than collect payments from the local saloon men. When he got the cold shoulder at the White Elephant, he started telling people there was "a combination against him" there led by Short. In particular he claimed that he "hadn't been treated with respect upstairs," which could have meant anything from being cheated at the gaming tables to having his credit cut off or the bar closed to him. Since Courtright was an indifferent gambler and a heavy drinker, any of these were possible.

Like most such feuds, this one simmered for a while, fueled by drinking bouts and long hours of brooding over perceived insults. For public consumption, Short steadfastly denied that there was any bad feeling between them, but his words rang hollow with those who knew the situation.[65]

Short had some premonition of trouble hurtling down the track toward him. On February 7, 1887, the day before the infamous shootout, he sold the gambling concession to Jake Johnson in a "little business deal" that netted him one thousand dollars and left just two of the original partners in place. Anyone who knew Short's past could also see in these developments a replay of Short's previous quick exits from Tombstone and Dodge City.

Beneath his dapper exterior, Luke Short had a hair-trigger temper, never went anywhere unarmed, and stepped aside for no man. Before coming to Fort Worth from Dodge City, he had plied his trade in Tombstone, Arizona, as a house dealer at the Oriental Saloon. One night a disgruntled gambler named Charlie Storms, in a drunken rage, challenged Short to a gunfight. Before the befuddled Storms could unholster his own gun, Short whipped out a little pocket pistol, stepped in close, and pumped three slugs into his opponent. Two years later, in Dodge City, Short spied a special policeman on the street one evening who had crossed him, and without so much as a warning he pulled his gun and began blazing away. The officer returned the fire but nobody was hit. Short had made his point, however, and word got around that there was no future in trying to buffalo the man they called "Little Luke." [66]

That reputation probably helped keep trouble away from the White Elephant those first two years when Short was running the gambling. He could handle things with a disarming smile and a slap on the back, or he could use hot lead. His professional reputation and managerial skills sufficed in those first two years (1885–87) to deter any poor losers from making trouble. He also succeeded beyond anyone's expectations in turning the upstairs into a cash cow for himself and his partners. The gambling concession was so profitable, in fact, that it attracted the avaricious attentions of Timothy Isaiah Courtright. The lawman-turned-extortionist pressured Luke to purchase some of his personal brand of "protection" in the winter of 1886–87, and when Short refused to cut the ex-marshal in on the profits, the stage was set for a showdown.

Courtright, motivated by hubris and greed in equal parts, told a friend that he had been treated disrespectfully at the White Elephant and would set things right with his six-gun.[67]

Meanwhile, the taciturn Short was playing it close to the vest about his own plans, saying only that he was not "contemplating any change of base" and would continue to call Fort Worth home. But the timing of his decision to sell out to Jake Johnson on February 7 suggests that he intended to "cash in his chips," as the gamblers put it, and move on to another town. Like most Western gamblers, Luke was rootless, following the action wherever it led and leaving a town whenever he wore out his welcome.

On the night of February 8, a liquored-up Courtright came calling at the White Elephant. He was through trying to muscle a piece of the action; what he wanted now was a piece of Luke Short. Pushing his way into the vestibule, he loudly demanded to see Short, who at that moment was having his shoes "blackened" while talking with friends at the bar. Short sauntered out to find Courtright and Johnson waiting for him, and the three men stepped out onto the sidewalk. Short and Courtright moved a little way up the block until they stood in front of a shooting gallery, an appropriate setting for what followed. Words were exchanged, quickly followed by gunplay, and when it was over, Courtright lay on the ground with five bullets in him from Luke's little hideaway pistol. He died on the spot.[68]

The coroner's inquest that met the next morning to "investigate the death of T. I. Courtright at the hands of Luke Short" found no cause to indict, calling it self-defense. This did not prevent plenty of grumbling about town that Short had literally gotten away with murder. Undaunted by the criticism, Short was ready to go back to work. He reconsidered his hasty decision to sell the gambling concession, but the deck had been reshuffled in just the ten days since that transaction. Jake Johnson had sold the concession to the third member of the partnership, giving Ward full control now over both the upstairs and downstairs.[69]

Short was forced to go to Ward, hat in hand, to reclaim the gambling concession. He approached Ward in October, and surprisingly perhaps, Ward agreed to sell it back to him for the same amount that had changed hands earlier (one thousand dollars). The transaction was done on the quiet, with nothing more than a handshake to seal it. This had to be some sort of record for a gambling concession trading hands.[70]

But if the price was right, some of the perks that went with the former arrangement were quite different. Luke and Hettie had to give up their fancy quarters upstairs. Furthermore, Luke was now reduced to working at a simple desk in Ward's downstairs office, although he still spent just as many hours at the saloon as before, and even had access to the combination safe.

With his kingdom taken away, the onetime "King of Fort Worth Gamblers" found that he had fewer important friends in the city. Some of the well-heeled customers who formerly patronized the upstairs took their business elsewhere. The nightly keno games, formerly such a draw, were canceled, too, much to the delight of the Law and Order Society.

The stress that came from the mounting criticism in addition to wondering if one of Courtright's friends was gong to put a bullet in him some dark night finally got to Luke Short. The man that colleagues called "thoroughly game" began to drink heavily, making him more pugnacious than ever. On the night of December 12, 1887, after too many rounds at the bar, he pulled his pistol and fired wildly into the floor. Other customers disarmed him and held him until the police arrived and hauled him off to jail. Fined twenty-five dollars for carrying the pistol and sentenced to twenty days in jail for the disturbance, Little Luke was washed up at the White Elephant. It was a sad end to a relationship that had started out as a match seemingly made in heaven.[71]

While the Short-Courtright gunfight has captured all the historical attention, it was not the last time gunfire was heard at 306–310 Main. Another homicide occurred only a month later, and like the previous shootout, just outside the front doors of the place. As before, it began with a falling out between members of the sporting fraternity over "money matters." Harry Williams, a visitor in town, was told by friends that Bob Hayward, a well-known local gambler, intended to "do him up" after Williams had gotten the better of him at the gaming tables. On the night of March 15, Harry was standing at the 310 entrance at 2:20 in the morning when a hack pulled up carrying Bob Hayward, who had been at the White Elephant earlier that evening, although not with Williams. Now, as he stepped out of the hack, the Fort Worth man was confronted by Williams, who demanded to know if the other man was looking for him. Snarled Hayward as he reached for his pistol, "Yes, you damned son of a bitch!"

Williams, too, was "heeled," but he waited coolly until his enemy's pistol had cleared leather; then faster than the telling, he drew his own pistol and put two slugs in Hayward. One of those shots hit the gambler in the right eye, causing instant death.

The crowd that came running to the scene included two policemen and a reporter for the *Fort Worth Gazette*. Before the officers hauled Williams off to jail, he calmly gave a statement to the newspapermen exonerating himself. Since he was the outsider in the affair while Hayward had been known as a man "popular among his associates for his liberality and genial ways," Williams could have been in serious trouble if the crowd had been in a vigilante mood. But there was a witness willing to speak in his behalf, and besides, both men were members of the sporting fraternity, among whom such affrays were normal.[72]

Hayward spent the night in jail, but he was turned loose at the coroner's inquest the next morning, thanks to the hack driver's testimony. He was on the next train out of town, but memory of the incident was not so easily banished from the public consciousness. For some time thereafter the curious came by 610 Main to gawk at the bloodstain on the sidewalk and cluck that the saloon seemed to be turning into a shooting gallery. It was not the kind of publicity that Bill Ward relished.

Nor did business benefit from what happened on the night of April 17, 1892. For the third time in less than five years gunfire erupted at the White Elephant. It was a Sunday night and this time the shooting was actually inside the saloon. A pair of self-styled sports, H. L. Cobb and James Nichols, had what others described as "some misunderstanding" in one of the clubrooms during the evening. These things usually arose over some perceived breach of gambling protocol. Cobb stormed off to his lodging to get a gun, and when he came back in the door at 306 Main, Nichols was waiting at the head of the staircase. With Cobb standing at the bottom of the stairs, the two men blazed away at each other with embarrassing lack of effect, firing a total of eight shots, all of which missed their target. When the smoke cleared, both men were still standing, but the frosted glass in the front doors had been shattered, and the second-floor paneling was well tattooed. Two members of the Fort Worth police department, who always seemed to be in the neighborhood whenever these things happened, raced to the scene and placed Cobb under arrest. They would have placed Nichols under arrest too, but he had taken advantage of the confusion to slip out the back door and take a cab home. By the time the police got to his house on West First, he had already flown the coop. Subsequently, it came out that Cobb had won the enmity of almost the entire local sporting fraternity, including Nichols, by regularly "cleaning them out" at the White Elephant. On the night of the shootout, Nichols had questioned Cobb's integrity, and gunplay followed.[73]

This string of violent incidents might have brought the full weight of the authorities down on the White Elephant and even gotten it shut down. But Fort Worth was still not that far removed from its frontier days, and things always seemed to return to normal after a bloody affair. After 1892, violence never again visited the White Elephant. Settling gambling disputes with pistols was becoming exceedingly unfashionable, and while gambling and liquor remained the key elements in the business, a certain level of refinement and respectability took hold. Perhaps the move to new digs that occurred in 1895 inaugurated the long reign of peace that followed. In any event, although the White Elephant would never be mistaken for a family establishment, it was still the premier entertainment palace of Fort Worth, which is not to say its preeminence went unchallenged.

After Bill Ward bought out his partners in 1887, Jake Johnson and Luke Short wasted no time before going into head-to-head competition with him. Johnson teamed up with another prominent saloon man, Vic Foster, to build their dream saloon just one block down from the White Elephant (406 Main). They gave it the grandiose name Palais Royal Saloon and had it ready for customers by October, 1888.

The Palais Royal followed Bill Ward's blueprint for success: elegant appointments, fully stocked bar, the finest dining, and high-class gambling behind closed doors. They even hired a "big name" gambler to run the gambling concession—Luke Short, who happened to be looking for a new home base about that time. The Palais Royal's grand open-ing on October 20 was written up as an "Event" in the pages of the *Daily Gazette*.[74] But the Johnson-Foster-Short partnership could never dis-place the reigning prince of Fort Worth saloon men. Johnson and Foster did not have the business smarts of Bill Ward, and Luke Short died of complications from "dropsy" (gout) in 1893.

Bill Ward was the one significant difference between the White Ele-phant and every other saloon in Fort Worth, including the Palais Royal. But Ward's power was as much about perception as reality, and the real-ity was that he never ran the whole show by himself. After his brother dropped out of the picture and Johnson and Short moved on, the man-agement picture became more muddled. By 1891 Ward felt the need to unburden himself of some of his responsibilities, so he took on a new partner and added a layer of what we now call "middle management" to the operation. It was a different organizational structure than he had em-ployed previously with either his brother or the holders of the gambling concession. His new partner was Louis Maas, a veteran saloon man who had spent most of the eighties running the Occidental Saloon. Before hooking up with Ward, Maas, in partnership with Giles H. Day, had run the bar at the Pickwick Hotel (formerly the El Paso). The Maas-Ward partnership proved to be short-lived; in 1892 Maas was back behind the Pickwick bar.

The middle management team in 1891 included Louis Maas's brother William and John H. Teller. They hired on about the same time, and both followed Louis Maas out the door within a year. Bill Ward was master of his domain again.[75] But the clock could not be turned back to 1884. The frontier saloon model of one-man-one-bar was being superceded by the corporate hierarchy of landlord, proprietor, and mul-tiple layers of management. The White Elephant was too big an opera-tion for one man.

Another management shake-up came in 1894 after Ward decided to move the White Elephant to new, larger digs. The relocation dragged on for months, causing the saloon to drop out of the business listings com-pletely in the 1894–95 city directory, but it reopened in time for the next edition (1896–97). During the interval it relocated to the 600 block of Main, right next door to the prestigious Commercial Club Building,

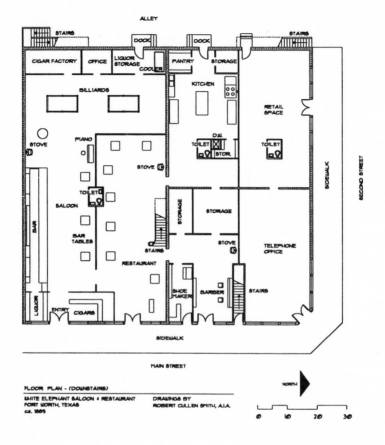

FLOOR PLAN - (DOWNSTAIRS)

WHITE ELEPHANT SALOON & RESTAURANT
FORT WORTH, TEXAS
ca. 1889

DRAWINGS BY
ROBERT CULLEN SMITH, A.I.A.

which anchored the southern end of the block. The White Elephant now occupied the Winfree Building (sometimes incorrectly spelled "Winfrey") and the building just to the north of it, separated by a narrow alleyway.

The Winfree possessed by far the better pedigree. It was a two-story brick structure built in 1885 by W. Glen Walker for "office building/ store" use and sold to C. V. Winfree and W. H. Loyd in April, 1889. Loyd exited the partnership, and it was known as the "Winfree Building" when the White Elephant moved in. As a result of cryptic leasing and subleasing arrangements over the next few years, the building acquired several proprietors of record before being sold to Winfield Scott in 1908 for twenty-five thousand dollars. By that date, it was widely known as the "White Elephant Building" and was sitting on land Scott had acquired in the fall of 1894 (block 97, lots 13–16).[76]

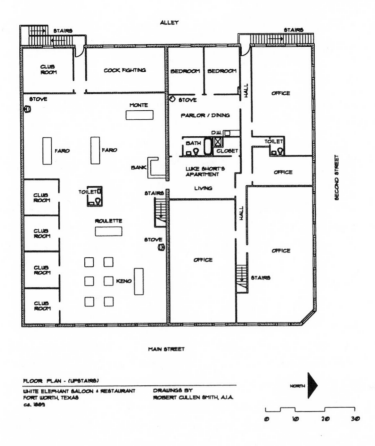

ALLEY

FLOOR PLAN - (UPSTAIRS)
WHITE ELEPHANT SALOON & RESTAURANT   DRAWINGS BY
FORT WORTH, TEXAS   ROBERT CULLEN SMITH, A.I.A.
ca. 1893

NORTH

MAIN STREET

The second building, directly north of the Winfree, lacks an established pedigree. Its only tenant of note was the White Elephant Saloon and Restaurant, and it was eventually torn down, to be replaced by the S. H. Kress Building in 1936.[77]

With the passage of time, Winfield Scott's association with the White Elephant would assume mythic proportions, but that was due to Scott's larger-than-life persona, not his personal involvement in the White Elephant. By the mid-1890s Winfield Scott was a man who had made one fortune as a cattle baron and was in the process of making a second as a real estate developer. He was the biggest "player" in the downtown real estate market, a virtual land baron who owned a checkerboard of prime property stretching from Courthouse Square to the Railroad Reservation. C. I. Dickinson was his trusty real estate agent, handling Scott's portfolio while the boss took the role of absentee landlord.

Among Scott's principal holdings were the railroad freight terminal and a slew of hotels: the Terminal, Worth, Metropolitan, and Majestic.[78]

At its new location in the 600 block of Main, the White Elephant was more swank than ever, beginning with the twin ivory elephants that flanked the saloon's front doors.[79] The business was more of a three-headed hydra than ever before—saloon, restaurant, gambling operation—taking up two separate buildings. At 610 Main the Winfree Building was occupied by the White Elephant Turf Exchange, while across the alleyway at 606–608 Main was the White Elephant Restaurant and Saloon. The restaurant occupied the south end of the building, just across the alley from the Turf Exchange, while the saloon was on the north end. Separate outside entrances kept up appearances for hungry customers who did not want to be seen entering a saloon, while an inside connecting doorway allowed customers to move easily between the two rooms.

The Turf Exchange was the new gambling center of the White Elephant, serving the same clientele who used to patronize the upstairs rooms at the former location. The "Turf Exchange" name was familiar to Fort Worth sports from the mid-1880s when there had been a saloon by that name at 304 Main, right next door to the old White Elephant.[80] It was also a classic case of using elevated language to disguise sordid behavior. The "turf" referred to racetrack betting; the "exchange" was a term borrowed from the world of business and finance for a central location where gamblers could place their bets on a variety of contests, like a horse race, a boxing match, or a ball game. In other words, the White Elephant had become a bookmaking joint!

In part, the metamorphosis was a reflection of the au courant "Progressive" attitudes, which frowned on casino-style gambling in any form, whether it be cards, roulette, or keno. The old-fashioned games could still be found upstairs at the Turf Exchange, but that fact was kept quiet by a conspiracy of silence. As far as the public was concerned, the White Elephant was simply a legitimate betting parlor for gentlemen. A telegraph hook-up brought in the latest reports of horse races, prize fights, and ball games from all over the country so that bettors did not have to wait for the morning edition of the newspaper. Gambling had gone high-tech. A modern business operation had replaced the sort of set-up Luke Short once ran, and the bookmaker had replaced the sporting man as the main player in the gambling profession. The owner of the building was now H. T. Huey and Company, a corporate entity not as concerned with its public image as the Winfree family had been.

Despite all efforts to disguise it, however, gambling was still gambling, and therefore still anathema to a vocal segment of the community. The moral watchdogs were quick to size up the White Elephant's new gambling operation, no matter how innocent the name sounded. Those who opposed gambling opposed it in all forms, even if it was done by a man sitting at a telegraph key behind a wire cage. The Turf Exchange lasted only about four years. By 1901 the Winfree Building had been partitioned into office space and rented to respectable tenants like Judge R. E. Beckham and the Texas Title Company.

Meanwhile, next door Bill Ward kept right on running the saloon and restaurant as he always had—winning customers' loyalty with the best in food, spirits, and service. He had severed his connection to the gambling operation except for sharing the "brand name" and the same landlord (Winfield Scott). With business going well and Ward devoting more time to his city council duties, he was forced to take on another manager in 1896, Charles E. Graham. The boss no longer came around every night to chat up the customers with his personal brand of blarney. He left that up to Graham, but the latter departed in 1900, and Ward again assumed the title and the duties of "General Manager."

If that was the full extent of his involvement in the 1907–1908 years, it appears on the surface to represent a sharp drop in power and prestige from his former days as "proprietor." On the other hand, his official title may have been nothing more than a public relations ploy by a man keeping one eye on his image as a city councilman.[81] There is no way of knowing Ward's exact legal connection to the saloon and restaurant at this time. What is clear is that in 1907 the two sides of the business went their separate ways.

The decade from 1896 to 1906 were the glory years of the White Elephant. It boasted all the refinements of any "fancy saloon," beginning with "ice cold" beer, kept chilled thanks to regular ice deliveries from one of the city's three ice factories. For those with more cultured tastes, "the finest [imported] brands of Scotch and Irish whiskies,

French brandy and Holland gin" were available, while customers of more modest means or simply a preference for the domestic stuff could order "the best brands of old sour mash in the state." [82] The quality and sheer variety of the bar stock was always a point of pride for Bill Ward.

When the beer stocks ran low, "reinforcements" were as close as the beer vaults of the Anheuser-Busch Brewing Company at Throckmorton and Third and the Texas Brewing Company on Jones Street between Ninth and Twelfth. Both delivered right to the back door with only a phone call. The hard stuff had to be brought in by train, but since Fort Worth was at the center of a dozen rail lines radiating in all directions, there was never any fear of being cut off from regular supplies.

The interior of the "new" White Elephant was, if anything, even more posh than the original. The front entrance to the Winfree building was now watched over by a liveried doorman whose job it was to open the door for the right sort of customers and shoo away the undesirable types. Just inside the front doors the tobacco apartment had been downsized to a tobacco stand set off to one side. Passers-by now had an unhindered view of the interior so they could see with their own eyes that nothing inherently immoral was going on inside. Past the tobacco stand, the customer could either head for the Turf Exchange or the bar and public area.

And that bar was something to behold. Located on the right side of the room, it stretched forty feet from one end to the other. It was fancier than the old Luke Short back-bar and longer than the Waco Tap's, which for years had held the title of "biggest bar in Fort Worth." [83] The rest of the room in front of the bar was taken up with chairs and tables for footsore drinkers and penny-ante poker players. Strategically placed about the room were a cast-iron, potbellied stove and an upright piano. The polished wood floors were buffed, swept, and mopped regularly, although they soon bore the scars of countless chairs being pushed back and countless booted feet, some with spurs, walking over them.

Among the notable amenities of the new location were electric lights in hanging chandeliers and several telephone jacks conveniently located about the room, allowing customers who had overstayed their visit to request a telephone and call in an excuse to the wife at home. There were also three indoor toilets or "water closets" as they were quaintly termed.

In the back were the usual billiard tables, where a man could retire with his drink and indulge in a little relatively quiet pool shooting with friends. Even with the high-tech and high-tone Turf Exchange, the billiard tables continued to do a steady business as part of the White Elephant's facilities, though "Billiard Hall" had long since been dropped from the business' name. Old-time cowboys who had come to Fort Worth in the early days seemed to particularly favor the back rooms at the White Elephant to gather and reminisce over their beers.

The total floor space taken up by the Turf Exchange and the saloon was about 4370 square feet (46' × 95'). This represented a smaller area than the main room at the previous site, but with the restaurant now located next door, there was more room for the gamblers and drinkers.

Ventilation, which was always a problem in nineteenth-century public buildings before electric fans, was taken care of by having louvers and windows on three sides. Those windows were the architectural reason for the narrow (five feet wide) alleys on two sides. They represented the earliest form of Texas "air conditioning."

The restaurant was first class, from its uniformed waiters right down to its linen napkins. That was a tradition that had been established at its first location. Josephine Earp, who was not particularly impressed with Fort Worth itself, nonetheless believed the White Elephant restaurant "offered a menu as good as that in any large-city eatery." [84] Bill Ward recognized that good food and drink went together and that serving both was more profitable than serving either by itself. He had replaced the free-lunch counter with a full menu and located the dining area up front where passers-by could look in the windows and see happy diners enjoying themselves. He even gave diners their own entrance when the restaurant was at 308 Main so they did not have to walk through the saloon to get to the restaurant. From such modest beginnings, the restaurant side of the business had grown until it got its own building at the 600-block location. [85]

Along the way, its service and food became legendary, the equivalent of a modern five-star eatery. It was furnished with high-grade, cut glassware and the finest in dishware, linens, and silver. Dining was transformed into a gourmet experience with such tasty fare as fresh fish, oysters, and game, in addition to the usual steaks and chops. The restaurant's advertising followed the dictum "If you have to ask how much it costs, you can't afford it" by promising, "Everything in season—The finest the market affords," without listing prices. The house specialty was oysters, served "any style" the customer requested. These were genuine Texas oysters, caught in the waters off the coast and shucked before shipping. Then they were packed into half-gallon wooden kegs with each keg nesting in a flour-sized barrel full of cracked ice. Keg, barrel, and oysters were then ready for quick shipment by rail straight to Fort Worth.[86]

In January, 1896, the menu included lake trout, Spanish mackerel, black bass, gulf trout, red fish, pickerel, and, incredibly for an inland city in the days of steam travel, fresh lobster. Citizens were urged to "Stop here for good dinner or lunch."[87] After a big meal fit for a king and queen, or a cattleman and his lady, patrons could top off their meal with a fine selection of "the choicest wines and liquors" plus cigars from the house stocks for the gentlemen.

The White Elephant even served a version of "take out," delivering hot meals to "patrons of the games" next door. There was no extra charge for this service, and it proved quite popular with men who did not wish to leave the table while on a winning streak.[88] For those good people who simply preferred eating to wagering, the White Elephant offered a refined, sit-down experience comparable if not superior to any hotel in the city.

Unlike most nineteenth-century restaurants during the heyday of Victorian propriety, the White Elephant allowed men and women to eat together in the same dining room either alone or in mixed couples. But the serving staff consisted entirely of male waiters, despite the advance in gender equality achieved by both J. M. Peers and Fred Harvey years before. In 1876 both men began using "female waiters" in their restaurants, Colonel Peers at his Peers House hotel in Fort Worth, and Harvey at his train station restaurant in Topeka, Kansas. But while the girls were described admiringly as "ornamental" and "exceedingly useful," and the practice was considered daringly progressive, waitresses did not catch on locally.[89]

While they were important, menus and fancy back-bars never defined the White Elephant; it was always the upstairs gambling rooms, which constituted the inner sanctum of the place. At the 300-block location narrow stairs on the north wall, reached by walking through the dining area, provided the only public access to the gambling rooms. That arrangement was corrected in a remodeling sometime before 1893, which saw the staircase moved over to the saloon side of the room (the 306 address).

When the new White Elephant reopened at 608–610, the narrow stairs had been replaced by a grand "sweeping staircase" up to the second floor, located just inside the doors between the two front entrances. That stairway was "carpeted with the most expensive carpet material," and at the head of the stairs was a table "stacked six inches high with gold coins."[90] It was a brilliant come-on: through the front doors and straight ahead lay the path to easy riches for the skilled gambler or the lucky stiff. The joke was that the coins were the unwilling donations of those who had climbed the stairs to gamblers' heaven only to come back down to reality with their pockets considerably lighter. Jokes aside, only the serious, well-heeled gamblers ever gained admission to the upstairs rooms.

Like the downstairs, the upstairs also got an image makeover in the move from the 300 block to the 600 block. The cockpit was banished, whether as a result of moral qualms, legal pressure, or simply fading customer appeal is unclear. Henceforward, cards, dice, and the roulette wheel were the tools of the gambling trade upstairs at the White Elephant, and the only chickens allowed on the premises were headed for the cooking pot. The second floor was divided into a series of small rooms, which could be entered off a central hallway, or, for more privacy, through doorways between rooms. As many as a dozen rooms were available for customers with good connections and a good bankroll.

According to legend the upstairs was the site of more than just gambling. The stories say that a bordello also operated there, although no one has ever suggested that Bill Ward was a flesh-peddler. If there was any hanky-panky, it occurred in the clubrooms that were rented out to private parties.

But the legend raises an important question about the relationship between the White Elephant and the world's oldest profession. Prostitution was the great unmentionable in the saloon business. Violence and drunkenness were accepted as part of the natural order, but prostitution seemed to be a genuine embarrassment even to hardened Westerners because however rough and untamed they were, these were still men raised on Victorian morality. Saloons in general got their bad reputations as dens of assignation from the dives on the low end of the business and from being lumped together by their critics with dance halls and variety theaters.

While men like Bill and John Ward were not saints, they were not pimps or procurers either. And they were several cuts above fellow saloon proprietor Henry P. Shiel. The former Fort Worth marshal (1874–75) ran a saloon in the city for six years where he rented "attached rooms" in the back to prostitutes. For shamelessly mixing the professions of barkeep and pimp, Shiel was considered a black sheep among Fort Worth saloon men.[91]

Variety theaters were the worst offenders. Saloon men tried to keep a discrete distance between their places and the theaters, although the lines were far from clear. The reasons for their uneasiness, however, are quite clear. The "actresses" who worked in the theaters were considered little better than prostitutes, and on top of that, the saloon men resented the competition with their main business of selling liquor. Pressured by the saloonkeepers and concerned about the odor of immorality exuded by the variety theaters, the Fort Worth City Council in 1890 decreed that theaters could no longer sell "intoxicants and keep 'beer jerkers' about their premises."[92] The immediate effect of this ordinance is unknown, but the lack of public reaction to it is a sure sign that it did not bring about much change.

The city's respectable saloonkeepers maintained an uneasy *entente cordiale* with the world's oldest profession. That relationship worked this way: Strictly speaking, it was not permitted for the girls to be in the saloons according to city ordinance.[93] Since the city's "soiled doves" were well known by name and reputation, it was impossible for them to slip quietly in through the front door to solicit. But everybody involved—the girls, the saloonkeepers, even the police—blatantly flouted the ordinance. The freelance girls (those who did not have a crib or parlor house to call home) used the back door to come and go. The wine rooms at the back of the nicer saloons were known to serve a double purpose:

storage area and meeting place where the girls sat and waited for customers to come to them. Regular customers knew the routine.

For parlor house girls, the situation was slightly different. Because they worked the "night shift," their days were their own. It was normal for them to go back and forth between their digs and nearby saloons where they sat in the back rooms and drank or ate their suppers before going on duty. The back room of a saloon was one of the few public places where they could congregate freely without the owner running them off.

The biggest surprise is that in Fort Worth both black and white girls were to be found in the back rooms of otherwise strictly segregated joints. Both groups were barred from being out front, but everybody knew where they could be found if a man was so inclined. And if violence broke out, the girls could skedaddle out the back exit because if the police found them on the premises when answering an official call, they would be arrested on the spot.

The White Elephant under Bill Ward's management was not the type of place to allow "floozies" to hang out in the public rooms. But this is not to say the saloon's wine room was never used for assignation purposes. There were no parlor houses within a several-block radius at either the 300- or 600-block location, but there was a convenient back alley at both addresses.

In its second incarnation, the connection between the White Elephant and prostitution in local lore is much stronger. At the 600-block address the dozen or so small rooms upstairs were perfect for discreet liaisons as well as for private gambling parties, and for years rumor had it that prostitution was indeed on the menu upstairs at the White Elephant. The girls, so the story went, slipped in and out through the back entrance, using the alley between the Winfree and Commercial Club buildings, in order to keep up the males-or-couples-only fiction. The lack of arrests or public outcry shows that management was effective at keeping it out of sight, not that it did not occur.[94]

While solicitation at the White Elephant is a matter of speculation, the rest of the operation is an open book, revealing a business as well managed and efficiently run as any in the city. Among the managers Ward employed to help run the saloon in the later years were John H.

Tiller, Charles E. Graham, and Lavin Martin. To manage the restaurant at different times, he hired Oscar Nowak, brothers J. K. and Fred Smalley, and another pair of gentlemen, John Coleman and Michael Max.

The most important staff, below the managers, were the men who worked on the saloon side of the business. In descending order of importance, those were the "dealers," a small platoon of bartenders, a barber, and a shoeshine boy. Not a single dealer's name at the White Elephant has come down to us today despite their elite status. Members of this exclusive profession were experts at the gamblers' art and adept at relieving "board whackers" of their money without sending away too many disgruntled customers.[95] They could deal blackjack, operate a keno "goose," a faro bank, or a roulette wheel, and consistently turn a profit for the house. Their skills were in such demand that even gender was not a barrier to membership in the profession. Indeed, women dealers were the "other profession" (besides actresses) sometimes allowed in respectable places, although there is no record of any ever being employed at the White Elephant.

The bartenders who worked behind the White Elephant's bar were as classy as the surroundings. They dressed immaculately in white aprons and jackets, white shirts with stiff collars, and bow ties. They did more than just "pull pints"; these gentlemen considered themselves "mixologists" in the elevated vernacular of the day. They knew how to chat up a customer, mix any drink in the book, and break up trouble before it got started. They could also be trusted as stakeholders when serious matters were being wagered. Of their drink-mixing talents, it was said, "They have artists at the White Elephant, and there's no drink known to modern or ancient times they cannot concoct with all the latest improvements.[96] The closeness of the bartending fraternity and its place on the social ladder was illustrated by the presence of a "bartenders' row" in a prominent section of Oakwood Cemetery, the city's premier public burial ground.

A haircut was another service available at the White Elephant and another sign that this was strictly a gentleman's saloon. The barbershop was a modest, one-chair operation located in a little nook off the main floor. On any given day, the resident barber could be found at his station. In 1885 George Hoeltzel ran the barbershop.[97]

The lowly shoeshine boy was a ubiquitous fixture who hovered in the shadows, eyes alertly roving over the faces in the room looking for anyone who needed a little spit polish. A customer could always get his shoes shined while he stood at the bar just by giving a "hi sign" in the boy's direction. The lad who did the work was probably a young African American lad, whose age and color did not bar him from the premises only because of the important service he performed. If an inebriated customer happened to miss one of the spittoons strategically placed along the rail, that shine became a necessity. Many of the customers ignored the shoeshine boy, but a "sport" always had to keep his boots blacked; it was part of the dapper image.[98]

At the end of the day, the White Elephant and places like it could only exist with the connivance of the local authorities. The fact that Bill Ward sat on the Police Committee of the city council did not hurt, but the collusion went deeper than that. Even before Ward won a seat on the council, the saloons were treated with kid gloves. They were allowed to hire their own "special policemen" who wore the uniforms and had all the authority of the regular force but were paid by the owners and therefore could apply the laws selectively to benefit their employers. On top of that, the saloon owners and members of the small, underpaid police force were on a first-name basis, taking care of each other in numerous ways. In 1902 Bill Ward provided an alibi for Fort Worth policeman Al Ray who had been arrested and fined in San Antonio for carrying a pistol in violation of both city ordinance and state law. Ward blithely stated that the officer had been on official duty investigating the theft of a suit of clothes from Ward and therefore authorized to carry the pistol.[99] Such small favors cultivated good relations between the saloon man and the boys in blue.

Because of this cozy arrangement between the authorities and the saloon, the White Elephant was never "raided," and very few arrests for any reason were ever made on the premises. Members of Fort Worth's Finest were much more likely to stop by for a drink than to answer an official call at the White Elephant.

The glory days of the White Elephant lasted from the mid-1890s to the middle of the next decade. The main competition during those years for the "carriage trade" (those who arrived in fine style via horse-drawn carriage) was Joseph G. Wheat's Stag Saloon at 702 Main. Like the White Elephant, it stocked "the best wines, liquors and cigars," including "Martin's Best Whiskey," which was manufactured and bottled right in the city by Martin Casey. The Stag's dining room also offered a lavish menu of fresh fish, oysters, game, and pastry dishes and was a gathering place for the city's young bulls.[100]

In 1901 Wheat flung the gauntlet down to Scott and Ward when he bought the six-story building in the 800 block of Main that later bore his name (the Wheat Building). Constructed in 1890, it was the city's first "skyscraper," and Wheat put its lofty height to good use by constructing an elegant roof garden restaurant. Yet, while it boasted two things the White Elephant could never aspire to, cool rooftop breezes and a panoramic view, it could never compete as a gambling emporium. The White Elephant was still king in that department.

Still, the White Elephant could not afford to ignore Wheat's brazen challenge. Ward's response was swift: a major redecoration of the saloon that necessitated closing it down for three months in the spring of 1901. When it reopened on June 8, the papers reported it as another grand "Event," stating that "thousands called on Mr. W. H. Ward" during the grand re-opening.[101]

Competition also came from private clubs like the Commercial Club (later the Fort Worth Club), the Cattle Exchange, and the Bank Exchange. All three, like the White Elephant, catered to the better class of customers, but they were even more exclusive with their restricted membership rolls. The White Elephant carried on at what it did best, filling a niche somewhere between the dives of the Acre and the private clubs uptown. Its advertising invited "transient customers" to come, but the unstated caveat was that they had to be well-heeled transients.[102]

Meanwhile, a different sort of competition had arisen from working-man's saloons owned and operated by the breweries. Powerful national companies like Anheuser-Busch and Miller preferred to control their own retail sales, thus cutting out the distributors and keeping competitors' product out of their saloons. This monopolistic practice became a trend in the late nineteenth century, one that accelerated in the early twentieth century. The company-owned (or leased) taverns had the advantages of deep pockets and political muscle that the independent saloons could not match. They could also offer expansive free-lunch buffets and cut-rate prices on their beer. From the turn of the century until World War I, Miller Brewery leased twenty-two taverns in Fort Worth. The effect of these joints on the White Elephant's business was like Chinese "death from a thousand cuts."

Other changes arrived with the changing times. A new breed of celebrities began coming through the doors of the White Elephant around the turn of the century: men who were not "heeled" or made their living with a deck of cards. They were "sports" of a different kind; men like New York Giants manager John "Iron Jaws" McGraw who brought his baseball team to Fort Worth for spring training; boxer James J. Corbett; and boxing promoter Tex Rickard. These were the sort of men who could stand at the bar with the locals crowded around them and never have to buy a drink all night. Their presence added an invaluable celebrity cachet and was shrewd advertising for the Turf Exchange.

Another visitor in those years who cared nothing for gambling or carousing was a brash young university professor and folk-song collector named John A. Lomax. In 1908 Lomax came to town with a five-hundred-dollar research grant from Harvard University and a hankering to record the music of genuine cowboys. He found his way to the back room of the White Elephant where he "cornered a bunch of Ediphone-shy cowboy singers" and asked them to record some of the old standards they had serenaded the longhorns with going up the Chisholm Trail. With the songs he recorded there, Lomax wrote a new chapter in the history of American folk music and won the appreciation of the bemused cowpokes who still cherished memories of Fort Worth as a trail town.[103]

Changing times, in the end, also brought about the demise of the White Elephant. Part of the uniqueness of the White Elephant had always been its successful integration of three different operations—gambling, drinking, and dining—under one sign. Burgower and his partners began that arrangement, and Bill Ward perfected it. This synergy was achieved not just by having everything under one sign, but in subtle ways. For instance, a customer could buy six dollars worth of tickets—good at the bar, the game rooms, or the restaurant—for only five dollars.[104] Tokens, the favored advertising medium of the day, were dispensed freely and honored at either the restaurant or the bar. Food delivered from the restaurant to the men sitting at the gaming tables was another profitable synergy.

Changing morality ultimately broke up this integrated, three-part operation. As professional gambling was forced behind closed doors and then outlawed completely, it could no longer flout the law. The "pass" it had enjoyed with the authorities for so many years had been a key element to the success of men like Luke Short. In those days, the White Elephant had the classiest public gambling rooms in the city, and a man could spend a pleasurable evening there without being harassed by the do-gooders.

After the turn of the century, as the first wave of Progressive reform swept the nation, gambling was forced further and further into the shadows. In 1907 the city council passed an ordinance outlawing gambling houses—for the umpteenth time in the city's history, but this time it seemed likely to stick. The Suffragists and Prohibitionists were both behind it, and Police Chief J. H. Maddox promised to enforce it. Despite the growing consensus against professional gambling, it is unlikely that the White Elephant cut all ties to it just because the reformers were in the ascendancy. What was true, however, was that a stranger in town could no longer expect to be directed to a friendly game just by inquiring on the street. He had to have the right "references," because under the new order, games were by "invitation only."

And it was not just gambling that was under attack. The town's toleration for the entire saloon culture had worn thin over the years. The first restriction on business hours with any teeth had come in 1889, on Sunday, September 15, when a new ordinance went into effect forcing all the saloons to close on "the Lord's Day." This was not the first time such an ordinance had been passed, but this one was enforced. That was new. The county attorney ordered notices posted in every establishment beforehand, and on that first Sunday they were all "hermetically sealed." [105]

As a crimp in business it was only a minor inconvenience, but as a harbinger of things to come, the Sunday closing ordinance got every saloon owner's attention. It was part of a larger prohibition movement being fought out in Texas. The first campaign to prohibit the sale of intoxicating liquors in the state occurred in 1887. It was narrowly defeated in a statewide referendum, but prohibition advocates continued to campaign vigorously in every major election for the next thirty years. Along the way, they lobbied for "local option" ordinances on the county level.[106] This unrelenting pressure put a damper on the saloon business.

The reformist tide against saloons was rising. In 1905 the city council passed an ordinance defining the boundaries of the "saloon district" and prohibiting any saloon from operating outside those boundaries.[107] A statewide Saloon Closing Law passed by the legislature in 1913 went further than any local ordinance heretofore. It required bars to close down for the night no later than 9:30 and not reopen until 6:00 A.M. the next morning on weekdays. They were to remain closed from Saturday night at 9:30 until 6:00 A.M. Monday morning. These hours applied not just to bars but also to any "grocery establishments or restaurants, bootblack stands, news stands, cigar stands and any character of business" connected to a saloon. Furthermore, saloon owners were not even allowed to enter their establishments on Sunday to clean up or turn out the lights.

The same law also aimed to eliminate the notorious "blind pigs" (unlicensed establishments) and backstreet dives that flourished in districts like the Acre. Now the interiors had to be open to scrutiny from passers-by on the street. This meant unshuttered windows and wide-open doors, the logic being that the best way to attack evil was to throw light on it, and the law aimed to do this literally.

The new get-tough attitude did not stop with the saloons alone. Even liquor ads could be banned from the local newspapers in dry counties according to a ruling by the state's attorney general.[108] And that same official decreed that combination restaurant-saloons like the White Elephant could not simply hang a curtain between the bar and the dining room and call the latter "closed" while the former stayed open. "The saloon must have a permanent and substantial closing," the ordinance stated, "and it is not sufficient even if the bar should be separated by curtains or other temporary partition from the rest of the house."[109] Such a provision aimed a dagger directly at the heart of places like the White Elephant. The intent of the reformers was not just to regulate saloons into line but also to regulate them out of business.

Unlike the crusaders who had launched previous campaigns, the new reformers were both organized and completely united. The Anti-Saloon League of Texas, led by J. B. Gambrell, editor of the *Baptist Standard*, was a political force to be reckoned with in these years, leading the charge for national prohibition. In November, 1913, the reform group announced their own "War on Liquor," one that was independent of milquetoast legislative enactments.[110] Meanwhile, popular Baptist preacher J. Frank Norris was denouncing vice operators by name from the pulpit in his Sunday sermons, creating enough of a stir to persuade someone to torch the First Baptist Church and the parsonage in separate incidents in 1912.[111]

As saloons fell into public disfavor, the White Elephant's dining room lost business because of its association with the bar. Decent folk preferred to eat elsewhere. The restaurant was finally sold to F. H. Reid, who converted it into a chili parlor in 1907. In the end, with two of the White Elephant's heads lopped off, all that remained was the saloon, and by the second decade of the twentieth century it was fighting a rearguard action against the surging forces of law and order.

Finally, Ward himself, the crown prince of Fort Worth gambling, was not getting any younger, and his other entertainment interests took up an ever-increasing share of his time after 1900. In 1904 he built Panther Park for the "Cats" baseball team. Running the park and the team itself was nearly a full-time job, which is why he sold the team in 1909.[112]

As the new century advanced, he was also one of the first impresarios to recognize the hot new trend in public entertainment, moving pictures. In 1907 Ward could look right out the White Elephant's front windows and see two storefront theaters across the street.[113] Increasingly after the turn of the century, old variety theaters and peep shows were being turned into movie houses, which attracted a broader audience and involved a lot less overhead than a saloon. Ward opened up a couple of places in Fort Worth where the new one- and two-reelers could be shown. Saloons would never go out of fashion, but movie theaters did not have to pay protection money, employ bouncers, or purchase a liquor license from the city.

Bill Ward the "city father" also found the old image of the White Elephant to be an embarrassing blot on his public image as a responsible businessman. His retirement from the saloon business was well timed. But what was good for the businessman proved fatal for the business. With declining profits and management turnovers, the White Elephant lived out its final years on past glories.

Even new management would not have helped because the price of being in the saloon business was no longer affordable. Those who were not shutting down voluntarily were being forced out. In March, 1913, seven Fort Worth bars had their liquor licenses yanked by the state comptroller. Their sin was opening for business on Sunday, thus violating a law formerly flouted with impunity. But this time the authorities moved promptly to shut down the offending establishments.

The White Elephant had not been the jewel in Winfield Scott's real estate portfolio for many years, and when the old cattleman died in 1911, it was left to Bill Ward to make final disposition of what had become more of a burden than an asset. After the crackdowns on business hours and open gambling, he could see the writing on the wall. He tried selling the place but could find no buyers. Saloons were no longer the cash cows they had once been.

On top of everything else, the new owner of the building and the land it sat on was adamant about not having a notorious saloon occupy the property. That had never been a problem so long as Winfield Scott was the owner, but Scott died on October 26, 1911, and his "vast fortune in real estate" passed to his second wife, Elizabeth. The successor owner was a very old-fashioned lady with the highest moral standards coupled with a willingness to speak her mind. She wanted to purge Scott's portfolio of unsavory properties, and that began with the White Elephant.[114] Bill Ward had the choice of closing the doors or re-inventing the White Elephant. He chose the former option. Conventional wisdom said the reason was "financial reverses," but Ward was neither broke nor in debt over his head. He was simply bowing to reality and cutting his losses.[115]

In the end, the White Elephant died a quiet death. There is no record of when the last round of drinks was served or who the last customer was, no public statements from Bill Ward revealing his personal feelings about leaving the business that had been so good to him for so long. Perhaps some of the old stockmen who had once "dealt stud" around the tables, "bucked the tiger" in faro games, or spent pleasant

A tantalizing view of the "second" White Elephant on the 600 block of Main Street, three blocks south of its first location. This view shows Main Street, ca. 1911, looking north from the east side of the 800 block. The Fort Worth Club building (with Haltom's Jewelers on the first floor) is on the corner of 7th and Main. Directly north of it, under the awning and the beer sign, is the Winfree Building with the White Elephant. Courtesy Fort Worth Club Archives

hours leaning up against the mahogany bar talking cattle prices may have raised a glass in salute at the end. But there was nothing to publicly mark the passing of a genuine local institution. A fitting epitaph might have borrowed the words of Prospero in Shakespeare's *The Tempest:* "Our revels now are ended."

When it closed, the White Elephant was one of the last visible connections to Fort Worth's wild and woolly days. For twenty-eight exciting years it had defined shady elegance in Fort Worth, from its magnificent back-bar to its exclusive private clubrooms upstairs. In the process it had seen some of the best and the worst characters come through its doors, but never the hoi polloi. The White Elephant brought national attention to Fort Worth—not all of it positive, to be sure—and set the local standard in food and bar service. Over the years it had seen its share of bloodshed, disreputable deals, illegal gambling, and shady characters. By 1913, the good citizens of Fort Worth were no longer proud of that heritage. Places like the White Elephant were viewed as anachronisms. With the frontier gone, even the name "White Elephant" no longer had any special meaning to a new generation of urbanites whose horizons tended to end at the city limits.

The "White Elephant" name was unofficially retired for the next six decades until the city began to take a new pride in its Western heritage. In 1976 a new ownership group consisting of Joe Dulle, Jane Schlansker, and Gene Miller resurrected the famous name for a popular bar on the city's historic North Side. "We brought back the White Elephant name," recalled Schlansker proudly when interviewed for a newspaper story later. In the years that followed, the legendary saloon was used to film scenes for the *Dallas* and *Walker, Texas Ranger* television series, was listed in *Esquire Magazine*'s "100 Best Bars in America," and earned an honorable mention in author Dan Jenkins's novel *Baja Oklahoma*. Not a bad record for the third incarnation of a frontier saloon! In 2002 the White Elephant was sold once again, this time to the owners of the Lonesome Dove Western Bistro. The new ownership promised to reinvigorate the venerable saloon. As one of the new owners said, "I don't want a museum. I want a fun saloon." [116]

If the White Elephant's customers today are not in the same league as the flashy dressers and big spenders of the old days, still, the current notoriety and hospitality of the place would make Bill Ward proud. And the annual restaging of the Short-Courtright gunfight in the street out front is a quaint reminder of the violent heritage associated with that once-legendary name.

The White Elephant's place in the history books is assured. It was the first place in Fort Worth to combine a bar and a first-class restaurant under one roof, providing luxurious surroundings for the prosaic pursuits of eating, drinking, and gambling. The combination of integrated operations and luxurious surroundings attracted the best clientele and made the White Elephant Fort Worth's saloon *par excellence* in its heyday.

The modern reincarnation of the White Elephant does not aspire to such exalted heights, but it is in the perfect location, where neighbors like the Stockyards Hotel and the Northside Coliseum serve new generations of customers. The ghosts of Bill Ward, Luke Short, and Winfield Scott must be smiling.

NOTES

1. Richard F. Selcer, *Hell's Half Acre: The Life and Legend of a Red-light District* (Fort Worth: Texas Christian University Press, 1991), 133. Years later, old-timers, interviewed for the Texas Writers' Project claimed that this was the hey-day of the wide-open saloon in Fort Worth history. See "Research Data: Fort Worth and Tarrant County, Texas," *Federal Writers' Project*, vol. 2 (Fort Worth: Fort Worth Public Library Unit, 1941), 507, located at Fort Worth Public Library Central Branch, Local History and Genealogy Dept.

2. "First Saloon," *Federal Writers' Project*, vol. 1, 56.

3. This picture, the earliest photographic image of Fort Worth, can be seen in Leonard Sanders and Ronnie C. Tyler, *How Fort Worth became the Texasmost City* (Fort Worth: Amon Carter Museum of Western Art, 1973), 27.

4. *Federal Writers' Project*, vol. 11, 4083.

5. Dewitt Reddick, "Reminiscences," in *Federal Writers' Project*, vol. 1, 129–30.

6. The first telephone was installed for Dr. W. B. Brook, connecting his home on Weatherford and Pecan Streets with his drug store at Second and Houston. *Federal Writers' Project*, vol. 11, 4088. For District Court, see Bill Fairley, *Fort Worth Star-Telegram*, Jan. 12, 2000, 6-B. For Rintleman's Saloon, see *Fort Worth Star-Telegram*, Jan. 10, 1909.

7. Interview with *Fort Worth Star-Telegram*, Mar. 23, 1933.

8. Robert L. Brown, *Saloons of the American West* (Silverton, Colo.: Sundance Publications, 1978), 15.

9. For San Antonio, see Frank H. Bushick, *Glamorous Days* (San Antonio: Naylor Company, 1934), 55; and George D. Hendricks, *Bad Men of the West* (San Antonio: Naylor Company, 1950), 173. For mention by a contemporary of White Elephants in Wichita Falls and Denison, Texas, see Jim McIntire, *Early Days in Texas: A Trip to Hell and Heaven*, ed. Robert K. DeArment (1902; reprint, Norman: University of Oklahoma Press, 1992), 86, 90. For "ecstasy" quote, see Robert K. DeArment, *Knights of the Green Cloth: The Saga of the Frontier Gamblers* (Norman: University of Oklahoma Press, 1982), 138. The building in Frededericksburg is still standing today and still has the figure of a white elephant over the door. For a list of White Elephant saloons in Texas, see William E. Fowler, et al., *TAMS Journal (Official Organ of the Token and Medal Society): The Trade Tokens of Texas* 13, no. 2 (Apr., 1973); with *Supplement 1*, vol. 19, no. 1 (Feb., 1979); and *Supplement 2*, vol. 24, no. 2. (1984); and Robert C. Smith, "Index to the Trade Tokens of Texas and Supplements Nos. 1, 2, and 3," unpublished ms., 1989.

10. For the Eagle City White Elephant, see Nyle H. Miller and Joseph W. Snell, *Why the West Was Wild* (Topeka: Kansas State Historical Society, 1963), 161–62. For Bingham Canyon's White Elephant, see photograph of faro players in collections of Denver Public Library, Western History Dept.

11. For "money pit" meaning, see William Morris and Mary Morris,

eds., *Morris Dictionary of Word and Phrase Origins* (New York: Harper and Row, 1977), 601.

12. For "great adventure" meaning, see Robert McCrum, William Cran, and Robert MacNeil, *The Story of English* (New York: Viking, 1986), 251–52. The expression seems to have been especially popular among the Forty-niners as they made their way to the California gold fields and was even incorporated into a trail song. See Brown, *Saloons of the American West*, 29.

13. Other Texas towns besides Fort Worth had Black Elephant Saloons around this time, such as San Antonio and Austin. Unlike the age-old debate about the chicken and the egg, there is no doubt that the White Elephants came before the Black Elephants. All evidence points to the fact that Black Elephant saloons were African American establishments, looked down upon by white citizens, including this remark in the *Fort Worth Record* on December 30, 1906: "For foul filth, nothing in the Acre can compare with the Black Elephant." For other Black Elephants, see Robert C. Smith, "Index to the Trade Tokens of Texas and Supplements Nos. 1, 2, and 3," unpublished ms. to accompany Fowler, et al., *TAMS Journal (Official Organ of the Token and Medal Society): The Trade Tokens of Texas* 13, no. 2 (Apr., 1973); with *Supplement 1*, vol. 19, no. 1 (Feb., 1979); and *Supplement 2*, vol. 24, no. 2.

14. The story of the Bull's Head sign is attributed by J. Frank Dobie to his father, cattleman R. J. Dobie, in J. Frank Dobie, *Cow People* (Boston: Little, Brown and Company, 1964), 68.

15. For advertising of both the Planter's House and Commercial restaurants, see *Fort Worth City Directory*, 1882.

16. Reported in *Dallas Weekly Herald,* Oct. 8, 1884, 4.

17. These numbers and the quotation come from an anonymous letter written July 1, 1888, to the *American Israelite,* preserved on microfilm at the American Jewish Periodical Center, Klau Library, Hebrew Union College, Cincinnati, Ohio. There are no official figures for Fort Worth's Jewish population in the 1880s, but oral traditions tell us it was small and quite transient. Moses Shanblum, who came to the city in 1887, found only six Jewish families "who worshiped in a private house on Holidays." See the *Jewish Monitor* [of Fort Worth], Dec. 11, 1925, 3 (Fort Worth Jewish Historical Society). Ms. Faye Brockman of the FWJHS estimates there were no more than one hundred Jews living in the city in the mid-1880s. The Burgowers, Berliners, Bornsteins, and Solomon Kahn represented a healthy percentage of the local Jewish population. The entire Jewish population of the West has been calculated at only about twenty thousand in 1876, roughly 8 percent of America's Jews. Charles Phillips and Alan Axelrod, eds., *Encyclopedia of the American West*, vol. 2 (New York: Simon and Schuster, Macmillan Reference USA, 1996), 781.

18. For Berliner's San Antonio connection, see Bushick, *Glamorous Days*, 55. See also obituary of Samuel Berliner in *San Antonio Express*, Apr. 30, 1919, 20.

19. See 1883–84 and 1885–86 *Fort Worth City Directories*.

20. Ron Tyler, et al., *The New Handbook of Texas*, vol. 6 (Austin: Texas State

Historical Assoc., 1996), 251–52; *Federal Writers' Project*, vol. 3, 1095 and vol. 7, 1113–15; "Grantee Index to Deeds, Tarrant County, Tex.," vol. 31, April 24, 1876, to Dec. 31, 1937, Tarrant County Deed Records Office, Fort Worth.

21. Nanny to "the Editor of the *Gazette*" (June 17), *Fort Worth Gazette*, June 28, 1884.

22. The so-called Sanborn Fire Maps were highly detailed schematics of the central business district, produced by the Sanborn Map and Publishing Company of New York for municipalities all over the country. They provided regular snapshots of Texas cities, at intervals of four to seven years from the 1870s through the early twentieth century and are invaluable to the urban historian today. The original maps of Fort Worth, starting in 1885, are at the Center for American History, University of Texas, Austin. Microfiche copies of same are in the collections of the Tarrant County Historical Commission, Fort Worth. In the late nineteenth century, entire saloon layouts could be purchased from specialized companies like Brunswick-Balke-Collender (BBC), who offered standardized "single-lot floor plans" to entrepreneurs starting from scratch. BBC offered two basic plans that could be purchased from the catalog as virtual "turn-key" operations. See Byron A. Johnson and Sharon Peregrine Johnson, *Wild West Bartenders' Bible* (Austin: Texas Monthly Press, 1986), 23.

23. *Fort Worth Press*, Feb. 25, 1973, 5-E.

24. Obituary for William Henry Ward, *Fort Worth Star-Telegram*, Oct. 13, 1934, 12.

25. Lots in the business district in 1885 were going for forty to sixty dollars per frontage foot. That price would rise to one hundred dollars per frontage foot in the next few years, and a prime corner lot at Main and Fifth would sell for eight thousand dollars in April, 1887. *Federal Writers' Project*, vol. 7, 2697 and 2712. In 1887, Luke Short bought a one-third interest in the White Elephant for one thousand dollars. *Luke Short vs. the State of Texas*, Court of Appeals of Texas, Case No. 5757, May 2, 1888, 25 TX. Ct. App. 379; 8 S.W. 281 (Hereafter referred to as *Luke Short vs. the State of Texas*).

26. *Federal Writers' Project*, vol. 51, 20,354. Centennial Edition, *Fort Worth Star-Telegram*, Oct. 30, 1949, "Commerce Section," 30. The "key toss" by tradition climaxed every new saloon opening in the old days. In Chicago, barkeeps on the "loop" tossed their keys into Lake Michigan. In Fort Worth, the street served the same function. George Ade, *The Old-Time Saloon* (New York: Ray Long and Richard R. Smith, Inc., 1931), 8. In Fort Worth the El Paso Bar, among many others, were proud to welcome customers day and night in an era when "last call" was unknown. See El Paso Bar advertisement in *Fort Worth City Directory*, 1882.

27. *Luke Short vs. the State of Texas*.

28. *Fort Worth City Directories* for 1888–89 and 1892–93; Directory of Leading Firms of Fort Worth, included in City Council Proceedings, June 1, 1897, in City Secretary's Office, unorganized files, Fort Worth City Hall and Municipal Building. Don Woodard, *Black Diamonds! Black Gold!* (Lubbock: Texas Tech

University Press, 1998), 36–37. Bill O'Neal, *The Texas League, 1888–1987: A Century of Baseball* (Austin: Eakin Press, 1987), 249, 350. The Fort Worth "Cats" were part of a proud local tradition of naming things after a wandering panther reportedly seen on the town's Main Street in 1875 by a Dallas visitor. Thereafter, Fort Worthers embraced the name proudly, slapping it on everything from grocery stores to the local baseball team. The abiding popularity of the name suggests that "White Panther" might have been a more appropriate name for the Ward brothers' saloon. See Sanders and Tyler, *How Fort Worth became the Texasmost City*, 46, 56, and 63*n* 21.

29. Tarrant County property records, Grantee Index to Deeds, vol. 40, 112, Tarrant County Courthouse.

30. Ward obituary, *Fort Worth Star-Telegram*, Oct. 13, 1934, 12. The semi-pro Fort Worth Panthers, the "Cats," were the pride of the local citizenry for many years and probably Ward's greatest legacy to his adopted town. The first public hall dedicated to motion pictures opened in McKeesport, Pennsylvania, in 1905. Within four years there were eight thousand more around the country, including Fort Worth, Texas. Brooks McNamara, *Step Right Up*, rev. ed. (Jackson: University Press of Mississippi, 1995), 148.

31. "Garish Saloons Followed the Last Chance of 1856," Centennial Edition of *Fort Worth Star-Telegram*, Oct. 30, 1949, "Commerce Section," 30.

32. J. B. Roberts, "Building Which Burned Friday Night . . . ," *Fort Worth Star*, Feb. 17, 1907, sec. 1, 12.

33. *Fort Worth Evening Mail*, Mar. 1, 1886, 8.

34. There is no record of how effective an alderman Bill Ward was, but the businessmen and well-heeled citizens who lived on the northern end of downtown continued to elect him for the next fifteen years. Oliver Knight, *Fort Worth, Outpost on the Trinity* (1953; reprint, Fort Worth: TCU Press, 1990), 270–71.

35. For a picture of Bill Ward's activities on the Police Committee see Fort Worth City Council Proceedings, June 1, 1897, and following dates, in City Secretary's Office, unorganized files, Fort Worth City Hall and Municipal Building.

36. The arrest of Tom Cheshire, described as a "stockman," is reported in the *Dallas Weekly Herald*, Dec. 4, 1884, 4. For "progress" on the case, see *Dallas Weekly Herald*, Feb. 5, 1885, 4.

37. *Fort Worth Evening Mail*, Mar. 1, 1886, 8.

38. One of the three pieces, the mirrored back-bar, has survived down to today. It is all that remains of the original White Elephant Saloon fixtures. In the process of relocating the saloon three blocks down the street in 1894–95, the back-bar was ripped out and sold to a San Antonio saloon. It next turned up in a Del Rio saloon, then in 1908 it came to Marfa, Texas, where it suffered the indignity of being installed in an ice cream parlor. Cherubic faces of children replaced the grizzled visages of cowboys looking back from the mirror. It remained in Marfa down through World War II. Throughout all these moves and changes in ownership, the connection to Luke Short was never forgotten. In 1946, its latest owners, Mr. and Mrs. O. L. Shipman, spent $150 to have it crated up and

shipped to El Paso, Texas, to install in their candy shop. When the candy shop closed its doors a few years later, the thing was crated up again and put in storage until the publisher of the *El Paso Times* bought it and moved it out to his New Mexico ranch, the Corralitos in the 1950s. The ranch changed hands, but the back-bar was still there in 1989 occupying a place of pride in the guest house.

The legend that Luke Short brought the bar with him when he came down to Fort Worth from Dodge City stretches credulity, and not just because there is no mention of it in Dodge City newspapers of the day. More to the point, Short's Dodge City departure in November, 1883, was rather hasty; he had little time to dismantle the Long Branch Saloon on the way out of town! On top of that, he was in Fort Worth more than two years before settling in at the White Elephant, which would already have had a serviceable bar when he moved in. Most gamblers did not cart something as large and cumbersome as a back-bar around with them on their travels.

This history of the back-bar was provided by Mr. and Mrs. Larry Foster of Fairacres, New Mexico, owners of the Corralitos Ranch in 1989, and newspaperman Art Leibson of El Paso. See also Leibson, "Famous Saloon Back Bar Becomes Part of Respectable Candy Shop," *El Paso Times*, May 10, 1949; and Leibson, "Seventh Generation Texans, Descendants of Moses Shipman, Live in Lower Valley," *El Paso Times*, Mar. 3, 1954.

39. Quoted in Irvin Farman, *The Fort Worth Club: A Centennial Story* (privately printed by Fort Worth Club, 1985), 20.

40. Today cockfighting is legal only in Oklahoma, Louisiana, and parts of New Mexico. In every other state it is outlawed as a barbaric sport, like bear-baiting. Cockfighting season currently comes in the fall every year, and the arenas are now known as "game clubs." It is still enormously popular with a certain class of Texans who, since they can't see legal fights at home any longer, swarm across the state borders every weekend come fall to attend the matches in Oklahoma and Louisiana.

41. See Sanborn Fire Map of Fort Worth, 1893, Center for American History, University of Texas at Austin. For "main event" see "Cocking Main at Fort Worth," *Austin Statesman*, Jan. 19, 1893. For Sullivan's visit, see *Fort Worth Record*, Apr. 9, 1905; and for early cock-fighting in Fort Worth, see Selcer, *Hell's Half Acre*, 48–50.

42. *Fort Worth Evening Mail*, Mar. 1, 1886, 8.

43. *Fort Worth City Directory* for 1882 and 1886–87; *Fort Worth Daily Gazette*, Feb. 3, 1890, 8. This is based on assessments of Real and Personal Property from state and county records, estimated at 50 percent of market value, or $29,700 valuation.

44. The *Dodge City Times* carried a small notice on November 22, 1883, saying that Short had left town a few days earlier headed for North Texas. The Fort Worth newspapers did not bother to announce his arrival. Selcer, *Hell's Half Acre*, 167.

45. *Topeka (Kansas) Journal,* May 18, 1883.

46. Luke's home base in Tombstone had been the Oriental; in Dodge City it was the Long Branch. See William R. Cox, *Luke Short: Famous Gambler of the Old West* (New York: Fireside Press, 1961); also published as *Luke Short and His Era* (Garden City, New York: Doubleday and Co., 1961).

47. Wayne Short, *Luke Short, A Biography* (Tombstone, Ariz.: Devil's Thumb Press, 1996), 196–97. For a good description of the workings of the game of faro see DeArment, *Knights of the Green Cloth,* 395n 1; and Elliott West, *The Saloon on the Rocky Mountain Mining Frontier* (Lincoln: University of Nebraska Press, 1979), 48.

48. Short, *Luke Short, A Biography,* 197. *Cf.* The *Fort Worth City Directory* of 1886–87 shows Luke Short residing at 311 Second Street, just around the corner from the White Elephant (308–310 Main).

49. Cox, *Luke Short and His Era,* 158.

50. Testimony by W. H. Ward in *Luke Short vs. the State of Texas.*

51. For Occidental scandal see *Fort Worth Gazette,* July 1, 1889 (also cited in "Consolidated Chronology," *Federal Writers' Project,* series I, vol. 2, 3515).

52. Ibid.

53. The story of the keno "turf battle" between Morris and Courtright is found in the *Fort Worth Daily Democrat,* Oct. 27, 1880. The hard feelings among certain elements of the community over Short's role in promoting keno did not get wide circulation until after the February 8, 1887, shootout between Short and Courtright. See *Dallas Morning News,* Feb. 9, 1887; and *San Antonio Daily Express,* Feb. 9, 1887.

54. DeArment, *Knights of the Green Cloth,* 101, 129, 137.

55. W. B. (Bat) Masterson, "Famous Gunfighters of the Western Frontier— Luke Short," *Human Life Magazine,* Apr., 1907, 20.

56. Alfred Henry Lewis, "The King of the Gun-Players, William Barclay Masterson," *Human Life Magazine,* Nov., 1907, 10.

57. Earp's early visits to Fort Worth are chronicled in the pages of the *Fort Worth Democrat* (e.g., Jan. 26, 1878). The source for later visits is Josephine Sarah Marcus (1861?–1944), who claimed to be married to the famous gunman, although documentation for that claim is suspiciously lacking. So far, the best evidence for the claim is an unpolished draft of her memoirs (the "Cason Manuscript"), "collected and edited" by Glenn G. Boyer: *I Married Wyatt Earp: The Recollections of Josephine Sarah Marcus Earp* (Tucson: University of Arizona Press, 1976), 122–23. The problem is, Boyer's editing has been thoroughly discredited because of his admission that he fabricated portions of *The Recollections.* The particular section about Fort Worth and the White Elephant has the necessary verisimilitude, however, because it would be almost impossible for anyone to know about the saloon's restaurant or the obscure Mansion Hotel unless they had been there at the time or spent many hours digging into obscure Fort Worthiana. Additional references to Earp's visits to Fort Worth can be found in Robert K. DeArment, *Bat Masterson: The Man and the Legend* (Norman: University of Okla-

homa Press, 1979), 294–95. For a discussion of the problems with *I Married Wyatt Earp*, see Neil B. Carmony, "Wyatt Earp's New Testament," *NOLA Quarterly* 25, no. 3 (July–Sept., 2001): 28–32.

58. Charlie Coe and Hugh Walters, *My Life as a Card Shark* (n.p., 1903), mentioned in Tom Bailey, "King of Cards," *New Magazine for Men*, May, 1958, 12–13. The same story is cited in DeArment, *Bat Masterson*, 294–95.

59. "A Mystery Man Found Dead in a Brothel," *Dallas Herald*, Oct. 6, 1884, 5.

60. *Old West Antiques and Collectibles* (Austin, Tex.: Great American Publishing Co., 1979), 114.

61. Letter to W. H. Nannie, introduced as evidence in *Luke Short vs. the State of Texas*.

62. All these accusations, threats, and denunciations are contained in letters from anonymous Fort Worth citizens to Short, et al., written in 1887 and subsequently entered as evidence in *Luke Short vs. the State of Texas*.

63. Letter to Mr. [Jake] Johnson, ibid.

64. Testimony by W. H. Ward in *Luke Short vs. the State of Texas*.

65. From testimony by witnesses at the coroner's inquest investigating the death of Jim Courtright, quoted in the *Fort Worth Daily Gazette*, Feb. 10, 1887; and from a jailhouse interview of Short by a *Gazette* reporter, quoted in the *Gazette*, Feb. 9, 1887.

66. Bill O'Neal, *Encyclopedia of Western Gunfighters* (Norman: University of Oklahoma Press, 1979), 284–86. Selcer, *Hell's Half Acre*, 191.

67. Testimony of W. A. James at coroner's inquest. Quoted in *Fort Worth Gazette*, Feb. 10, 1887, 5.

68. See Short's testimony in *Fort Worth Gazette*, Feb. 10, 1887. For the full story of the famous gunfight, see Selcer, *Hell's Half Acre*, 165–95.

69. *Fort Worth Gazette*, Feb. 17, 1887, 8.

70. Testimony of W. H. Ward in *Luke Short vs. the State of Texas*.

71. For "game," see *Fort Worth Daily Gazette*, Feb. 9, 1887. For details of conviction, see *Luke Short vs. the State of Texas*.

72. *Fort Worth Daily Gazette*, Mar. 17 and 18, 1887, 8 (both).

73. *Fort Worth Gazette*, Apr. 18, 1892, 1.

74. *Fort Worth Daily Gazette*, Oct. 21, 1888. See also *Fort Worth City Directories*, 1890–95, under "Saloon" listings and "Jake Johnson."

75. The movements of Louis Maas must be pieced together from the *Fort Worth City Directories*, starting in 1885. Every year of Maas's saloon employment can be accounted for up through the 1890s except 1891, because that year's directory has not survived. An undated advertisement in this author's collections (see *Hell's Half Acre*, 174) is probably from that directory. It shows Louis Maas and Ward as co-proprietors with Bill Maas and John Teller working for them and is obviously from the first era because the address on the ad is "308 and 310." Maas and Ward could only have been together at that address in 1891.

76. The purchase of the White Elephant by Winfield Scott is reported without citation or even a date in Knight, *Fort Worth: Outpost on the Trinity*, 157. But

Knight suggests it was before 1896, which is demonstrably untrue. For the changing legal status of the building and property, see Tarrant County, Tax Assessor's Abstract of City Property, No. 106 in "Original Town" plat, block no. 97, lots 11–12; Tarrant County Deed Book, Warranty Deeds, vol. 55, 557; and information assembled by Allen Eyler on the Kendavis Industries International, Inc., Building, from the Abstract of Titles, etc., 1984, Tarrant County Historical Commission, Vertical Files. For Scott's other properties on the same block, see Grantee Index to Deeds, Tarrant County, vol. 31, Deeds Records Office, County Courthouse. For reference to "White Elephant Building," see *Fort Worth Star,* Jan. 11, 1909 (reprinted in *Federal Writers' Project,* vol. 8, 2882).

77. Carol Roark, *Fort Worth Central Business District, Tarrant County Historic Resources Survey* (Fort Worth: Historic Preservation Council for Tarrant County, Tex., 1991), 95.

78. For a discussion of Winfield Scott's various property holdings at this point, including the White Elephant, see *Fort Worth Star,* Jan. 11, 1909.

79. Those elephants are part of the recollections of Will Lake, as told to his wife Mary Daggett Lake many years later. See June 8, 1948, notes in Mary Daggett Lake Papers, Fort Worth Central Library, Local History and Genealogy Dept.

80. See *Fort Worth City Directory,* 1886–87.

81. For Ward as "General Manager," see undated White Elephant advertisement in vertical files of Tarrant County Historical Commission. The ad comes from an unidentified *Fort Worth City Directory,* probably 1895, soon after the place reopened at its new address. Unfortunately, there are no surviving copies of the 1894–95 directory.

82. For imported liquors, see White Elephant letterhead in collections of James Kattner of Spring, Texas. For "sour mash," see *Fort Worth Daily Mail,* Nov. 7, 1885.

83. Centennial Edition, *Fort Worth Star-Telegram,* Oct. 30, 1949, "Commerce Section," 30.

84. Boyer, ed., *I Married Wyatt Earp,* 123. (See footnote 47 for discussion of credibility problems with Boyer's editing.)

85. The natural synergy that exists between the gambling business and restaurant business has long been a given: In Depression-era Fort Worth, Top O' the Hill Terrace, the area's "top gambling palace," was also known for serving the best food around, counting both legitimate and shady establishments! Bill Fairley, "Tarrant had top gambling palace," *Fort Worth Star-Telegram,* Feb. 11, 1998, sec. B, 8.

86. There is no record that any of the White Elephant's customers ever became sick from eating bad oysters (*Vibrio* poisoning) though there was a definite danger posed by the sort of bacteria-contaminated shellfish that came from Gulf waters, especially in the warm summer months. Ice-packing and quick shipping were the key. See Laurence A. Johnson, *Over the Counter and on the Shelf: Country Storekeeping in America, 1620–1920* (New York: Bonanza Books, 1961), 84.

87. "Season" and "market" quotes come from the 1891 advertisement in the

Fort Worth City Directory (dated incorrectly 1881 in *Hell's Half Acre*). For the 1896 menu and advertising copy, see *Fort Worth Morning Register,* Jan. 6, 1896.

88. *Federal Writers' Project,* vol. 51, 20,355.

89. Fred Harvey's uniformed hostesses, fondly dubbed "Harvey Girls" by his loyal customers, first began serving meals to passengers on the Atchison, Topeka, and Santa Fe line at the Topeka, Kansas, station in 1876. They eventually became a fixture at terminals all over the West, including Fort Worth's Union Station after the turn of the century. By contrast, the Peers House "girls" were curiosities, not trendsetters. For "Harvey Girls," see Mike Flanagan, *The Old West, Day by Day* (New York: Facts on File, 1995), 276. For Peer House girls, see *Fort Worth Standard,* Oct. 5, 1876.

90. "Where the West Begins," essay in *Federal Writers' Project,* vol. 51, 26,354–55.

91. Shiel was a witness in a murder trial where he testified reluctantly about his own business interests. See *Martin McGrath vs. the State,* No. 849, Court of Criminal Appeals of Texas, 35 TX. Crim. 413; 34 SW 127; 1896 TX. Crim. Appeals, Lexis 28.

92. The ordinance apparently went unnoticed in Fort Worth, but it was written up in Dallas. See the *Dallas Daily Times Herald,* Aug. 30, 1890, 2.

93. This information and what follows comes from a perusal of the old newspapers, in particular the report of a killing in the Santa Fe Saloon (corner of Twelfth and Main) on July 31, 1884. *Fort Worth Daily Gazette,* Aug. 26, 1884, 8.

94. The only reference for this legend today comes from an article with no by-line, "Kiii [*sic*] Buildings Have Colorful Histories," in *The Sixth Street Journal,* an in-house publication of Fort Worth's Kendavis Industries, Oct., 1984, 1 and 3.

95. "Board whackers," according to author Stephen Crane in his short story "The Blue Hotel," were the gamblers who got excited when they held winning cards and snapped each card down on the table with a flourish, thus marking themselves for rank amateurs.

96. For bartenders' attire, see "Where the West Begins," introductory essay in *Federal Writers' Project,* vol. 51, 20,354. For "artists," see *Fort Worth Daily Mail,* Nov. 7, 1885.

97. *Fort Worth Evening Mail,* Nov. 27, 1885.

98. On the evening of February 8, 1887, when Timothy Courtright came looking for Luke Short, the suave gambler was in the bar of the White Elephant getting his boots blacked and did not come out until he had finished. See testimony in *Fort Worth Gazette,* Feb. 9, 1887, 8.

99. *Al Ray vs. the State,* Case No. 2278, Court of Criminal Appeals of Texas, 44 TX. Crim. 158; 70 S.W. 23, 1902.

100. In 1901 Wheat used his substantial profits from the Stag Saloon to buy Fort Worth's first skyscraper, rechristen it the "Wheat Building," and put an elegant roof garden on top. By contrast, Ward preferred to invest his profits in theaters and baseball teams. Mack Williams, "Fiddlers on the Roof," *In Old*

Fort Worth (Fort Worth: privately published by Mack and Madeleine Williams, 1975), 27.

101. *Fort Worth Register,* June 9, 1901, 8.

102. See advertisement in 1891 *City Directory* (illustration).

103. John A. Lomax, *Adventures of a Ballad Hunter* (New York: Macmillan Company, 1947), 41–42.

104. See advertisement in 1891 *City Directory* (illustration).

105. *Austin Daily Statesman,* Sept. 18, 1889.

106. B. B. Paddock, ed., *History of Texas: Fort Worth and the Texas Northwest Edition,* vol. 2 (Chicago: Lewis Publishing Co., 1922), 505–506.

107. *Charter and Revised Ordinances,* Fort Worth, Texas, 1906, chapter 8, section 110, 64–66, Fort Worth Public Library, Central Branch, Local History and Genealogy Dept.

108. *Fort Worth Record,* Dec. 9, 1913, 1.

109. Ibid., Oct. 24, 1913, 8.

110. Ibid., Nov. 11, 1913, 1.

111. Homer G. Ritchie, *The Life and Legend of J. Frank Norris, The Fighting Parson* (Fort Worth: privately printed, 1991), 81–92.

112. Jeff Guinn with Bobby Bragan, *When Panthers Roared* (Fort Worth: TCU Press, 1999), 25–27.

113. According to some sources (see *Fort Worth Star-Telegram,* Apr. 12, 1998), Fort Worth got its first movie house in 1910, but already in 1907 there were two storefront theaters directly across the street from the White Elephant (607 and 609 Main). They are listed in the City Directory for that year.

114. Roze McCoy Porter, *Thistle Hill, The Cattle Baron's Legacy* (Fort Worth: Branch-Smith, Inc., 1980), 269, 274, 293, 299. See also Mack Williams, "The Real Winfield Scott," *In Old Fort Worth: The Story of a City and Its People as Published in the News-Tribune* [a compendium of Williams' columns published over many years] (Fort Worth: privately printed by Mack H. and Madeline C. Williams, 1986), 83–84.

115. *Fort Worth Press,* Feb. 25, 1973, section C, 10.

116. Sandra Baker, "Entertaining a Plan," *Fort Worth Star-Telegram,* Nov. 1, 2002, 1 and 7C.

Epilogue

"Last Call"

Saloons and the men who ran them were a vital element of Western culture from the late nineteenth century through the early twentieth century. The saloon itself served a variety of functions in a frontier town, over and above being a headquarters for men to drink and gamble, more functions than we can cover here. It could also be the stagecoach "stand" (terminal), local post office, and courtroom. Often it served as the town's first courthouse, giving added meaning to the phrase, "appearing before the bar." Gouhenant's Saloon in Fort Worth was the seat of the district court for North Texas when it came to town, a service for which the owner charged the government $7.50 per session. A similar if more famous arrangement was "Judge" Roy Bean's Jersey Lilly Saloon in Langtry, Texas, where the self-styled jurist dispensed his eccentric brand of frontier justice for many years. The saloon was woven into the fabric of community life in the West. It was a drinking and gambling emporium, but it was far more. Ben Dowell's saloon served as El Paso's city hall while he was mayor, and Virgil Earp maintained his marshal's office over a saloon in Tombstone, Arizona. Many Western lawmen, in fact, headquartered out of a saloon, Austin's Ben Thompson and Fort Worth's Jim Courtright being two of the more famous.

After the turn of the century, Fort Worth's El Toro Bar occupied a prime location at 301 Main Street, in the same block (across the street) where the first White Elephant had stood. By the time this picture was taken (ca. 1909–1911), saloons no longer had Western-style bat-wing doors or hitching posts out front. Instead they tried to fade into the background of neigh-boring businesses. Courtesy *Bob Smith of Fort Worth, Texas*

Just like in the real estate business, location in the saloon business was important, if not quite everything. The most successful owners located their places on Main Street, by either custom building or buying an existing structure. They took advantage of the lack of zoning laws to practically take over the central business district until there was nothing but solid saloons up and down both sides of the street. It was no accident that the premier saloons in San Antonio, Austin, Fort Worth, and El Paso were all located on Main Street.

The men who ran the big saloons in frontier towns were more than just barkeeps; they were always counted among the leading businessmen in their communities. And many of them were more than just businessmen; they were also political power brokers on the local scene. Ben Dowell served at different times as mayor, alderman, and county commissioner in El Paso. Bill Ward was a city councilman and commissioner in Fort Worth for several years around the turn of the century.

As a group, saloon men were unsung business pioneers who demonstrated their shrewd grasp of good business principles by introducing such innovations as the "free lunch," the "good-for-one-drink" token, and other forms of advertising. Old photographs from the earliest days of many frontier towns tell the same story: the first large commercial signs erected on Main Street were put up by the saloons. The heavy competition and often cutthroat nature of the business demanded innovation and produced an entrepreneurial class of remarkable, if not always admirable, accomplishments. As captains of business, they have been overlooked because their principal product was not oil or steel but liquor.

Fancy saloons tended to be known by their owners, such as Neff's Iron Front Saloon in Austin and Jack Harris's Vaudeville in San Antonio. This custom extended to the sign over the door, which prominently featured the owner's name. Reputation of owner and saloon were thus inseparably intertwined. And the proprietor's persona infused the saloon's operations. Until the brewers and distillers began to take over, there were no impersonal corporate boards or absentee owners calling the shots. A saloonkeeper was an entrepreneur of the highest order.

The four cities that are the focus of this book were all regular stops on the "gamblers' circuit," that unofficial collection of towns stretching across the western half of the United States that welcomed members of the sporting fraternity. No one can explain how a town or a saloon came to be included on the circuit; by some mysterious process it just happened. In addition to Fort Worth, El Paso, San Antonio, and Austin, the gamblers' circuit included Tombstone, Arizona, and Dodge City, Kansas, among other wild and wooly burghs. It is clear that the four communities that are the focus of this book were on the circuit because the same (famous) names kept turning up in town to ply their trade. A roll call of the "usual suspects" includes people like "Rowdy Joe" Lowe, Luke Short, Ben Thompson, Bat Masterson, the Earp brothers, and their pal Doc Holliday. Periodically, one or more celebrity members of the gambling fraternity would put in an appearance and before long cards were being cut, whiskey was being poured, and the game was afoot. Sometimes such men stayed for only a few days; sometimes, if things did not get too hot, they settled in for months or even years, but never permanently. Theirs was a rootless existence. A first-class saloon in one of the towns on the gamblers' circuit just naturally attracted the high rollers, and each member of the fraternity gained something from facing off against the best. As for the saloonkeepers, they were happy to roll out the red carpet whenever a legend came to town.

Financially, saloons depended on gambling more than drinking to meet the bottom line. All the drinks sold in a typical evening could not begin to equal the house's take from gambling operations, whether faro, keno, ten-pins, or whatever. That is why the gambling concession was such a valuable piece of the action for a place like the White Elephant or the Vaudeville. The house ran the bar, but it turned over the gambling concession to a professional sporting man who enjoyed *carte blanche* in all things related to his area. That is also why management always catered to the gambling fraternity, just like Las Vegas casinos do today. Food and drink are and were merely inducements to bring in the customers. In the biggest saloons, the bar was an adjunct to the gaming area, not vice versa. The gaming area was physically separated by either being located upstairs or in smaller side rooms off the main floor. The death knell rang for the Western saloon when laws began being enforced against all forms of gambling on the premises. The first to go were the cockfights, but they were followed by the keno banks, bowling alleys, and other games of chance. Until Prohibition came along, the law scarcely touched bar operations in most towns.

Famous saloons seldom die; they are just recycled as modern-day tourist traps in the manner of Ben Dowell's Saloon in El Paso and the White Elephant in Fort Worth. The new places lay claim to a famous old name, taking advantage of the rich history associated with it and the lack of copyright protection for something as prosaic as a saloon's name. Famous names aside, what has certainly changed in modern times is a *way* of doing business. The old landmarks were part of a highly romanticized institution with their good and their bad sides. Today, we no longer have saloons with personality, merely bars.

Index

Abbott, Alice, 140–41
Abilene, Tex., 57, 89, 90
Abraham, Arthur, 66
Acme Saloon (El Paso), 135, 146, 148
actresses, 15, 66, 67, 71, 72, 79, 105, 270;
  as prostitutes, 81, 268
Adam, Anton, 102
Adams, "Captain" Warren, 56
Adelphi Theater (San Antonio), 60
advertisers, and advertising, 7, 58, 175–
  176, 185, 191, 240, 244, 272, 273, 275
African Americans, 5, 20, 24, 64, 143, 151,
  180, 215, 231, 269
"After the Ball" (tune), 7
Alamo Plaza (San Antonio), 75
Alamo Sample Room (Fort Worth), 228
Alberts, Lulu, 69
Amarillo, Tex., 29
American National Bank (Austin), 170,
  220, 221
Anderson, J. E., 161
Andrews, W. T., 7
Anheuser-Busch Brewing Company, 145,
  264, 272
Anti-Saloon League, 28–29, 31, 276
Ardmore, Okla., 24
artwork, in saloons, 7, 8, 9, 50, 109, 186,
  187, 247
Astor House Saloon (El Paso), 152, 154
Atheneum Theater (New York City), 67
Atterbury, Bill, 241
Austin, Tex., 10, 25, 31, 87, 108, 128, 129,
  169, 170, 204, 218, 219; and Ben

Thompson, 88–91, 94, 96, 103, 195,
  206, 211; and gambling, 83, 86, 178,
  194, 217, 293; saloons, 5, 173, 176,–77,
  189, 191, 194, 215, 292
Avenue Hotel (Austin), 193

Babel, Oscar, 67
Baker, Newton D., 157
Baker, and Maurice, 70
Baldwin, B. C., 23
"balloon frame" building construction,
  233
Bank Exchange Saloon (Fort Worth), 236,
  272
bar area, 10, 14, 15, 17, 18, 20, 32, 33, 43,
  45, 50, 51, 63, 108, 137, 143, 146, 152,
  170, 186, 188, 193, 205, 215, 228, 233,
  236, 242–43, 258, 259, 270, 272, 273,
  275, 294; back bar 63, 242, 264, 266,
  278, 283n38
barbers, and barbering, 12, 245, 270
barkeeps, and saloonkeepers, 6, 8, 11, 15,
  16, 20, 26, 34, 43, 44, 45, 48, 49, 60,
  152, 154, 158, 159, 174, 189, 190, 192,
  220, 233, 240, 242, 258, 259, 268, 271,
  274, 275, 292, 294; as arbiters of justice, 21–22; as businessmen, 292–93;
  as counselors, 17; as father-confessors,
  126; fraternity of, 190; hospitality of,
  191, 214–15; job description, 17–18; as
  retirement plan, 24; types of, 24
Barrymore, Lionel, 68, 116n31
bar tab (credit), 20

bartenders, 7, 10, 22, 23–24, 26, 32, 47, 74, 90, 108, 135, 150–51, 43, 46, 47, 135–36, 138, 150–51, 159, 188, 193, 242, 270, 263; as bouncers, 48; as confidantes, 150; as enforcers, 48; as mediators, 48; as pimps, 82; as public benefactors, 49; unionization of, 49
bartenders' row, 270
bartending manuals, 47
bar tokens. See saloon tokens
Barton, Jerry, 48
baseball, 239–40, 273
bat-wing doors, 20, 32, 33, 143, 146, 153, 185–86, 291
bawdy houses, 60, 69, 73, 82, 83, 138–40, 153, 161, 180, 181, 183, 267, 268
Baylor, Captain George W., 136
Bean, Roy, 291
Beckham, R. E., 263
beer, 10, 11, 12, 13, 137, 145, 243, 263–64, 265, 273; and beer halls, 3, 229
Beeson, Chalkey McArtor "Chalk," 4, 24
Beeson and Fox (vaudeville team), 95
Bella Union Theater (San Antonio), 77, 78
Ben Dowell's Saloon (San Antonio), 124–25, 126, 128, 129, 130, 132, 141, 144, 147, 152, 155, 162, 294
Bennett, Harry, 84
Benton, G. R., 155
Berliner, Samuel, 84, 232–33
Bernauer, Henry C., 155
Bexar County, Tex., 31, 54, 98
Bexar Exchange (San Antonio), 55
billiards, and pool, 7, 13, 126, 128, 132, 137, 174, 179, 186, 187, 188, 193, 219, 232, 233, 236, 238, 242, 245, 265
Billy Miner's Saloon (Fort Worth), 34
Bird Cage Saloon and Theater (Tombstone, Ariz.), 37n29, 78
Bismarck Saloon (Fort Worth), 18, 31, 230
Black Elephant Saloon: in Austin, 213; in Forth Worth, 230, 231, 281n13
blackjack, 270
blacks. See African Americans
Blevins, Tom, 15, 33,
blind pigs, 27, 46, 275
blind tigers. See blind pigs
Bloodgood, Fannie, 68
blue laws. See Sunday closing laws
Board of Trade (Chamber of Commerce), 186
Board of Trade Saloon (Fort Worth), 19, 240
bookmakers, and bookmaking, 262, 263

Boone, J. H., 153, 154
bootleggers, and bootlegging, 158
bordellos. See bawdy houses
Bornstein, Nathaniel, 232–33
Borodino, F. A., 231–32
Bosslington, Miss, 95
bouncers, 71, 73, 74, 75, 82, 276
Bougereau, Adolphe William, 8
Bowen, Jane (Mrs. John Wesley Hardin), 147
Bowen, W. A., 204
bowling, and bowling alley, 13, 294
boxing matches, 141
Boyd and Hart (vaudeville team), 66
Brandy, 10, 125, 243, 264
Brawn, Dick, 68
Brennan, Joe, 17
Brewer, Sallie, 73, 83. See also "110" House
brewers, and breweries, 8, 12, 29–30, 45, 145, 272; monopolies, 29–30
Brewery Exchange Bar (Fort Worth), 26
Bronson, D. G., 58, 59
Brook, Dr. W. B., 280n6
Brown, Frank, 68
Brown, Jim, 241
Brown's Saloon (Virginia City, Nev.), 5
Brunswick-Balke-Collender Company, 45, 49, 187
bucking the tiger, 84, 277. See also faro
Buckler, Julius A., 134
buffalo hunters, 5, 19, 228
Bull's Head Saloon (Abilene, Kans.), 89, 231
Burgower, Gabriel, 232–33; G. Burgower & Co., 232, 234, 235, 236, 237, 251, 273
Burton, Will C., 67
Bushick, Frank, 64, 66, 83, 84

cabarets, 3
Cabinet Saloon (Fort Worth), 19
Cactus Saloon (El Paso), 141
Cahill, Bob, 142–43
Callaghan, Bryan, 75
Camino Real Hotel (El Paso), 125, 133, 134, 155, 163. See also Hilton Camino Real of El Paso; Hotel Paso del Norte (El Paso); Hotel Westin Paso del Norte
Campbell, George, 134
Campbell, Thomas, 31
Capital State Fair, 190
card players, 270
card sharps, 17

Cardwell, John, 180, 181, 182, 214

Carleton, Miss, 95

Carranza, Venustiano, 157

carriage trade, 271–72. *See also* high-rollers

Casey, Martin, 272

cash register, 9

casino gambling, 248. *See also* gamblers, and gambling fraternity

Cassidy, Butch (Robert Leroy Parker), 86, 87

Cats. *See* Fort Worth Cats baseball team

cattle drives, 57

Cattle Exchange Saloon (Fort Worth), 230, 245, 250, 272

cemetery, 102, 174, 202, 222, 270

Central Hotel (also Grand Central Hotel) (El Paso), 125, 127, 133, 137

Chadwell, John, 101

chair warmers, 65, 69, 72

Chamberlain, Glanton, 54

Chamizal Convention, 131. *See also* Rio Grande

champagne, 191

Charles, Sam, 68

Charlie Townsend's Saloon (El Paso), 151

Chenneville, John, 213

Cheshire, Tom, 241

Chicago, Ill., 25, 45, 72

Chief Saloon (El Paso), 151

Chinese, 64, 107, 138, 143, 151, 152

Chisholm Trail, 5, 273

chuckaluck, 84

Church in Action Against the Saloon 28. *See also* Anti-Saloon League

churches, 154, 228

Churchill, Bob, 101

cigar factory, 243–44

cigar girls, 12

cigars. *See* tobacco, and tobacco products

cigar stand. *See* tobacco apartment (stand)

Citizens' League for Reform, 153

City Cemetery No. 1 (San Antonio), 102

city councils, 18, 29, 30, 74, 130, 133, 139, 151, 154, 180, 182, 205, 241, 268, 271, 274, 275

city marshals, 21, 133, 196, 197, 204, 205, 206, 227, 241, 268; as pimps, 24; races for 133–34, 197–98, 210, 214

Ciudad Juarez. *See* El Paso del Norte, Mexico

Civil War, American, 33, 44, 57, 88, 89, 97, 127, 128–29, 172, 173, 175, 176, 179, 194, 234

Clanton family, 92; Ike, 25

Clark, Etta, 140–41

Clark, Richard B. S. "Dick," 84, 250–51

Clarke, Gaylord, 129–30

clean-up drives. *See* reform, and reformers

Clemente, Nellie, 81

Clements, Emanuel Mannen, III, 149–50

clientele. *See* customers

club rooms, 6, 13, 137, 143–44, 246, 247, 248, 250, 252, 267, 278

Club Room Saloon (Fort Worth), 229

Cobb, H. L., 257–58

cock fighting, 244–45, 284n40, 294; cock pit, 245, 267

cocktails, 50

Coe, Charlie, 251, 286n58

Coe, Phil, 90, 231

Coldwell, Colbert, 131

Coleman, John, 270

Coliseum Saloon (Manning's Saloon) (El Paso), 133, 134, 135, 137

Columbus, N.Mex., 157

Colvin, Bessie, 140–41

Commercial Club, and Commercial Club Building (Fort Worth), 259–60, 269, 272

Commercial Restaurant (Fort Worth), 232

con men, 43

Coney Island Saloon (El Paso), 149

concert saloons 16. *See also* variety theaters

Conly, Patrick, 213, 226n70

conspiracy, to commit murder, 148–49, 120n116

Corbett, James J., 8, 272

cordials, 10, 243

coroner's jury, 127, 134, 136, 255

Cortez, Ignacia, 82

Cosmopolitan Hotel (San Antonio), 55

Cosmopolitan Saloon (San Antonio), 57

Cotton Boll Saloon (Fort Worth), 228

Courthouse Square (Fort Worth) 228, 261

Courtright, Timothy Isaiah "Longhair Jim," 227, 250, 252, 253, 254–55, 291

Courtright-Short gunfight, 227, 256, 279

Cowboy Saloon (Fort Worth), 18,

cowboys, 4, 5, 12, 17, 18, 19, 32, 34, 46, 64, 143, 176, 203, 228, 244, 265, 273

cowtowns, 19, 34, 44, 228

Coy, Jacob S., 73, 75, 99, 117n40, 120n116

craps, 174, 191, 179, 203, 267

Creary, Edward, 197, 198, 222, 226n70

Creede, Colo., 25

cribs, 77, 183, 268. *See also* prostitutes, and prostitution

Criswell, Luther, 48

Crystal Palace Saloon: in El Paso, 155; in Tombstone, 24

Crystal Saloon (Austin), 170–71, 172, 185, 187

Cummings, Samuel M. "Doc," 134, 135, 136

cuspidors. *See* spittoons

Custer's Last Stand (painting), 8

customers, 10, 14, 16, 17, 20, 24, 25–26, 31, 32–33, 46, 47, 49, 63, 64, 65, 76, 78, 79, 81, 82, 104, 107, 111, 126, 128, 138, 142, 144, 146, 150, 151, 152, 163, 171, 176, 177, 182, 183, 186, 187, 189, 191, 195, 197, 200, 211, 212, 215, 217, 221, 228, 229, 230, 233, 235, 236–67, 240, 241–42, 248–49, 262, 263, 264, 265, 267, 271, 272, 277, 278, 279, 294; code of conduct, 193, 270; by ethnic type, 18

Dallas, Tex., 34, 83, 241

dance halls, 89, 137, 139, 150, 268

Davenport, Millie, 95

Davis, Edmund, 129

Davis, Ella, 68

Davis, Warren, 95

Day, Giles H., 259

DeAlarcon, Martin, 53

DeArment, Robert, 178

Dearwood, Blanche, 69, 82

Debarlehan, H. R., 205

DeHaven, Emma, 69, 72

DeHaven, George, 95

Denison, Tex., 86, 237

Deno, Lottie, 84

Denver, Colo., 26, 138

Devine and Atwater's Drugstore, 55

Democratic Party politics, 215

Devine, Dr. J. M., 55

Devine and Atwater's Drugstore (San Antonio), 55

dice. *See* craps

Dickinson, C. I., 261

dime novelists, 253

disease: Spanish influenza, 159; venerial diseases, 139, 161

disreputable houses. *See* bawdy houses

distillers, and distilleries, 8, 10, 49

Dixie Saloon (Fort Worth), 228

Doane, Rufus, 128

Dobie, J. Frank, 17

Dodge City, Kans., 5, 10, 11, 24, 57, 72, 84, 172, 243, 247, 254, 293

dog fights, 141

Dome bar, in Camino Real Hotel (El Paso), 163–64

doorman, 6. *See also* porters

Dowell, Benjamin Shacklett, 123, 124–65, 128, 130–31, 164, 193, 292

Dowell, Juan (son), 127

Dowell, Juana, 127 (wife), 132

Dowell, Mary (daughter), 127

Dowell's Saloon. *See* Ben Dowell's Saloon

Drake, Georgia, 79–81

drugs, and drug usage, 70, 81, 105, 108

drug stores, 18

drummers, 64, 90, 183, 203

drunkenness, and drunkards, 19, 21, 25, 27, 28, 204, 207, 208, 252, 254, 268

drys. *See* prohibition movement

Duff, Harry H., 189, 190–92, 218

Dulle, Joe, 278

Durand, Loa, 66. *See also* Belle Storms

Duval, Claude, 82, 83

Dwyer, Jerry J., 69

Dyer, John D., 94, 95

Eagle Pass, Tex., 104

Earp brothers, 291; Virgil, 24, 291; Warren, 26; Wyatt, 4, 86, 87, 90, 91, 92, 236, 250, 251, 118*n*66, 143, 285*n*57

Earp, Sarah Josephine Marcus, 86, 90, 265, 118*n*66, 285*n*57

Eastern Cattle Trail, 229. *See also* Chisholm Trail

Eastern Grill Restaurant (El Paso), 155

Edgar, Henry, 251

Eighteenth Amendment. *See* prohibition movement

Eikemeyer, Rudolph, 143

electricity, and electric lights, 75, 110, 132, 188, 264

Elite Hotel (San Antonio), 113

Ellsworth, Kans., 57, 90

El Paso, Tex., 10, 31, 130–31, *132*, 133, 136, 137, 140, 149, 156, 157, 158, 292, 293; and Ben Dowell, 125, 127, 128, 164; saloons, 5, 129, 137–38, 143, 144, 150, 153, 154, 163; and violence, 126, 127, 129, 146, 147

El Paso Brewery, 133

El Paso County, Tex., 31, 128, 153

El Paso del Norte, Mexico (Cuidad Juarez), 127, 130–31, 133, 141, 147, 155, 156, 157, 158, 159, 160, 161; re-named, 128; valley of, 125, 128

El Paso Hotel (El Paso), 133

El Paso Hotel (Fort Worth), 232, 259. *See also* Pickwick Hotel

El Paso Hotel Company (San Antonio), 155–56. *See also* Hotel El Paso del Norte

El Toro Bar (Fort Worth), *292*

Elwood, Miss, 95

Emerson, Jesse M., 101

extortion, 254. *See also* protection racket

Fall, Albert B., 149–50

Farmer's Saloon (Fort Worth), 228, 230

faro, 20, 23, 84, 85, 107, 142–43, 174, 178, 196, 208, 229, 247, 270, 271

Fashion Theater (San Antonio), 66, 77

"Fatal Corner" (San Antonio), 53, 56, 95, *104*, 113

fees, and fines system, 139,151, 153, 154, 180

female boarding house. *See* bawdy houses

feuds, 19, 25. *See also* gunplay

Fey, Josie, 74

fiddle player, and fiddle playing. *See* music, and musicians

fire department, 177, 209

fireproof, 55

fires, 63, 142, 176

First and Last Chance Saloon (Fort Worth), 228

First Baptist Church (Fort Worth), 276

First Texas Mounted Volunteers, 173

First Ward (Fort Worth), 241

Fisher, Joby, and Lucinda Warren, 97

Fisher, John King, 9, 8, 24, 53, 86, *96*, 97, 98, 104, 113, 206; death of, 100–103, 104; funeral of, 103; grave of, 120*n*114

Fleming, Henry, 24

Flemmons, Jerry, 33

foot rail, 9, 186

Ford, Bill, 126

Ford, Bob, 24–25

Ford County, Kans. *See* Dodge City, Kans.

Ford, Will, 84

Fort Allen (San Antonio), 82

Fort Bliss, N.Mex., 157, 159, 161

Fort Concho, Tex.. *See* San Angelo, Tex.

Fort Worth Cats baseball team, 239, 276, 283*n*30

Fort Worth Club 272. *See also* Commercial Club

Fort Worth, Tex., *6*, 18, 25, 43, 48, 108, 172, 231, 232, 234, 245, 273; and gambling, 83, 86, 87, 153, 247, 251, 254; John and Bill Ward, 237–39, 245; saloons, 5, 10, 11, 15, 29, 30, 31, 32, 34–35, 227–28, 229, 235, 242, 264, 265, 292–93

Foster, Joseph C. "Joe," 85–86, 98, 99, 100, 103, 204, 206

Foster, Victor, 95, 258; Foster-Short-Johnson Partnership, 259

Fountain, Albert, 129–30

Fourth Estate. *See* news, and newspapers

Frank, Naomi, 95

Franklin House Hotel, 128

Fred Jones Building Company Contractors, 155

free-hearted fellows, 169, 194

free (bar) lunch, 6, 36*n*9, 50, 63, 144, 228, 235, 236, 265, 272

Freemasons. *See* Masons, and Masonic Order

French, A. H., 129, 130

French, James H., 75

Frye, Charles, 69, 95

Gaines, W., 205

Galena, Ill., 237

Gallagher's Saloon (San Antonio), 99

Galveston, Harrisburg & San Antonio Railroad, 75

gamblers' circuit, 83, 133, 229, 293

gamblers, and gambling fraternity, 3, 12, 13, 15, 19, 23, 26, 43, 46, 54, 57, 58, 65, 76, 77, 83, 84, 85, 87, 89, 90, 132, 137, 138, 139, 140, 143, 147, 150, 151, 152, 159, 160, 161, 164, 169–70, 173, 174, 176, 177–79, 181–83, 184, 187, 191, 194, 196–97, 204, 211, 215, 216, 217–18, 219, 220, 227, 236, 241, 244, 245, 246, 250, 252, 254, 262, 265, 266–67, 276, 279, 293–94; Big Games, 198–201, 203, 251; brace game, 197, 248; casino gambling, 248; Gamblers' Mecca, 228; gamblers' luck 142; invitation-only games, 274; on credit, 249, 253; open gambling, 141–42, 154, 218, 229, 247, 277; state law against, 153, 154

gambling concession, 196, 197, 205, 207, 236, 254, 255–56, 258, 294

gambling hall, 88

Gambrell, J. B., 276

Gandsor, F. M., 188–89

gas lighting, 63, 65, 107, 110, 141

Gem Saloon and Theater (El Paso), 132, 141–43, 144, 147, 151, 155, 159; as Jewel Saloon, 143

Gem Variety Theater (Deadwood, Dakota Terr.), 60, 78

General Stoneman (statue), 152

George, J. V., 86

George Holland's Theater (Fort Worth), 20

German population, 18, 24, 45, 138

Gibson, Lily, 82

Gilded Age, 27

gilded palaces, 49. *See also* saloons, fancy

Giles, Alfred, 76

Gillett, James B., 136, *144*, 203

Ginger, Lew, 66

Ginnochio, C. A., 32

Ginnochio's Saloon (Fort Worth), 32

Glanton, John, 54–55

Globe Restaurant (El Paso), 135

Gordon, Jack, 126–27

Gouhenant, Adolphus, 9, 36*n*12, 228

Gouhenant's Saloon (Fort Worth), 36*n*12, 291

Gounah, Adolphus. *See* Gouhenant, Adolphus

Government Hill (San Antonio), 75, 76

Graham, Charles E., 263, 270

Grand Central Hotel (El Paso). *See* Central Hotel

Grant, Ulysses S., 237

Gray, Ada, 99

Grayson, Ida, 95

Grayson, Mark, 95

Great War. *See* World War I

Greeley, Horace, 10

Green River, Utah, 25

Greenback Party, 215

Green Front Saloon (San Antonio), 79

Greenwall's Opera House (Fort Worth), 245

Grimes, Bob, 26

gunfighters' code, 136

gunplay, 19, 25–26, 39–40*n*53, 125, 126, 127, 128, 129–30, 133, 134, 140, 142–43, 146, 147, 148, 172, 180, 199, 207, 208, 212, 255, 258

Guy Town (Austin), 180. *See also* red-light districts

hail, and hail storm, 11

Hale, Johnny, 134, 135

Hall, Captain Lee, 110

Hall, Jeff, 127

Hamilton, A. J., 129

Handly, Henry, 212–13, 226*n*70

Happy Hour Theater (El Paso), 155

Hardin, John Wesley, 13, 146–48, 194–95; death of, 146; as 'King of the Saloon Brawlers', 26

Harding, Warren G., 149

Harlan, M. A., 161

Harris, Jack, 53, 57, *58*, 60, *61*, 70, 72, 75, 83, 108, 193, 203, 204, 205; funeral of, 94. *See also* Vaudeville Saloon and Theater, Jack Harris's

Harris, Moses C., 25

Harris, William H., 4

Harris-Bronson (vaudeville team), 66

Harrison, Stuart, 25

Hart, Bill, 83

Hart, Sim, 62, 65, 72, 73, 74, 101

Harton, Hattie, 66

Harvey Fred, 266, 288*n*89

Hays, "Coffee" Jack, 173

Haywood, Bob, 256–57

Haywood, Lizzie, 69, 72

Hazel, Lena, 95

Headquarters Saloon (Wilcox, Ariz.), 26

Hearne, Tex., 213

Hell's Half Acre (Fort Worth), 15, 27, 228, 238, 241, 244, 272, 275

Henry, O. (also William S. Porter), 219

Henry, William "Big Henry", 56

Herndon, Richard, 219

Herndon Lodging House (El Paso), 147

Hickock, William "Wild Bill", 26, 231

hideaway gun, 173, 255

high-rollers, 33

Highsmith, Capt. Samuel, 173

Hilton Camino Real of El Paso, 163. *See also* Hotel Westin Paso del Norte; Camino Real Hotel (El Paso); Hotel Paso del Norte

Hispanics, 5, 24, 138, 143, 151

history, Hollywood-style, 4, 17, 203

Hixson, W. T., 155

Hoeltzel, George, 270

Hole in the Wall Saloon (El Paso), 159–60

Holland, George, 20

Holliday, John "Doc", 25, 293

Holman, Bob, 208, 210, 212

Hord, Frank, 106

horse racing, 245, 262

hospitality. *See* barkeeps, hospitality

Hotel Paso del Norte (also Hotel Del Norte) (El Paso), 134, 155–56, 158, 163. *See also* Camino Real Hotel (El Paso)

Hotel Westin Paso del Norte, 163. *See also* Camino Real Hotel (El Paso); Hilton

Camino Real of El Paso; Hotel Paso del Norte
Houck and Dieter Wholesalers 145. *See also* liquor interests
Houston, Tex., 85, 108
Howard, Jennie, 95
Hubbard, Louis H., 146
Hudspeth, Claude B., 158
Huey, H. T. and Company, 263
Hunter, J. Marvin, 150
Huntsville State Prison (Tex.), 80, 89, 97
Hyorth, Fred, 95

ice, and ice making, 11, 12, 199
Illinois Central Railroad, 237
Imperial Restaurant (Austin), 209
incorporation, of cities, 130, 138
Indians. *See* Native Americans
inquest. *See* coroner's jury
International and Great Northern Railway, 75
International Saloon Beer Garden (El Paso del Norte, Mex.), 133
Irish, 4, 18, 24
Irish Town, 19
iron building construction, 184–85
Iron Front Saloon (Austin), 8, 33, 58, 86, 169, 171, 172–73, 175–76, 177, 180, 182, 183, 184, 188, 189, 193, 194–95, 196, 198, 200, 201, 202, 203, 205, 206, 207, 208, 210, 212, 213, 214, 215, *220*; as meeting hall, 215; destruction of, 224*n*46; Jobe's Saloon, 170; John Neff's Iron Front Saloon, 187, 190; new Iron Front, 221; secret stairway, 187, 222; tombstone story, 200–202

Jack Harris's Saloon and Vaudeville Theater. *See* Vaudeville Saloon and Theater, Jack Harris's
Jackson, Jim, 202
Jack Wright Saloon (Comanche, Tex.), 26
jails, and jailhouses, 76
James brothers, 195; Frank, 195; Jesse, 195
Jenkins, Dan, 278
Jersey Lilly Saloon (Langtry, Tex.), 291
Jewel Saloon (El Paso). *See* Gem Saloon
Jews, and Jewish community, 24, 232
Jim Burns's Saloon (El Paso), 155
Jim Crow laws, 20, 231, 269. *See also* racism
Jobe, Phillip, 173, 174, 189, *196*, 222
Jobe's Saloon. *See* Iron Front Saloon
John Leer's Comique Theater and Saloon (Fort Worth), 241

Johnson, Bill, 134–35, 208
Johnson, Harry, 43, 51*n*7
Johnson, Jacob G. "Jake", 241, 245, 247, 254, 255, 258; Johnson-Short-Foster partnership, 259
Johnson, R. F., 145, 151
Jones, Melina, 74
Joyce, Milt, 32
Juarez, Benito, 128
justice of the peace court, 154

KATY Railroad. *See* Missouri, Kansas, and Texas Railroad
Kansas City, Mo., 244
Keating, Paul, 133
Keating's Saloon (El Paso), 133
Keg Saloon (Fort Worth), 10
Kelly, John, 198
Kelly, Ned, 95
keno, 84, 86, 105, 174, 178, 196, 197, 203, 204, 208, 209, 210, 211, 216–17, 249, 251–52, 256, 270, 285*n*53, 294; keno craze, 250
Kimmel, Emmanuel, 26
Kirk, J. R., 198
Knights of Labor, 18
Knights of Pythias Hall (Fort Worth), 245
Knights of the Green Cloth, 4, 35*n*6. *See also* gamblers
Krempkau, Gus, 134
Kussatz, Herman, 235

La Grange, Tex., 189
Lake, Will F., 232, 287*n*79
Langtry, Tex., 291
Lanham, John, 79, 80
Laredo, Tex., 83
last call, 7–8
Last Chance Saloon (generic), 230
laudanum. *See* drugs, and drug usage
Lavascoeur, Miss, 95
Law and Order League (El Paso), 151
Law and Order Society (Fort Worth), 252, 256
lawman, 46, 160. *See also* city marshals; police, and police departments
Leadville, Colo., 32
Lee, J. T. W., 209
Leer, John, 241
Legal Tender Saloon (El Paso), 154
legislature. *See* Texas legislature
Lemps, William J., Brewing Company, 145. *See also* brewers, and breweries
Leonard, Minnie, 69

Lewis, Callie (Mrs. John Wesley Hardin), 147

licensing, of saloons, and liquor licenses, 16, 27, 30, 46, 151, 234, 276, 277

limestone block construction, 55, 76, 185

Lindell Hotel (Fort Worth), 247

Linn, Charles M. "Buck", 142–43

liqueurs, 10

liquor, by the drink, 145, 161, 183, 187, 194, 212, 240, 243, 266, 268, 272, 274; as medication, 18

liquor interests, and dealers, 21, 27, 130, 158, 159; monopolies, 29–30; retail, 29; wholesale, 11, 29–30, 45, 145 LIT Ranch, 170

lithographs, 8, 50

Littlefield, George W., 169–70, 219, 220, 222

Littlefield Building, 170

Lobby Saloon (El Paso), 160

local option, 20–21, 160, 274; elections, 16, 157, 158, 163

Local Option Saloon, 11

Lomax, John A., 273

Lombard, R. H., 101

Lonesome Dove Western Bistro (Fort Worth), 278

Long Branch Saloon (Dodge City, Kans.), 4–5, 23, 24, 247

Long, John, 200, 201

Look, George, 143, 149

Loraine, John A., 207, 208

Louis Vidal's Saloon (El Paso), 154

Louisville, Ky., 140

Look, L. C., 213

Love, Frances Taylor, 219

Lowe, Joseph "Rowdy Joe", 26, 48, 293

Loyd, W. H., 260

Lung, Wing, 193

Maas, Louis, 259, 286n75

Maas, William, 259

madams, 69, 81, 83, 140, 181, 248

Maddox, J. H., 274

Magoffin, Joseph, 139, 145–46

Majestic Hotel (Fort Worth), 262

Main Plaza (San Antonio), 53, 54, 57, 61, 65, 75, 76, 82, 104, 106

Malone, James, 43

Manning brothers, 134; Frank, 132, 136, 137; G. F. "Doc", 136; James "Jim", 132–33, 135, 136; John, 132–33

Manning's Saloon (El Paso). See Coliseum Saloon

Mansion Hotel (Fort Worth), 245

Marcross, Professor, 7

marketing. See advertising

Marretta, Rose, 68

Mart. H. Watrous's Saloon (Denver, Colo.), 26

Martin, John, 73, 74

Martin, Lavin, 270

Martin, Thomas Alonzo "Lon", 8, 193, 202, 221

Martinez, Felix, 155

Martinez, Oscar J., 159

Martinez Cocktail, 44

Masons, and Masonic Order, 128, 131

Masterson, William Barclay "Bat", 4, 86, 87, 88, 90, 118n67, 196, 250, 251, 293

Matagorda County, 31

Maverick Hotel (San Antonio), 76

Max, Michael, 270

mayor's court, 210, 213. See also recorder's court

McDaniels, James A., 132, 133

McDonald, J. H., 55

McDonald, Red, 84

McElroy, William (William Blair), 126

McGill and Reardon (vaudeville team), 70, 73

McGrath, Martin, 18, 22, 23

McGraw, John "Iron Jaws", 272, 273

McNary, J. G., 155

McQuatters, A. J., 157

Mechanic's Bar (Fort Worth), 230

Menger Hotel (San Antonio), 76, 91, 93

Merrill, Mamie, 95

Methodist Mission Home and Training School (San Antonio), 83

Metropolitan Hotel (Fort Worth), 262

Metz, Leon, 148

Mexican Revolution (1910), 156

Mexicans. See Hispanics

Mexican War (1846–48), 54, 173

Middleton, Doc, 24

military, prisoner escort duty, 52

Military Plaza (San Antonio), 67, 75, 76, 77, 82, 98, 102

Miller, Gene, 278

Miller, Max, 154

Miller, William, 126

Miller Brewery, 29, 272, 273

Mills brothers: Anson, and W. W., 127; W. W., 127, 128, 129

Milton, Annie, 69, 72

Milwaukee, Wisc., 145

mining camps, 44

Mint Saloon (El Paso), 151, 160,
Missouri, Kansas, and Texas Railroad
  (KATY), 237
mixologists, and mixology, 43, 45, 46, 47,
  49, 50, 270. *See also* professors, of
  drink; bartenders, and bartending
Mobeetie, Tex., 24, 33
Moncrief, Ed, 95
Monroe, Frank, 74
monte. *See* Spanish monte
Monte Carlo of the West, The (El Paso), 143,
  147, 154
Monte Carlo Saloon (El Paso), 151, 154
Morehead, Charles R., 153
morphine. *See* drugs, and drug usage
Morris, John C., 250
Morton, Mrs. Fruzie, 15
movie theaters, 276, 289n113
moving pictures, 276
Mroz family: Beulah, 147–48; Martin,
  147; Martin's murder, 147–49
Mullins, Frank, 88
Mundy, J. J., 155
Murphy, J. C., 74
music, and musicians, 6–7, 58, 64, 65, 100,
  109, 112, 160, 264, 273
My Office Saloon (Fort Worth), 230
My Option Saloon (Fort Worth), 230
mythology, of Old West, 5, 50, 208,

Nanny. W. H., 234
Nash, Kid, 84
Natatorium (Fort Worth), 245
National Protective Bureau, 30
Native Americans, 5, 20, 173, 222
Neff, John B., 8, 58, 189–91, 192, 193,
  213, 218, 221, 222
Negroes. *See* African Americans
New Braunfels, Tex., 200
Newman, C. M., 155
news, and newspapers, 14, 26, 31, 80–81,
  95, 126, 133, 136, 137, 140, 141, 161,
  171, 172, 181, 188, 191, 200, 206, 210,
  213, 215–16, 218, 229
New York, N.Y., 3, 67
Ney, Elisabeth, 219
Nichols, Blanche, 74
Nichols, James, 257–58
"Nigger Town" (Fort Worth), 19
Niggli, Ferdinand, 103
nine-pins. *See* bowling, and bowling alley
non-alcoholic beverages, 11, 50
Norris, J. Frank, 276
Northfield, Minn., 195

Northside Coliseum (Fort Worth), 279
Nowak, Oscar, 270
Nueces Strip, Tex., 97

Oakwood Cemetery (Austin), 174, 202,
  222
Oakwood Cemetery (Fort Worth), 270
Obenchain, S. J., 133
Obenchain's Saloon (El Paso), 133
Obregon, Alvaro, 156–57
Occidental Saloon (Fort Worth), 19, 236,
  248, 259
Old Cabinet Saloon (Miller's Place, El
  Paso), 144
Olive, Mary, 66
Olympic Theater (New York), 67
"110 House" ("Brewer House"), 83. *See
  also* Berewer, Sallie
Opera Saloon (Fort Worth), 25
opium: addict, 72. *See also* drugs, and drug
  usage
Oriental Saloon: generic, 230; Tombstone,
  Ariz., 23, 32, 236, 247, 254
Outlaw Trail, 88

Pabst Brewing Company, 145. *See also*
  brewers, and breweries
Pacific House Hotel (San Antonio), 76
Pacific Saloon (Fort Worth), 10
Paddock, Buckley B., 229, 118n65
paintings. *See* artwork, in saloons
Palace Hotel Saloon (Fort Worth), 23
Palace Saloon (San Francisco), 32
Palais Royal Saloon (Fort Worth), 258, 259
Palmer House (Chicago, Ill.), 32
Panic of 1893, 30
Panther Park (baseball), 276
Panthers. *See* Fort Worth Cats baseball
  team
Pantherville (also Fort Worth), 10
Pap Wyman's Saloon (Leadville, Colo.), 32
parlor houses. *See* bawdy houses
patrons. *See* customers
Peers, J. M., 266
Peers House (Fort Worth), 266
Pershing, John J., 157
pets, 9, 10
Phillips, Aurelia "Chella", 162
Phillips, Bill, 214
Phoenix, Ariz., 48
piano, and piano player. *See* music, and
  musicians
Pickwick Hotel (Fort Worth), 245, 259. *See
  also* El Paso Hotel (Fort Worth)

Pierce, Johnny, 66
Pierce, Hattie, 66
pikers. *See* Spanish monte
Pikes Peak, Colorado, 44
pimps, 268
Pioneer Palace. *See* Texas Frontier Centennial Celebration
Planter's House Restaurant (Fort Worth), 231
Plaza House Hotel (San Antonio), 54, 56
poker, 84, 137, 142, 174, 198, 200, 202, 225*n*55, 249, 252, 264
police, and police departments, 22, 23, 57, 74, 89, 139, 140, 157, 159, 161, 180, 197, 203, 205, 209, 210, 211, 213, 214, 217, 218, 248, 257, 258, 268, 269; bonding of, 22; detectives, 23; interrogation methods, 213. *See also* "Special Policemen"
Police Committees, 18, 139, 241, 271
Pollock, Charles, 149
Ponce de Leon, Juan Maria, 124, 125, 164*n*2
Ponder, J. D., 141, 142
pool. *See* billiards
porters, 20, 46, 47, 48, 74, 108, 150, 188, 201, 212, 215
private clubs, 31
private detective, and agency, 253
professor, of drinks, 45, 46, 48, 50. *See also* mixologist, and mixology
professor, of music, 7, 67
Progressives, and Progressive Era, 31, 50, 262, 274
prohibition movement, 27, 28, 30, 31, 47, 50, 160, 163, 216, 274–75, 294; Eighteenth Amendment, 158, 159; elections, 21, 30. *See also* temperance movement
Prohibition Party, 31, 216
prostitutes, and prostitution, 4, 14, 15, 16, 17, 27, 60, 66, 77, 78, 79, 81, 82, 147, 157, 159, 161, 179–182, 218, 267–68, 269; code of silence, 181
protection racket, 253, 254
pubs, English, 3, 7

Quinn, Kitty, 95

racism, in saloons, 5, 107, 231. *See also* Jim Crow laws
raffle, public, 191

Railroad Reservation, 261
railroad towns, 17
railroads, 57, 128, 131, 133, 135, 136–37, 139, 180, 184, 195
Ralston the Dwarf, 95
Ranch Saloon (El Paso), 143
Ray, Alton G., 23, 271
Raymond House Hotel (Austin), 174
Raynor, Billy, 142
recorder's court, 181. *See also* mayor's court
red-light districts, 5, 16, 82, 139, 140, 150, 158, 160, 161, 180, 228, 241. *See also* saloon district
Red Light Saloon (El Paso), 106
Red Light Saloon (Fort Worth), 7
Red Lion Saloon (Fort Worth), 231
reforms, and reformers, 14, 20, 27–29, 30, 31–32, 139, 151–53, 157,159, 161, 181, 183, 216, 219, 263, 274, 275–76; strategy of, 28–29
refrigeration, 13
Regulators, 97
Reid, F. H., 276
Rennick, R. B., 142–43
Republican Party Politics, 129, 215
Reservation Ordinance of 1890, 139. *See also* red-light districts
restaurants, 163, 193, 227, 233, 240, 245, 248, 262, 263, 265–66, 270, 272, 274, 275, 276, 279; menus, 144, 162, 236, 265–66, 272, 287*n*86
Retail Liquor Dealers' Association. *See* liquor interests, retail
revues, stage. *See* variety shows
Revolving Light Theater (San Antonio), 76, 106
Rhode, Oscar, 192
Rice, Frank, 95
Richard, Frank, 155
Richmond, Lottie, 70
Rickard, Tex, 272
Rintleman, A. G. "Gus", 229
Rintleman, C. H. "Chris", 11, 229
Rio Grande, 55, 130, 131, 159, 161
Robertson, J. W., 182
Robey, L. T., 161
Robinson, Bute, 198, 202–203
Robinson, Gussie, 69, 73
Robinson, John H., 176, 189, 212
Robinson, Lizzie, 95
Rocky Mountain Punch, 50. *See also* liquor, by the drink
Rost, Sophie, 67

roulette, 12, 13, 84, 142, 143, 178, 203, 229, 247, 267, 270

Royal Gorge War, 195

Rushing, Bill, 23

Russell, Edward, 126

Russell, H. H., 28

Ryan, Si, 152. *See also* Astor House Saloon

Saint Louis, Mo., 45, 127, 137, 145, 201

saloon business, and industry, 27, 33, 49, 90, 159, 170, 175, 183, 187, 189, 190, 192, 193, 216, 229, 232, 234, 238, 240, 258, 262, 263, 265, 267, 269, 270, 274, 275, 277; monopolies, 29–30

Saloon Closing Law, 275. *See also* Sunday Closing Law

saloon district, 25, 26, 275. *See also* red-light districts

saloon equipment (saloon outfits), 45, 49

saloon hopping, 19

saloonkeepers. *See* barkeeps, and saloonkeepers

Saloon No. 10 (Deadwood, Dakota Terr.), 26

saloon proprietor. *See* barkeeps, and saloonkeepers

saloons, Eastern, 4

saloons, fancy, 5, 6, 7, 15, 30, 32, 76, 187, 229, 235, 242, 263, 293

saloons, Western, 3, 4, 5, 10, *12*, 30, 32, 34, 55, 58, 72, 124, 137, 140, 150, 174, 176, 187, 242, 294; company-owned, 50; as courtrooms, 291; democratic culture, 20, 33, 229; franchising, 49; Golden Age of, 43–44, 50; grand openings, 238, 241, 272; legacy of, 35; liquor clubs, 157; as male preserves, 4, 9, 31, 183, 215; model, 259; naming of, 18–19; and politics, 130, 145–46; as polling places, 127; as post offices, 291; public image of, 17, 32, 34, 190, 213, 214, 236, 241, 236, 241, 257, 267, 276; as public meeting halls, 4, 215; as self-policing, 6, 197; as stagecoach terminals, 291; synergy of, 274; violence in, 25, 26, 27, 80, 124, 126, 127, 128–29, 135–36, 142, 145, 146, 148, 150, 202, 209, 212, 213, 257, 258, 267, 269, 279

saloons, working man's, 6

saloon tokens, 6, 7, *8*, 221, 244, 273–74

saloon trust. *See* liquor interests

Sam Smith's Saloon. *See* Bexar Exchange

San Angelo, Tex., 33

San Antonio, Tex., 11, 17, 25, 30, 31, 53, 55, 76, 77, 80, 61, 83, 125, 127, 195, 200, 271; and Ben Thompson, 86–87, *87*, 91, 98, 204, 206; and Jack Harris, 57, *61*, 211; saloons, 5, 10, 15, 20, *61*, 63–64, 94, 106, 112, 292, 293; and vaudeville, 67–68, 73–75

Sanborn Fire Insurance Co., 113, 184, 186, 235, 244, 282*n*22

San Elizario, Tex., 126, 138

San Francisco, Calif., 25, 44, 72, 140, 141

San Jacinto Plaza (El Paso), 163

San Marcos, Tex., 200

Santa Maria, Calif., 48

Saroney, Nellie, 66

Sautley, Belle, 69

Scarborough, George, 146, 147, 149

Schilder, Carl, 30–31

Schlansker, Jane, 278

Schuler, A. J., 160

Schubert, "Frenchy", 211

Schueber, J. W., 230

Schutz, Sam, 143

Scott, Daisy, 70

Scott, Elizabeth (Mrs. Winfield Scott), 277

Scott, Mr. and Mrs. Billy (vaudeville team), 67

Scott, Hugh, 157

Scott, Winfield, 235, 260, 261, 263, 272, 27, 279, 286*n*76

Seamon, H., 66

Seamon and Pierce (vaudeville team), 67

Second Texas Cavalry, 57

"seeing the elephant", 230–31

segregation. *See* Jim Crow laws

Selman, John, 146, 148; death of, 149

Selman, John, Jr., 148–49

Senate Saloon (El Paso), *144*

Seventy-six Saloon (Santa Maria, Calif.), 48

Shakespearean actors, 31, 67, 70, 114

Shamrock Saloon (Fort Worth), 18

Shardein, Phillip, 101, 103

Sheehan, John, 241

Shelton, Anna, 34

Sherrington, Laurie, 95

Sherwood, Pearl, 69, 73

Shiel, Henry P., 15, 23, 268

Shipman, O. L., 243, 283*n*38

shoe shines, and shoeshine boys, 12, 270, 271

Short, Hettie (Mrs. Luke Short), 247, 256

Short, Luke, 4, 70, 87, 92, 196, 227, 243, *246*, 247, 250–51, 252, 253, 254–55, 256, 258–59, 263, 274, 279, 293; as 'Gambling King of Dodge City', 246; as 'King of the Fort Worth Gamblers', 248, 256; Short-Foster-Johnson partnership, 259
Short-Courtright gunfight, 227, 256, 279
showgirls, 16, 133. *See also* actresses
Sibley, H. H., 127
Silver City, N.Mex., 82
Silver Dollar Saloon (Fort Worth), 228
Silver King Saloon and Gambling House (San Antonio), 67
Sim Hart's Tobacco Shop (San Antonio), 62
Simmons, Josie, 95
Simms family, 72, 95, 203; William H. "Billy", 72, 85, 92, 94, 95, 96, 99, 100, 104, 111, 112, 203–204, 211; James M., Jr. 211; James M., Sr., 203, 211, 213, 222
Simms, Pink, 24
Simon, Isaac S., 191, 209, 210, 212
Smalley brothers: Fred, 270; J. K., 270
Smith, Charles A., 213
Smith, Johnny, 58
Smith, Marvin and Kitty (vaudeville team), 67
Smith, Sam S. "Big Beard", 54
Smith, Will G., 105
Smith, William T., 125
Sommers, Annie, 66
Sommers, Mollie, 66
Sons of Temperance, 27
Southern Hotel (San Antonio), 76, 106
Southernwood, George, 175–76, 192–93
Spanish monte, 84, 85, 143, 174, 178, 247
Sparrow, Frank, 8, 67, 68, 69, 70, 71, 72, 78, 79
"Special Policemen", 74, 75, 109, 254, 271
spittoons, 7, 9, 186, 229, 271
sporting men, 4, 32, 70, 71, 85, 133, 294; in Austin, 171, 173, 174, 183, 191, 192, 203, 214; Ben Thompson as, 197–98, 203, 206, 209; in Fort Worth, 240–41, 245, 248, 256–57, 258, 263, 271, 272; Jack Harris as, 60–61
Squires, Gilbert, 80
Stag Saloon (Fort Worth), 272
stage managers, 73
stage shows. *See* variety theaters
Stanniforth, Sid, 82
Star Saloon (Austin), 190
State National Bank (Austin), 170

state university (Tex.), 182, 196, 219
Stewart, Perry, 4
stock companies, and stock players, 65, 67, 68, 78, 95
Stockyards Hotel (Fort Worth), 279
Storms, Belle, 66
Storms, Charlie, 254
Stoudenmire, Dallas, 133–34, 135, 136; death of, 136
streetcars, 220
Strum, Henry, 11
Sullivan, John L., 244
Sundance Kid (Harry Longabaugh), 87
Sundance Square (Fort Worth), 34
Sunday closing laws, 153, 154, 274, 277. *See also* Saloon Closing Law
swinging doors. *See* bat-wing doors
Sylvester, Ed, 95

Tarrant County, Tex., 31
tavern, 4, 272
taxes, and taxation, 18, 21
Taylor, J. J., 143
Teatro Real (San Antonio), 68
Teepee Saloon (El Paso). *See* Wigwam Saloon
telegraph, 146
telephone, 12, 13–14, 75, 132, 188, 264, 279*n*6
Teller, John H., 259
Telluride, Colo., 12
temperance movement, 11, 16, 20, 27–28, *28*, 30
Templeton, John D, 234
ten-pins. *See* bowling
tenderloin district, 6, 15. *See also* red-light districts
Terminal Hotel (Fort Worth), 262
Terrazas family: Luis, Jr., 142; Luis, Sr., 165–66*n*44
Terrell, Ed, 228
Terry's Texas Rangers, 170
Texas and Pacific Coal Company, 238
Texas Brewing Company, 264
Texas Frontier Centennial Celebration (1936), 34
Texas League Baseball, 239
Texas legislature, 21, 27, 130, 151, 158, 182, 216, 275
Texas Title Company, 263
theaters. *See* movie theaters; variety theaters
Third Ward (Fort Worth), 18
Thomas, George, 133

Thomas, Jerry, 43, 45

Thomas, W. P., 241

Thomas's Saloon (El Paso), 133

Thompson, Ben, 53, 70, 86, *87*, 88, 89, 90, 91, 92, 93, *96*, 97, 98, 100, 101, 104, 109, 113, 182, 189, 194, 195, *196*, 197–98, 200–201, 202, 203, 204–205, 206–209, 210–11, 212, 214, 222, 231, 291, 293; autopsy, 103; death of, 98–102, 103, 206; funeral, 103, 206; indictment, for murder, 93

Thompson, Billy, 88, 99, 100, 101, 103, 195

Thompson, Catherine (Mrs. Ben Thompson), 88, 89, 90

Thorne, Grace, 68

Thurber, Tex., 238

Tiller, John H., 269–70

Tivoli Beer Hall: in El Paso, 133; in Fort Worth, 235

Tivoli Theater (San Antonio), 76, 106

tobacco, and tobacco products, 12, 107, 144, 213, 272

tobacco apartment (stand), 12, 65, 242, 245, 264

tokens. *See* saloon tokens

Tombstone, Ariz., 23, 24, 32, 72, 254, 291, 293

Tom Burchell's Saloon (El Paso), 161

Tooley, W. L., 155

Topeka, Kans., 266

tourism, and tourists, 160

trail towns. *See* cowtowns

Travieso family, 54; Vincente Alverez-Travieso, 54

Trinity City, Tex., 13

Trost and Trost Architects, 155–56

Turf Exchange (Fort Worth), 262, 263, 264, 265, 272

Turfman, 245. *See also* horse racing

Turner's Variety Hall (San Antonio), 99

Tuscon, Ariz., 72

United Friends of Temperance, 216. *See also* temperance movement; Sons of Temperance

Upchurch, J. T., 16

Uranga, Jose Maria, 131

Utah Street (El Paso), 138, 140, 148, 150, 154, 158

Uvalde County, Tex., 206

variety theaters (shows, and halls), 7, 15, 16, 58, 64, 66, 67, 68, 70, 72, 73, 74, 77,

81, 90, 114–15*n*14, 124, 133, 137, 141, 240, 268, 276; bookings, 95

vaudeville circuit, 71

Vaudeville Saloon and Theater (San Antonio), 33, 53, 55, 56, 57, 58, 62, 63, 65, 71, 76, 77, 78, 79, 81, 82, 83, 85, 86, 92, 94, 99, 101, 105, 110, 111, 115–16*n*27, 206, 294; Jack Harris's, 15, *56*, 183, 203, 53, 57, 58, 59, 60, 61, 65, 76, 79, 86, 91, 94, *104*, 105, 107, 112, 113, 211; management of, 115–16*n*27; new, 95; remodeling of, 95

vaudeville theater, 114–15*n*14. *See also* variety theaters

venereal diseases, 139, 161

ventilation, 265

vice districts. *See* red-light districts

Victorian America, morality of, 15, 266, 268

Villa, Francisco Pancho, 157

Villaneua, Santiago, 7

Vincent, May, 95

Virginia City, Nev., 5

Vivian, Sarah (Mrs. John King Fisher), 97

Vivienne, Ida, 74

Vogue Department Store (El Paso), 155

Waco, Tex., 83, 154

Waco Tap (Fort Worth), 7, 264

Wainwright, Marie, 68

Walker, Maude, 69

Walker, W. Glen, 260

Walker, William, 57

Walton, William Martin "Buck", 173, 178, 206, 209

Wambold, Horace, 67, 116*n*28

War of the Rebellion. *See* Civil War, American

War on Liquor, 276. *See also* reform, and reformers

Ward brothers, 237, 242, 253; John L., 236, 237, 238, 239, 242, 268; William "Bill", 18, 193, 235, 237, 238, *239*, 241, 242, 244, 245, 247, 248, 253, 255, 257, 259, 263, 264, 265, 267, 268, 269, 271, 272, 273, 276, 277, 279, 283*nn*34, 35, 287*n*81, 292

Warner, Matt, 25

Washington Theater (San Antonio), 77

water closet, 112, 264

Watson, Burt, 95

Watts, Luke, 200

Wedig, Frank C., 192–93

Wells, Kitty, 69, 72

Wells Fargo & Co., 147

West, Zoe, 74

"West of the Creek" (vice district, San Antonio), 82

Western saloons. *See* saloons, Western

Wheat, Joseph G., 272

Wheat Building (Fort Worth), 272

whiskey, 10, 11, 14, 35, 48, 50, 64, 72, 73, 108, 137, 146, 242, 243, 263–64, 272; cost of, 10; Martin's Best Whiskey, 272; Monarch brand, 11; names for, 10; whiskey money, 14; W. H. McBrayer's, 144

White, Owen, 137, 149, 150, 154

White, Zachary, 134, 155, 158, 162

White Elephant, origin of name, 230–31, 278

White Elephant Saloon: in Bingham Canyon, Utah, 230; in Butte, Mont., 230; in Denison, Tex., 230; in Eagle City, Idaho, 230; in El Paso, Tex., 230; in Fort Worth, Tex., 32, 33, 58, 193, 196, 227, 230, 232, 233, 234, 236, 238, 239, 241, 243, 244, 245, 247, 248, 250, 251, 252, 253, 254, 255, 256, 257, 259, 260, 262, 265, 269, 270, 271, 272, 273, 275, 277, 278, 292, 294; —, remodeling of, 272; —, second (new), 260–61, 264, 269, 278; in Fredericksburg, Tex., 230; in San Antonio, Tex., 76, 101, 106, 117n43, 230; in Wichita Falls, Tex., 230

White Elephant Saloon and Billiard Parlor (Fort Worth), 236. *See also* White Elephant Saloon

Whitman, Charlie, 84

Whitney, C. B., 90

Wholesale Liquor Dealers' Association. *See* liquor interests, wholesale

Wigwam Saloon (El Paso), 141, 146, 147, 148, 151, 154; as Teepee Saloon, 143

Willard, Frances, 16

Williams, Benjamin Franklin "Frank", 129–30

Williams, Harry, 142, 256–57

Williams, John E., 214

Wilson, C. W., 229

Wilson, Mark, 90

wine, 10, 125, 144, 187, 240, 243, 266, 272

wine rooms, 10, 15, 16, 17, 65, 69, 72, 80, 149, 268

Winfree, C. V., 260

Winfree Building (Fort Worth), 260, 263, 264, 269

Wing, J. Q., 205

Winslow, E. D., 7

Winter, Annie, 95

Witcher, Joe, 23

W. L. Sallis's Saloon (Fort Worth), 26

women, and women's rights, 16–17, 20, 28, 38n37, 139, 177, 215; as customers, 138. *See also* prostitutes, and prostitution

Women's Christian Temperance Union (WCTU), 31, 40n57, 152, 153, 216

Woods, John, 128

Wooten, Dudley Goodall, 182, 219, 220

working girls. *See* prostitutes, and prostitution

World War I, 159

Worth Hotel (Fort Worth), 262

Wright, Jack, 26

Wyman, Pap, 32

York and Voltz's Senate Saloon (Junction City, Kans.), 9

Young, Tommie Lee, 26

Younger brothers, 194–95; Bob, 194; Cole, 194; James, 194; John, 194

Zaurine, Marie, 74